Advance Praise for
Vajrayāna and the Culmination of the Path

"This series of volumes presents an engaging, methodical, step-by-step guide for the whole of the Buddhist path to awakening. The foremost aim of this tenth volume is "to demystify Vajrayāna—to clarify what it is and what its practice entails." And in clear, immediate, and fluid language, the volume more than delivers on that objective! Apart from Lama Thubten Yeshe's *Introduction to Tantra* and His Holiness's own discussion of Tantric practice in *The World of Tibetan Buddhism*, this comprehensive treatment is the absolute best we have! Moreover, this distinctive and fundamental series of teachings, taught by His Holiness the Dalai Lama and assisted by Venerable Thubten Chodron, is a publishing triumph for our time."
—Jan Willis, professor of religion, emerita, Wesleyan University

"In this final volume of the monumental series, His Holiness the Dalai Lama and Venerable Thubten Chodron once again present an important aspect of the Buddhist path in precise language that is accessible to the general reader. This volume, like its predecessors, will be valuable to scholars and practitioners alike. The presentation of Vajrayāna Buddhism demonstrates both its continuity with the broader Buddhist path and the distinctiveness of Tantric practice and the theory that underlies it. This library is now complete, and what a gift it is to the world!"
—Jay Garfield, Doris Silbert Professor in the Humanities and Professor of Philosophy and Buddhist Studies, Smith College and the Harvard Divinity School

THE LIBRARY OF WISDOM AND COMPASSION

The Library of Wisdom and Compassion is a special multivolume series in which His Holiness the Dalai Lama shares the Buddha's teachings on the complete path to full awakening that he himself has practiced his entire life. The topics are arranged especially for people not born in Buddhist cultures and are peppered with the Dalai Lama's unique outlook. Assisted by his long-term disciple, the American nun Thubten Chodron, the Dalai Lama sets the context for practicing the Buddha's teachings in modern times and then unveils the path of wisdom and compassion that leads to a meaningful life, a sense of personal fulfillment, and full awakening. This series is an important bridge from introductory to profound topics for those seeking an in-depth explanation from a contemporary perspective.

Volumes:

1. *Approaching the Buddhist Path*
2. *The Foundation of Buddhist Practice*
3. *Saṃsāra, Nirvāṇa, and Buddha Nature*
4. *Following in the Buddha's Footsteps*
5. *In Praise of Great Compassion*
6. *Courageous Compassion*
7. *Searching for the Self*
8. *Realizing the Profound View*
9. *Appearing and Empty*
10. *Vajrayāna and the Culmination of the Path*

THE LIBRARY OF WISDOM AND COMPASSION · VOLUME 10

Vajrayāna and the Culmination of the Path

Bhikṣu Tenzin Gyatso,
the Fourteenth Dalai Lama

and

Bhikṣuṇī Thubten Chodron

Wisdom

Wisdom Publications
132 Perry Street
New York, NY 10014 USA
wisdom.org

Library of Congress Cataloging-in-Publication Data
Names: Bstan-'dzin-rgya-mtsho, Dalai Lama XIV, 1935– author. | Thubten Chodron, 1950– author.
Title: Vajrayāna and the Culmination of the Path / Bhikṣu Tenzin Gyatso, the Fourteenth Dalai Lama; Bhikṣuṇī Thubten Chodron.
Description: First edition. | New York: Wisdom Publications, 2024. | Series: The library of wisdom and compassion; 10 | Includes bibliographical references and index.
Identifiers: LCCN 2024010057 (print) | LCCN 2024010058 (ebook) | ISBN 9781614299578 (hardcover) | ISBN 9781614299806 (ebook)
Subjects: LCSH: Tantric Buddhism. | Dge-lugs-pa (Sect)—Doctrines. | Yoga—Buddhism.
Classification: LCC BQ7935.B774 V35 2024 (print) | LCC BQ7935.B774 (ebook) | DDC 294.3/420425—dc23/eng/20240604
LC record available at https://lccn.loc.gov/2024010057
LC ebook record available at https://lccn.loc.gov/2024010058

ISBN 978-1-61429-957-8   ebook ISBN 978-1-61429-980-6

28 27 26 25 24
5 4 3 2 1

Photo credits: cover, Gen Heywood; pp. vi, 214, 356, Olivier Adam; pp. xx, 178, 270, Gen Heywood; p. xxiv, Yeshe Ochirova; p. 150, Louise Lu for Amitabha Buddhist Centre Singapore
Cover and interior design by Gopa & Ted2. Typeset by PerfecType, Nashville, TN.

Printed on acid-free paper that meets the guidelines for permanence and durability of the Production Guidelines for Book Longevity of the Council on Library Resources.

Printed in Canada.

Publisher's Acknowledgment

The publisher gratefully acknowledges the generous help of the Hershey Family Foundation in sponsoring the production of this book.

Contents

Preface by Bhikṣuṇī Thubten Chodron xiii

Abbreviations xxi

Introduction by His Holiness the Dalai Lama 1

1 Method and Wisdom in Sūtra and Tantra 9

Method and Wisdom 9

Wisdom in Pāramitāyāna and Vajrayāna 12

Method in Pāramitāyāna and Vajrayāna 15

Method and Wisdom Practiced Together 19

The Inseparability of Method and Wisdom 22

What Makes Vajrayāna Fast 27

2 Introduction to Tantra 33

The Meaning of Vajrayāna 34

The History of Tantra 34

Tantric Deities 37

The Purpose of Vajrayāna 39

Abandoning False Expectations of Vajrayāna 41

Terminology 44

Tantric Masters 46

Tantric Practitioners 50

3 ENTERING TANTRAYĀNA 57
Empowerment, Permissory Rites, and Oral Transmission 57
Preliminary Practices 60
Empowerment 62
Rituals 65
After Receiving Empowerment 68
Tantric Ethical Restraints and Commitments 69
Empowerment Taken Prematurely 72
The Practice of Sādhanas 74
Women and Vajrayāna 77
Unusual Behavior 78
The Four Classes of Tantra and the Nine Vehicles 80
Practicing Vajrayāna in a Gradual Manner 83

4 ALL-ENCOMPASSING YOGA 85
The Method 87

5 THE PATH OF KRIYĀ TANTRA 91
Becoming a Suitable Vessel 92
Keeping the Ethical Restraints and Commitments Purely 94
Practicing the Close Approximation 96
Achieving the Actual Attainments (Siddhi) 106
Training in the Body, Speech, and Mind of a Buddha 108
Yoga with Signs and Yoga without Signs 110

6 THE PATHS OF CARYĀ TANTRA AND YOGA TANTRA 111
Caryā (Performance) Tantra 111
Becoming a Suitable Vessel 111
Keeping the Ethical Restraints and Commitments Purely 112
Practicing the Close Approximation 112
Achieving the Actual Attainments (Siddhi) 117
Yoga Tantra 117
Becoming a Suitable Vessel 117

Purely Keeping the Ethical Restraints and Commitments 118
Practicing the Close Approximation 118
Achieving the Actual Attainments (Siddhi) 121
Concluding Comments on the Three Lower Tantras 122
Vajrayāna and the Five Paths and Ten Grounds 123

7 Highest Yoga Tantra 125
Levels of Meaning 126
Distinguishing the Four Classes of Tantra 126
How Vajrayāna Brings Awakening 128
Meditational Deities and the Ultimate Nature of Desire 131
Excellent Features of Highest Yoga Tantra 133
Utilizing Afflictions in the Path 134
Cultivating Serenity and Insight in Highest Yoga Tantra 137
Meditation on Emptiness in Vajrayāna 139
Bliss and Emptiness 142
Meditation Sessions in the Generation Stage 143
Post-Meditation Time 146
Meditation Sessions in the Completion Stage 147

8 The Tantric Perspective of Body and Mind 151
The Tantric View of Body and Mind 152
The Body 156
The Mind 158
Mental Consciousness 160
Knowing an Object 161
Supersensory Perception and Karmic Winds 163
Death, Bardo, and Rebirth 164
Taking Death, Bardo, and Rebirth into the Path to the Three Buddha Bodies 171
Purifying the Basis of Purification 174
Near-Death Experiences and the Illusory Body 175
Preserving Good Qualities from Life to Life 177

9 THE PATH OF HIGHEST YOGA TANTRA 179
Becoming a Suitable Vessel 179
Keeping the Ethical Restraints and Commitments Purely 180
The Path to Follow—Generation Stage 181
Uncommon Factors to Be Abandoned by the Generation Stage 182
The Coarse and Refined Yogas of Single Mindfulness 185
Generation Stage and Completion Stage 189

10 INTRODUCTION TO THE COMPLETION STAGE 191
Putting Together the Elements of the Path 191
The Vast and Profound 194
Levels of Completion-Stage Practice 195
Paths That Overcome Ordinary Death, Bardo, and Rebirth 199
The Nine Mixings 203
More about the Nine Mixings 208
Advice 212

11 GOING DEEPER INTO THE COMPLETION STAGE 215
Isolated Body 215
Isolated Speech 220
Isolated Mind 222
Practice with a Mudrā 224
The Inseparability of Bliss and Emptiness 228
The Completion-Stage Practice of the Two Truths 229
Illusory Body 229
Correlations between the Basis, Path, and Result 234
Conduct Enhancing the Path 235
Meanings of "Clear Light" 239
Actual Clear Light 241
Learners' Union—the Inseparability of the Two Truths 242
The Union of the Two Truths 249
The Five Paths according to Vajrayāna 250
The Completion Stage according to Other Highest Yoga Tantras 251
How to Manifest the Results 253

12 THE PATH OF KĀLACAKRA TANTRA 257
Becoming a Proper Vessel 258
The Ethical Restraints and Commitments to Keep Purely 258
Practicing the Path of Kālacakra: The Generation Stage 259
Practicing the Path of Kālacakra: The Completion Stage 260
Six Branches of the Completion Stage 262
Heartfelt Advice 266

13 THE FOUR TIBETAN TRADITIONS 271
Nālandā and the Four Tibetan Traditions 271
The Texts Shared in Common in the Four Tibetan Traditions 275
How to Approach the Various Tibetan Buddhist Traditions 277
The Nyingma Tradition 278
The Kagyu Tradition 284
The Sakya Tradition 287
The Gelug Tradition 289
Similarities among Traditions 290
Are Sentient Beings Already Awakened? 292
Sūtra and Tantra Methods to Meditate on Emptiness 296
Dzogchen, Highest Yoga Tantra, and Madhyamaka 299

14 COMING TO THE SAME POINT 307
Differences in Approach, Unity in Results 308
Confusion Involving Terminology 309
Mind as the Creator 311
Presentations from Different Perspectives 313
Avoiding Misunderstandings 314
Self-Empty and Other-Empty 316
The Jonang Tradition 317
The Mind and I 321
Different Perspectives on the Clear-Light Mind 324
Bliss and Emptiness 326

15 A Song of the Four Mindfulnesses and the Culmination of the Path 331
Mindfulness of the Guru 331
Mindfulness of Compassion and Bodhicitta 333
Mindfulness of the Body as a Divine Body 333
Mindfulness of the View of Emptiness 335
Why Vajrayāna Is the Culmination of the Path 337

16 Epilogue: Advice for My Disciples 341
Entering Tantrayāna 344
Learning, Reflecting, and Meditating 346
Skillful Practice 352
The Importance of Daily Practice 353

Notes 357
Glossary 367
Recommended Reading 391
Index 399
About the Authors 429

Preface

THE *LIBRARY OF Wisdom and Compassion*, of which *Vajrayāna and the Culmination of the Path* is the tenth and concluding volume, began in the mid-1990s when I requested His Holiness the Dalai Lama to write a short text that Tibetan lamas could use when teaching non-Tibetans. This request arose because Westerners and others who did not grow up Buddhist who wanted to learn Tibetan Buddhism needed more introductory background than the stages of the path (*lamrim*) literature provided. The lamrim—a brilliant way of systematizing the Buddha's teachings—was based on knowledge that we were not familiar with, such as the nature of mind, rebirth, karma and its effects, and buddhahood, to name a few. His Holiness's response to this request has resulted in the ten volumes comprising the *Library of Wisdom and Compassion* and, prior to these, *Buddha: One Teacher, Many Traditions*. Now with this concluding tenth volume, which gives a brief introduction to Vajrayāna, there is a feeling of fulfillment for completing a task as well as a sense of wanting to do more.

Vajrayāna, which is regarded as the culmination of the path to buddhahood in Tibetan Buddhism, is sometimes misunderstood and regarded as a degenerate form of the mixture of Buddhism and Hinduism. But when studied with teachers who practice it, we discover that it is in line with Buddhist tenets.

In the West, some people say there are three Buddhist traditions: Vipassana, Zen, and Vajrayāna. This is not accurate. Buddhists usually speak of two traditions: the Fundamental Vehicle and the Mahāyāna (Universal Vehicle).[1] Alternatively, the scriptures speak of three vehicles: the Śrāvaka, Solitary Realizer, and Bodhisattva Vehicles.

In Asia, vipaśyanā (P. *vipassanā*) is a meditation technique found in Theravāda Buddhism as practiced in South and Southeast Asia. It is not regarded as a distinct Buddhist tradition. In the broader Buddhist context, vipaśyanā (insight) refers to the teachings and meditations that bring insight into selflessness and emptiness. As such, vipaśyanā is found in all Buddhist traditions, although they may have different approaches to it.

Zen is Japanese for the Chinese *Chan* and Indian *Dhyāna* meaning meditative stability. Popular in East Asia, Zen is one branch of Mahāyāna, which includes Pure Land, Huayan, Tiantai, Vajrayāna, and so on. Vajrayāna—also called Tantrayāna—is a branch of Mahāyāna, and Mahāyāna is based on the teachings and practice of the Fundamental Vehicle. Esoteric Buddhism (Zhenyan, Mizong) or Vajrayāna was established as a distinct tradition in China during the Tang Dynasty. In the eighth century, Kūkai brought it to Japan where it is called Shingon. Although it was not widely practiced in China in later years, Vajrayāna influenced the other Buddhist traditions there. In Tibet it became very popular and is found in the four principal Tibetan traditions: Nyingma, Sakya, Kagyu, and Gelug. This book is an introduction to Vajrayāna as practiced in the Himalayan region.

We have several aims for this volume. Foremost is to demystify Vajrayāna—to clarify what it is and what its practice entails. In the past these points have been misunderstood. Although Vajrayāna is regarded as the culmination of the path to buddhahood in Tibetan Buddhism, it is sometimes misunderstood and regarded as a degenerate mixture of Buddhism and Hinduism or as magic performed to bring wealth. In fact it is none of these. When qualified disciples practice Vajrayāna methods properly under the guidance of a qualified spiritual mentor, they can attain the same state of buddhahood as the Buddha did.

Another aim of this volume is to clarify points for people interested in practicing Vajrayāna. Based on questions from his students, His Holiness explains empowerments, the ethical restraints and commitments that are taken during them, how Vajrayāna differs from Sūtrayāna, and the unusual behavior of some of the mahāsiddhas of ancient times. He differentiates and delineates the practices of the four Tantric classes and of the various Tibetan traditions. This book does not give meditation instructions—students receive these only after receiving a Vajrayāna empowerment—but it does give the necessary background so people can decide if tantric practice is suitable for them at this time given their current level of understanding of the Dharma.

The common teachings we find in Tibetan Buddhism—on the four truths, two truths, renunciation of saṃsāra, bodhicitta, and the correct view of emptiness or selflessness—are contained in the first nine volumes of the *Library of Wisdom and Compassion* and in other books on the stages of the path to awakening. Because practitioners of Vajrayāna should already be familiar with these teachings and be practicing them, they are not explained again here. Rather, the outline of how one progresses through the paths and grounds of Vajrayāna is the central topic.

An Overview

Just as every field of knowledge from science to philosophy to music has its own vocabulary and common concepts, so does Buddhism. You encountered new terms in the previous volumes and they are present in this volume too. Buddhist students are not expected to understand a teaching completely the first time they hear or read it (or even the second, third, or fourth time), but if you go over the material repeatedly, gradually it will become clearer. Think about and meditate on what you currently understand. Put the discussions that are currently over your head aside for the moment and come back to them as you learn and practice more. While some points may not seem useful now, they may be later on, so keep an open mind and accept the challenge to investigate the ultimate nature of your mind.

Vajrayāna and the Culmination of the Path begins with discussing method and wisdom—the two wings of the path needed to complete the causes for full awakening. Method includes bodhicitta and the first three perfections (generosity, ethical conduct, and fortitude), wisdom includes the last two perfections (concentration and wisdom), and joyous effort, the fourth perfection, applies to both. Chapter 1 gives a summary of the way method and wisdom are practiced in both the Pāramitāyāna (the vehicle of the bodhisattva perfections) and Vajrayāna (the vajra vehicle), the differences between them, and how method and wisdom are practiced together in both vehicles. It then reveals the qualities of Vajrayāna that make it quicker than the Pāramitāyāna, when practiced correctly and with the proper motivation of bodhicitta.

Chapter 2 introduces us to Tantra—its history and purpose, the qualities of its masters and disciples. Chapter 3 continues this introduction by discussing empowerments—the way to enter the Vajrayāna—and the commitments and precepts we undertake when taking empowerments. Vajrayāna is said to be faster than Pāramitāyāna, but that does not mean it is easier. We must be much more attentive to the actions of our body, speech, and mind and the ethical restraints that steer them away from nonvirtue and toward virtue. Chapter 4 explains all-encompassing yoga, a practice cultivating both bodhicitta and wisdom. His Holiness does this practice daily and encourages us to do the same.

Tantrayāna practice may be categorized in various ways, one way being into four: Kriyā, Caryā, Yoga, and Highest Yoga Tantras. The first three are called the lower tantras, although there is nothing simple about them. They involve meditating on emptiness, dissolving ourselves into emptiness, and then imagining that the wisdom realizing emptiness appears as the central deity and as the deity's environment that form the supporting and supported maṇḍala. We then do various practices to cultivate serenity and insight through the tantric method. Chapters 5 and 6 cover this.

In chapter 7 we are introduced to Highest Yoga Tantra. Practicing it—especially the completion stage—leads us to work with the subtle body and its channels, winds, and drops to make manifest the fundamental innate mind of clear light, the subtlest consciousness that is latent in our busy, distracted lives. Chapter 8 describes the Tantric perspective of the body and mind; this knowledge is necessary to practice the two stages of Highest Yoga Tantra: the generation stage and completion stage. Chapter 9 shows the practice of the generation stage and chapter 10 introduces us to the practice of the completion stage.

In chapter 11, we learn the five (or six) stages within the completion stage.[2] Isolated body, isolated speech, and isolated mind isolate our ordinary body, speech, and mind from our ordinary view and ordinary way of conceiving and grasping them. The example clear light at the end of isolated mind is a condition for manifesting the impure illusory body—a body whose substantial cause is the subtlest mind. It is said to be impure because practitioners still haven't eliminated the afflictive obscurations. They have attained a high meditative state, where most of the winds have dissolved in the indestructible drop at the heart, but not all of them. Eliminating the afflictive obscurations is accomplished when yogis enter meditative equipoise on emptiness and dissolve all winds into the indestructible drop at the heart, thereby making manifest the actual clear light. After further meditation, they emerge from that equipoise with a pure illusory body that is totally free from the afflictive obscurations. With continued meditation, they then attain union—the union of the two truths, of purified body and mind—and attain buddhahood and a buddha's three bodies: the truth body, enjoyment body, and emanation body. As buddhas they then fulfill their bodhicitta aspiration to be of the greatest benefit to sentient beings, especially by leading them on the path to full awakening.

Chapter 12 introduces the Kālacakra Tantra, whose completion stage differs from the general pattern of other tantras. Chapters 13 and 14 delve into the four Tibetan traditions of Nyingma, Sakya, Kagyu, and Gelug. The Pāramitāyāna portion of their practice is the same, the differences among them being due principally to the perspectives of the Indian and Tibetan lineage masters who brought those tantras to Tibet and spread their practices.

Chapter 15 shares the inspiring poem "Song of the Four Mindfulnesses" by the seventh Dalai Lama, which summarizes the essentials of tantric practice in five verses, and His Holiness's commentary on it. At the end of this chapter His Holiness gives a brilliant concise explanation that ties everything together on why Vajrayāna is the culmination of the path. To conclude this volume, as well as the *Library of Wisdom and Compassion* series, His Holiness gives heartfelt advice to those readers who consider him their guru. This advice is precious; if our spiritual aim is to become a fully awakened buddha to be of the greatest possible benefit to all sentient beings, we should keep this advice in our hearts and live according to it.

Please Note

Although this series is coauthored, the majority of the material is His Holiness's teachings. I researched and wrote the parts about the Pāli tradition and Chinese Buddhism, wrote some other passages, and composed the reflections.

"A Song of the Four Mindfulnesses" by the Seventh Dalai Lama passed from Tsongkhapa to Jetsun Sherab Senge. The present translation was done by Geshe Dorji Damdul, and His Holiness's commentary was translated by Jeffrey Hopkins.

His Holiness advises us to read several books on Tantra. The English, Sanskrit, and Tibetan titles are noted when known, although many of these books have not yet been translated into English.

For ease of reading, most honorifics have been omitted, but that does not diminish the great respect we have for the most excellent Buddhist sages, learned adepts, scholars, and practitioners. Foreign terms are given in italics parenthetically at their first usage. Unless otherwise noted with "T," indicating Tibetan, italicized terms are Sanskrit. Sanskrit spelling is given for Buddhist terms in common usage (nirvāṇa, Dharma, arhat, ārya, and so forth). To maintain the flow of a passage, it is not always possible to gloss all new terms on their first usage, so a glossary is provided at the end of the book. Tantrayāna has some unique vocabulary. The glossary contains the most important terms. You will learn the others later, when your study and practice of Tantra progresses.

"Sūtra" refers to Sūtrayāna, and "Tantra" to Tantrayāna—the Sūtra Vehicle and Tantra Vehicle, respectively. When these two words are not capitalized, they refer to two types of practices or scriptures. "Mahāyāna" here refers principally to the bodhisattva path as explained in the Sanskrit tradition. In general, the meaning of all philosophical terms accords with the presentation of the Prāsaṅgika Madhyamaka tenet system. For ease in reading, "yogi" refers to both male and female practitioners who meditate on emptiness. Unless otherwise noted, the personal pronoun "I" refers to His Holiness.

In general, readers of books on Tantra are restricted to those who have received the suitable Vajrayāna empowerment. However, concerned that people learn about Tantra from reliable sources, H. H. the Dalai Lama has given his permission for people without empowerment to read this volume.

Throughout this book, His Holiness recommends that we study and practice according to specific texts. These have been listed in the Recommended Reading section according to those authored by Indian pandits, Tibetan scholar-adepts, and Western practitioners.

Appreciation

My deepest respect goes to Śākyamuni Buddha and all the buddhas, bodhisattvas, and arhats who embody the Dharma and with compassion teach us unawakened beings. I also bow to all the realized lineage masters of all Buddhist traditions through whose kindness the Dharma still exists in our world.

This series appears in many volumes, so I express my appreciation to those involved in each individual volume. This final volume has depended on the abilities and efforts of His Holiness's translators—Geshe Lhakdor, Geshe Dorji Damdul, and Mr. Tenzin Tsepak. I am grateful to Geshe Chodrak (Dadul Namgyal) and Bhikṣuṇī Sangye Khadro for checking the manuscript, and to Samdhong Rinpoche for his encouragement. The staff at the Private Office of His Holiness kindly facilitated the interviews, and Sravasti Abbey supported me while I worked on this volume. Mary Petrusewicz skillfully edited the manuscript. I thank everyone at Wisdom Publications who contributed to the successful production of this series. All errors are my own.

Bhikṣuṇī Thubten Chodron
Sravasti Abbey

Abbreviations

AKC *Advice to Kunzang Chögyal*, by Dza Patrul Rinpoche. Translated by Karen Lilienberg. https://www.zangthal.co.uk/files/Advice_to_Kunzang_Chogyal.pdf.

BCA *Engaging in the Bodhisattvas' Deeds* (*Bodhicaryāvatāra*), by Śāntideva.

CTA *Cutting Through Appearances*, by Geshe Lhundup Sopa and Jeffrey Hopkins. Ithaca, NY: Snow Lion Publications, 1989.

DC *Dzogchen: The Heart Essence of the Great Perfection*, by the Dalai Lama. Ithaca, NY: Snow Lion Publications, 2000.

DIR *Death, Intermediate State, and Rebirth in Tibetan Buddhism*, by Lati Rinpoche, Jeffrey Hopkins et al. Ithaca, NY: Snow Lion Publications, 1985.

DY *Deity Yoga*, by H. H. the Dalai Lama, Tsong-ka-pa, and Jeffrey Hopkins. Ithaca, NY: Snow Lion Publications, 1981.

EOE *The Essence of Other-Emptiness*, by Tāranātha. Translated by Jeffrey Hopkins. Ithaca, NY: Snow Lion Publications, 2007.

GP *Fifty Verses on the Guru* (*Gurupañcāśikā*), by Aśvaghoṣa. Dharamsala: Library of Tibetan Works and Archives, 1975.

GR *Illuminating the Intent: An Exposition of Candrakīrti's "Entering the Middle Way,"* by Tsongkhapa. Translated by Thupten Jinpa. Somerville, MA: Wisdom Publication, 2021.

GSM *Great Exposition of Secret Mantra,* vol. 2, *Deity Yoga*, by Tsongkhapa. Translated by Jeffrey Hopkins. Boulder, CO: Shambhala Publications, 2017.

HM *The Heart of Meditation: Discovering Innermost Awareness,* by the Dalai Lama. Translated by Jeffrey Hopkins. Boulder, CO: Shambhala Publications, 2016.

J. Japanese

KCI *Kindness, Clarity, and Insight*, by His Holiness the Dalai Lama. Ithaca, NY: Snow Lion Publications, 2012.

LC *The Great Treatise on the Stages of the Path to Awakening* (*Lam rim chen mo*), by Tsongkhapa, 3 vols. Translated by Joshua Cutler et al. Ithaca, NY: Snow Lion Publications, 2000–2004.

LP *Atisha's Lamp for the Path to Enlightenment*, by Atisha. Translated by Ruth Sonam. Ithaca, NY: Snow Lion Publications, 1997.

LPH *Liberation in the Palm of Your Hand*. Edited by Trijang Rinpoche. Translated by Michael Richards. Boston: Wisdom Publications, 2006.

LS "A Lamp to Illuminate the Five Stages: Tsongkhapa's Reformatory Work on Guhyasamāja Tantra," by Gavin Kilty. In *Tsongkhapa: The Legacy of Tibet's Great Philosopher-Saint*, edited by David Gray. Somerville, MA: Wisdom Publications, 2024.

MD *Mountain Doctrine: Tibet's Fundamental Treatise on Other-Emptiness and the Buddha Matrix*, by Dol-bo-ba Shay-rap-gyel-tsen. Translated by Jeffrey Hopkins. Boulder,CO: Snow Lion Publications, 2017.

MIS *Manjushri's Innermost Secret*, by Kachen Yeshe Gyaltsen. Translated by David Gonsalez. Somerville, MA: Wisdom Publications, 2019.

MMA *Supplement to the "Treatise on the Middle Way"* (*Madhyamakāvatāra*), by Candrakīrti.

MNM *Meditation on the Nature of Mind*, by the Dalai Lama, Khonton Peljor Lhundrub, and José Cabezón. Boston: Wisdom Publications, 2011.

OBT *Overview of Buddhist Tantra: General Presentation of the Classes of Tantra, Captivating the Minds of the Fortunate Ones*, by Panchen Sonam Dragpa. Translated by Martin J. Boord and Losang Norbu Tsonawa. Dharamsala, India: Library of Tibetan Works and Archives, 1996.

RC *Resurrecting Candrakīrti*, by Kevin Vose. Boston: Wisdom Publication, 2009.

RR *Reflections on Reality: The Three Natures and Non-Natures in the Mind Only School*, by Jeffrey Hopkins. Los Angeles: University of California Press, 2002.

SM *The Hundred Thousand Songs of Milarepa*, by Garma C. C. Chang. New York: Oriental Studies Foundation, 1962.

T. Tibetan

TBD *The Tibetan Book of the Dead: Liberation through Understanding in the Between*. Translated by Robert A. F. Thurman. New York: Bantam Books, 1993.

TK *Tsongkhapa: A Buddha in the Land of Snows*, by Thupten Jinpa. Boulder, CO: Shambhala Publications, 2019.

TW "A Tree in the West: Competing Tathāgatagarbha Theories in Tibet," by William Magee. Taipei: Chung-Hwa Buddhist Journal 19, 2006.

VT *Vajramālā Tantra*.

YT *Yoga Tantra: Paths to Magical Feats*, by H. H. the Dalai Lama, Dzong-ka-ba, and Jeffrey Hopkins. Ithaca, NY: Snow Lion Publications, 2005.

Introduction

Vajrayāna, or the path of Tantra, is a branch of Mahāyāna that is based on the practice of the four truths as taught in the Fundamental Vehicle. It is infused with the heart of bodhicitta—the aspiration to attain full awakening in order to benefit all sentient beings most effectively, and its core is the wisdom realizing emptiness, dependent arising, and their complementary nature.

Vajrayāna is found principally in Tibet, Mongolia, and Japan; it spread to China in ancient times but did not become popular there. Since Vajrayāna was more widespread in India when Indian and Tibetan sages brought Buddhism to Tibet, Sūtrayāna and Vajrayāna teachings spread in Tibet and became popular at the same time.

Vajrayāna is also called the Secret Vehicle (Guhyayāna), which in some people's minds evokes notions of hidden, mystical, and fantastical practices that make a practitioner powerful and magical, not to mention famous. Actually, *secret* indicates that tantric practitioners are discreet; they don't announce their meditative experiences to the world or seek fame. For that reason, the texts advise them not to display the pictures of the deities whose practices they do, or their tantric implements such as vajra, bell, and inner offering. Secrecy is to protect practitioners from the eight worldly concerns as well as to prevent the public from having misconceptions about the practice.

Vajrayāna practice involves visualization of meditational deities and maṇḍalas, recitation of mantras, and pūjās or offering ceremonies. Being unfamiliar with Vajrayāna teachings and practice, some people have glamorous or outlandish notions about Vajrayāna practitioners. It is very important as modern Buddhist practitioners that we debunk these misconceptions. The tantric path involves the same aims as the Fundamental Vehicle—to uproot the afflictions that bind us in saṃsāra and, like the Pāramitāyāna, to eradicate the latencies of these afflictions that prevent the full awakening of a buddha.

All sentient beings—no matter our physical form or other distinguishing characteristics—want equally to be happy and avoid suffering. Each human being has the same human mind with its unique human potential, and all of us have to deal with the same mental defilements. All religions and cultures encourage us to develop ethical conduct and a kind heart, to abandon harming one another, to help others as much as possible, and to forgive ourselves and others when we act in harmful ways. Even though we may feel more comfortable living in our own culture because it is more familiar, it is only suitable to respect the good aspects of all cultures and learn from them. However, romanticizing other cultures—for example, thinking Tibet is Shangri-la[3]—blinds us to what they actually are and causes us to ignore the good qualities of our own culture. Although some people may want to live in a culture or practice a religion other than that of their family, we will benefit from appreciating the good qualities of our birth culture and religion while adopting Buddhist perspectives and practices. This book, therefore, is our attempt to present Vajrayāna as practiced in Tibet in an accurate way, explaining some of the philosophy that lies behind it so that people don't get too distracted by its more colorful aspects.

Two Aspects of the Path

To attain full awakening, the practice of both the method and wisdom aspects of the path are necessary. The method aspect is exemplified by the aspiration to be free from saṃsāra and generate bodhicitta, whereas the wisdom aspect emphasizes understanding emptiness and impermanence. These two need to be combined so that they mutually reinforce each other. We may have a strong determination to free ourselves and others from saṃsāra and to attain buddhahood in order to do so, but without uprooting the principal cause of saṃsāra—the ignorance grasping inherent existence—this is impossible. The wisdom realizing emptiness is the factor that frees our minds from defilements, and without doing this we will still circle in saṃsāra and be unable to lead others to liberation and full awakening. Likewise, we may realize emptiness, the ultimate nature of reality, but if we lack love and compassion for all sentient beings and the altruistic intention to benefit them, we will be content to attain our own liberation from saṃsāra. Although we may wish others to be free from duḥkha, we won't necessarily act to bring this about.

How do these two aspects of the path complement and enhance each other? One way is to see that the sentient beings for whom we feel love and compassion are empty of inherent existence. Understanding this increases our compassion, for we can see that ignorance obscures their minds and causes them to repeatedly create the causes for saṃsāra's duḥkha. The wisdom realizing emptiness is the antidote to saṃsāra. We need to actualize this wisdom and free ourselves from saṃsāra so that we are fully capable of guiding others on the path to generate this wisdom and free themselves from saṃsāra too. In this way bodhicitta encourages the practice of wisdom.

In addition, wisdom supports the practice of bodhicitta. In the early stages of meditation on emptiness, some practitioners fall to the extreme of nihilism and mistakenly believe nothing exists. However, emptiness does not mean nonexistence. Emptiness is a quality of all phenomena; it is their ultimate nature, their deepest mode of existence. As such, wherever and whenever a particular phenomenon exists, so does its emptiness. They are one nature—a phenomenon and its emptiness are inseparable. This means that the ultimate nature of each and every sentient being is their emptiness of inherent existence. The two truths—ultimate truth (emptiness) and conventional truth (the variety of phenomena, including persons)—exist and complement each other. The sentient beings we want to benefit exist conventionally and at the same time lack inherent existence. Because they lack independent or inherent existence, they are dependent on causes and conditions.

Knowing that ignorance and other afflictions are adventitious and not in the nature of the mind, we know that sentient beings' duḥkha is not a given. It is not fixed and everlasting. Because duḥkha and its causes are empty, they can be altered. When ignorance, the afflictions, and their seeds are eradicated by the wisdom realizing emptiness, the duḥkha that depends on them gradually ceases. Thus this wisdom is the key to fulfilling our compassionate aspiration of bodhicitta.

Together with wisdom and bodhicitta, serenity—the ability to remain focused on a meditation object without laxity or restlessness—is necessary to attain awakening. Tantrayāna has a special method for generating serenity (meditative concentration) and insight (the realization of emptiness). The union of these two facilitates yogis to fulfill the accumulations of method and wisdom more quickly than in the Sūtra path. This is one of the chief reasons Tantrayāna is highly praised.

Unfortunately, nowadays when some people think of Tantrayāna, their first thought is of lamas wearing big hats, sitting on high thrones, ringing bells and playing drums, while mumbling magical mantras in Sanskrit. It is as if some people think the less they understand of a ceremony, the greater the blessing they receive—their wealth will increase, they will obtain special powers, and their worldly affairs will flourish.

However, increasing our saṃsāric pleasures—which are transient and eventually lead to pain and loss—is not the purpose of tantric practice. Once I watched a television program about Tibetan Buddhism. The film showed lamas holding the bell in their right hands—it is normally held in the left hand—sprinkling water here and there. There were colorful prayer flags all around and the room was filled with paintings of deities and lavish offerings of food, light, and so on. What the film didn't show was Buddhists studying and debating the Buddha's teachings for twenty years or more in the monasteries. It omitted their practice of disciplining their body, speech, and mind, and it neglected to show them teaching the Dharma to help others subdue their clinging attachment, anger, confusion, jealousy, arrogance, and so on. From that television program, it would seem that Tibetan lamas did rituals to earn their living and increase their reputation and wealth. If such were their motivation, that is not Dharma practice, no matter its external appearance.

It is important to understand what practicing Dharma means. Its purpose is to subdue and abolish our disturbing emotions and wrong views. The Nālandā tradition from India, as embodied in Tibetan Buddhism, emphasizes the use of reason and logic. Eschewing blind faith, it encourages faith based on understanding the teachings and having a reasoned conviction in them. This begins with listening, reading, and studying the teachings; continues with discussing and debating them; and leads to deep meditation on the meaning of the teachings to integrate it with our minds.

One of the excellent texts I recommend to people as the basis of their spiritual practice is *Engaging in the Bodhisattvas' Deeds* (*Bodhicaryāvatāra*) by the eighth-century Indian sage Śāntideva. Consider this book as your guru and your trusted friend. Read it again and again; become very familiar with it. Then whenever you face problems or difficulties, you will know what chapter to read to counter the affliction disturbing your mind at that time. For example, when you suffer from anger, resentment, and jealousy, read and contemplate chapter 6 on fortitude and patience. When you're carried away by attachment and lust, refer to the first part of chapter 8, and to deal with competition, arrogance, and self-preoccupation, practice the teachings in the second part of chapter 8 to calm your mind, subdue your self-centered attitude, and water your seeds of compassion.

With wisdom and compassion, faith and joyous effort, ethical conduct and concentration, we'll now explore the Vajrayāna. But first, a short overview of the Buddha's teachings to put Vajrayāna in context.

Three Turnings of the Dharma Wheel

The *Extensive Play Sūtra* (*Lalitavistara Sūtra*) relays in chapter 24 the words our teacher, the Buddha, said after he attained full awakening under the bodhi tree:

> Profound and peaceful, free from elaboration, clear light,
> unconditioned—
> I have found a nectar-like Dharma.
> Yet if I were to teach it, no one would understand,
> so I shall remain silent here in the forest.

In this statement the Buddha underlined the profundity of the ultimate reality that he had discovered. Thinking that others could not understand this, immediately after his awakening he turned away from giving teachings. He abided in silent contemplation in the forest until gods such as Brahmā and Indra came and pleaded with him to teach, saying there were beings who had "little dust in their eyes" and would benefit from hearing the Dharma. Accordingly, he "turned the wheel of Dharma," teaching the Dharma in three sets.

Profound and peaceful refers to the first turning of the wheel of Dharma, which speaks of four truths of the āryas as well as dependent arising. *Free from elaboration* indicates the second turning, which includes the Perfection of Wisdom sūtras. These emphasize the ultimate nature of all persons and phenomena—their emptiness of inherent existence. *Clear light, unconditioned* refers to the third turning of the Dharma Wheel. Whereas the second turning contained teachings on emptiness—the object clear light—the third turning speaks of the cognizing subject, the clear-light mind that knows emptiness. In this short verse, the Buddha summarized the teachings he would give.

His first teaching was to five human disciples—the wandering mendicants who had been his companions during his six years of ascetic practices. When they requested him to teach, he explained the four truths of the āryas from the point of view of their nature, how to engage with them, and the result of realizing each truth. Regarding their *nature*, he said, "This is the truth of duḥkha—unsatisfactory experiences; this is the truth of the origin of duḥkha, this is the truth of the cessation of duḥkha and its origins, and this is the path leading to that cessation." With respect to *engaging* with each truth, he said, "Duḥkha is to be known, its origin is to be abandoned, its cessation is to be actualized, and the path is to be cultivated." Regarding the *result* of understanding each truth, the Buddha said, "True duḥkha is to be fully understood, but there is no duḥkha to understand; true origins are to be abandoned, but there are no origins to abandon; true cessation is to be actualized, but there is no cessation to actualize; and true paths are to be cultivated, but there are no paths to cultivate."[4] In saying this, the Buddha is speaking about the ultimate nature of all phenomena—they are empty of inherent existence. There is no inherently existent duḥkha to know, no inherently existent origins to abandon, no inherently existent cessation to actualize, and no inherently existent path to cultivate. Thus, while the four truths exist conventionally, on the ultimate level they are empty of having any independent, self-instituting nature.

True origins—the afflictions and polluted karma—are described in detail in the second turning of the Dharma Wheel, as is the way to abandon them by practicing the true path, the wisdom realizing selflessness. *Free from elaborations* refers to true cessations and to emptiness. Both of these are free from the elaborations of inherent existence and grasping inherent existence. This shows the possibility of overcoming the afflictions by understanding dependent arising free from the eight extremes of (inherently existent) ceasing, arising, discontinuation, permanence, coming, going, difference, and identity, as Nāgārjuna said in his homage to the Buddha in *Treatise on the Middle Way*.

The third turning of the Dharma Wheel consists of two sets of sūtras: The first set are for those disciples who found it difficult to understand the literal meaning of the teachings on emptiness in the second turning. They interpreted them by speaking of the three natures: dependent phenomena, imaginaries (imputed), and the consummate or perfect nature (nonduality—i.e., directly knowing the world as "representation only" in the nondual deeper layer of our consciousness). These form the basis for the Yogācāra school of Mahāyāna Buddhism as explained by Asaṅga and Vasubandhu in the fourth century CE.

The second set of sūtras in the third turning include the *Tathāgata Essence Sūtra* (*Tathāgatagarbha Sūtra*), the root sūtra that is the topic of Maitreya's *Sublime Continuum* (*Uttaratantra*), in which the basic element, the tathāgatagarbha, is explained. "Clear light" and "unconditioned" refer to this. This basic nature of mind itself is luminous, whereas the afflictions are distorted conceptions rooted in ignorance. Here "luminous" does not mean radiating light but has the connotation of being vivid and capable of knowing an object. When ignorance is overcome by the realization of emptiness, the other mental afflictions have no basis and they too cease. Dependent arising is the "monarch of reasoning," and understanding it correctly brings about this cessation.

By bringing together the two points taught in the second and third turnings of the Dharma Wheel—emptiness (object clear light) and the clear-light nature of the mind (subject clear light)—we can feel the possibility of attaining nirvāṇa. The basic nature of the mind is clear light in that it is empty of inherent existence, and the afflictions are adventitious because they are not imbedded in either the conventional or ultimate nature of the mind.

By speaking of the subject clear light, the third Dharma Wheel hints at Tantra, which explains the subtlest mind, the fundamental innate clear-light mind, and how to make it manifest so that it realizes emptiness. Teaching the tathāgatagarbha is a prelude to this.[5]

The tantric teachings speak of the coarse, subtle, and subtlest minds. The subtlest mind becomes manifest at the time of death after the three visions of white appearance, red increase, and black near-attainment dissolve during the dying process. At this time the eighty indicative conceptions, most of which are subtle afflictions, also dissolve, leaving the fundamental innate clear-light mind, which is free from the three visions and the eighty conceptions. In some explanations, this is understood to indicate *zhentong* (other-emptiness), but here it refers to levels of consciousness, not to the ultimate nature of phenomena.

Ultimately this innate clear-light mind is the basis of all appearances in the universe. Dzogchen terminology includes the words "basis" (T. *gzhi*) and the "expression or appearance of the basis" (T. *gzhi gnang*). The latter refers to various appearances, including the white appearance, red increase, black near-attainment, and the eighty conceptions. At the time of death, all these dissolve into the basis, the subtlest clear-light mind.

When meditators already have the correct view of emptiness, the subtlest clear-light mind can be used to realize emptiness nonconceptually. This further purifies the actual clear-light mind, which then becomes the wisdom truth body of a buddha. The emptiness of this mind and its true cessations are known as the nature truth body of a buddha. From the subtlest wind that is one nature with a buddha's mind arises the enjoyment body and the emanation bodies. Buddhas use their enjoyment body to teach the ārya bodhisattvas in a pure land and their emanation bodies to teach ordinary sentient beings. These two form bodies of a buddha serve the purpose of others by guiding them on the stages of the path to liberation and full awakening, and the two truth bodies serve that buddha's own purpose by being actualized upon their attainment of buddhahood.

Bhikṣu Tenzin Gyatso, the Fourteenth Dalai Lama
Thekchen Choling

1 Method and Wisdom in Sūtra and Tantra

IN *MY LAND and My People*, I related my experience of going in 1956 to Bodhgaya, the site of the Buddha's awakening in north India. I had been invited to participate in the celebration of the 2,500th anniversary of the Buddha's parinirvāṇa. This momentous occasion was attended by thousands of people from all over the world who had faith in the same teacher, the awakened Buddha. I too felt a deep personal connection and appreciation of the Buddha and his Sūtrayāna and Tantrayāna teachings, because by learning, reflecting, and meditating on them, I have received incomparable benefit. Sūtrayāna is the system of practice taught in the sūtras, the teachings the Buddha gave while appearing in the aspect of a monastic. These include the paths of śrāvakas, solitary realizers, and bodhisattvas. Tantrayāna (Tantric Vehicle) consists of the practices and paths taught in the tantras, the teachings the Buddha gave to a special audience while appearing in the aspect of Vajradhara.

Method and Wisdom

A bird needs two wings to fly. Similarly, a meditator needs two principal types of practice to accomplish the path to awakening—method and wisdom. The method aspect of the path correlates with the collection of merit, and the wisdom aspect of the path correlates with the collection of wisdom. In Sūtra, some examples of method are the meditation on the ugliness of the body; the determination to be free from saṃsāra; the aspiration for liberation, bodhicitta, and all the meditations leading up to it; and the first four perfections. Through engaging in these practices, we principally collect great merit. The collection of merit includes mind, mental factors, and the seeds of virtuous karma.

Examples of the wisdom aspect of the path are meditations on ultimate truth and the emptiness of inherent existence. In Sūtra, wisdom refers to the wisdom realizing the sixteen aspects of the four truths, and specifically the wisdom realizing emptiness. This may be either a correct conceptual understanding or a direct perceiver that knows the four truths without the veil of a conceptual appearance. These meditations increase our wisdom, leading to the collection of wisdom.

In the Pāramitāyāna, the Sūtra branch of Mahāyāna, the practice of wisdom principally leads to the truth body of a buddha and the practice of method principally leads to the form body of a buddha. Both wisdom and method need to be complete for the actualization of either the form body or the truth body. Wisdom and method and the two buddha bodies also correlate with the two truths. Meditations on the method side correspond with veiled truths, for they understand the multifarious types and aspects of conventional truths. This relates to the varied form bodies of the Buddha that manifest to benefit sentient beings. Meditations on the wisdom side see all these diverse phenomena as of one taste; in terms of the way in which they exist, all phenomena are equally empty of inherent existence.

COLLECTION	ASPECT OF PATH	ASSOCIATED TRUTH	BUDDHA BODY
Merit	Method	Veiled truths	Form body
Wisdom	Wisdom	Ultimate truths	Truth body

To reach the awakening of any of the three vehicles—the Śrāvaka, Solitary Realizer, or Bodhisattva Vehicles—practitioners must collect both merit and wisdom. These collections can be spoken of in two ways. *Fully qualified collections* lead to the highest awakening, the awakening of a buddha. These practices are motivated by bodhicitta and are engaged in by bodhisattvas. *Ordinary collections* are those motivated by the aspiration for liberation. These are practiced by those on the Śrāvaka and Solitary Realizer Vehicles and lead to the awakening of their respective vehicles.

The collections may be either actual collections or similitudes of the collections. *Actual collections* are those accumulated once practitioners have entered a path—that is, they have attained the path of accumulation of any of the three vehicles. The actual collection of wisdom refers to realizing emptiness either inferentially or directly; it does not necessitate the union of serenity and insight on emptiness—thus it can be the inferential realization of emptiness on the path of accumulation.

Similitudes of the collections are the merit we create and the wisdom we gain in our daily practice as ordinary beings before entering the path of accumulation. Through these similitudes of collections, we plant the seeds and build up our potential to be able to accumulate the actual two collections later. For example, someone who aspires to enter the Pāramitāyāna and has generated contrived bodhicitta builds up a similitude of a bodhisattva's collection of merit and wisdom. When she generates actual bodhicitta and enters the Mahāyāna path of accumulation, she begins to accumulate the actual two collections. Although śrāvakas and solitary realizers also accumulate merit and wisdom, theirs are considered similitudes of the two collections because they are not supported by bodhicitta.

In general, meditations on the method side of the path are said "not to cognize the object," whereas those on the wisdom side "cognize the object." This relates to two types of meditation described earlier: meditation to transform our subjective experience and meditation on an object.[6] To review these, when we meditate on compassion, we don't ascertain sentient beings or their duḥkha. We *experience* compassion and transform our minds into this wish for sentient beings to be free from duḥkha. But during meditation on emptiness, we seek to ascertain emptiness, which is the apprehended object of that mind.

Although the collection of merit created by method is a necessary support for wisdom, moving from one path to a higher path is spoken of in terms of wisdom—meditating minds that perceive the object, the emptiness of inherent existence. Except for the first path, the other four paths and the ten grounds are not demarcated in terms of minds on the side of method but in terms of the clarity of our wisdom and the strength of that wisdom to eradicate defilements.

Wisdom is the ultimate antidote that eliminates the afflictions from our mindstream so that they never arise again. Meditations on the method side are temporary antidotes. For example, meditation on love reduces the force and frequency of anger, but it does not uproot the seed or potential of anger in our mindstream. This is only done by the wisdom directly realizing emptiness. In short, method and wisdom are essential elements for the practice of both Sūtra and Tantra. Tsongkhapa says in his *Great Exposition on the Stages of the Path* (LC 2:99):

> This training in method and wisdom comprising the six perfections is, as explained earlier, common to both the Mantra and Perfection Vehicles. For in many tantric classics, we find repeated mention of the complete path of the perfections—the six perfections, the thirty-seven harmonies with awakening, the sixteen emptinesses, and so on—in the context of explanations that the entire celestial mansion and the array of resident deities are the inner qualities of mind. Therefore, know that all the explanations in the Perfection of Wisdom literature about what is to be adopted and what is to be discarded are comprehensively shared with the Mantra Vehicle, except in the case of the tantric teachings for certain exceptional persons in which they must take the experience of sensory objects as the path, and so forth.

Wisdom in Pāramitāyāna and Vajrayāna

The way in which method and wisdom are practiced in Sūtra and Tantra is similar in some respects and different in others. The Prāsaṅgika Madhyamaka view of emptiness is common to all vehicles and all tantric classes. In terms of the object of realization, the emptiness of inherent existence, practitioners of all Buddhist traditions and vehicles must realize the same emptiness of inherent existence to attain liberation or awakening.

However, Pāramitāyāna and Vajrayāna differ from the viewpoint of the subject, the consciousness realizing emptiness. Although in Pāramitāyāna the wisdom realizing emptiness is a more subtle consciousness than our usual daily consciousnesses, it is nonetheless coarse in comparison to the subtler levels of consciousness spoken of in Vajrayāna, particularly in Highest Yoga Tantra. In that tantric class, the fundamental innate clear-light mind (T. *gnyug sems*), which is the source of saṃsāra and nirvāṇa, is the subject—the mind realizing emptiness. By using bliss as the method, practitioners dissolve the coarser winds and coarser levels of mind to make manifest this subtlest clear-light mind. Transforming the subtlest mind into the wisdom realizing emptiness is a distinctive feature of Highest Yoga Tantra.

Why is meditation on emptiness more effective when done with subtler levels of mind? When meditation on emptiness takes place using the coarse levels of mind, the primary approach to emptiness is analytic. Analysis is used to deconstruct what ignorance grasps as existent—inherently existent persons and phenomena. When the level of mind being used to meditate on emptiness is the subtlest consciousness, the mode of meditation on emptiness is stabilizing, allowing the mind to be fully concentrated and immersed in the ultimate nature of reality.

Analysis is a coarser consciousness. In Sūtrayāna, analytical meditation is required to cultivate insight because analysis brings greater clarity to the ascertainment of emptiness. However, in Vajrayāna, where the meditative approach is primarily nonconceptual, greater clarity of the ascertainment of emptiness is attained by making manifest ever more subtle states of mind. This is done by dissolving the coarser winds and minds through stabilizing meditation and making manifest the subtlest mind, which is then used to ascertain emptiness. Since analysis would make the coarser levels of mind return, tantric yogis who have gained the correct view by following the Sūtra path now engage in stabilizing meditation so that the subtlest mind is in deep concentration on its own ultimate nature. Thus the role analysis plays in Sūtrayāna meditation on emptiness is fulfilled in Vajrayāna by stabilizing meditation done with increasingly subtle levels of mind. The subtlest mind is the actual substantial cause of the omniscient mind. This approach is shared in the Highest Yoga Tantra meditations of mahāmudrā, dzogchen, and the indivisibility of bliss and emptiness.

The primordial innate clear-light mind is devoid of the elaborations of the temporary, coarser states of mind. When this subject—the innate clear-light mind—perceives the object—clear light (emptiness)—it eradicates obscurations very quickly. In contrast, the wisdom realizing emptiness as described in Pāramitāyāna is not as strong, and thus it takes eons longer to eliminate obscurations. The tenth-ground bodhisattvas in the Pāramitāyāna know the object clear light—emptiness—very clearly and purely and are absorbed in it nondually in meditative equipoise. However, they are not successful in knowing the subject clear light, for the method to actualize this is taught only in Highest Yoga Tantra. By employing techniques to make manifest the innate clear-light mind, which is totally freed from all pollutants and the dualism of the coarser levels of mind, tantric bodhisattvas quickly eliminate defilements. When all obscurations have been eliminated, they actualize the union of no-more-learning of the illusory body and clear light.[7] This is the attainment of buddhahood.

Furthermore, to actualize an omniscient mind, we must cultivate its substantial cause. This is not just any consciousness but a consciousness with an enduring continuity. Polluted states of mind, such as the afflictions, are adventitious and temporary. They arise at certain times and then disappear, whereas the mind whose nature we want to realize in order to become omniscient should be eternal, because buddhahood does not cease. In addition, we want to realize the emptiness of the mind that has never been polluted by afflictions or their latencies. This unpolluted, everlasting mind is the fundamental innate clear-light mind.

Sometimes it is said that the view in Sūtra and Tantra is the same. Here, view refers to the object, emptiness. This is the same in Sūtra and Tantra. However, view can also mean the subject, the consciousness that views. In this case, as noted above, there is a difference in views between Sūtra and Tantra in that in Tantra, the consciousness viewing emptiness is the great bliss, a subtler consciousness that is not spoken of in Sūtra.

The Tibetan sage Sakya Paṇḍita (1182–1251) said that Sūtra and Tantra are not differentiated in terms of their view of emptiness. Nevertheless, in the Sakya tradition four different views are presented in the four empowerments. This is not contradictory, because when Sakya Paṇḍita said Sūtra and Tantra are not differentiated by view, he was referring to "view" as emptiness, the object to be realized. But when he sets forth different views in the four empowerments of Highest Yoga Tantra, "view" refers to the subject, the consciousnesses realizing emptiness. Similarly, when the Gelug master Jamyang Shepa (1648–1721), in his *Great Exposition of Tenets* (T. *Grub mtha' chen mo*), said that Tantra supersedes Sūtra in terms of the view, here too "view" refers to the mind perceiving emptiness, the wisdom of great bliss. Kagyu and Nyingma texts also say that Tantra is superior to Sūtra in terms of the view, and here too they are referring to the view as the very subtle mind realizing emptiness.

In summary, the paths of the three vehicles taught in Sūtrayāna and the paths taught in the four tantric classes can overcome all afflictive obscurations and bring arhatship. However, only the path taught in Highest Yoga Tantra is capable of overcoming all cognitive obscurations completely. A bodhisattva who practices the Sūtra path must enter the Tantra path on the tenth ground at the latest to attain full awakening. The *supreme object*—the emptiness of inherent existence—is taught in Sūtrayāna and the three lower tantric classes, but the *supreme subject*—the innate great bliss—is hidden and not taught there. Similarly, the *principal defilement*—the subtle, small cognitive obscurations—are taught in Sūtrayāna and the three lower tantric classes, but the *supreme antidote* at the end of the tenth ground—the actual clear light and great bliss of Highest Yoga Tantra—is hidden. To attain buddhahood, all conceptuality and karmic winds must be completely stopped and the only antidote that can halt them is the great bliss of Highest Yoga Tantra. For this reason, all bodhisattvas must eventually practice Highest Yoga Tantra.

Method in Pāramitāyāna and Vajrayāna

In both Pāramitāyāna and Tantrayāna, the method aspect of the path is based on bodhicitta. However, in Tantra, practitioners should see sentient beings' duḥkha as inexorably unbearable and want to attain awakening as quickly as possible in order to be of the utmost benefit to them. These bodhisattvas seek to attain full awakening quickly so that sentient beings don't need to wait for their help for a long time.

Thus the compassion of bodhisattvas who practice Vajrayāna is much more intense, propelling them to seek awakening in this very lifetime rather than in three countless great eons through the practice of Pāramitāyāna. Although the intention of meditation on bodhicitta—the aspiration for sentient beings to be free from duḥkha—and the entity of bodhicitta—the aspiration for oneself to attain full awakening—are the same in Pāramitāyāna and Vajrayāna, the intensity of bodhicitta is far greater in the latter. Bodhicitta isn't just about being a nice person who is kind and considerate of others; it is based on cherishing others more than ourselves and wanting to exchange ourselves with others in the sense of taking on their pain and misery and giving them our happiness and good opportunities. For example, during the revolutions in Mongolia and later in China, many great scholars were executed. One was a tutor to Jamyang Shepa. It seems he was executed for the crime of having many disciples. When he was about to die, he asked for a moment to say a prayer, and then he said, "O my guru, please inspire me so that the harmful deeds and negativities of all sentient beings ripen on me and all my virtues ripen for them." Then he passed away peacefully.

Both Pāramitāyāna and Vajrayāna practitioners engage in the essential bodhisattva activities of the six perfections and the four ways of gathering disciples. The difference in the method side between these two vehicles is that method in Vajrayāna also involves taking the result into the path—that is, practitioners imagine having the four purities: the pure body of a buddha, the pure environment of the maṇḍala, pure enjoyments, and the pure actions of an awakened one. This enables them to accumulate merit quickly.

Why is method in Tantra superior to method as presented in Sūtra? A buddha possesses a truth body and a form body. The truth body is said to primarily fulfill one's own aims and the form body to primarily fulfill the aims of others. In Sūtra the principal cause for the form body is the collection of merit by means of the six or ten perfections. Since a result must be concordant with its cause, the special mental body attained by ārya bodhisattvas is the substantial cause for a buddha's form body, according to Sūtra. However, the causes of the mental body are the latencies of ignorance and unpolluted karma. How can this mental body born from the impurity of the latencies of ignorance serve as the substantial cause of a buddha's enjoyment body? There would be some disparity between the impure nature of the cause and the undefiled nature of the effect.

In Tantra the Buddha's enjoyment body is explained on the basis of the subtlest wind that always accompanies the subtlest mind, making the nature of the cause and effect in accord. The substantial cause for the form body is the illusory body—the body of the deity created from the subtle winds and assumed by a yogi on the completion stage. Preliminary to this, practitioners meditate on the pure appearance of themselves as the deity and on the divine identity of being the deity on the generation stage.

In Sūtrayāna the causes for the truth body and form body are created separately because method and wisdom are practiced by different minds. During meditative equipoise on emptiness, the wisdom realizing emptiness (wisdom) is complemented by bodhicitta (method). In post-meditation the bodhisattva actions to benefit others are supported by a factor of wisdom. In Sūtra, it is not possible for both the wisdom and method factors of the path to be present in one consciousness. Thus the union of method and wisdom is not complete in Sūtra: while method and wisdom are not isolated from each other, they are not completely united either.

Only in Tantrayāna do we find the complete union of method and wisdom that leads to the complete unity of the form body and truth body in the resultant state of buddhahood. This unity comes about through deity yoga. In the generation stage, practitioners meditate on the emptiness of themselves and the deity and then imagine this wisdom consciousness appearing in the divine form of the deity—this is the method aspect. At the same time, the meditator ascertains and is mindful of the emptiness of the deity—this is the wisdom aspect. In other words, just visualizing oneself as the deity is not deity yoga; one must also include meditation on emptiness and the wisdom realizing emptiness appearing in the form of the deity.

On the generation stage, meditators cultivate a sense of divine identity of being the deity and contemplate that these two—the wisdom realizing emptiness and the mind of deity yoga (that is, the wisdom consciousness appearing in the form of the deity) are one nature. Here the composite of method and wisdom—the appearance of the deity that is empty of inherent existence and like an illusion—is an affirming negative. Inherent existence is negated, and simultaneously the deity appears to the meditator's mind.

Then on the completion stage, meditators generate the illusory body from the subtlest wind and the subtlest mind, which is the clear-light mind realizing emptiness. The subtlest wind and subtlest mind are one nature, and so are the illusory body and the clear-light mind generated on the completion stage. These causes for the form body and the truth body are cultivated simultaneously in one consciousness and are directly concordant with the two resultant bodies of a buddha, which are also one nature.

When meditating on emptiness in Sūtra, all conventional appearances vanish, whereas in Tantra, one trains to maintain the conventional appearance of oneself as the deity performing compassionate actions while simultaneously meditating on emptiness. Here, the conventional appearance of the deity is not the I of an ordinary saṃsāric being with polluted aggregates but the I as a deity with aggregates that are manifestations of wisdom. Cultivating the clear appearance of oneself as the deity and the divine identity of being the deity overcomes the perception and grasping of oneself as an ordinary, polluted sentient being. This helps to actualize our potential for buddhahood.

As mentioned above, in Vajrayāna, the result is taken into the path. This entails imagining your body, the beings around you, the environment, your actions, and everything you use and enjoy as pure, like those in a pure land. This is done for a specific purpose—it acts as an antidote to afflictions. This meditation does not make impure phenomena become pure. Sentient beings who suffer in saṃsāra still exist, and we must engage in compassionate activities to benefit them. Similarly, our impure body does not become the deity's body. Instead, we meditate that it is empty of inherent existence and then imagine that the blissful wisdom mind that realizes emptiness itself appears as the deity. The I is designated in dependence on this base, and divine identity is cultivated on oneself as the deity. When practitioners attain an illusory body on the completion stage, they manifest many different forms and go to various buddha fields to make offerings to the buddhas there. They also appear in diverse forms to benefit sentient beings throughout the universe. The mental body of ārya bodhisattvas practicing the Pāramitāyāna engages in similar activities, but this body and the illusory body differ. Pāramitāyāna bodhisattvas think of themselves as bodhisattvas when doing these activities, whereas Vajrayāna bodhisattvas think of themselves as buddhas. Pāramitāyāna bodhisattvas emanate and offer gorgeous objects, whereas Vajrayāna bodhisattvas offer objects that are the nature of bliss and emptiness.

Believing everything to be literally pure is a wrong consciousness (T. *log shes*), because everything is not pure. Developing a wrong consciousness will not produce a correct result. For example, the meditation in which we see the whole earth filled with skeletons is done only at the level of imagination, for a specific, beneficial purpose—to decrease desire and attachment to saṃsāra. Practitioners of this meditation do not believe that the world is in fact filled with bones, for that would be a wrong consciousness. In addition, it would be very strange indeed to relate to everything around us as bones. In the same way, the meditation on pure view done by tantric practitioners does not mean that the people and environment around them become deities and the maṇḍala.

Method and Wisdom Practiced Together

Generating insight by alternating stabilizing and analytical meditation until the analysis can induce pliancy is common to the Sūtrayāna, as well as to the three lower tantric classes. However, Vajrayāna contains some special techniques for doing this. In all four tantric classes, practitioners meditate on emptiness and then generate their wisdom realizing emptiness into the deity. Examining the details of the deity's body is analytical meditation. Focusing single-pointedly on the deity's body is stabilizing meditation. In deity yoga, analytical and stabilizing meditation are thus mutually supportive and are cultivated in the same meditation session.

However, in Sūtrayāna, serenity and insight are cultivated separately because stabilizing meditation interferes with analysis and analysis interferes with stable concentration. Sūtrayāna practitioners gain full serenity by going through the nine mental abidings, and after that they cultivate insight, whereas Vajrayāna practitioners cultivate serenity and insight together.

The three lower tantric classes contain special concentrations that are a union of serenity and insight realizing emptiness. For example, in Action Tantra, the initial class of tantra, practitioners first engage in meditative stabilizations with repetition, followed by meditative stabilizations without repetition. Meditative stabilizations without repetition consist of the meditative stabilizations of abiding in fire, abiding in sound, and bestowing liberation at the end of sound, practices that will be described in a later chapter. At the end of the latter, through alternating stabilizing and analytical meditation, practitioners attain a special concentration that is a union of serenity and insight. Similarly, Performance Tantra and Yoga Tantra contain uncommon techniques for quickly generating this special concentration.

In Highest Yoga Tantra the methods for attaining serenity and insight are not separate, and the two can be practiced simultaneously. Even while training in serenity, practitioners can engage in more intensive analysis without harming the factor of stability. This is due to concentrating on special focal objects—for example, the entire maṇḍala within a tiny drop—and to meditating on special places within the body, such as the essential channel points. Although analytical meditation on emptiness is not done when visualizing these special objects, by cultivating stability and analysis together, practitioners more easily attain the union of serenity and insight on emptiness when they switch to emptiness as the object of meditation.

It is crucial that a practitioner seeking insight prevents analysis from interfering with the single-pointedness of serenity. Instead, analysis must be able to induce pliancy and thus serenity. On the refined generation stage of Highest Yoga Tantra, practitioners who already have attained serenity focus on themselves as the deity and imagine a tiny drop at the top or bottom of their central channel. In this drop, they imagine an upright vajra. This vajra multiplies to become two vajras, then four, eight, and so forth. Then the vajras gradually dissolve back into each other until only one vajra remains. Doing analytical meditation in this way helps the winds to enter the central channel, thus making the mind subtler and enhancing the power of concentration. In this way, insight is attained easily.

The mind goes wherever its mount, the winds, go. By focusing on various parts of the body in the practices of the channels, winds, and drops, Vajrayāna practitioners on the completion stage make the winds enter, abide, and dissolve in the heart cakra. This makes manifest the fundamental innate clear-light mind, which is then transformed into the wisdom realizing emptiness. This is the meaning of actualizing innate great bliss focused on emptiness. With this as method, insight into emptiness becomes more powerful and can quickly eradicate both afflictive and cognitive obscurations.

In addition to employing these special techniques to make manifest the subtlest consciousness, in meditations subsequent to meditative equipoise on the generation and completion stages, yogis practicing Highest Yoga Tantra engage in analytical meditation on emptiness. However, the advanced yogis who have developed firm concentration on the vital points of the body do only stabilizing meditation on emptiness during the completion stage. At that time, they do not do the analytical meditation of insight described above.

In short, the differences between Sūtra and Tantra lie in the method aspect of the path that facilitates the eradication of the cognitive obscurations. Some of the factors that differentiate Highest Yoga Tantra from Sūtra and make it more profound are:

- The urgency of one's wish to become a buddha to benefit sentient beings is stronger in Tantra, which brings forth special effort to practice Vajrayāna.

- The method in Tantra is great bliss, which makes manifest the subtlest mind of clear light.
- The subtlest mind, the fundamental innate mind of clear light, is used to realize emptiness, and meditating with this mind quickly eliminates obscurations.
- The path of the union of bliss and emptiness that leads to an illusory body is a unique cause for attaining the form body of a buddha.
- The illusory body and actual clear light are the substantial causes that are directly concordant with the resultant form and truth bodies, respectively.
- Method and wisdom are cultivated simultaneously in the entity of one consciousness—that is, in a single mental event. This enables the accumulation of method and wisdom to occur simultaneously.
- Practitioners train in perceiving the two truths simultaneously, which prepares them for buddhahood, where conventional and ultimate truths are perceived at the same time.
- The object with which one cultivates serenity is the divine body of the deity or the subtle drops in the deity's body. This leads to deeper concentration.
- There are special techniques for cultivating refined analysis by focusing on tiny objects visualized in the deity's body.
- Analytical and stabilizing meditation are mutually supportive and are cultivated in the same meditation session, thus bringing about the union of serenity and insight more quickly.
- Stabilizing meditation that employs subtle levels of mind increases the clarity of the ascertainment of emptiness.
- Due to special meditative techniques, serenity and insight are attained simultaneously.
- The paths practiced in Tantrayāna are concordant with the four perfect results at buddhahood: (1) the pure body of the deity, (2) the pure maṇḍala or environment, (3) pure objects of enjoyment and resources, and (4) pure awakened activities, such as emanating forms that eliminate the suffering of sentient beings.

REFLECTION

1. What constitutes the actual collections and similitude collections of merit and wisdom?
2. What are the similarities between the method and wisdom aspects of the Sūtrayāna and the Tantrayāna?

The Inseparability of Method and Wisdom

Although method and wisdom become completely inseparable at buddhahood, Sūtra and Tantra have different approaches to cultivating their inseparability. In Sūtra, practitioners train by conjoining one with the other, whereas in Tantra, practitioners train to make both manifest within a single consciousness.

In Sūtrayāna, method and wisdom are separate entities. To practice them together, before entering into single-pointed meditation on emptiness (wisdom), practitioners generate bodhicitta (method) as the motivation for meditating. Their meditation on emptiness is influenced by and conjoined with bodhicitta, but bodhicitta is not manifest at that time. Some scholars say it is latent, while others say that at the time of directly realizing emptiness, all minds on the method side are not present. Tsongkhapa explains in *Small Stages of the Path* (GSM 2:214):

> If at the beginning of a session, one initially establishes firm bodhicitta, then, when set in meditative stabilization on emptiness, it will be conjoined with the force of that bodhicitta, which nevertheless is not actually present.

After arising from meditation on emptiness and during the times of subsequent attainment, wisdom is conjoined with method. At this time, practitioners generate bodhicitta and practice generosity, ethical conduct, and fortitude. They teach the Dharma and serve sentient beings. Although ārya bodhisattvas do not directly perceive emptiness while they go about their daily activities, they reflect that the agent of generosity (themselves), the gift they give, the action of giving, and the recipient are all empty of inherent existence yet appear like illusions. In a similar way, when practicing ethical conduct and fortitude, they reflect that the agent, object, and action are empty. Tsongkhapa says in the *Small Stages of the Path* (GSM 2:214):

> If one's wisdom realizing emptiness is strong, then when one gives gifts, pays homage, circumambulates, and so forth, the mind that observes those, although not realizing emptiness, will be in possession of the power of that mind [realizing emptiness].

In his *Great Exposition of the Stages of the Path* (LC 2:93–94), he says:

> Deeds imbued with the philosophical view and wisdom imbued with method may be understood by way of an analogy. When a mother stricken with grief at the death of her beloved child engages in activities such as discussing other topics with people, although all of her feelings may be influenced by grief, not every one of them is grief. Similarly, if the wisdom that knows emptiness is very strong, even though the states of mind associated with giving, making obeisance, circumambulating, or reciting are not cognitions of emptiness, this still does not preclude those thoughts being influenced by the force of the cognition of emptiness. For instance, at the start of a meditation session, if you first generate very strong bodhicitta, this bodhicitta is not manifest when you then enter meditative equipoise in a concentration on emptiness. Yet this does not preclude this concentration's being imbued with the influence of bodhicitta.
>
> It is this sort of thing that is referred to by the term "non-apprehending generosity." It is not the complete absence of a generous attitude, wherein giving is not feasible. Understand the remaining perfections in a similar way. Know also that this is how method and wisdom are inseparable.

In this way, a yogi alternates meditative equipoise on emptiness and bodhisattva activities in a mutually supportive manner. Wisdom is prominent in meditative equipoise on emptiness, and method is prominent when engaging in generosity and so forth. Each is conjoined with the other, but the two do not occur simultaneously. This is the meaning of practicing method conjoined with wisdom and practicing wisdom conjoined with method in Sūtrayāna.

In Tantrayāna a practitioner endeavors to make manifest both method and wisdom in a single consciousness. This is done through the practice of deity yoga, which is much more than simply visualizing a deity. First a practitioner meditates on emptiness and dissolves all appearances of inherently existent phenomena, including herself. Then, the mind realizing emptiness itself appears in the form of a deity, and again the practitioner meditates on the emptiness of the deity and the emptiness of the I that is now merely designated in dependence on the basis of the purified aggregates of the deity. This inseparability of method and wisdom in Tantra is the unity in one consciousness of the vast practice of deity yoga and the profound practice of wisdom realizing emptiness. For example, in the Action Tantra meditation called "the concentration bestowing liberation at the end of sound," the consciousness that appears as both the sound of the mantra and the deity's body also realizes their emptiness. Such indivisibility of method and wisdom is the meaning of the word "vajra" in Vajrayāna.

Focusing on the body of the deity and developing the aspect that it lacks inherent existence is not meditation on the indivisibility of method and wisdom, because such a practice is also found in Sūtrayāna. For example, while visualizing the Buddha, a Sūtra practitioner meditates that the Buddha lacks inherent existence. Meditating on such a pure object as the Buddha is the method side of the path and the collection of merit, and ascertaining the Buddha's lack of inherent existence is the wisdom side of the path and the collection of wisdom. But this is not the inseparability of method and wisdom spoken of in Tantra. The difference is that in deity yoga, practitioners generate themselves as the deity after having meditated on the emptiness of both themselves and the deity, and the mind realizing emptiness itself appears in the form of the deity.

In Sūtrayāna, when we inferentially realize the emptiness of a particular object, let's say a sprout, does that sprout appear to the mind that realizes its lack of inherent existence? There are two lines of thinking. According to some scholars, the sprout, as a conventional truth, does not appear to the mind inferentially realizing its emptiness. According to others, it does.

According to these latter scholars, there is no problem in Tantrayāna with saying that when a meditator realizes the lack of inherent existence of herself as the deity, the image of the deity can still appear.

Even those who say that the sprout does not appear to the mind that inferentially realizes its emptiness assert that in Tantrayāna the image of the deity can appear to the mind of the person realizing its emptiness. Panchen Sonam Drakpa clearly says that the imagined deity appearing to the mind realizing its reality is totally different from the case of the sprout. Why is this? Tantra has the added dimension of deity yoga. Here a meditator meditates on emptiness, and then that very wisdom realizing emptiness arises in the form of the deity, and again the meditator reflects on the empty nature of the deity. There is a certain reflexive quality in that the wisdom mind is meditating on itself appearing as the deity. Meditation on emptiness in deity yoga is not meditating on an external object but on the form of the deity that is the appearance of our own mind fused with emptiness.

Furthermore, the deity we have visualized is something we have freshly cultivated mentally, not a sprout that is an external object perceivable by others. It is easy to realize that the deity has no objective existence, because it is imagined by the mind. In addition, this imagined deity is a much subtler object than a sprout. It is the appearance of the mind realizing emptiness, and we again meditate on its emptiness.

In the three lower tantras, the practice to develop the inseparability of method and wisdom is done by first dissolving ordinary appearance and counteracting ordinary grasping by meditating on emptiness. Within that state of emptiness, a practitioner's wisdom mind arises in the form of a deity and reflects on the ultimate nature of that deity. Arising as the deity is done on an imagined level, whether or not a practitioner has realized emptiness. Imagining whatever understanding of emptiness a practitioner has appearing as the deity is appropriate, because when a practitioner later enters Highest Yoga Tantra, familiarity with this practice will lead to the actual realization of the unity of body and mind.

In Highest Yoga Tantra, the inseparability of method and wisdom is explained differently than in the three lower tantras. In Highest Yoga Tantra, practitioners develop the wisdom that is the ultimate or actual clear light directly realizing emptiness. From this, they actualize a pure illusory body that arises from that clear light. After attaining the pure illusory body, when they again enter into clear light, both method and wisdom arise simultaneously, as one entity in actuality. This is called "the stage of learners' union," which is a profound realization of the completion stage of Highest Yoga Tantra. Those who have attained this are very close to buddhahood. Through continued meditation, when they eliminate all cognitive obscurations, they become fully awakened buddhas.

In short, the method found in Highest Yoga Tantra excels because it presents a path leading to the inseparability of body, speech, and mind at the resultant stage of buddhahood. The Buddha's body, speech, and mind are called "the inconceivable three secrets of the Buddha" because our ordinary mind cannot conceive of the total indivisibility of body and mind that occurs at full awakening. This indivisibility is possible because at the ordinary level, our subtlest mind—the fundamental innate clear-light mind—is inseparable from its mount, the subtlest wind. This indivisibility, which is part of our fundamental nature, makes it possible for our body and mind to be totally indivisible upon attaining full awakening. And a distinctive feature of Highest Yoga Tantra is that it presents a path in which method and wisdom are combined and become inseparable.

Some Highest Yoga Tantra practices emphasize focusing on both the subtlest wind and subtlest mind to attain the form body, while others emphasize focusing only on the subtlest mind. In the New Translation schools, most tantric systems, including Guhyasamāja, Cakrasaṃvara, and Yamāntaka, use the former method. Kālacakra Tantra, dzogchen, and mahāmudrā emphasize meditation on the subtlest mind.

Some systems rely on meditation on the channels, winds, and drops to manifest the fundamental innate clear-light mind. Of these, some—such as Guhyasamāja—emphasize wind yoga, and others—such as Cakrasaṃvara—emphasize the four joys. Other systems, such as dzogchen and mahāmudrā, emphasize remaining in a nonconceptual state as a means to manifest this subtlest mind.

The tantric practice of inseparable method and wisdom is found in both mahāmudrā and dzogchen, where it is explained in terms of the basis, path, and result. The mind that is the originator of the universe is called *rigpa*. On the level of the basis or ground, rigpa has two principal qualities: spontaneous presence (T. *lhun grub*), which is the nature of the ground, and primordial purity (T. *ka dag*), which is its essence. In their nature, these two qualities are inseparable. All appearances and their perceptions in our mind arise as the play of rigpa.

On the path, the practice of leap-over (T. *thod rgal*) is related to spontaneous presence, and the practice of breakthrough (T. *khregs chod*) is related to the primordial purity. Leap-over practice creates the causes to actualize the form body and involves seeing all appearances as arising naturally and spontaneously from rigpa. The practice of breakthrough creates the causes to actualize the truth body and is the practice of clear light. These two aspects of the practice of method and wisdom lead to the two buddha bodies. Through leap-over, the outer lucidity (T. *phyi gsal*) of spontaneous presence leads to the form body, and the inner lucidity (T. *nang gsal*) of primordial purity leads to the truth body.[8] The latent inner state of buddhahood becoming fully evident to the practitioner is the inner lucidity of the truth body, and the natural radiance of the mind manifesting for the benefit of others accounts for all the pure and impure form manifestations and is the outer lucidity of the form body. This is the inseparability of wisdom and method in dzogchen. While the terminology used in dzogchen is unique, its meaning is parallel to the systems of Highest Yoga Tantra. This chart abbreviates what was just explained.

	BASIS OR GROUND	PATH	RESULT
Method side of the path	Spontaneous presence, the nature of the basis (T. *lhun grub*)	Leap-over (T. *thod rgal*)	Outer lucidity of the form body
Wisdom side of the path	Primordial purity, the essence of the basis (T. *ka dag*)	Breakthrough (T. *khregs chod*)	Inner lucidity of the truth body

What Makes Vajrayāna Fast

All four classes of tantra speak of attaining awakening within this one lifetime; however, the way they do it differs. In the three lower tantric classes, awakening is accomplished by extending practitioners' lifespan so that they have more time to create the merit necessary to attain awakening. In Highest Yoga Tantra, it is accomplished by generating great bliss, dissolving all the winds into the heart cakra, accessing the subtlest mind, and generating the illusory body.

The Three Lower Tantras

The explanation and practices of the three lower tantras are similar. Since Action (Kriyā) Tantra, the lowest tantric class, is more widespread than Caryā and Yoga Tantras, it is used in this discussion. Action Tantra has several qualities that makes its path quicker than Pāramitāyāna. First, the wisdom consciousness realizing emptiness manifests as the deity's body, speech, and mind. This enables a practitioner to quickly accumulate the collections of merit and wisdom, which lead to the actualization of a buddha's form body and truth body.

Second, the techniques for attaining serenity in Action Tantra are superior to those in the Pāramitāyāna. Action Tantra has special meditation techniques, such as binding vitality-exertion by stopping the breath, that speed the attainment of serenity. In addition, observing subtle internal objects, such as fire and sound in the meditative concentrations abiding in fire and in sound, focuses the mind more quickly and deeply, facilitating the attainment of serenity.

With the attainment of serenity, practitioners have a fully qualified concentration (samādhi) and can then switch the focal object of their meditation to emptiness, where they analyze emptiness with the powerful mind of serenity. Still, they need to skillfully alternate analytical and stabilizing meditation so that one does not harm the other, until they attain the union of serenity and insight realizing emptiness. This practice is done during the concentration bestowing liberation at the end of sound, which is the yoga of signlessness. When they attain the union of serenity and insight, they enter the bodhisattva path of preparation.

Third, by means of the special techniques involved in the concentrations with and without repetition, practitioners can go from the path of accumulation to the path of seeing much quicker than in Pāramitāyāna, where this may require one countless great eon. By attaining the siddhis (feats) of the concentration bestowing liberation at the end of sound, they can accomplish many more actions to benefit sentient beings and thus accumulate greater merit. In addition, they come under the direct care of the buddhas and bodhisattvas, who guide their practice. Furthermore, they can utilize special feats, such as clairvoyance, extending the lifespan, and knowing all treatises immediately upon reading them. These feats hasten the direct realization of emptiness and empower yogis' wisdom at the concentration bestowing liberation at the end of sound so that it can eliminate the cognitive obscurations. Thus both deity yoga and the feats achieved through it enhance the wisdom realizing emptiness, enabling practitioners of Action Tantra to attain awakening more quickly than in Pāramitāyāna.

Highest Yoga Tantra

The practice of Highest Yoga Tantra enables a practitioner to attain awakening even more quickly. In Pāramitāyāna, it is said that once a bodhisattva enters the first path, the path of accumulation, it takes three countless great eons to complete the accumulations of merit and wisdom necessary to attain the form body and the truth body of a buddha. The special techniques of the path of Highest Yoga Tantra enable a practitioner to do this much quicker.

The first countless great eon in Pāramitāyāna is spent practicing the path of accumulation and the path of preparation. Here practitioners work to accumulate great merit on the path of accumulation and to attain the union of serenity and insight in order to progress to the path of preparation. Highest Yoga Tantra speeds this process by means of special methods: a practitioner dissolves into emptiness, imagines the mind realizing emptiness appearing in the form of the deity, and meditates on the simultaneous emptiness and appearance of the deity's form. In deity yoga, not only do meditators imagine having the body of the deity, but they also imagine living in the residence of the deity, enjoying the deity's resources, and engaging in the activities of a buddha,[9] such as benefiting sentient beings and leading them on the path to awakening. With the power of deep single-pointed concentration, yogis make great offerings to the buddhas and contemplate the emptiness of the circle of three—the agent, object, and action. In this way they swiftly accumulate merit and wisdom. In addition, the union of serenity and insight is attained quickly through special stabilizing and analytical meditations on the subtle drops and syllables in the deity's body. All of these practices are accomplished on the generation stage.

In Pāramitāyāna the second countless great eon occurs from the time a practitioner directly realizes emptiness and enters the path of seeing until all afflicted obscurations have been removed and they attain the eighth ground. By using great bliss as method, completion-stage practitioners of Highest Yoga Tantra can dissolve the winds into the central channel and make manifest the subtlest mind, which then realizes emptiness. This mind is extremely powerful and can eliminate all afflicted obscurations quickly—in one meditation session—on the fourth-stage clear light of the completion stage.

The third countless great eon occurs in Pāramitāyāna on the eighth, ninth, and tenth grounds, during which a practitioner vanquishes the cognitive obscurations. This is accomplished quickly in the Highest Yoga Tantra by generating the illusory body and uniting the actual clear light and pure illusory body again and again. Due to skillfully working with the subtle system of winds, the two truths are cognized simultaneously and the ultimate union of the purified subtlest body and subtlest mind are attained. In addition, the illusory body can quickly accumulate great merit through doing many virtuous deeds. For these reasons, the path of the Highest Yoga Tantra is said to lead one to awakening quickly.

Speaking from the viewpoint of Tantra, the way one traverses the five paths and ten bodhisattva grounds is slightly different than in Pāramitāyāna. Although the paths and grounds have the same names in Sūtra and Tantra and are equivalent, they are not the same. We can see this in the way Tsongkhapa outlines the paths in Highest Yoga Tantra in *Lamp Illuminating the Five Stages of the Completion Stage* (*Rdzogs rim rim lnga gsal sgron*), a commentary on Guhyasamāja practice (LS 57):

> The path of accumulation extends from the common paths up to but not including the ability to directly induce the empties by causing the winds to enter and dissolve in the central channel by the power of meditation. The path of preparation extends from the capacity to do that up to but not including the illusory body directly realizing suchness through bliss. The path of seeing, the ground of the Very Joyful, extends from the actual clear light up to but not including the attainment of union. The nine grounds of the path of meditation extend from the learners' union up to but not including attainment of nonlearners' union.

Here "common paths" are the minds cultivated in common in both Sūtra and Tantra practitioners, such as the aspiration to be free of saṃsāra, bodhicitta, and wisdom realizing emptiness. These form the basic structure of the path for all Mahāyāna practitioners. By learning and then contemplating the structure of the path and the way method and wisdom work together in Sūtra and Tantra, we see the superiority of Tantrayāna. This, in turn, will inspire us to create the causes to enter Tantrayāna by developing a firm foundation in the three higher trainings, the six perfections, and in receiving empowerment. Then, we will proceed to keep our tantric ethical restraints and commitments purely, practice deity yoga in six sessions daily, and gain the realizations of the generation and completion stages. By relying on the guidance of fully qualified tantric spiritual mentors and making ourselves into fully qualified tantric practitioners, we will abandon all defilements to be abandoned, actualize all excellent qualities to be actualized, and become fully awakened buddhas.

2 | Introduction to Tantra

VAJRAYĀNA IS A branch of Mahāyāna. Practiced on the basis of the Fundamental Vehicle and the general Mahāyāna, Vajrayāna was widespread throughout Tibet and remains so now among those who follow Tibetan Buddhism worldwide.[10] Vajrayāna spread to China in the eighth century but was not widely practiced there. In Japan, Vajrayāna is called Shingon.

Where does Tantra fit in the three higher trainings? In the Sūtra Vehicle, the path is cultivated by practicing the thirty-seven harmonies with awakening as explained in texts such as Maitreya's *Ornament of Clear Realizations* (*Abhisamayālaṃkāra*). The path is also cultivated through the ten perfections, which texts such as Candrakīrti's *Supplement to the "Treatise on the Middle Way"* (*Madhyamakāvatāra*)[11] explain. Both of these Sūtra Vehicle approaches are based on ethical conduct, concentration, and wisdom. In general, the greatness of the Vajrayāna comes from its sophistication in cultivating concentration and meditation practices. For this reason, of the Three Baskets (*Tripiṭaka*) of Buddha's discourses, Vajrayāna teachings are included in the second, the Sūtra Basket, which is correlated with the higher training in concentration. This emphasizes that one of the unique features shared by all four tantric classes is the method to cultivate concentration. However, this does not mean that Vajrayāna lacks ethical conduct and wisdom. On the contrary, the tantric path is not complete without them.

The Meaning of Vajrayāna

Vajrayāna is also called Tantrayāna (Tantra Vehicle) and Mantrayāna (Mantra Vehicle). *Vajra* refers to two entities—in this case wisdom and method—that are inseparably joined. *Wisdom* refers to the wisdom realizing emptiness and *method* is bodhicitta and the perfections. Just as a vajra is diamond-hard and unbreakable, so too are method and wisdom conjoined unbreakably.

Tantra means "continuum," referring to the continuum of the path taught by the Buddha in the form of Vajradhara and the teachings describing this path that have been passed down, without interruption, to your own root guru. *Tantra* also refers to the continuum of consciousness. In the context of Highest Yoga Tantra, this is the subtlest consciousness, the fundamental innate mind of clear light, which continues without interruption from one life to the next in saṃsāra and when purified becomes the dharmakāya of a buddha.

Mantrayāna indicates that this vehicle protects the mind from defilements and takes you to the other shore, full awakening. Reciting mantras helps to calm and transform the mind. Practices such as vajra recitation involve the body with its winds, channels, drops, and cakras. When these are employed to generate a blissful consciousness, the innate clear-light mind can realize emptiness and purify defilements.

Vajrayāna is also called the Resultant Vehicle because practitioners imagine having attained the resultant buddhahood while they practice. They imagine being the central deity in a maṇḍala, the environment of deities. Surrounded by an entourage of subsidiary deities who are like their disciples, they give and receive offerings in the nature of bliss and emptiness and engage in effortless awakening activities that benefit sentient beings. Like children who dress up and play being adults, practitioners imagine being the buddha they want to become in the future.

The History of Tantra

The Buddha gave the Tantric teachings during his lifetime as Śākyamuni Buddha as well as afterward in various pure lands. In general, when the Buddha taught a Tantra, he did so in the form of the principal deity of the maṇḍala of that particular tantra. It is also said that the Buddha taught many tantras in the form of Vajradhara (T. Dorje Chang) and that he taught a few of the action tantras in his normal form of a fully ordained monk. Such was the case when he taught the maṇḍala of Buddha Śākyamuni. He assumed the celestial appearance of a universal monarch when he taught Yoga Tantra. In these ways, he gave tantric empowerments and teachings to a group of select individuals. This illustrates that, unlike the sutras and Nāgārjuna's and Asaṅga's texts, which are general teachings to be taught to the public, tantric teachings are prescribed according to the individual because the subtle body of channels, winds, and drops differs from person to person. The Vajrayāna teachings were later compiled by Vajrapāṇi, a deva who was also a bodhisattva.

The Buddha taught the various Buddhist tantras at particular times and places, and there are several ideas about this. In the *Kālacakra Tantra* the Buddha said that when he delivered the second turning of the Dharma Wheel at Vulture's Peak, he also gave tantric teachings at Dhānyakaṭaka (Amarāvatī). But some Tibetan scholars say that the Buddha gave tantric teachings on the full-moon day one year after his awakening, while others say that he taught the tantras a month prior to his parinirvāṇa. Many tantras are said to have been taught in Oḍḍiyāna, although people have varying ideas where that is. Places such as Śambhala, which is spoken of in the *Kālacakra Tantra*, cannot be found in our world.

To understand the origination and evolution of Vajrayāna teachings, we should not be confined to notions of time and place in the conventional sense of historical years and physically identifiable locations. Just because these descriptions cannot be verified if taken literally, we should not negate them. Applying our conventional notions of time and place is not suitable because tantric teachings were given in a different dimension and to an exceptional audience.

Some tantric teachings may have come about through the experience of Buddhist practitioners with deep concentration fully exploring the potential in the body. As a result, they gained deep realizations of the Dharma, had visions of buddhas who manifested in the forms of meditational deities, and received tantric teachings from them. In this way, some tantras appeared after the life of the historical Buddha Śākyamuni.

Most of the great Indian scholar-practitioners practiced tantra. Āryadeva and Śāntarakṣita wrote tantric texts, and in *Stages of Meditation*

(*Bhāvanākrama*), Kamalaśīla quoted tantric texts. Professor Jaganath Upadhaya from the Varanasi Sanskrit University told me that in Nepal he found a palm-leaf scripture on the Highest Yoga Tantra written in Sanskrit. Because the writing style was same as in the *Four Hundred* (*Catuḥśataka*), he concluded that Āryadeva was its author. If Āryadeva practiced Tantra, surely his teacher Nāgārjuna must have also (RC 30). In his *Lamp for the Path of Enlightenment* (*Bodhipathapradīpa*), Atiśa discussed not misusing Tantra, showing that he, too, was familiar with and practiced Tantra. Tsongkhapa read and impartially studied all the scriptures in the Kangyur and Tengyur available in his time. He concluded that Tantra is higher than Pāramitāyāna and leads to the accomplishment of the two siddhis—the common and transcendental attainments. All this demonstrates that these great sages considered Tantra the Buddha's teachings and a viable and sophisticated path to full awakening.

Tantra is not unique to Buddhism. In ancient India there were Hindu and Jain tantric practitioners, and those tantric traditions exist in the present day. One Hindu practitioner told me that they make maṇḍalas, visualize deities and maṇḍalas, and practice concentration meditation. They also meditate on the channels, cakras, drops, and winds; do certain physical or yogic exercises; meditate on *tummo* (*caṇḍālī*); and perform fire offerings. However, Buddhist and Hindu practices in each of these areas differ: the deities are different, and Buddhist Tantra is practiced with refuge in the Three Jewels, supported by renunciation of saṃsāra, motivated by bodhicitta, and imbued with the Madhyamaka or Yogācāra view of emptiness. The discussion in this book concerns Buddhist tantric practice.

Unfortunately, misconceptions about Vajrayāna practice abound due to the lack of proper information. In the past, without receiving explanations about the symbolic nature of the practices and deities, some people developed their own conjectures of Vajrayāna and spread these misconceptions to others. Other people have reduced Vajrayāna to the performance of rituals that are carried out with a worldly motivation seeking wealth or power. Others do rituals, thinking that by merely reciting mantras or prayers an external deity will grant them long life or wealth. All these wrong views contribute to the degeneration of the Buddhadharma. In this chapter I shall endeavor to eliminate some of these misconceptions and to lay out the route through which sincere and serious practitioners can enter the Vajrayāna.

Tantric Deities

Some paintings of tantric deities illustrate them in sexual union. Others depict fierce looking deities. People who aren't familiar with Vajrayāna wonder: If sexual desire is to be abandoned on the Buddhist path, why do some deities, who are said to be awakened beings, appear in sexual union? If buddhas are compassionate, why are some deities wielding weapons and glaring ferociously? How can meditating on such strange figures bring awakening?

The fact that the Buddha—or Vajradhara, the tantric aspect of the Buddha—appears in peaceful and wrathful forms does not mean that, like worldly beings, he has different aspects of his personality, one kind and the other angry. There is a purpose for these various appearances. From the buddhas' perspective, the truth body, which is total peace and free from conceptual elaborations, is the fulfillment of their own purpose, whereas the form bodies that appear to sentient beings are the fulfillment of the purpose of others. Because of the variation in sentient beings' interests, dispositions, and physical constituents, the buddhas appear in whatever form that will benefit them the most. For example, to Togden Jampel Gyatso, one of Tsongkhapa's close disciples, Mañjuśrī appeared in a friendly manner with a sense of humor, whereas in Tsongkhapa's visions of Mañjuśrī, his manner was reserved.

These deities are appearances of a buddha's omniscient mind in a physical form that enables them to relate to sentient beings. All the deities in a maṇḍala are the nature of the pristine wisdom of bliss and emptiness; they are not separate, unrelated individual beings. The Buddha manifests in the form of the central deity and the other deities in a maṇḍala when there are people who will benefit from those particular manifestations.

The large number of tantric deities is due to the great variety of practitioners' dispositions. The form bodies of a buddha appear effortlessly in response to sentient beings' karma, to benefit these beings. Just as a reflection of a face in the mirror depends on the face, the mirror, and surrounding conditions such as light and lack of dirt on the mirror, the appearance of a buddha in the form of a deity depends on the minds of the sentient beings to whom they appear and the capacities or lack of obscurations in their minds. For those who would benefit from the buddha appearing as a monastic, he appears in that form. For those who would benefit from the Buddha appearing in the aspect of enjoying the five sense objects as a method to overcome afflictions, the Buddha appears in the form of a tantric deity. The Buddha manifests as fierce deities for those who are capable of taking anger into the path, and as a couple in union for those who are able to take desire into the path so that they can more effectively eliminate those afflictions.

In addition, there are vast differences in practitioners' physiological, mental, and emotional states. Given this diversity in practitioners, a variety of yogic practices are taught in Tantra, and different maṇḍalas and deities are associated with them. For example, the scholar and lama Taktsang Lotsawa said in his *General Exposition of the Kālacakra Tantra* that the detailed explanation of the breathing process and flow of the winds found in the *Kālacakra Tantra* exactly matched his personal meditation experience, whereas the explanation in the *Guhyasamāja Tantra* did not. Nevertheless, another practitioner may find that the description in the *Guhyasamāja Tantra* corresponds to their experience. This is how I understand the diversity of Vajrayāna meditation practices.

Because of the great significance of utilizing a blissful mind to realize emptiness, many of the meditational deities in Highest Yoga Tantra are depicted in union with consorts. Here the male deity symbolizes the method aspect of the path and the female deity symbolizes the wisdom aspect of the path. These meditation deities are not overwhelmed by sexual desire and attachment to the pleasure of this life! Buddhas have the full bliss of awakening within them; they are not interested in ordinary sexual intercourse, and having totally eliminated sexual desire, they do not engage in it.

Like peaceful deities, wrathful deities are also manifestations of compassion and wisdom. They appear in that form to illustrate the power and clarity of compassion and wisdom used in the proper way. The sādhana of the fierce deity Yamāntaka says, "Although the truth body has neither attachment nor hatred, to tame all nefarious ones of the three realms with compassionate means you display the body of the king of anger." The ferocity of wrathful deities is directed toward the real enemies that destroy sentient beings' well-being—self-grasping ignorance, afflictions, and self-centeredness. These deities are not demons, nor do they attack sentient beings with harmful intent.

Some Buddhists incorrectly think of meditational deities as external gods that are to be worshipped. This is especially easy for practitioners who grew up in cultures that believe in an external creator or god. Even though tantric sādhanas—manuals describing the visualizations and meditations of a deity's practice—contain bowing, offerings, and request prayers to the gurus and deities, the tantric path is not concerned with worshipping an external being so that he or she will bless us and grant us nirvāṇa. The Buddha emphasized that awakening is attained by transforming our own minds. These devotional practices are tools to effect that change, and they are done with the bodhicitta motivation and sealed with contemplation of the circle of three—the emptiness of the agent, object, and action.

People may pray to wrathful deities to remove obstructions to gain realizations of the path, and to peaceful deities to bring attainments. However, simply requesting a wrathful deity to expel our disturbing emotions and wrong views, or requesting a peaceful deity to grant realizations, does not bring this about. We must practice the methods the Buddha taught. Propitiating external deities to accomplish the path for us and expecting them to do the work for us would be to distort the Buddhadharma and make it a theistic religion. Practicing the path is like eating and sleeping—we must do it ourselves; we cannot request or hire someone else to do it for us.

A tantric deity is an embodiment of all the realizations of the stages of the path to awakening. Seeing a deity in this way enables us to integrate the paths of Sūtra and Tantra. If we want to become close to the deity, we must meditate on the stages of the path and generate the three principal aspects of the path in our mind. Being close to the deity does not mean having sparkling visions of the deity, just as being close to the guru does not mean staying in the guru's physical presence. Closeness is a state of mind. The more our mind becomes the Dharma, the closer we are to the gurus, buddhas, and deities.

The Purpose of Vajrayāna

As much as people associate visualizing deities and maṇḍalas, reciting mantras, and meditating on the channels, winds, and drops of the subtle body with Tantra, these are not its unique features. As noted above, other spiritual traditions contain similar practices. Hindus visualize deities. Christians, Hindus, and Sufis recite certain phrases repeatedly, counting the repetitions on prayer beads. Hinduism has kundalini practice, complete with meditations on the channels, winds, and drops.

It cannot be repeated too often that what makes these meditation techniques Buddhist practice is that they are supported by refuge in the Three Jewels, by the determination to be free from saṃsāra, by bodhicitta, and by the wisdom realizing the emptiness of inherent existence. Within the framework of these attributes, deity yoga, mantra recitation, and meditation on the subtle nervous system become Buddhist Tantra. If our practice is not supported by these, we may spend days and years meditating intensely, but we will not attain awakening. Dza Patrul Rinpoche, a very forthright lama who speaks his mind, said (AKC 21–22):

> Those who have not practiced the essential bodhicitta for even one session,
> yet supposedly practice generation- and completion-stage "meditation," and
> so-called recitation of mantras—such sham practitioners
> are like excrement you should chuck into the gutter!
>
> My friend, if you want to practice some real Dharma,
> train your mind, train your mind, train in compassion, bodhicitta!
> Having reflected on this vital point, repeated many times over,
> tame your mind with the Dharma: that is the essential point.

Our faith in Buddhadharma in general and in Tantra specifically must be firm and based on reason. Our goal is buddhahood with a buddha's truth body (dharmakāya) and form body (rūpakāya). At that stage, a buddha's body, speech, and mind are inseparable; they are indivisible and one nature.

Our present coarse body and mind are not one nature. They have different continuums and separate after death, whereas the subtle body, speech, and mind are one nature. Once they are developed in tantric practice, then wherever the subtle mind goes, the subtle body and subtle speech also go.

To gain a buddha's inseparable body, speech, and mind, we must create the causes that can lead to this. Such a practice or path exists only in Tantrayāna. Only Highest Yoga Tantra explains the method for making that subtlest mind, which is one nature with the subtlest body or wind, manifest. The subtlest wind manifests as our voice; it is the expression or tone (T. *gdangs*) of that wind. Thus the subtlest body and subtlest speech are indivisible, and both are inseparable from the subtlest mind.

The principal Vajrayāna practice is deity yoga, and its purpose is to create a union of method and wisdom. This embodies the meaning of Vajrayāna or Vajra Vehicle: "vajra" refers to inseparable method and wisdom. Method is the subtlest wind manifesting in the form of the illusory body, and wisdom is the blissful innate clear-light mind realizing emptiness. Their inseparability is the vehicle that takes us to awakening.

Method and wisdom are united in Vajrayāna through a gradual process of training, centered around the practitioners' wisdom consciousness that realizes emptiness appearing as a deity. In Highest Yoga Tantra, this is done first in the generation stage by practitioners meditating on emptiness and dissolving all appearance of inherent existence into emptiness. They then imagine their wisdom realizing emptiness appearing in the form of the deity. This sets the stage for the completion-stage practice in which their subtlest wisdom mind and subtlest wind actually arise as an illusory body. This comes about by minimizing the coarser levels of consciousness and making manifest the blissful, innermost subtlest mind. Once that subtlest mind becomes active, it is transformed into the wisdom understanding emptiness.

Although a coarser level of consciousness that realizes emptiness can act as an antidote to defilements, as is done in Sūtrayāna, utilizing the subtlest mind to realize emptiness is more powerful and has a far greater effect in removing obscurations. For even the subtlest consciousness to be purified of all obscurations, it must realize emptiness directly. Furthermore, practitioners meditate on method (the appearance of the deity as the illusory body) and wisdom (the actual clear-light mind realizing emptiness) in one consciousness. These are special features of deity yoga in Highest Yoga Tantra.

Abandoning False Expectations of Vajrayāna

The most important element of Buddhist tantra that distinguishes it from other Buddhist and non-Buddhist practices is transforming the fundamental innate mind of clear light into a meditative yogic state. All other practices directly or indirectly contribute to this realization. In this context, yoga is a realization, the core of which is realizing our own ultimate nature, the emptiness of inherent existence. For this wisdom to become a condition for attaining omniscience, bodhicitta is indispensable. Thus, no matter what tantric practice one does, it is important that it is imbued with bodhicitta and the realization of emptiness.

Certain tantric practices such as meditating on the cakras in the form of wheels, employing special substances, reciting mantra, and meditative concentration can enable the meditator to attain the power to perform the activities of peace, increase, control, and wrath. However, if these practices are not tempered with bodhicitta, they can easily be abused. Gungthang Rinpoche said that those who employ the practices of Secret Mantra only to remove obstacles in this life—for example, by extending the lifespan, making oneself or others invulnerable to spells, or eliminating enemies through mantra—are imbeciles who are seeking unfortunate rebirth by means of Dharma practice. One tantra says, "Even though a sandalwood tree can provide cooling shade, if someone lights a fire to it, it becomes worthless coal." In the same way, although tantric practices are means to overcome suffering, if improperly employed—for example, with a self-centered motivation, arrogance, or lack of proper knowledge of the technique—they can become conditions to further our suffering.

How do we avoid the pitfalls of either wasting our time by practicing incorrectly or harming ourselves and others by having incorrect motivations? One factor is to receive teachings on Sūtra and Tantra texts from a qualified guru and to study them well. If we have a firm and broad understanding of Buddhadharma, we will not fall prey to misconceptions, such as thinking that mantra recitation alone will bring spiritual attainments. Through study we will know that there are mantras to be recited by generation-stage practitioners and mantras to be recited by completion-stage practitioners. In completion-stage practice, the mantra that a practitioner recites is the ultimate mantra, which refers not to a series of orally recited syllables but to meditation on emptiness, especially on the indivisibility of bliss and emptiness.

Another factor is to have realistic expectations for a person of our level. We hear that one can attain awakening through tantric practice in three years and three phases of the moon, but for the vast majority of people this is not true. Among several billion people, perhaps one or two have accumulated sufficient collections of merit and wisdom from previous lives to bring this about. Otherwise it is not possible, because most of us are not yet at a stage of realization whereby we are capable of creating all the causes for awakening in one lifetime.

Therefore, it is much safer to maintain a long-term view and resolve to practice for eons. This will give us inner strength. Otherwise, we risk having too many expectations, which are grounds for disappointment. Doing retreat for three or six years is good, but that does not ensure we will emerge with great realizations. We may just come back with a bigger ego! Thus, whether we do retreat or not, we must improve ourselves year by year and be willing to cultivate good qualities for eons to attain awakening.

A third factor is to be practical and first cultivate a proper foundation in Sūtrayāna practice. Hearing that Vajrayāna is the quick path to awakening, some people are overly eager to begin practicing it immediately, while others have irrational fears based on superstitious rumors that Vajrayāna is black magic or that meditation can make one crazy. A middle way is needed. Studying and practicing the Sūtra path establishes proper understanding and internal strength of mind so that when we receive Vajrayāna empowerment, we will abide in the tantric ethical restraints and commitments and will approach tantric practice realistically and with a bodhicitta motivation.

Just like piloting a plane, Vajrayāna practice requires much preparation. Simply having the wish to fly doesn't give us the ability to do so, and attempting to fly a plane before we are thoroughly trained is dangerous. Yet once we are well trained, the ability to pilot a plane is marvelous. Navigating our way through Vajrayāna practice is similar.

It is said that Vajrayāna teachings and practices should remain secret. This refers to how an individual should practice. Tantric practitioners should not boast about the empowerments they have received or advertise to others that they do Vajrayāna practice. They should keep their Vajrayāna images and personal implements private, taking them out only when doing the sādhana privately.[12] In this way, they will avoid the danger of self-centeredness stepping in to claim, "I know the most advanced teachings. They are secret, and I'm special because I practice them." Such an attitude would clearly hinder spiritual progress.

Terminology

In Sūtra and Tantra, the usage of certain terms vary according to the context, so it is important to get an overall understanding of a topic and see what the meaning of a certain term is in that context. For example, the word "nonconceptuality" is used in a variety of circumstances where it has different meanings. Some states of nonconceptuality are common to Buddhists and non-Buddhists. Within Buddhism, there are nonconceptual states in both Sūtra and Tantra. In Sūtra, some of these are included in serenity, others in the direct realization of emptiness. In Tantra, there are nonconceptual states in the generation and completion stages, and within the completion stage there are the nonconceptual states of āryas and of ordinary beings.

Here we see that there are different levels of nonconceptuality and different meanings of the word according to the context. Let's look at some of them. One is a state of mind where we don't conceive of any particular way of existence, such as existing, not existing, being something, not being something. When someone is in deep sleep, we say they are in a state of nonconceptuality. Another is when we are very tired and have no particular thoughts. This resembles well-fed rabbits that don't sense any danger; they drop their ears and sit in a state of what looks like nonconceptuality. Another occurs when someone has the deliberate intention of not letting their mind go to any thought—for example, by the power of some concentration practices associated with serenity, someone could enter a deep state of nonconceptuality. Another form of nonconceptuality occurs when we are engaged in single-pointed analysis of a topic. Although analysis may involve thought, this is called "nonconceptual" because the mind is not allowed to go to any other object. The wisdom realizing emptiness may be nonconceptual in two senses: the mind lacks any thought whatsoever and it is focused only on emptiness without wandering to other objects.

In Tantra, we speak of nonconceptuality in a relative sense, when one mind is subtler than another. For example, in general the clear-light mind of an ordinary person at the time of death is conceptual in nature. But compared to coarser adventitious minds, on many occasions it is said to be nonconceptual because it is the subtlest mind with the least conceptuality.

Furthermore, there are many types of conceptuality (T. *rtog pa*) such as conceptuality in the context of the two levels of analysis that examine an object such as impermanence. One type of analysis is called "analysis" and the other is called "investigation." Here, analysis is detailed examination and investigation is a superficial examination of the object.

Another example occurs in Sūtra when the meanings of "selflessness" and "emptiness" differ according to the four tenet systems. In the completion stage of Guhyasamāja, four empties are mentioned. These are four subtle states of mind that can be used to realize emptiness, although they are neither emptiness itself nor the pristine wisdom realizing emptiness. These states of mind occur as the coarser winds and coarser consciousnesses dissolve[13]: (1) *the empty* that is the vivid white appearance occurs when the eighty conceptions accompanying the coarse mind dissolve, (2) *the great empty* that is the red increase occurs as the winds continue to dissolve, (3) *the very empty* that is the black near-attainment arises when the winds dissolve even more, and (4) *the all empty* is the fundamental innate clear-light mind. This mind is "fundamental" in that its continuum is beginningless and endless; it exists while the person is in saṃsāra and after they attain nirvāṇa and full awakening. The fundamental innate mind of clear light is also called the "all good" or Samantabhadra and the "basis of all" (*ālaya*).[14]

As we see, "clear light" has different meanings in Sūtra and Tantra. Although our natural tendency is to apply one meaning to a word, it is best to exercise caution and listen to each teaching freshly in order to discern the meaning of each term in that context. Within the four principal Tibetan traditions, one word may have different meanings, and different words may have the same meaning. Therefore, it's best to listen carefully and avoid assuming that different terminology and different meanings necessarily mean that the fundamental point differs.

Furthermore, not all words or phrases are to be understood literally. You may hear the expression "the Tathāgata is to be killed" and "by killing the Tathāgata one will attain supreme awakening." In a Sūtra context, the "tathāgata" to be destroyed is our grasping the Tathāgata as truly existent. In Tantra, these phrases mean that the coarse levels of wind and mind are to be dissolved into the central channel, which leads to the manifestation of the subtlest mind that is used to realize emptiness.

Tantric Masters

In *The Foundation of Buddhist Practice*, two chapters are devoted to the topic of discerning qualified spiritual mentors and establishing a healthy and beneficial relationship with them. Because of the type of practice done in Tantrayāna, it is even more important to select and properly rely on a tantric lama. Tsongkhapa cautions (LC 1:32–33):

> Nowadays those making effort at yoga have studied few [of the classic texts],
> while those who have studied much are not skilled in the key points of practice.
> They tend to view the scriptures through the eyes of partisanship,
> unable to use reason to discriminate the meaning of scriptures [and] . . .
> lack the path pleasing to the wise,
> the supreme complete instructions, the key points of the teaching.

To practice Mantrayāna successfully, a practitioner must become part of a continuum of inspiration (blessings) from previous tantric lamas. Although a continuum of inspiration is mentioned in the Sūtra system, it is especially important in Tantra. The initial source of entry into this continuum lies in receiving empowerment (*abhiṣeka*), which practitioners must request a qualified tantric lama to give. Before requesting an empowerment, it is important to examine if that spiritual mentor (*guru*, T. *lama*) has the necessary qualifications. Even if it takes many years to discern this, taking the time to do it is worthwhile.

Checking the qualities of a guru is difficult to do if a teacher arrives at a Dharma center and gives a general teaching, gives an empowerment the next day, and departs on the third. Instead, it would be far better if he or she gave teachings on the general path, especially the three principal aspects of the path for at least a week or two, to prepare potential students for empowerment and to give students the opportunity to determine if they want to form a relationship of tantric guru and disciple with this person. Tantric ethical restraints and commitments should be clearly explained to students, either by the tantric lama or by a senior disciple, before the empowerment is given so that people will be clear what they are committing to. After receiving empowerment, students should request teachings on the practice and on the bodhisattva and tantric precepts so that they will know how to keep them properly.

In addition to the qualities of a Mahāyāna spiritual mentor, as described in chapters 4 and 5 of *The Foundation of Buddhist Practice*, Aśvaghoṣa explains the qualities of a suitable vajra lama in *Fifty Verses on the Guru* (GP v7):

> Reliable, disciplined, and wise,
> patient, honest, and without deceit,
> [having] knowledge of mantras, tantras, and [ritual] actions,
> compassionate, an expert in the explanatory texts,
> possessing the two sets of ten qualities,
> skilled in drawing maṇḍalas,
> having knowledge of the activities of explaining mantra,
> full of faith and subdued senses.

Such spiritual mentors are reliable and disciplined due to mindfulness of their body, speech, and mind. Having great wisdom, they are patient toward those who cause harm, understand the hardship entailed in practicing the Dharma, and revere the profound Dharma. They are honest and trustworthy, have compassion for all sentient beings, and know the Dharma well. Qualified tantric lamas possess the two sets of ten qualities of a tantric lama and are skilled in drawing sand maṇḍalas and explaining the mantra path to disciples. They have stable faith in the Vajrayāna and have subdued their senses so as not to be carried away by attachment.

Furthermore, qualified Vajrayāna lamas guard their body, speech, and mind from destructive actions, practice the three higher trainings, are knowledgeable in both Sūtra and Tantra, and are free from pretention and deceit.

The ten outer qualities of an excellent tantric lama are especially important for gurus of Action Tantra (Kriyā Tantra) and Performance Tantra (Caryā Tantra):

1. Skill in drawing the outer maṇḍalas and in meditating on the inner maṇḍalas.
2. Skill in the concentrations, such as the initial preparation and so on.
3. Skill in the hand gestures (*mudrā*).
4. Skill in ritual dances.
5. Skill in sitting in vajra posture, the posture of Vajrasattva, and so on.
6. Skill in proclaiming mantras.
7. Skill in performing fire pūjās.
8. Skill in offering rituals.
9. Skill in the ritual actions of pacification (of disputes, famine, and illness), increase (of lifespan, knowledge, and wealth), control (to influence others), and ferocity (eliminations of negative forces and interferences).
10. Skill in invoking meditational deities and requesting them to return to their places.

The ten inner qualities are important for Yoga Tantra and Highest Yoga Tantra.

1. Skill in eliminating obstacles through meditating on the protection wheel.
2. Skill in preparing and consecrating protection cords and amulets to expel interferences.
3. Skill in giving the vase (*kalaśābhiṣeka*) and the secret empowerments (*guhyābhiṣeka*) to plant the potentials to attain a buddha's form bodies.
4. Skill in giving the wisdom (*prajñājñānābhiṣeka*) and the fourth empowerments (*caturthābhiṣeka*) to plant potentials to attain a buddha's truth bodies.
5. Skill in separating enemies from their protectors.
6. Skill in making torma offerings.
7. Skill in the various types of recitation, such as mental recitation, vajra recitation, commitment recitation, palanquin recitation, fierce recitation, wrathful recitation, heap recitation, and so forth.
8. Skill in performing fierce actions to disperse interferers when this cannot be accomplished through other means.

9. Skill in rituals to consecrate statues, images, and so forth.
10. Skill in making offerings to the maṇḍala, performing the meditation practice, and taking self-empowerment.

In the first three tantras, a lama should have the ten outer qualities, and in Highest Yoga Tantra the vajra lama should also have all ten inner qualities.[15]

It is good to remember these qualities not only when seeking a qualified tantric lama but also when thinking of becoming one. We should not be eager to sit on a throne and confer empowerments when we ourselves are lacking in qualities. Doing this is detrimental to ourselves as well as others.

However, it may not be possible to find such a tantric lama. Puṇḍarīka said in *Cluster of the Ultimate Meaning* (MIS 205):

> Owing to the time of the five degenerations,
> faults and virtues are mixed in the guru.
> No one is found to be completely perfect.
> Therefore after thorough examination, disciples should rely on
> whoever has a dominance of good qualities.

Fifty Verses on the Guru also describes attributes that are not suitable for a qualified vajra lama: lack of compassion, full of spite, governed by strong attachment or anger, having little knowledge or practice of the three higher trainings, boastful of the little knowledge they have, manipulative, and seeking offerings, reputation, and respect from disciples.

The *Kālacakra Tantra* says that if we have a choice between a guru who is a fully ordained monastic, a novice, or a lay practitioner, the fully ordained monastic is best regardless of their personal realizations, due to the disciplined way of life they have chosen. This relates to the important statement of the Buddha that where the practice of Vinaya is present, his teachings are present, but where the practice of Vinaya is missing, his teachings are also missing.

In the case of general Dharma teachings, listening to Dharma talks from a spiritual brother or sister is fine, but to receive teachings with a guru-disciple relationship, we must be very careful. Both the guru and disciples should observe each other to determine their respective qualifications. If you skip this step and without proper investigation immediately consider someone your tantric guru, after a while you may find faults. This could cause you to lose faith, which would be harmful to your Dharma practice.

Since we cannot evaluate someone's mind, how do we investigate their inner qualities? A Vinaya text compares this to knowing that a fish is swimming under the water's surface by seeing the ripples, although the fish itself cannot be seen. Similarly, by observing someone's external behavior, we can infer his or her inner qualities.

It is important for tantric gurus to teach in accordance with the general structure of the Buddhist path, taking this as the framework within which to train the students. Tantric masters should not arrogantly think that they are almighty and can do or say whatever they want within the circle of their disciples and expect them to follow. A Tibetan proverb advises, "Even though you may rival the deities in terms of your realizations, your conduct should conform with that of other human beings."

Tantric Practitioners

In terms of the method side of the path, Vajrayāna practitioners must have stronger bodhicitta than Pāramitāyāna practitioners. Qualified tantric practitioners find the three types of duḥkha that sentient beings constantly undergo in saṃsāra unbearable and want to attain awakening as quickly as possible to lead others out of saṃsāra and to awakening. In terms of the wisdom side of the path, tantric practitioners need either stable wisdom realizing emptiness or the ability to activate that wisdom easily. To be a special practitioner for whom the practice of tantra was specifically taught, one must have very sharp faculties. Average tantric practitioners can be of sharp or modest faculties. Yogācārins are considered secondary practitioners of tantra: they can only advance to a certain point in the Tantra Vehicle before having to adopt the Madhyamaka view.

The union of method and wisdom is taught in both Sūtra and Tantra. In Sūtra, the practice of method and the practice of wisdom are conjoined with the force of the other. In Mantrayāna they are conjoined in one consciousness such that method and wisdom are one undifferentiable entity; this is a distinguishing feature of Tantra. Thus the special practitioner for whom Vajrayāna was specifically taught wishes to attain buddhahood quickly for the benefit of all sentient beings and is interested in practicing the path of method and wisdom as one undifferentiable entity. This person admires a path with both the vast and profound aspects. From the viewpoint that is in common with Sūtrayāna, this is a path with bodhicitta and wisdom realizing emptiness. From the uncommon tantric viewpoint, this is a path that unites the experience of great bliss with the wisdom realizing emptiness. Great bliss is experienced by the subtle consciousness, after the coarse consciousnesses have ceased. In the context of Kālacakra, it is a path uniting immutable bliss and empty form. Furthermore, qualified tantric disciples engage in tantric practice in a skillful manner, without arrogance: they value the tantric practice and take it seriously.

Those best prepared to receive tantric empowerment and begin tantric practice are practitioners with effortless realizations of the three principal aspects of the path: the determination to be free (renunciation), bodhicitta (altruistic intention), and the correct view of emptiness. For tantric practice to be most effective, you need some experience of emptiness, and to become an antidote to the cognitive obscurations, the realization of emptiness must be complemented by bodhicitta. Without bodhicitta and the wisdom understanding emptiness, it is impossible to actually receive Highest Yoga Tantra empowerment even if you're physically present at the empowerment ceremony. However, if you wait until you have realized these two, there may not be time in this life to enter Vajrayāna. Thus, the time to begin tantric practice is when you have true understanding of the three principal aspects of the path and the intention to generate those realizations, although these understandings do not yet arise effortlessly within you. In that case, continue meditating on the three principal aspects of the path and do your daily sādhana commitments as a way of planting seeds on your mindstream in order to be familiar with tantric practice and gain tantric realizations in future lives.

Regarding suitable vessels for empowerment into Highest Yoga Tantra, in *Lamp for the Path to Enlightenment*, Atiśa says (LP 64–67):

> Because the *Great Tantra of the Primordial Buddha*
> forbids it emphatically,
> those observing pure conduct should not
> take the secret and wisdom empowerments.

> If those observing the austere practice of pure conduct
> were to hold these empowerments,
> their ethical code of austerity would be impaired
> through doing that which is proscribed.
>
> This creates transgressions that are a defeat
> for those observing [monastic] discipline.
> Since they are certain to fall to a bad rebirth,
> they will never gain accomplishments.
>
> There is no fault if one who has received
> the [vajra] master empowerment and has knowledge
> of suchness listens to or explains the tantras
> and performs burnt-offering rituals,
> or makes offerings of gifts and so forth.

"Those observing pure conduct" are monastics and lay practitioners holding the precept of celibacy. These ordinary beings practicing pure conduct should not take the actual secret and wisdom empowerments that involve consort practice, because doing so would violate their celibacy precept and lead them to an unfortunate rebirth. The situation is different for those practitioners who have high spiritual realizations, such as the union of serenity and insight that nonconceptually perceives emptiness. Nevertheless, ordinary beings may receive and give the secret and wisdom empowerments by using imagination and visualization. If they have received the vajra master empowerment, they may engage in various tantric activities such as listening to and teaching the tantras, performing consecrations and fire pūjās, and engaging in the four activities of peace, increase, control, and wrath.

Regarding the traits of suitable disciples to receive tantric empowerment, the *Vajra Garland, an Explanatory Tantra of Guhyasamāja* (*Vajramālā Tantra*) says (OBT 68):

> Faithful and full of respect for the guru,
> abiding always in the practice of virtue,
> with wrong views completely abandoned,
> such a one must have received many teachings.

Free of the faults of killing and harming,
with his or her mind intent on liberating beings,
always diligent and very pure,
these and others are the virtues one should have,
but the best of all is strong faith.

The faith of such a disciple is not blind faith that idolizes the guru. It is faith born from examining and practicing the Buddha's teachings, faith that will not waver when difficulties arise. Such trust is cultivated over time; we cannot force ourselves to have it.

Tantric texts instruct that empowerments be given only to people who are properly prepared, not to newcomers who lack understanding of the fundamentals of Buddhist practice. In spite of this, some Tibetan masters allow or even encourage everyone to attend empowerments. Older students, thinking that they are being compassionate, may unwittingly pressure people into prematurely taking empowerment by saying, "You may not have another chance to receive empowerment, and this master is very high." People do not want to miss out on something good, so these newcomers take empowerments prematurely. Later on, many of them become confused because the practice is too advanced for their present level and abandon it. This is a sad situation.

Some people who are relatively new to Buddhism delve into Vajrayāna, mahāmudrā, or dzogchen practice with great enthusiasm to become a buddha in this very lifetime. But when they do not see immediate results from practicing what is said to be the quick path, they become disillusioned and stop practicing. This occurs because their expectations are too high. To prevent this, I strongly recommend that sincere students spend years training in the preliminary stages of the path—which are not easy—as well as developing the basic qualities of a Buddhist practitioner and building a good foundation for further practice. You will see the change in your mind by doing these practices, and that will give you a strong foundation in the Dharma as well as confidence in yourself and in the path. On that basis, you can later receive empowerments and permissory rites and engage in Action and Performance Tantra. Later you can receive empowerments and permissory rites in Yoga and Highest Yoga Tantra practices.

Some people seek Vajrayāna for the wrong motivation—for example, simply to have long life and good health, to become wealthy, or to overcome obstacles to their worldly success. Others seek supernormal powers, thinking that they will then have power over others and receive respect and offerings. Such motivations are completely contradictory to Vajrayāna. Vajrayāna is done to benefit all sentient beings, whereas these people are thinking of benefiting only themselves. Sometimes their mental obscurations are so strong that they clothe their motivation in altruistic terms even in their own minds.

To avoid the misuse and degeneration of tantra practice, Highest Yoga Tantra empowerments must remain secret—that is, restricted to those few individuals with the basic qualifications. Teachers should not give empowerments without carefully examining the students first, and empowerments of the Highest Yoga Tantra should not be advertised in flyers distributed to the general public. Dharma centers could institute a process of screening and preparation before tantric empowerments are given, making Vajrayāna available only to those who are properly prepared. This protects both the purity of the Buddhadharma and the minds of Dharma students.

When I offer the Kālacakra empowerment, which is usually given to a large group, my basic aim is not the empowerment itself but the opportunity to explain the fundamentals of the Buddhist path and the way to develop a kind heart to a large group of people. Many people come, but only those with the proper preparation can be said to have received the empowerment. Meanwhile, the majority of the audience remains peaceful for those days and hears teachings about love, compassion, and wisdom. If, as a result, people develop an appreciation of the kind heart, the event has been worthwhile.

I have heard that some teachers are motivated to give empowerments and some Dharma centers want to host them because such events bring many people and thus increased income. Such an attitude is totally wrong and outside the scope of the Buddhadharma.

Although Vajrayāna in India was restricted to qualified practitioners, in Tibet it became very popular. Many Tibetans recite mantras and visualize deities, but very few can respond if we ask them who the Buddha is. This is not a good sign. The Indian masters emphasized the four truths, the two truths, renunciation, bodhicitta, the wisdom realizing emptiness, and the six perfections. We should follow their example, studying and practicing these for some time to build a good foundation. Then slowly we can begin Vajrayāna practice.

My senior tutor, Kyabje Ling Rinpoche, requested only teachings and empowerments that he knew he could practice. In Tibet a monk who did retreat at Taklungdrak Hermitage would tell Rinpoche whenever Takdrak Rinpoche was giving important teachings. Once, the monk informed Ling Rinpoche that Takdrak Rinpoche was giving the empowerments of the Hundred Practices of Mitrayogi (Mitra brgya rtsa) and asked if he would attend. Rinpoche said that he would be unable to do the practices and so declined. This is an excellent example of wisely assessing whether we should take an empowerment rather than indiscriminately gathering empowerments like some people collect stamps.

In summary, I do not recommend attending all empowerments that are offered. Think carefully about the commitments before receiving an empowerment. Can you keep them? Do you have the time and the wish to do the daily practice? Accumulating many empowerments so that you can boast to your friends is not prudent. To some extent, Tibetans are already spoiled in this regard, but non-Tibetans should not copy them. The great sage Atiśa said that in India people did the practice of one deity and through that actualized one hundred deities, whereas Tibetans took empowerment into one hundred deities but actualized none.

As disciples go deeper into Vajrayāna practice, they usually emphasize the practice of one deity. The decision as to which deity will be our principal deity should be made jointly by the guru and disciple. Although disciples may have many daily commitments, they should emphasize the practice of their principal deity.

Having examined a prospective spiritual mentor and decided that he or she is a qualified Vajrayāna master, you establish a guru-disciple relationship by receiving an empowerment from that person. After that, rely on that person in the way prescribed for tantric gurus. Although you have high regard for your Vajrayāna master, do not think that since your guru is very precious, they will protect you with their blessings if you are careless. Such an attitude contradicts the law of karma, which holds that we are responsible for our actions and create the causes for our experiences. The Buddha said, "I show you the path to liberation. Whether you attain liberation or not is up to you." He never said, "I will give you spiritual realizations and awakening."

In the colophon of his *Lamp Illuminating the Five Stages*, a text on the completion stage of Guhyasamāja, Tsongkhapa wrote (TK 265):

> If you do not understand just what the superior paths are superior to, and if you do not properly understand the lower tenets, you will not understand the subtle and exclusive features of those superior paths and of the higher tenets. Especially if you do not truly discover the ultimate definitive meaning that is the profound emptiness and the definitive teachings of the Buddha by using analytical intelligence trained well in the subtle paths of reasoning presented by the master Nāgārjuna, then you will not discover the general points of the paths to liberation and omniscience. In particular you will not properly recognize the innate pristine wisdom that arises from a practice that has bliss and emptiness united, which is the essential subject matter of the two kinds of nondual tantra (father and mother tantra). Though you may have great liking for it, it will never go beyond mere faith. Realizing this, I trained myself well in our and others' traditions of the Universal and Fundamental Vehicles, in the Mantra and Perfection Vehicles, and in the four tantra classes of Vajrayāna.

REFLECTION

1. What are the qualities of an excellent tantric spiritual mentor? Why is each of these qualities important to examine before taking someone as your tantric guru?
2. What are the qualities of an excellent student of Tantra?
3. Why is each of these qualities important to cultivate? Which qualities do you want to work on cultivating now?

3 | Entering Tantrayāna

Empowerment, Permissory Rites, and Oral Transmission

One enters the Vajrayāna through receiving an empowerment (T. *dbang*), a ritual in which the tantric master has generated him- or herself as the deity and then leads the disciples in doing various meditations and visualizations so that they can make a connection to that deity. The reason for receiving an empowerment is to do the practice, and the reason to do the practice of that deity is to attain buddhahood in order to benefit all sentient beings most effectively.

People may not attend an empowerment as an observer or out of curiosity; they should be interested in doing the practice. The only exception is Kālacakra. Because this practice concerns society and emphasizes uniting people to form a virtuous community, I allow people who are not Buddhists or who are not yet ready to do tantric practice to remain in the room as neutral observers during the empowerment. They do not take the tantric ethical restraints and commitments and do not receive the Kālacakra empowerment. They are not entitled to engage in the Kālacakra practice, but for that time their mind is likely in a virtuous state. However, neutral observers are not permitted to be present when an empowerment for any other deity is given.

A *permissory ritual* (T. *rjes gnang*) is a shorter ritual that gives permission to do the practice of a deity to practitioners who have already received an empowerment into the practice of a deity of a higher class. Permissory rituals involve receiving the blessing and inspiration of a deity's body, speech, and mind. There are numerous permissory rites for deities of Action Tantra, but fewer for Highest Yoga Tantra deities. Examples of the latter are the permissory rites of Cittamaṇi Tārā and of Vajrayoginī, which is a blessing of the four empowerments.

The difference between an empowerment and a permissory ritual can be confusing because both *dbang* and *rjes gnang* are often translated as "empowerment" in English. The empowerment for a deity empowers the person to engage in the practice of that deity, including the self-generation, where the practitioner meditates on emptiness and then imagines arising as that deity. The practitioner is also empowered to do retreat on the deity and the concluding fire pūjā. After that, they may do the self-empowerment.

A permissory rite for a deity gives the practitioner permission to do the practice of that deity only after they have first received either an empowerment within that deity's lineage in the case of Action Tantra or an empowerment of a deity from a higher lineage. Here we can see that it is not allowed, nor is it beneficial, to read about a deity, do the sādhana practice, or learn the hand mudrās without having received the proper empowerment or permissory rite.

Empowerments usually occur over the course of two days, with the preparations on the first day and the actual empowerment on the second day, although sometimes both parts are done in one day. The preparations on the first day include purification, generating the bodhicitta motivation, making requests, entering the maṇḍala, taking precepts, and so forth. The actual empowerment on the second day will differ according to which of the four classes of tantra the deity is in. In the New Translation schools of Kagyu, Sakya, and Gelug, there are four classes of tantra—Action, Performance, Yoga, and Highest Yoga, going from the lowest to the highest. Action Tantra contains the vase and crown empowerments; Performance Tantra adds to these the empowerment of the five buddha families. Yoga Tantra consists of all of the above plus the vajra-master empowerment, and Highest Yoga Tantra adds to these the three higher empowerments—the secret, wisdom, and word (or fourth) empowerments.

During an empowerment, after receiving the corresponding ethical restraints and commitments, the tantric master instructs disciples to meditate on emptiness and dissolve all appearances of themselves as truly existent. They then visualize this pristine wisdom manifesting as the deity, entering the maṇḍala of the deity, and receiving the empowerments. By awakening potentials in their mindstream and making connection with the deity, the empowerment enables them to do the self-generation practice of visualizing themselves as the deity. Unless people have previously received the empowerment of another deity, a permissory ritual does not permit them to visualize themselves as the deity.

An *oral transmission* is the reading of a text or the recitation of a mantra by a spiritual mentor while the students listen attentively. Students are encouraged to follow along in the text as the mentor reads it aloud. Oral transmissions may be of a sūtra, commentary, tantric sādhana, or mantra. As with empowerments and permissory rituals, it is important that the person giving a particular oral transmission has received it from a teacher who has received it through an unbroken lineage.

With the advent of modern technology, people have asked if empowerments, permissory rituals, and oral transmissions can be given over the internet, by telephone, or via an audio or video recording. According to the Vinaya, in ancient times if a candidate for ordination was unable to be present in the room where the ordination ceremony was given because she was ill or because traveling to the ordination site was dangerous, a messenger could notify her of the time of the ordination in advance and instruct her what to think and recite at that time. The preceptor, the ordaining saṅgha, and the ordinee were all aware that this was happening. The preceptor and saṅgha had the intention to ordain that person, and the ordinee had the intention to receive ordination from them at that time.

By extension, I believe it would be permissible for someone to receive an empowerment, permissory ritual, or oral transmission through the internet or telephone at the same time the ceremony is being conducted elsewhere if some conditions were met. First, the people wishing to receive the empowerment, permissory ritual, or oral transmission should request the spiritual master before the ceremony begins. Second, they must actively participate. That is, they do not lie down, chat, or eat snacks while watching the empowerment on the computer screen. They should sit up, pay full attention, do the visualizations as instructed, and recite the appropriate verses as if they were at the actual site of the empowerment in the presence of the tantric master. However, I do not think empowerment and so forth could be received by audio or video recording or by downloading the ceremony from the internet and viewing it at a later time.

Receiving empowerment and so forth through the internet or by telephone should be done only in exceptional situations—for example, if someone is in prison or is extremely ill, or during a pandemic. However, this should not become common practice. There could be many disadvantages for the practitioner, spiritual mentor, and lineage if sacred ceremonies were conducted in a haphazard way without proper constraints.

Preliminary Practices

Preliminary practices are designed to help students become suitable vessels to receive tantric empowerment and engage in tantric practice. The preliminaries are of two types: those that form the primary teachings of Sūtrayāna and those done specifically to purify the mind and accumulate merit in preparation for tantric empowerment. Calling them "preliminary practices" does not imply that these foundational practices are easy or that they can be skipped.

The Sūtrayāna foundational teachings are similar in the four principal Tibetan traditions, although they may have varying names. In the Nyingma and Kagyu traditions, they are called "the four thoughts that turn the mind"—precious human life, death and impermanence, karma, and the disadvantages of saṃsāra. The Sakya tradition calls them "turning away from the four clingings"—clinging to this life prevents becoming a Dharma practitioner, clinging to saṃsāra hinders generating the aspiration to be free from saṃsāra, clinging to self-centeredness prevents generating bodhicitta, and grasping inherent existence interferes with gaining wisdom realizing emptiness. In the Gelug tradition, they are the three principal aspects of the path: the aspiration to be free from saṃsāra and attain liberation, bodhicitta, and the correct view of emptiness. Understanding the stages of the path is common to both Sūtra and Tantra. Without them, we lack the proper motivation and view to even consider ourselves Buddhists.

When we hear the term "preliminary practices," we tend to think that they must be easy practices done by beginners. In fact, the above preliminaries are not easy or simple. They are essential understandings that require study, reflection, and meditation for a long time. Integrating these foundational teachings with our mind and outlook on the world makes tantric practice worthwhile.

Although the great masters in all four traditions emphasize the importance of these preliminary practices, some students with inflated ideas of their preparedness and intelligence dismiss them or rush through them. In discussing the preliminaries to enter the Guhyasamāja practices and Tantra in general, Tsongkhapa says (LS 100):

> If you do not train well in the stages of the paths common to both vehicles as explained above, you will not cut the attachment to this life, and no firm desire to practice Dharma will arise. Sincere faith will not develop, and consequently you will not give yourself completely to the objects of refuge. You will not find a true conviction in cause and effect, and any guarding and protecting of whatever precepts and vows you may have becomes coarse and superficial. There will be no genuine turning away from the attachment to saṃsāra, and "striving for freedom" simply becomes an academic understanding. Uncontrived bodhicitta built on love and compassion will not grow, and you will be a Mahāyānist in name only. There will be no strong desire to practice bodhisattva activities in general, and consequently there will be no genuine generation of the bodhisattva ethical restraints. There will be no pure understanding of serenity and insight in general, and therefore you will become prone to error on even the smallest samādhi and will not find any right conviction concerning the view of no-self. Therefore, if you wish not to go this way, you should train in the path common to both Mahāyāna vehicles [Pāramitāyāna and Vajrayāna].

Practitioners should follow the path outlined in the *Ornament for Clear Realizations* and the *Stages of the Path* that constitutes the general structure of the Buddha's teachings, whereas instructions in the tantras are specialized teachings. Only by first immersing ourselves in the general structure of the Dharma can we appreciate the qualities of the specialized teachings. In Tibet, we placed undue emphasis on the specialized teachings of Tantrayāna, sometimes at the expense of the general structure. This is one reason why in exile I have urged monasteries and nunneries to study the general structure of the teachings.

The second set of preliminary practices, commonly referred to by their

Tibetan name *ngondro* (T. *sngon 'gro*), can be enumerated in several ways, according to the lineage, be it Nyingma, Kagyu, Sakya, or Gelug. The benefit gained from practicing these tantric preliminaries is proportional to our understanding of the common preliminaries—the stages of the path. Some spiritual mentors have their students complete the ngondro practices before receiving Highest Yoga Tantra empowerment, others before engaging in long retreats. Some teachers advise doing them in the context of a retreat, others as a daily practice. Some teachers instruct their students to complete one preliminary practice before embarking on another, while others have their students do two or more preliminary practices at the same time. For this reason, practitioners consult with their spiritual mentors and receive the oral transmission or permission, as well as instructions on how to meditate on these practices, before beginning one of them.

In general, there are nine preliminaries: (1) prostrations, (2) maṇḍala offerings, (3) taking refuge, (4) Vajrasattva (Dorje Sempa) meditation and recitation, (5) guru yoga, (6) Samayavajra (Damtsig Dorje), (7) Vajraḍāka (Dorje Khadro), (8) water bowl offerings, and (9) making images of the Buddha or meditation deities. Sometimes bodhicitta is added as another preliminary practice.

Guru yoga is done when we have, from our heart, taken someone as our root guru. Guru yoga is often done in relation to our tantric guru, and here we practice seeing the inseparability of the guru and the deity. In this regard it is important to differentiate the interpretive and definitive gurus, the interpretive guru being the person who embodies excellent qualities and bestows the empowerment and the definitive guru being the Buddha's mind of bliss and emptiness. Unifying the definitive guru, the deity, and our own wisdom mind then becomes possible when our subtlest clear-light mind, through practicing the path, becomes the blissful wisdom realizing emptiness.

Empowerment

Empowerment is the door to enter Vajrayāna. Therefore, receiving empowerment from a qualified tantric guru is of crucial importance before engaging in tantric practice. The *Drop of the Great Seal* (*Mahāmudrātilaka Tantra*) says (OBT 66):

> Without empowerment, there are no attainments,
> just as no butter will come from squeezing sand.

Although we may be inspired by hearing about tantra or feel attracted to a specific meditation deity, we should not pick up a book or attend a teaching on that practice without first receiving the empowerment. Furthermore, tantric masters must take care and give tantric empowerments, especially those of Highest Yoga Tantra, only to qualified and serious disciples.

The empowerment procedure or ceremony is fairly uniform among the three lower tantras, while the ceremony for Highest Yoga Tantra is more complex. During an empowerment ceremony for a particular deity, the practitioner receives different empowerments according to the tantric class. In Action Tantra, two types of empowerment are important, the water and crown empowerments. In Performance Tantra, the empowerment of the five wisdoms is crucial, while in Highest Yoga Tantra, the vase, secret, wisdom, and word empowerments form the core. The four empowerments in Highest Yoga Tantra are ripening factors for different stages of the completion-stage path:

- The vase empowerment empowers the practitioner to meditate on the generation stage.
- The secret empowerment empowers the practitioner to undertake the practices of the illusory body and the three isolations—isolated body, isolated speech, and isolated clear mind—which are preliminaries to that. The three isolations are the first three of the five stages that comprise the completion stage of Guhyasamāja.
- The wisdom empowerment empowers the practitioner to meditate on clear light.
- The fourth or word empowerment empowers the practitioner to meditate on the union of illusory body and clear light, which is the union of the two truths in Highest Yoga Tantra.

The four empowerments in Highest Yoga Tantra correspond to the progressive stages of the tantric path, ripening practitioners' minds so they can practice and realize the fruit of each stage. These form a series of correspondences between the empowerment, the path, and the result of each stage. For that reason, Tsongkhapa explains the essence of Tantra in terms of the meaning of the four empowerments, and the Sakya lamdre similarly structures the tantric path in terms of the four empowerments. Sakya Paṇḍita, in *Clear Differentiation of the Three Ethical Codes* (*Sdom gsum rab dbye*), explains the attainment that corresponds to each of the four empowerments: (1) The vase empowerment is correlated with culmination of attainment that is the inseparability of saṃsāra and nirvāṇa. (2) The secret empowerment is correlated with culmination of attainment that is clearly distinct and utterly complete. (3) The wisdom empowerment is correlated with culmination of attainment that is blissful emptiness of the lesser extent. (4) The word empowerment is correlated with culmination of the attainment that is blissful emptiness of greater extent.

The terms for the empowerments vary in different traditions. For example, in the Nyingma tradition, the vajra-master empowerment is called the "empowerment of illusion" and the disciple empowerment is called the "beneficial empowerment." There is also an all-encompassing vajra empowerment. In dzogchen, the fourth empowerment is further divided into four—the empowerments with elaboration and so forth.[16]

The word "empowerment" has different connotations depending on the context. In general, there are the causal empowerment that is a factor ripening the practitioners' mind, the path empowerment that is the actual path of realization, and the resultant empowerment that is the purified result. Dzogchen mentions an additional empowerment, the empowerment of the basis. This refers to the clear light that is the basis on which all other empowerments can be received. If sentient beings lacked this subtle clear-light mind, no other empowerments could take place.

Receiving empowerment should make an impact on our subtle mind. During the empowerment ritual as well as the subsequent practice we do, single-pointed concentration on the visualization, supported by bodhicitta and understanding of emptiness, is important. Empowerment must be received from a living human being, and this person must have some experience based on receiving the empowerment from their own guru, with the empowerment lineage being ultimately traced back to the Buddha himself. For this reason, it is crucial to know the attributes of a qualified tantric master and to investigate if a prospective guru has them. It also explains why guru yoga is important in tantric practice.

To engage in the coarse and refined stages of the generation stage, it is necessary to receive the vase empowerment, which includes the five common empowerments of the five buddha families and the uncommon empowerment of the vajra guru. If people haven't received the vase empowerment, or if they have but neglect to keep the tantric ethical restraints and commitments purely, even if they seem to do the generation stage, it is like squeezing sand to get oil. When receiving the vase empowerment, pay attention and meditate. When the vase is touched to the crown of your head, imagine various nectars flowing down into your body, purifying your body and mind of all defilements. When your body is filled with the nectars, your mind experiences great bliss. This is the conscious factor of the empowerment. When you experience purification and great bliss, a seed is planted in your mindstream so that in the future you will attain the body of a buddha. Of the three types of impermanent phenomena—form, mind, and abstract composites—this seed is an abstract composite. Thus, in each empowerment two factors become the nature of the empowerment: the conscious factor that is great bliss and a seed that is an abstract composite placed on the mindstream.

Similarly, when the crown or any other implement is touched to the crown of your head during the empowerment, it is important that you think a strong seed has been placed on your mindstream that will ripen in the future as the attainment of the resultant stage. This is the significance of the Sanskrit word *abhiṣeka* that is repeated when you receive the empowerment. *Abhiṣeka* has the connotation of sprinkle, in the sense of sprinkling seeds in a field that will then grow and mature into a result. Feel that a seed has been sprinkled onto your mindstream that will yield excellent results in the future.

When I give empowerment, my emphasis is on helping disciples understand Tantra. I could go into detail explaining the meaning of the specific tantra—for example, explaining the complex ritual of how the mantra is composed. However, I prefer that disciples gain a broad understanding of the deeper significance of Tantra and therefore focus on the essential points.

Rituals

To conduct an empowerment, a maṇḍala—the divine abode of the deity—is required. There are different types of maṇḍalas: those created by concentration, painted maṇḍalas, sand maṇḍalas, and in Highest Yoga Tantra the body maṇḍala and the maṇḍala of conventional bodhicitta. Among these maṇḍalas, the sand maṇḍala is principal because it is the one used to consecrate the site and so forth. In some cases, a ritual dance consisting of various hand gestures and steps is done in the presence of the sand maṇḍala.

In general, *maṇḍala* means "that which extracts the essence." Its usage varies according to the context. One type of maṇḍala is the offering of the entire world system. Disciples visualize the universe accepted in ancient India with its major and minor continents, offering goddesses, and auspicious articles, which are offered to the holy beings. This is the maṇḍala offering done before and after teachings and in our daily practice. There are also painted maṇḍalas and so forth used in tantric empowerments, as mentioned above. All of these are called maṇḍalas because when disciples do practices with them, they extract meaning. Although there are pictures and constructed depictions of tantric maṇḍalas, the main meaning is that practitioners enter a maṇḍala and extract an essence in the sense of receiving blessing and inspiration. Gaining magnificence and attaining realization is the meaning of extracting essence that occurs in a maṇḍala.

Ritual dances are of different types. One is done when consecrating the site where the maṇḍala will be built and the empowerment held. Another is performed after the completion of the maṇḍala. Another type of ritual dance is called *cham*, which is associated with counteracting obstacles. Many small monasteries are expert in performing these ritual dances, but I wonder how well they understand their significance and symbolism. Most people consider them to be a theatrical performance, done for amusement or to preserve Tibetan culture. This indicates the sad fact that Tantrayāna is degenerating. One factor that contributed to the degeneration of the Buddhadharma in India was the excessive public performance of tantric rituals, which unfortunately led many people to consider Tantra as mere ritual similar to theistic worship. In actuality, the philosophy supporting tantric practice is very profound, but when only the external elements are seen and no explanation given, such misunderstanding easily occurs.

Rituals are aids to meditation. A tantric ritual text, such as a sādhana or pūjā, is recited when visualization does not come automatically. It guides us through the stages of practice. Once we can mentally generate the sequence of visualizations by the power of familiarity, reciting the text is no longer necessary. We can simply do the visualization and meditate.

Certain aspects of tantric rituals, such as the offerings, are based on Indian customs and can be adapted to Western cultures. However, an exception exists: although the forms of the Buddhist deities, their ornaments, garments, and maṇḍala houses are influenced by ancient Indian culture, no Tibetan master has suggested that these be adapted to Tibetan culture. Thus my personal view is that Western practitioners should not change the appearance of the deities, their garments, the mantras, or the design of the maṇḍalas. Other than that, however, you can adapt the offerings, the musical instruments, and the melodies for the chants to your own culture rather than relying on Asian forms.

Some examples of cultural adaptation occur when I give empowerments in the West. I sometimes use cookies or biscuits for a torma (a ritual offering of food) because the material used for tormas, as well as their size and shape, depend on the culture and can be changed. In addition, I ask the audience to recite the verses for generating aspiring bodhicitta in English, not in Tibetan. By understanding the words of the ceremony, people will have a stronger experience of the meaning, and that gives them more confidence in their practice.

Playing Tibetan musical instruments, such as the short or long horns, during rituals is not necessary, although you may play them if you like. The purpose of playing instruments is to offer music to the Buddha, and for that you can use Western instruments such as the piano or guitar.

I recommend that lay followers who have completed a three-year retreat but who are not celibate do not shave their heads or wear the robes of an ordained, celibate monastic. Those wishing to wear some sort of robe could wear a white upper or lower robe and have long hair. In the Tibetan tradition, a person who takes the eight precepts with celibacy can wear monastic robes. However, lay followers with the five precepts cannot. Unfortunately, although I have said this publicly to the Tibetan community, some Tibetan lamas with families still wear garments that resemble monastic robes. This creates confusion for people, who cannot understand why a person who dresses like a monastic does not keep monastic precepts.

After Receiving Empowerment

Because the great majority of those who receive Vajrayāna empowerment these days have not yet attained effortless and genuine realizations of the three principal aspects of the path, generating these should remain the emphasis of our Dharma practice. The more we understand these three—especially emptiness as explained in Sūtra—the more we'll understand the method and purpose of generating oneself as a deity in Tantra. Therefore I strongly recommend that newcomers to tantric practice emphasize the meditations on refuge, bodhicitta, and emptiness included in the sādhana, as well as continue with analytical meditation on the stages of the path. In this way, meditation on the three principal aspects will enrich our practice of deity yoga, and deity yoga will, in turn, help our understanding of the Sūtra path. This becomes the practice of combining Sūtra and Tantra in a mutually beneficial way. There is a Tibetan saying, "Whether or not a cake is delicious depends on the butter." Similarly, whether or not our tantric practice is successful depends on our understanding and realization of the Sūtra path. With deep experience of the determination to be free, bodhicitta, and the wisdom realizing emptiness, we will be able to practice tantra genuinely and effectively. Without these, even if we recite many sādhanas and meditate on the completion-stage practices, our spiritual practice will not progress.

Some people say, "I've been practicing tantra for years and have no results." This is because they lack a deep understanding of the three principal aspects of the path. They may do retreat on Yamāntaka or Vajrayoginī and recite many sādhanas and mantras, and visualize many deities, but their practice isn't Highest Yoga Tantra, because they lack bodhicitta. Only when our motivation accords with Highest Yoga Tantra does our practice become a practice of Highest Yoga Tantra. Therefore, when our tantric practice feels dry, it indicates we should meditate more on the Sūtra path to nourish our motivation and enrich our understanding.

The Indian yogis said that someone may do the generation-stage practice of visualizing themselves as the deity, but without meditating on emptiness first, this will produce more conceptual thought, making it difficult to eliminate the root of saṃsāra, grasping at inherent existence. The very purpose of imagining ourselves as a deity is to reflect on the ultimate nature of the deity—to meditate on emptiness and dependent arising. This is the focus of deity yoga. When we visualize deities and offerings emanating and absorbing, the main point is to keep emptiness and dependent arising in mind. For that reason, cultivating the wisdom realizing emptiness is extremely important for Vajrayāna practice. Without it, little difference exists between visualizing ourselves as a deity and daydreaming.

You should develop yourselves gradually in the tantric path. In Tibet, people received advanced teachings or oral transmissions on texts describing completion-stage practices, such as the six yogas of Nāropā, but they didn't immediately put these teachings into practice. Instead, they continued to practice at the level they were at, knowing that hearing these oral transmissions and teachings planted good seeds in their mindstream. These seeds ripen later, when practitioners are capable of doing those practices.

Tantric Ethical Restraints and Commitments

For advanced practice such as Tantra to bring good results, it is essential that we maintain good ethical conduct, beginning with the prātimokṣa precepts. Thinking that we can ignore "lower-level" ethical restraints in the name of being a tantric practitioner is a huge mistake. The *Tantra Requested by Subāhu* says (LPH 495):

> I, the Victorious One, taught the prātimokṣa ethical restraints;
> do not forsake its pure ethics.
> Lay tantrists, abandon the signs and rituals [of monastics,]
> but practice all the rest [of the trainings].

And the *Mañjuśrī Root Tantra* says:[17]

> The lord of sages did not prescribe mantra practice
> for the ill disciplined,
> as it would not lead to the city,
> land, or even the direction of nirvāṇa.
>
> For a debased fool such as this,
> how could his mantra succeed?

For a person fickle in his discipline,
what pleasant state could be found?

Heaven is not for him,
nor a happy departure from this world,
let alone an attainment
of mantras taught by the Victorious One.

Practitioners may be slack in ethical conduct due to laziness or to arrogance, thinking they are too advanced to pay attention to "trivial" precepts such as abandoning stealing, lying, and so forth. Such attitudes and behavior prevent our spiritual growth no matter what practice we engage in. Learning and practicing the stages of the path, on the other hand, creates great merit and stabilizes our mind and behavior, making them suitable for more advanced practices.

Tantric practice mainly deals with eliminating the appearance of ourselves and our surroundings as ordinary and our grasping them as ordinary. Thus most of the tantric ethical restraints and commitments are concerned with reducing the view that we, our companions, environment, enjoyments, and activities are ordinary and exist inherently.

Since the path to be cultivated is different in each of the four tantric classes, the empowerments ripening the practitioners' mindstream also differ. Practitioners of the two lower tantric classes (Action Tantra and Performance Tantra) are required to take the bodhisattva precepts, but the tantric ethical restraints are not given. A practitioner also assumes some commitments that are to be kept.

In the two upper classes (Yoga Tantra and Highest Yoga Tantra), practitioners must take the tantric ethical restraints and commitments. This is done on the basis of having taken the bodhisattva precepts, which, in turn, is based on having taken either monastic precepts or refuge in the Three Jewels, and preferably all five lay precepts, although having refuge and some of the five lay precepts is also acceptable. All of these constitute the higher training of ethical conduct of a Vajrayāna practitioner. We can see that for Tantra practitioners, ethical conduct is more exacting than for Sūtra practitioners.

The Kālacakra Tantra has an additional set of twenty-five rules of conduct that practitioners take at the time of empowerment into the Kālacakra maṇḍala. One of these is to abandon taking alcohol and intoxicants. As mentioned before, the Kālacakra Tantra says the ideal lay practitioner keeps all the monastic precepts but doesn't wear robes, so maintaining celibacy is important for practitioners of this tantra. This is because the way of actualizing the form body of a buddha in Kālacakra involves generating an empty form. To accomplish this, a yogi must stack up the twenty-one thousand white and red drops in the central channel. Emitting these drops through ejaculation, then, is counterproductive.

Being vegetarian when practicing the three lower tantras is important. While I recommend that people in general be vegetarian, some people require meat in their diet. In such a case, they should do all their Action, Performance, and Yoga Tantra commitments before eating meat that day.

Highest Yoga Tantra contains a practice concerning five meats and five nectars.[18] Fully qualified practitioners of Highest Yoga Tantra can transform these five meats and five nectars into purified substances through the power of meditation. These advanced practitioners can then use those substances to enhance the body's winds, which facilitates the yogic practices. If someone tries to justify eating meat by claiming to be a practitioner of Highest Yoga Tantra, they should partake of all five meats and five nectars impartially and enjoy all of them equally, without relishing some and rejecting others in disgust.

After receiving empowerment, we must study the tantric ethical restraints and commitments we have taken and try to keep them as best as we can. These should be regarded as treasured ornaments, not as burdens or as a tax you have to pay to take the empowerment. Abiding in the tantric ethical restraints and commitments creates the container in which tantric practice can be successful and our spiritual goals can be actualized. The ethical restraints and commitments describe how a fully awakened being acts. By abiding in them purely, we come closer to the physical, verbal, and mental activities of a buddha.

Avoid the extremes of being nonchalant about our ethical restraints and commitments or emotionally fearful of transgressing them. Keeping the tantric ethical restraints and commitments well brings great benefits, whereas transgressing them brings undesirable repercussions. Tsongkhapa says (LC 3:364):

> You should then listen to the pledges and tantric precepts to be taken [at the time of empowerment], understand them, and maintain them. If you are stricken by root infractions, you may take [these precepts] again. However, this greatly delays the development of the qualities of the path in your mind. You should strive fiercely not to be polluted by those [root infractions] . . . but in the event you are polluted, use the method for restoring [your precepts]. . . . Someone who talks about practicing the path without maintaining the pledges and tantric precepts has completely strayed from the tantric path.

If we overstep the boundaries of our ethical restraints and commitments, we should confess and restore them by receiving the empowerment again, doing one hundred thousand recitations of the Vajrasattva mantra, or performing the self-empowerment. The latter is a way of entering the maṇḍala and receiving empowerment ourselves, and it can be done after we have completed the approximation retreat and the concluding fire pūjā.

Empowerment Taken Prematurely

The prātimokṣa ethical codes, with the exception of the one-day precepts, are taken for the duration of our lives. If we have obstacles in our practice, we may offer these precepts back to avoid breaking them from the root. The bodhisattva precepts and the tantric precepts are taken until awakening, and they remain as long as we do not commit a root infraction.

If someone is not sure that they can keep the tantric ethical restraints and commitments, it is best to wait before taking the complete empowerment. In the meantime, they can participate in the ceremony until the point just after having entered the maṇḍala and then depart.

Some people enthusiastically take empowerment because they hear the tantric master is very famous or tantric practice is very high. Later they do not feel able to keep the ethical restraints and commitments received at the time of empowerment. This situation can be likened to someone who impulsively buys a rare item, but after taking it home, thinks that he really doesn't want it. What should he do? He doesn't throw it out, because it is valuable. He keeps it for a later time when he will need it. Likewise, if someone takes tantric empowerment prematurely and lacks understanding and faith in tantric practice, it's best not to discard it but to respectfully put it aside for the time being. Later, at a more suitable time, one can return to it.

On the other hand, some disciples take an empowerment and accept the tantric ethical restraints and commitments, including the commitment to practice the meditation of that deity by reciting and meditating on a sādhana every day. They have faith in Tantra, but the commitment to recite and meditate on the sādhana every day becomes a burden for them. These disciples can abbreviate their practice—for example, by reciting some verses once instead of three times and doing the visualization quickly rather than reciting the long description. But they should not omit the essence of the sādhana—dissolving themselves into emptiness and imagining their wisdom realizing emptiness appearing in the form of the deity and the maṇḍala. After that, they can recite the mantra and then dedicate the merit.

If someone still has faith and interest in the Buddhadharma but does not want to do Vajrayāna practice at this time, I recommend that they recite the one-hundred-syllable mantra of Vajrasattva for purification and then focus on cultivating bodhicitta and the correct view of emptiness in their practice. Developing bodhicitta and the correct view are more practical for these people, and practicing bodhicitta and meditating on emptiness are the best way to purify.

Other people who have stopped living in their tantric ethical restraints and commitments may want to take up Vajrayāna practice later. I recommend that they resume following the tantric ethical restraints and commitments and receive empowerment again whenever it is possible.

For the people who do not want to keep the tantric ethical restraints and commitments, and do not regret this, there is nothing much to say.

On a broader note, some people ask me what to do if their friends lose faith in the Dharma. If someone comes to us for help, we should give them suitable advice. But if they have made up their mind and feel happy to relinquish the Dharma, there's nothing much you can say. Even the Buddha would be helpless in that situation.

After attending an empowerment or permissory rite, some newcomers discover that there are tantric ethical restraints and commitments to keep and become confused. Here we have to consider each individual case. If they did not consciously know they were taking the bodhisattva precepts or the tantric precepts at the time they were being given, they did not receive them and therefore are not responsible to keep them. However, without consciously taking the precepts during the empowerment, they do not receive the empowerment and thus are not entitled to do the self-generation practice of that deity.

The Practice of Sādhanas

Sādhanas—the texts outlining the meditation practice of a deity—were originally written in Sanskrit or other Indian languages and translated into Tibetan. Only the mantras remained in the original language. Similarly, except for the mantras, sādhanas can now be translated into Western languages. Reciting the sādhana in a language that you do not understand does not help you to remember the steps of the practice, so the main purpose of meditating on a deity is lost. Although you may enjoy chanting in Tibetan, do that only if you understand the meaning. Otherwise do the practice in your own language. You must understand the meaning of the words to do the meditation properly. Having accurate translations of sādhanas is important.

The practice of a sādhana is not the recitation of the text. Nor is deity yoga mere words. The words act as a reminder of the steps of the practice and how to meditate during them if we find it difficult to remember all the details. But if we know the details of the visualization and meditation, recitation of the text isn't necessary. In ancient times, the texts did not exist; the guru would explain the practice to the disciple through his or her experience, and the disciple would remember and meditate in accord with the explanation. But as time went on, some people found it difficult to remember all the steps in the meditation. In addition, some unqualified people began to practice Vajrayāna, so there was danger of incorrect explanations. Thus great masters composed the sādhanas.

Many sādhanas—for example, the Six-Session Guru Yoga—have long and short versions. Optimally, only tantric masters would recite the short sādhanas, because they are already familiar with the meditation, and those who don't know the practice well would recite the longer sādhanas. But now it's the opposite! The people who don't know the practice want to do it quickly to get on with other activities, while the masters take time to do the practice slowly and accurately. We should follow the example of the great masters and try to become like them.

For this reason, after giving an empowerment, I often require practitioners to recite or meditate on the long sādhana. At one occasion when I was requested to give the Yamāntaka empowerment in Dharamsala, many people came on the first day for the preparation to the empowerment, and I cautioned them, "If you take the empowerment but don't practice properly, it will shorten the guru's life. Please take the empowerment only if you have determination to keep the tantric ethical restraints and commitments and meditate and recite the sādhana. The next day only half the people came back to receive the actual empowerment. I was pleased that they listened to my advice. I prayed to Yamāntaka to care for those who didn't receive the empowerment for their mindstream to mature so that they may receive it in the future.

We are very surprised if someone asks a child to hold a fragile and valuable cup. Ḍākinīs feel similarly astonished if empowerments and tantric teachings are given to those who aren't yet mature enough to do the practice. These teachings are precious and should be valued and treated respectfully once they are received. Therefore, we should properly recite and meditate on a sādhana not only to further our own Dharma practice but also to repay the kindness of the guru who gave us the empowerment.

Some people take an empowerment and initially keep the commitment the tantric master has given to meditate on the sādhana daily. But after a while their interest in tantra diminishes and they no longer want to do the sādhana. If that happens to you, do not stop your tantric practice. Instead, do the Six-Session Guru Yoga daily, and at the point when the merit field dissolves into you, instead of arising as Vajradhara, arise as the deity and say the number of mantras you promised to recite each day. Then finish the rest of the Six-Session Guru Yoga. This condensed way to keep the commitment to do the sādhana daily is only for those who no longer feel sufficiently engaged in tantra.

Some practitioners may initially find it easier to do the self-generation practice of a deity that is the same sex as they are. For example, some men find it difficult to imagine themselves as Tārā, and some women feel strange imagining themselves as Mañjuśrī. This occurs due to your familiarity with and grasping to your coarse body. However, self-generation has nothing to do with your coarse body, which is dissolved into emptiness before you reappear as the deity. As your understanding of emptiness deepens, visualizing yourself as the deity will become easier.

Astute practitioners bring their understanding of the lamrim into their practice of tantric sādhanas—for example, by meditating on refuge and bodhicitta at the beginning of the sādhana, contemplating relating to a spiritual mentor during the guru yoga section, and so forth. The entire sādhana is best done within an awareness of emptiness and dependent arising. Without this important element, thinking of yourself as a truly existent deity will not bring you closer to awakening.

Before doing the self-generation, the sūtra instructs you to meditate on emptiness after reciting the mantras *oṃ svabhāva-śuddhāḥ sarva-dharmāḥ svabhāva-śuddho 'ham* and *oṃ śūnyatā jñāna vajra svabhāva ātmako 'ham*. Here, recall your previous understanding of emptiness and meditate on emptiness. Then, motivated by bodhicitta, begin the self-generation visualization.

If your understanding of emptiness is superficial, after saying the mantras recite these experiential verses from the "Song of the Direct View" by the Seventh Dalai Lama:

> All phenomena in saṃsāra and nirvāṇa are merely designated by mind. Mind itself, when investigated, is beyond arising or ceasing. Abiding in the ultimate mode of being, *emaho*! Most wondrous!
>
> Just as autumn clouds dissipate in the sky, within the sphere of emptiness, emptiness and my mind become indivisible. Within this, all the elaborations of experiences (pain and pleasure) and appearances (of form and so forth) dissolve.
>
> I, an unborn yogi of space, see that nothing truly exists, all things are falsities. I understand the great show of illusion-like sights and sounds. By experiencing the joyous union of appearance and emptiness, I find certainty in the nondeceptive nature of dependent arising.

The first verse indicates that because all phenomena in saṃsāra and nirvāṇa exist by being merely designated by mind, they are empty of inherent existence and cannot be found when searched for with ultimate analysis. After reciting the second verse, dissolve everything into emptiness, recalling that if phenomena existed inherently, they would not depend on any other factors; they would be permanent and self-enclosed. But nothing exists like that. Focus on emptiness single-pointedly.

The first two verses dispel the extreme of absolutism, while the third verse counteracts nihilism by affirming that all phenomena exist as falsities, as mere designations, having no inherent essence. This appearance is phenomena's conventional existence that is established after emerging from meditation on emptiness. Finding certainty in the infallibility of dependent arising, ascertain that phenomena both lack inherent existence and appear falsely, like illusions.

REFLECTION

1. What is the difference between an empowerment and a permissory rite?
2. What are the benefits of following the ethical restraints and commitments you receive by taking an empowerment or permissory rite? What are the disadvantages of not following or transgressing them?
3. How can you determine when it is a good time for you to enter Vajrayāna and when it is premature to do so?

Women and Vajrayāna

Women form half of the world's human population, and in most countries the great majority of people who attend religious services and teachings are women. Women have sincere spiritual aspirations and the potential to actualize them.

According to the Vinaya texts, men and women have equal opportunity to ordain,[19] and the Buddha said both are capable of attaining liberation. Nevertheless, following the social standards at the time of the Buddha and even today, fully ordained monks are objects of respect and veneration, whereas nuns are not as respected and receive less support. From this point of view, we could say there is some gender discrimination.

In Sūtrayāna, bodhisattvas may be either men or women, until they reach the highest level of the path, when, before attaining buddhahood, they must be male. Bodhisattvas attain buddhahood in Akaniṣṭha Pure Abode. Someone in their last life as a bodhisattva who is born there as a female deva must transform into a male deva prior to attaining full awakening. This is the same in the three lower tantric classes.

Highest Yoga Tantra is different. Here, even the first step of receiving empowerment is possible only on the basis of an assembly of male and female deities. Many deities are female, such as Vajrayoginī, Tārā, Nairātmya,[20] Sarasvatī, and Siṃhamukhā (Lion-Faced Ḍākinī). In addition, ḍākinīs, who are highly realized practitioners, are included in the Saṅgha Jewel as objects of refuge. The *Guhyasamāja Tantra* clearly and explicitly states that a female practitioner can attain awakening in that lifetime. To despise a woman, thinking that she has a lower rebirth (than a man), is a transgression of one of the root tantric precepts; there is no corresponding precept regarding despising men.

In Highest Yoga Tantra practitioners develop the latent potency within themselves—the fundamental innate clear-light mind. Since both women and men possess this, both can actualize full awakening in that lifetime. Thus, from the viewpoint of Highest Yoga Tantra, which is the ultimate teaching, there is no distinction in the capabilities of men and women, and women are to be respected.

Unusual Behavior

Some people rightly question, "Why do some people, who call themselves practitioners of Highest Yoga Tantra, drink alcohol?" This must be understood in its proper context. In the completion stage of Highest Yoga Tantra, practitioners meditate on the subtle winds, channels, and drops of their body in order to dissolve the winds into the indestructible drop at the heart cakra. For yogis with stable renunciation, powerful bodhicitta, and profound wisdom realizing emptiness, who are at the level of the completion stage called "isolated mind," taking alcohol and having sexual relations are allowed because they facilitate the dissolution of the winds. This practice is extremely advanced and only a handful of people nowadays are at that stage. Those people are discrete and follow the tantric precepts regarding such practices.

Ordinary practitioners of tantra, including most people who attend tantric empowerments these days, are not at that level, and those who have taken the precept to abandon intoxicants should abide by that. Highly realized yogis have developed a special ability whereby they can transform excrement and urine into nectar and consume it. I do not think that most Buddhists who drink alcohol have that kind of power! People should practice at their own level and not have delusions of grandeur, thinking they are high yogis when they are not.[21]

Highly accomplished siddhas attain a stable practice of the inseparability of method and wisdom in Highest Yoga Tantra. Sometimes these highly realized adepts may engage in strange behavior, such as hunting animals, which seems far beyond acceptable behavior for a genuine practitioner. Why would highly realized siddhas, who are intimately familiar with the subtlest clear light and have gone beyond conceptuality, act in this manner? Hunting animals is not done for mere sport. It is to benefit the animal, because those yogis have the ability to transfer its mindstream to a more fortunate birth.

Needless to say, such practices are limited to those with very high, stable realizations. To engage in such behavior, they must have "attained capacity." Padma Karpo (1527–92), a great Drukpa Kagyu scholar and adept, said this means they have the power to overcome the skepticism and loss of faith that arises in others who see them engaging in such actions. Since these yogis don't want others to disrespect or lose faith in the Dharma—harmful attitudes that would spiritually damage them—these yogis must be able to prevent others from generating these harmful mental states. Only then would they be considered capable of engaging in unusual behavior. Tilopa acted in strange ways with his disciple Nāropa, but he had the ability to overcome any skepticism and loss of faith Nāropa may have had. Such seemingly inappropriate behavior is permitted in the case of these highly realized yogis because these practices enhance their special qualities. Although these highly accomplished practitioners are capable of practicing in this way, it is neither appropriate nor beneficial for those of us who lack their realizations to try to do so. We must focus on the gentler practices that accord with the norms and mores of society.

Some people may pretend to be highly realized yogis and try to show off their supernormal powers or fierce behaviors. Naïve people may believe them for some time, but when these people lose faith in them, charlatans blame their lack of faith on the bad karma or impure view of those people.

In conclusion, Vajrayāna teachings are very precious and must be studied and understood properly for practitioners to benefit from them. Thus, if you aspire to practice Tantra, you must make yourself into a suitable vessel for tantric empowerment by practicing all the previous stages of the path and gaining familiarity, if not actual experience, in them. Then seek a fully qualified Vajrayāna master who can grant empowerments, and keep the tantric ethical restraints and commitments you have taken as purely as possible. Request a tantric master to give instructions on the sādhana and practice according to those instructions. When tantric practice is approached in a thoughtful and respectful manner, it is very beneficial. However, if it is approached with recklessness, conceit, or attachment, you will not benefit and instead may create difficulties for yourself and others.

The Four Classes of Tantra and the Nine Vehicles

There is a great difference between the Pāramitāyāna and the Tantra Vehicle concerning the mind that understands emptiness. In Tantrayāna, the mind realizing emptiness is in the nature of great bliss. Within blissful consciousnesses, four types of bliss are found, and four classes of tantra are differentiated based on this: Action (Kriyā), Performance (Caryā or Upa), Yoga, and Highest Yoga (Anuttarayoga). Together these are known as tantras from the New Translation school, which includes the Kagyu, Sakya, and Gelug traditions. These four classes of tantras are described in the explanatory tantra *Vajrapañjara*.

The tantras are classified into four according to their functions. In Action Tantra, external actions such as hand gestures (mudrās) and bathing are considered very important. In Performance Tantra, inner yoga and external actions are equally emphasized, while in Yoga Tantra, inner yoga is more important. In Highest Yoga Tantra, inner yoga greatly supersedes external actions.

Because the profound and unique qualities of Tantra are consummated in Highest Yoga Tantra, the lower tantras are seen as steps leading to it.

Thus, when you enter Tantrayāna, it is best to receive empowerment into Action Tantra and engage in that practice first.

The Nyingma explanation of the nine yānas or vehicles can be helpful in understanding the progression from Sūtra to Tantra, and within Tantra, from the lower tantras to the higher. The nine vehicles are divided into three groups, each of which has three subdivisions:

1. Sūtrayāna. These three vehicles are called "vehicles countering the origin of duḥkha" because they explain the path that leads to liberation by abandoning the afflictions and karma that are the origin of duḥkha.

    1. Śrāvaka Vehicle
    2. Solitary Realizer Vehicle
    3. Perfection Vehicle (Pāramitāyāna)

2. Vehicle of the Ritual and Ascetic Practices. Also called the "external vehicles," these include the recitation of mantras, certain hygienic conduct, and so on.

    4. Action Tantra
    5. Performance Tantra
    6. Yoga Tantra

The above six vehicles do not contain teachings on the method to actualize the fundamental innate mind of clear light, thus they lack a complete method for totally overcoming the discursive thought processes that are the coarser levels of mind. In Action, Performance, and Yoga Tantras, there are many rituals pertaining to purity that are important to do, and one has to observe conventions, such as the distinction between purity and impurity.

3. Vehicle of the Method for Gaining Mastery, or "Inner Vehicle." The name of this vehicle indicates that it contains the unique methods to make manifest the subtlest mind and wind and to master and take afflictions into the path. Through these means, practitioners overpower the afflictions by understanding their true nature. They place their mind in a state of deep meditation beyond the discrimination of

good and bad or pure and impure, enabling them to transcend worldly conventions by means of wisdom.

7. Mahāyoga
8. Anuyoga
9. Atiyoga

The following chapters contain a presentation of the stages and paths of the four classes of Tantra. By studying this, in the future you'll be better prepared to study more scriptural texts on Tantra, which in general are far more extensive and complicated than Sūtrayāna texts, and are thus more difficult to understand and gain insight into. Learning an abbreviated presentation is useful for the future when you delve into more elaborate texts.

The great Atiśa proclaimed his skill in the tantric teachings and was somewhat proud of it. However, in a dream, ḍākinīs showed him tantric texts that he'd never seen before, and his pride decreased. He thought, "Well, even though I didn't know of the texts that were revealed in the dreams, I still can boast of my knowledge of the tantric texts extant in the world." However, when he went to Tibet, he saw in various temple libraries so many great tantric texts no longer extant in India that had been translated from the first flowering of Dharma in Tibet, spearheaded by Guru Rinpoche Padmasambhava, Śāntarakṣita, and other early scholars, that his pride about knowing all the tantric texts in the human world decreased even further. Since the tantric teachings and texts explaining them are all-encompassing, deep, profound, and difficult to understand, it is important to study presentations that abbreviate the essential points and set them out in an orderly fashion.

Followers of the Fundamental Vehicle can attain liberation from saṃsāra in a minimum of three lifetimes. To reach the higher attainment, buddhahood, practitioners must practice the Mahāyāna path. Within the Mahāyāna, those who practice the Pāramitāyāna accumulate merit for a minimum of three countless eons to attain awakening. Those who follow the three lower classes of Tantra may attain awakening in one lifetime. However, this is not an ordinary lifetime, it is one that has been extended through the practice of special tantric methods. Followers of Highest Yoga Tantra may attain buddhahood within this very short lifetime. They do this by correctly and intensely practicing special instructions found in Highest

Yoga Tantra. Although attaining buddhahood in this life sounds enticing, don't think this is easy or requires little effort.

Practitioners must first have complete proficiency in the three preliminaries—the determination to be free from saṃsāra, bodhicitta, and the correct view of emptiness. In addition, they must practice in a proper and perfect fashion and be willing to experience difficulties and hardships along the path. Great effort is required. Furthermore, they must not be motivated to attain awakening for the sake of their own happiness and fulfilling their own aims. These prerequisites are emphasized in many tantric texts. To learn and practice them, please study and practice the Sūtrayāna teachings explained in the previous volumes of the *Library of Wisdom and Compassion.*

Practicing Vajrayāna in a Gradual Manner

When people are properly prepared to enter Vajrayāna practice, they should in general begin with Kriyā Tantra and do that practice for a long time. This practice is simpler and safer, yet very profound. It will be easier for people new to Tantra to cultivate spiritual experiences and realizations through Kriyā Tantra practices.

To help qualified practitioners transcend ordinary appearance and ordinary grasping, Highest Yoga Tantra speaks about eating meat, drinking alcohol, and using sexual intercourse in the path. In earlier times, this practice was kept strictly secret to prevent unqualified people from engaging in practices that could be harmful to them and to prevent others from misunderstanding these practices. However, now that books about Highest Yoga Tantra can be found in stores and empowerments are given openly, many misunderstandings have arisen. This is one reason why I recommend that people interested in Vajrayāna engage in Kriyā Tantra practices first. These are, for example, the practices of One-Thousand-Armed Avalokiteśvara, Tārā, Mañjuśrī, Vajrapāṇi, and Medicine Buddha. By familiarizing themselves with these practices, they will get a good idea of the meaning and purpose of Tantra. On that basis, they can smoothly progress over time and become a suitable vessel to receive empowerment into and practice Highest Yoga Tantra.

It is challenging enough to visualize Kriyā Tantra deities and do their practices, let alone those of Highest Yoga Tantra. Maintaining a clear visualization of the thousand arms of Avalokiteśvara single-pointedly is not easy! I think for many people it is more suitable to visualize a maṇḍala with Śākyamuni Buddha, a monk, in the center, and do the self-generation of Śākyamuni Buddha. The Buddha looks like a human being with just two hands, and he is a monk keeping excellent ethical conduct. Imagining ourselves in this form can be beneficial. It is easier, and yet we can still do the practice of the inseparability of method and wisdom. The yoga with signs and the yoga without signs are very profound. The practices contained in these—the fourfold repetition of self, other, letter, and sound; the concentrations on fire and on sound; and the concentration bestowing liberation at the end of sound—lead a practitioner to attain serenity, insight, and the union of serenity and insight (see chapter 5).

4 All-Encompassing Yoga

BEFORE WE LOOK more closely into Vajrayāna, let's generate an exceptionally virtuous motivation for doing so. My main practices are bodhicitta—the aspiration to attain awakening to benefit all sentient beings—and the wisdom of emptiness. My Dharma friends, to practice the Dharma properly, it is important for you too to practice bodhicitta and the view of emptiness. To show one way to do this, I will lead you in the practice of the all-encompassing yoga, which comes from tantric texts. It is usually done as part of an empowerment, but now we'll do it as a separate practice since it is extremely important to develop both conventional and ultimate bodhicitta.

Begin by contemplating conventional bodhicitta. In the *Supplement to the "Treatise on the Middle Way,"* Candrakīrti says in his verse of homage:

> Compassion alone is seen as the seed
> of a conqueror's rich harvest, as water that nourishes it,
> and as the ripened fruit that is the source of long enjoyment.
> Therefore, at the start I praise [great] compassion.

Candrakīrti doesn't pay homage to the buddhas and bodhisattvas as we might expect him to. Rather, he praises great compassion.[22] He does this because no matter how profound our wisdom may be, only when it is supported by great compassion can it become a cause for the omniscient state of buddhahood. Even if you have great meditative abilities and the superknowledges,[23] without compassion you cannot attain the resultant two bodies—the truth body and the form body—of a buddha. So first we must cultivate great compassion. All the magnificent buddhas have become awakened in dependence on developing great compassion. For that reason, Candrakīrti praises it at the beginning of his treatise.

In *Engaging in the Bodhisattvas' Deeds*, Śāntideva counsels us (BCA 8.129–31):

> Whatever joy there is in this world
> all comes from desiring others to be happy,
> and whatever suffering there is in this world
> all comes from desiring myself to be happy.
>
> What need is there to say much more?
> The childish work for their own benefit,
> the buddhas work for the benefit of others.
> Just look at the difference between them!
>
> If I do not actually exchange my happiness
> for the suffering of others,
> I shall not attain the state of buddhahood,
> and even in saṃsāra I shall have no joy.

All sentient beings—from the eight-billion-plus human beings on Earth down to the smallest insects and creatures in the ocean—want happiness and not suffering. But they don't know what the cause of suffering and the cause of happiness are. We human beings have an intelligent human brain, but our self-centered desires and greed often turn this intelligent brain into a tool of harm. We have the ability to think about the future and the effects of our actions. If we use our intelligence constructively, we can create a happy and peaceful life and a world in which people live in harmony, share resources, and cooperate with one another.

In general, scientists emphasize research on material phenomena, but now they are gradually turning to examine the mind and mental phenomena. One scientist commented to me that science usually investigates the causes of illness and harm to the body but neglects to examine happiness and its causes. But now scientists are coming to understand that happiness is based on having a peaceful mind free from afflictions such as disturbing emotions, harmful attitudes, and incorrect views. Buddhist psychology can contribute to scientific knowledge through sharing its methods to cultivate love, compassion, generosity, and cooperation. We must put effort in this direction.

Environmentalists warn that within the next few decades, climate change will become more serious and affect the lifespan of beings on this planet. To counteract this, we must stop harming and exploiting one another and cooperate for the common purpose of preserving life. It is our responsibility to increase our love for others and to share the methods to cultivate compassion. This must be the basis for educating future generations.

To do this, people need not be religious, because kindness is a universal value. We must put our energy in this direction, transforming our own minds and encouraging others to do the same. No one else can do this for us. Educating people in the methods found in the Buddha's teachings to generate affection, care, and concern for others can be done without linking it to religion.

In addition to generating compassion and bodhicitta, meditation on the ultimate nature of all phenomena is essential. Nāgārjuna's six texts on reasoning and Candrakīrti's *Supplement to (Nāgārjuna's) "Treatise on the Middle Way"* are excellent texts for you to study and base your meditation on emptiness on. In verses 6.35–37 of the *Supplement*, Candrakīrti emphasizes the logical inconsistencies of believing that all phenomena exist inherently. He stresses that although phenomena lack inherent existence, they appear and exist within being empty of inherent existence; they exist by being merely designated.[24]

The Method

To practice all-encompassing yoga, follow these steps. You may go through them quickly or slowly contemplate each one, depending on the time you have available.

1. Contemplate that all sentient beings want happiness and not suffering, as described above. Everyone is equal in this regard. Contemplate the benefits of cherishing others as described in *In Praise of Great Compassion*, and meditate on cherishing all sentient beings equally. Make a determination to help them as much as you can, and if you can't do that, resolve at least not to harm them.

2. Then contemplate the four immeasurables:

> May all sentient beings have happiness and its causes.
> May all sentient beings be free from duḥkha[25] and it causes.
> May all sentient beings never be separated from sorrowless bliss.
> May all sentient beings abide in equanimity, free of bias, attachment, and hatred.

3. Generate bodhicitta, the primary mind that is preceded by the aspiration wishing others to be free from all duḥkha and accompanied by the aspiration to attain full awakening for their benefit. Make the determination, "To be able to guide all sentient beings to be free of duḥkha and its causes, first I must become a buddha endowed with the three buddha bodies—truth body, enjoyment body, and emanation body—who has full wisdom, compassion, and skillful means to benefit others most effectively. I now aspire to attain the state of a buddha with these qualities." When you reflect on bodhicitta repeatedly, your confidence that it is possible to attain buddhahood will grow. Contemplate Atiśa's moving words in *Lamp for the Path to Enlightenment* (LP 29):

> I have no craving to attain awakening
> quickly for myself.
> I will live for infinite lives
> for the sake of a single sentient being.

4. If you have received the empowerment or permissory rite for Avalokiteśvara, for example, you may visualize yourself transforming into Avalokiteśvara, and with the determination to become a buddha for the benefit of all sentient beings, imagine your bodhicitta appearing in the center of your chest (your heart cakra) in the form of a radiant, horizontal, flat moon disc. If you have not received the Avalokiteśvara empowerment or permissory rite, do not visualize yourself as Avalokiteśvara, but imagine the moon at your heart cakra. The love and compassion it embodies fills your heart. Rest your mind on this for a few minutes.

5. To fulfill this aspiration to free sentient beings from duḥkha and its causes, we must know the causes of duḥkha, the chief of which is the igno-

rance that misapprehends how persons and phenomena exist. Only the correct understanding of reality—the wisdom knowing that all persons and phenomena are empty of inherent existence—can abolish this ignorance.

6. Now investigate the ultimate nature of reality. When you try to search for the true identity of persons and things, no independent essence can be found within that object or person. You cannot even find your self! Contemplate the unfindability of inherent essence.

But the lack of findability under ultimate analysis doesn't mean that things and persons don't exist. They exist; we know they affect us, bringing benefit or harm. When you emerge from meditation on emptiness, there is a sense of I. This I exists by being merely designated in dependence on the collection of mental and physical aggregates. Nāgārjuna says (MMK 22.1):[26]

> Neither [one with] the aggregates, nor different from the aggregates;
> the aggregates are not [based on] him, nor is he [based on] the aggregates.
> The Tathāgata does not possess the aggregates.
> What is the Tathāgata?

This verse speaks of searching for the Tathāgata, the Buddha, but I find it helpful to substitute "I" for "Tathāgata," and examine how *I* exists. Contemplate, "The five psychophysical aggregates are not me, but they are my aggregates. I do not exist separate from the five aggregates, but I am not identical to them either." This causes you to wonder, "Who am I?" Of course, the I that possesses the body and mind exists. But when you search for its identity within the five aggregates, nothing can be pointed out as being I. Nor can you identify anything apart from the aggregates that is you. You will come to a point when it seems that you do not exist. But that does not mean you do not exist at all. It indicates that the solid I that is the object of your grasping I does not exist. However, you, your aggregates, and all other phenomena exist through worldly conventions.

7. The mind that is absorbed in emptiness is the ultimate bodhicitta. I firmly believe that all phenomena are empty of inherent existence. Other than that, there is no other option regarding the ultimate nature of phenomena. Although you may not have realized emptiness yet, meditate with

strong conviction that you are completely absorbed in emptiness, and have conviction that you do not exist ultimately. Let your mind rest in the experience of the emptiness of inherent existence.

8. The mind of ultimate bodhicitta now transforms into a white five-spoked vajra, standing upright on the moon disc (the conventional bodhicitta) at your heart. Your mind is now in the form of a vajra standing on a moon, symbolizing the two bodhicittas. This is the mind of all-encompassing yoga.

9. When you arise from this contemplation, carry bodhicitta and the wisdom of emptiness with you all day.

When the mind of all-encompassing yoga is done during an empowerment, after the above visualization, imagine a replica of the radiant moon disc and vajra goes from the guru's heart and absorbs into the moon and vajra at your heart as the guru recites the mantra and you repeat after him: *om sarva yoga citta upataya mi*. When doing this practice by yourself, it is good to recite the mantra, but it is not necessary to do so.

I meditate daily on the all-encompassing yoga, which is conventional bodhicitta and ultimate bodhicitta conjoined. Meditating on bodhicitta and emptiness every day will bring great benefit. Over time, you will see change in yourself. All my spiritual mentors have practiced and realized these two in their own minds. All previous lineage masters have also practiced them, and through such practice they have become fully awakened. Thus, I request you to reflect on the two bodhicittas daily.

REFLECTION

1. Go back to the beginning of this chapter and meditate along with the instructions in it.
2. What was your experience? Try doing this practice daily and see how you change.

5 | The Path of Kriyā Tantra

A FOLLOWER OF KRIYĀ (Action) Tantra practices either the yoga with signs or the yoga without signs and emphasizes external activities over internal activities. Certain Kriyā Tantra sādhanas—for example, the text of the fasting retreat of Avalokiteśvara (T. *smyung gnas*)—emphasize external activities such as keeping cleanliness and performing ritual ablutions.

Four main tantras or texts are followed in Kriyā Tantra: the *Secret Tantra Concerning the General Rituals for All Maṇḍalas* (*Sarvamaṇḍalasāmānyavidhiguhya Tantra*), the *Complete Fulfillment of All Deeds* (*Susiddhikāra Tantra*), the *Tantra Requested by Subāhu* (*Subāhuparipṛcchā Tantra*), and *Analyzing the Stages of the Subsequent Concentration Tantra* (*Dhyānottarapaṭalakrama*). These four texts are also found in the Chinese canon.

The presentation of Kriyā Tantra based on these four main texts has four points:

1. How to become a suitable vessel for meditating on the paths of Kriyā Tantra
2. Having become a proper vessel, purely keeping the ethical restraints (*samaya*, T. *dam tshig*)
3. Abiding in the ethical restraints, how to do the close approximation—the practice
4. Having become a suitable vessel by means of this close approximation, how to achieve the actual attainments (*siddhi*)

Becoming a Suitable Vessel

As explained in the lamrim texts, first train your mindstream well in the common paths of the initial- and middle-level practitioners. Then properly devote yourself to a fully qualified Tantrayāna guru in the manner explained in tantric texts.

All Buddhist tantras stress the necessity of meditating on emptiness before doing the self-generation, whether or not the sādhana explicitly states this. Meditation on emptiness is essential as a precursor to imagining your wisdom realizing emptiness transforming into the appearance of the deity. Although appearing as the deity is initially done on the level of imagination, it serves as a rehearsal for generating the illusory body (*māyādeha*) on the completion stage and culminates in attaining the resultant body of a buddha. Those who lack an understanding of emptiness according to the Yogācāra or Madhyamaka view find tantra practice difficult because they miss this essential element.

Tantric meditation involves cultivating the profound and vast paths. The *profound path* is meditation on emptiness—not just the emptiness of any object but specifically the emptiness of the deity you have visualized. Meditation on the *vast path* has two aspects: developing a clear visualization of the deity and cultivating the divine identity of being the deity. The appearance of your wisdom realizing emptiness in the form of the deity is the practice of method or the vast aspect of the deity. The profound path or the practice of wisdom involves frequently reaffirming your mindfulness of the empty nature of the deity. Meditating on method and wisdom in this way is called the "great seal" (mahāmudrā) according to Action Tantra. It ripens the practitioner's faculties in order to actualize a buddha's form body.

It is helpful to have already attained serenity before engaging in tantric practice, but if not, it can be cultivated during the sūtra practice after generating yourself as the deity but before the mantra recitation. Here the form of your own deity body is the focal object of serenity meditation.

To be a suitable vessel to hear the teachings and engage in the practice of a tantric deity, it is necessary to receive the empowerment of that deity from a proper maṇḍala. A suitable maṇḍala may be a maṇḍala made with powdered sand, a maṇḍala drawn on cloth, or a maṇḍala of meditative concentration that some specially qualified persons can use to confer empowerment. Kriyā Tantra empowerments are not conferred from a body maṇḍala, a maṇḍala of relative bodhicitta, a maṇḍala of the womb, or a maṇḍala of ultimate bodhicitta, as these are found only in Highest Yoga Tantra.

In general, four types of empowerments—the vase, secret, wisdom, and word empowerments—are received from various maṇḍalas. The three lower classes of tantra have conferral of only the vase empowerment. The number of empowerments conferred in the vase empowerment differs in the four classes of tantra. In Kriyā Tantra, only the water empowerment and the crown empowerment together with the concluding ceremonies are conferred.

In addition to these, in Caryā Tantra, the vajra, bell, and name empowerments are given. In other words, Caryā Tantra contains the empowerments of the five buddha families together with the concluding ceremonies. However, the *Vajra Mālā Supreme Maṇḍala* text (*Vajrāvalī*) by Abhayākaragupta explains that the five empowerments of the five buddha families are given in both the Kriyā and Caryā Tantras. The stages of the path followed in these two tantras are very similar.

FIVE BUDDHA FAMILIES AND THEIR EMPOWERMENTS IN THE ACTION AND PERFORMANCE TANTRAS

	VAIROCANA	RATNASAMBHAVA	AMITĀBHA	AMOGASIDDHI	AKṢOBHYA
AGGREGATE	Form	Feeling	Discrimination	Miscellaneous factors	Consciousness
COLOR	White	Yellow	Red	Green	Blue
DIRECTION IN MAṆḌALA	Center	South	West	North	East
SYMBOL	Wheel	Jewel	Lotus	Double vajra	Vajra
EMPOWERMENT	Name	Crown	Vajra	Bell	Water
ELEMENT	Water	Earth	Fire	Wind	Space

Yoga Tantra adds to these the vajra guru (vajra ācārya) empowerment with the concluding ceremonies. In addition to all these previous empowerments, Highest Yoga Tantra adds the secret, wisdom, and word empowerments. A special Highest Yoga Tantra, the Kālacakra Tantra, contains several empowerments: the empowerments of entering like an infant, the four higher empowerments, and the four highest empowerments. The empowerment of entering like an infant includes the seven parts of the vase empowerment (the water, crown, and five Buddha family empowerments). Furthermore, Kālacakra contains the four higher, the four highest, and the great master vajra ācārya empowerment, totaling sixteen empowerments.

TANTRIC CLASSES AND THEIR EMPOWERMENTS

EMPOWERMENTS GIVEN	ACTION TANTRA	PERFORMANCE TANTRA	YOGA TANTRA	HIGHEST YOGA TANTRA	KĀLACAKRA TANTRA
Vase (water crown)	x	x	x	x	x
Vase (vajra, bell, name)		x	x	x	x
Vajra guru			x	x	x
Secret				x	x
Wisdom				x	x
Word				x	x
Entering like a child, 4 higher, 4 highest, great master vajra ācārya					x

Keeping the Ethical Restraints and Commitments Purely

The basis for receiving a Kriyā Tantra empowerment is having one of the seven classes of prātimokṣa ethical restraints (male and female practitioners with the five lay precepts, male and female novice monastics, training nuns, bhikṣus, and bhikṣuṇīs). Someone must at least have taken refuge and abide with the ethical basis of abandoning the ten nonvirtuous actions. The bodhisattva ethical restraints are also conferred during the empowerment. Conferral of the tantric ethical restraints are not included in Kriyā and Caryā Tantras empowerments. Having received the bodhisattva ethical restraints, practitioners must safeguard themselves from transgressions of the eighteen root and forty-six auxiliary precepts.

Practitioners of the Avalokiteśvara yoga method also adhere to four ascetic practices: not to respond to insult by insulting others in return, not to get angry with those who are angry with you, not to strike or beat someone who physically strikes or beats you, not to observe the faults of others who point out your faults. These practices may be difficult, but they are very virtuous and extremely valuable. Becoming a bodhisattva without them is almost impossible.

The bodhisattva ethical restraints can be learned from Mahāyāna scriptures.[27] In addition, many samayas unique to Kriyā and Caryā Tantras are to be kept. Some of these are to consecrate food before eating with *om ah hum* and to offer it to yourself as the deity; to keep your residence, body, and clothes very clean; to abstain from certain foods such as onions, garlic, and leeks that are said to increase the energy of desire;[28] to abandon sleeping on metal or grass; to abstain from sleeping on your back or stomach, but in the position the Buddha lay when he passed away; and to avoid stepping on things offered to the deity. You can learn them by studying the *Susiddhikāra Tantra*.

All downfalls and transgressions come from four doors: (1) ignorance of the ethical restraints, what to abandon and what to practice; (2) lack of respect for the ethical restraints, disregarding their importance; (3) carelessness, a lack of conscientiousness that values ethical conduct; and (4) having strong afflictions that overpower the mind even when we know they are to be abandoned.

Likewise we should apply four methods to prevent committing transgressions: (1) acquire knowledge, wisdom, and understanding regarding the ethical restraints; (2) develop greater faith in and respect for these ethical restraints so that we see their value and importance for our Dharma practice; (3) care and conscientiousness in our actions to avoid transgressing any of the ethical restraints; and (4) application of the antidotes to afflictions that subdue them.[29]

If we transgress any of the ethical restraints and/or commitments, we should purify them immediately. Those committed in the day must be purified by the evening, and those committed at night must be purified by the morning. Try to avoid abiding with transgressions.

Practicing the Close Approximation

The outline below describes the practice of the deity whose empowerment you have received. This has two points: meditative concentration with recitation and meditative concentration without recitation.

1. Meditative concentration with recitation of mantra. This has three points:

(1) Generating yourself as the deity by the sixfold self-generation (the deity as emptiness, the deity as sound, the deity as letters, the deity as form, the deity as mudrā, and the deity as sign)
(2) Invoking the wisdom beings, making offerings, and so forth
(3) Fourfold recitation, conjoined with *prāṇāyāma* (binding the wind—that is, holding the breath)

(1) Generating yourself as the deity by the sixfold self-generation

In general, the generation of yourself as the deity involves a deity from one of the three buddha families or lineages of Kriyā Tantra: the tathāgata family, lotus family, or vajra family. The "lord of the family"—that is, the prominent deity—of the tathāgata family is Mañjuśrī. In the lotus family, it is Avalokiteśvara (Chenresig, Kuan Yin), and in the vajra family, Vajrapāṇi. Texts such as *Clarifying the Meanings of Kriyā Tantra* (*bya rgyud dongsal*), a Kriyā Tantra sādhana of the Great Compassionate One (Avalokiteśvara), explains the members of the three Kriyā Tantra families. I encourage you to study these great texts to learn the details of Kriyā Tantra.

THE THREE BUDDHA FAMILIES OF KRIYĀ TANTRA (DY 237)

	TATHĀGATA	LOTUS	VAJRA
PRINCIPAL OF THE FAMILY	Teacher Śākyamuni Buddha	Amitāyus	Akṣobhya
LORD OF THE FAMILY	Mañjuśrī	Avalokiteśvara	Vajrapāṇi
FEMALE DEITY OF THE FAMILY	Marīci	Ārya Tārā	Analapramohani
OTHER DEITIES OF THE FAMILY	Uṣṇīṣavijayā, Sitātapatrā, Chundi	Hayagrīva, Sitatārā (White Tārā),	Amritakundali, Vajra Garuda

The fourfold recitation consists of being absorbed on yourself as the basis, being absorbed on the other as the basis, being absorbed at the heart, and being absorbed in sound.

Regarding the first, being absorbed on yourself as the basis, first generate yourself as the deity. Here the meditation on Avalokiteśvara is an example, but this method can be applied to meditation on the other Kriyā Tantra deities too.[30]

1. The *ultimate nature of the deity* entails meditating on the emptiness of inherent existence of both yourself and the deity. There is no difference in the meditation on emptiness as described in the Pāramitāyāna and in the Tantrayāna. Analyze the ultimate nature of yourself and the deity and absorb your mind in the emptiness of inherent existence.
2. To meditate on the *deity as sound*, think that the wisdom realizing the nondual emptiness of yourself and the deity appears as the sound of the mantra. Imagine that the entirety of space is filled with the reverberation of the mantra, *om mani padme hum*. Focus on the sound of the mantra filling all of space.
3. In the meditation on the *deity as syllables*, imagine your mind as a flat white moon disc. On it the sound of the mantra crystallizes into the form of the written syllables of the mantra that stand clockwise on the moon. Feel the energy of the mantra as it consolidates and appears as syllables on the moon disc.
4. To meditate on the *deity as form,* imagine your mind as the moon disc with the syllables *om mani padme hum* standing around its edge. From the mantra syllables, light rays shine forth. Touching all sentient beings in the three realms, the light eliminates their duḥkha, teaches them the Dharma, and leads them to the awakened state of buddhahood. They transform into Avalokiteśvara. Again, light radiates from the moon disc and the mantra syllables; it carries elegant offerings to all the buddhas and bodhisattvas in the ten directions, who receive them and experience bliss. The buddhas and bodhisattvas of the ten directions, together with all the sentient beings who have been transformed into Avalokiteśvara, recollect and absorb back into yourself as the moon disc and the syllables.

   This transforms into the form of Avalokiteśvara. This could

be any of the forms of Avalokiteśvara, but here we will focus on Thousand-Armed Avalokiteśvara specifically. This Avalokiteśvara has eleven heads. Of the faces on the first level of three heads, the center face is white, the right face is green, and the left face is red. On the second level, the center face is green, the right is red, and the left white. On the third level, the center face is red, the right white, and the left green. Above that is the blue wrathful head of Vajrapāṇi, and on top of that is the red head of Amitābha Buddha.

His two central hands hold a jewel. On the right, the top hand holds a mālā, the next hand is in the mudrā of protection, and the last hand holds a Dharma Wheel. On his left side, the top hand holds a lotus, the next hand[31] a vase, and the third hand a bow and arrow. The thousand arms are arranged in five circular rows, and each hand has an eye in its palm. The first row has twelve arms. Like spokes coming from the center of a wheel, the next row of arms has fourteen arms stemming from each of the twelve arms in the first row. The third row of arms consists of sixteen arms coming from each of the fourteen arms in the second row. Then eighteen arms come from each of the sixteen arms to make the fourth row, and twenty arms come from each of the eighteen arms to form the fifth row. Altogether, this makes one thousand arms. Avalokiteśvara wears beautiful silk garments. In this way, generate yourself in the form of Thousand-Armed Avalokiteśvara.

You could also arise as one of the other forms of Avalokiteśvara, such as Four-Armed Avalokiteśvara holding a jewel in the central two hands, a lotus in upper left hand and a rosary in his upper right hand. You could also visualize the Khasarpaṇi form of Avalokiteśvara, who is standing. He has one head and two arms, with the right hand in the giving mudrā and the left at his heart holding the stem of a lotus that blooms by his ear. You could visualize the form of Avalokiteśvara called the Protector Who Brings Liberation to Those in the Lower Realms. He is seated and is white in color, with one head and two arms. His right hand is on his knee in the giving mudrā, and his left hand is in back. He is leaning back, his right leg extending down like Tārā's leg. On his right is green Tārā and on his left is blue Ekajaṭī holding a skullcup and cleaver.

5. For the meditation on the *deity as mudrā*, put your hands in the mudrā

of the lotus family—palms open and the hands placed with your little fingers side by side. Touch this to your heart, forehead, throat, right and left shoulders while saying the mantra of the lotus family, *om padma udbhavaye svaha*.

6. For the *deity as sign*, visualize a white *om*, red *ah*, and blue *hum*—symbolizing the deity's body, speech, and mind—at your crown, throat, and heart, respectively, and visualize the mantra on a moon disc at your heart.

The way that a deity is generated out of emptiness differs in various sādhanas. Refer to the sādhana of each deity you practice and make an effort to receive teachings on the practice of each deity.

(2) Invoking the wisdom beings, making offerings, and so forth

After generating yourself as Thousand-Armed Avalokiteśvara, to increase the feeling of being the deity of compassion, invoke the wisdom beings, make offerings to them, and dissolve them into yourself as the deity. Then invoke the initiating deities and make offerings to them. They initiate you with the water of the vase and then absorb into you.

(3) Fourfold recitation, conjoined with prāṇāyāma (restraining vitality-exertion, binding the wind)

The meditative concentration with recitation of mantra also consists of the fourfold recitation together with binding the wind. Binding the wind is practiced during the fourfold mantra recitation to prevent mental wandering. Since the mind and the winds are inseparable, when the winds or breath are agitated and move a lot, you experience a lot of mental wandering and many extraneous thoughts. To prevent mental wandering and restless thought, three practices are recommended to draw the breath in—that is, to prevent the breath and wisdom from leaving. This practice is known as *prāṇāyāma*, or holding the breath.

The fourfold recitation of mantra consists of the following:

1. The mind *absorbed on yourself* as the basis is the sixfold self-generation as Avalokiteśvara described above.
2. The mind *absorbed on the other* as the basis is to generate the supporting

and supported maṇḍala of Avalokiteśvara in front of you, making offerings, contemplating the seven-limb prayer, and so forth.

3. The mind *absorbed at the heart.* Visualize your mind in the form of a moon disc at your heart and concentrate on it.
4. The mind *absorbed in sound* is the mind's attention absorbed in the sound of the mantra *om mani padme hum* emanating from the moon disc and mantra syllables at your heart. The mind absorbed at the heart and the mind absorbed in sound refer to a moon disc in your Avalokiteśvara body and in the Avalokiteśvara visualized in front of you as well.

Whispered and mental recitations

The meditative concentration with recitation may be done with whispered recitation or mental recitation of the mantra. *Whispered recitation* is verbally reciting the mantra quietly so that only you can hear it. *Mental recitation* involves visualizing the mantra syllables at your heart. Recite the mantra mentally in your mind, imagining the sound without saying it out loud. Holding the breath—also known as restraining vitality and exertion—is done only with mental recitation.

Meditative stability and concentration

The meditations of the fourfold mantra recitation involve two types of meditation: meditation with meditative stability (*dhyāna*) and meditation with meditative concentration (*samādhi*). The dhyāna meditation is done to gain clarity on your visualized deity-body. To do this, focus on your body as the deity's body, locating and identifying each part—the deity's head, eyes, torso, arms, and so forth. This is a form of analytical meditation in which your focus moves from one part of the body to another to become familiar with the deity's body. After reviewing each part of your deity-body, focus on the entire body.

In the *meditation with concentration*, choose one particular aspect of your deity-body and focus single-pointedly on that without analyzing and going back over all the various parts. In short, the meditative concentration with recitation of mantra involves dhyāna meditation and samādhi meditation. It is only when you become tired of doing these two practices that you refresh your mind by doing the actual recitation of the mantra.

Binding the wind

When appropriate, the practice of binding the wind is done while engaged in the meditation with meditative stability or the meditation with concentration. Here, wind refers to the wind that goes through the doors of the senses and pores of the skin. The wind is also the medium that conveys consciousness. Binding it means not to let it go out through the pores, the sense organs, and other openings in the body. Kriyā Tantra doesn't speak of the three channels, drops, and so forth found in Highest Yoga Tantra. So here, when you bind the wind by holding the breath, it's held in the body in general, not at a specific place, although some people like to focus more at the navel when doing this.

When you remember an object of attachment during meditation, your concentration on the deity decreases. To stop distraction away from the main meditation object, the deity, we need to "bind" the wind that is the conveyance of the mind so that it doesn't stray to other objects. By binding the wind or life, our memory (mindfulness) is also bound to the object of concentration, thus enhancing concentration.

Binding the wind is done like a tortoise contracting limbs. Close orifices of the body as you draw the wind inside. Inhale gently from the nose and hold the breath. Focus on yourself as the deity and cultivate the clear appearance of yourself as the deity. Also cultivate the divine identity of being the deity. When holding the breath becomes uncomfortable, exhale. After a pause, repeat this. Drawing the wind in from the orifices first is easier, then do it from the sense organs. The purpose of this meditation is to eliminate distraction and increase concentration. This practice is done only during mental recitation, because during the whispered meditation the breath is used to recite the mantra out loud.

Clear appearance and divine identity

Two important abilities to cultivate in Kriyā Tantra are clear appearance and divine identity. Clear appearance is to clearly visualize yourself as having the body of the deity, and divine identity is holding the identity of being the deity. In the lower tantras, the meaning of isolated body, speech, and mind is to separate yourself from ordinary appearance and ordinary grasping. Ordinary appearance is the appearance of ourselves as an ordinary, limited sentient being with afflictions and faults. Ordinary grasping is to grasp ourselves as being such a person. Clear appearance is the antidote to ordinary appearance; it involves concentrating on your body being the deity's pure body made of light, and cultivating serenity on that object. Divine identity overcomes ordinary grasping that thinks of yourself as a truly existent sentient being who can never improve. Divine identity is cultivated by thinking, "I am the deity. I have the deity qualities such as great compassion, bodhicitta, and the wisdom realizing emptiness." Hold the identity of being the deity—imagine having impartial compassion for every sentient being and the wisdom that accurately knows both conventional and ultimate truths.

To cultivate clear appearance and divine identity, it is imperative to first meditate on emptiness. Your ordinary body and self that you grasp as inherently existent I and mine don't become the deity. When seen as empty, the inherently existent body disappears, and your conventional I manifests as the deity. Specifically, your wisdom realizing emptiness manifests as the deity and you identify "This is me." Since it's simply a matter of time until you become a buddha, designating I on the basis of the deity's aggregates is suitable, whereas designating I on an apple is not.

The idea behind clear appearance and divine identity is that to become something, you have to be able first to imagine being like that. This is similar to a child putting on the uniform of a fireman, a nurse, or a teacher and pretending to be such a person. Using your imagination in this way gives you the confidence to cultivate the causes for buddhahood.

Profundity and clarity

In the practice of deity yoga—uniting your body, speech, and mind with those of the deity—we cultivate profundity and clarity. Profundity is the understanding of emptiness; this understanding of emptiness itself becomes the clarity of the appearance of the deity. Clarity of your appearance as the deity entails the analytic and stabilizing meditations done after meditating on the self-generation as the deity. Profundity is cultivated by meditating on the emptiness of the deity that you are. That is, the deity appears but it is empty of inherent existence. It is empty but it still appears. You go back and forth between the deity-body's appearance and its emptiness. While on the path, the conventional appearance of the deity and its emptiness cannot be perceived by the same consciousness, whereas at buddhahood, one consciousness can simultaneously cognize both the appearances of conventionalities and their emptiness. This meditation on profundity and clarity brings about that ability unique to a buddha.

The main practice

We usually think that the main practice of a meditation session on a deity is the mantra recitation, whereas in fact it is the meditative concentrations of dhyāna and concentration. The object of meditation in both of these is your deity-body, and the purpose is to develop the mind's clarity of that object. These practices aid in cultivating serenity.

Mantra recitation is done when you are tired after meditating on clear appearance and divine identity. In other words, the meditations above are the most important part of the practice, and mantra recitation is secondary. Unfortunately, nowadays many people rush through the meditations—barely stopping to meditate on emptiness or to cultivate serenity—and then focus on reciting many mantras.

2. Meditative concentrations that do not depend on recitation

After meditating on the fourfold recitation conjoined with binding the wind, progress to the three meditative concentrations that do not depend on recitation. These are done in order, beginning with the first one, to develop serenity and insight.

1. To do the *meditative concentration abiding in fire*, visualize a flat horizontal moon disc in your heart cakra, inside your body in the center of your chest. On top of the moon is a flame. Your own wisdom dwells within the flame and appears as the sound of the mantra *om mani padme hum*. The sound of the mantra is emitted from the flame and you listen to it.
2. The *meditative concentration abiding in sound* entails visualizing a small Avalokiteśvara called a wisdom being at your heart. At the heart of this tiny Avalokiteśvara is a moon disc upon which is a flame. Inside the flame are the seed-syllable *hrih* and the mantra syllables. They resonate with the sound of the mantra. Do not recite the mantra, but listen to its sound in the flame as if it were being recited

by someone else. This and the above meditation are done to attain serenity.

3. The *meditative concentration of the ultimate sound that confers liberation* is meditating on the ultimate nature with the mind of deity yoga that itself realizes emptiness. Although emptiness is the main object, your deity-body and the sound of the mantra haven't disappeared. The deity's body and the mantra appear to the appearance factor of that mind, but only emptiness is ascertained by the ascertainment factor of that mind. That is, while Avalokiteśvara and the sound of the mantra appear to the mind, that mind ascertains only emptiness. This is the union of the two truths in Tantra—the consciousness that realizes emptiness appears in the form of the deity and the mantra (conventional truths) and simultaneously realizes emptiness (ultimate truth). This leads to the union of serenity and insight on the emptiness of inherent existence, which actually brings liberation. It acts primarily as a cause for attaining a buddha's truth body (dharmakāya).

To realize emptiness, it is extremely important to know and practice the teachings explaining this profound topic. These are detailed in *Searching for the Self* and *Realizing the Profound View*, volumes 7 and 8 of *The Library of Wisdom and Compassion*. Do not neglect the teachings on emptiness; doing so risks wasting time meditating on an incorrect view that will only impede the growth of wisdom. However, if you have a good foundation in the stages of the path, your tantric meditation will bear fruit.

First gain a conceptual understanding of emptiness. Then, through repeated meditation on emptiness, the conceptual appearance of emptiness is worn away and the nonconceptual direct realization of emptiness dawns. As the result of continued practice and meditation, you will eventually attain the dharmakāya.

If your meditation has too much analysis, discriminating awareness causes the loss of meditative stability. If your meditation focuses too much on stability, the understanding of emptiness could decline. The union of serenity and insight is gained by alternating stabilizing meditation and analytical meditation on emptiness. Rely on the practices of the Pāramitāyāna as explained in texts such as Maitreya's *Discrimination of the Middle and Extremes* (*Madhyānta-vibhāga-kārikā*) and *Ornament of Mahāyāna Sūtras*

(*Mahāyānasūtrālaṃkāra*), as well as Asaṅga's *Śrāvaka Grounds* (*Śrāvakabhūmi*). From these, you will learn the method to attain perfect serenity by progressing through the nine stages of sustained attention (placing the mind, continual placement, repeated placement, close placement, taming, pacifying, thoroughly pacifying, making single-pointed, and placement in equipoise). This is done by overcoming five faults (laziness, forgetting the instruction, restlessness and laxity, nonapplication of the antidote, and overapplication of the antidote) and cultivating the eight antidotes to them (confidence, aspiration, effort, pliancy, mindfulness, introspective awareness, application of antidotes, and equanimity). Progress through the nine stages occurs by means of applying the six powers (hearing, reflection, mindfulness, introspective awareness, effort, and complete familiarity) and the four attentions (painstaking attention, interrupted, uninterrupted, and effortless attention).

This is followed by cultivating mental and physical pliancy and the bliss of physical and mental pliancy, which culminate in serenity. All of these are described in detail in *Following in the Buddha's Footsteps*. In general, the lower tantras' method for generating serenity is consistent with the explanation in the classical texts of Maitreya, Asaṅga, and other sages. However, they differ in their meditation objects; in Tantra they are the deity's body, drops, syllables, and so forth.

As set out in Kriyā Tantra, the five paths leading to buddhahood are similar to those of the Pāramitāyāna. The path of accumulation begins with the generation of uncontrived bodhicitta. Practitioners proceed to the path of preparation when they attain insight—which is actually the union of serenity and insight—on emptiness. They attain the path of seeing when they have the direct, nonconceptual realization of emptiness. This is followed by the path of meditation, where the innate afflictions are removed, and the path of no-more-learning, which marks the first moment of buddhahood.

REFLECTION

1. What are clear appearance and divine identity? How do you cultivate them and why are they important?

2. What are the six steps to generate yourself as the deity? Why is the first step the most important?

3. Why is imagining yourself as the deity and holding the identity as the deity not a wrong consciousness?

---

*Achieving the Actual Attainments (*Siddhi*)*

To attain the special actual attainments (*siddhis*) as described in Kriyā and Caryā Tantra, it is necessary to be experienced in the fourfold mantra recitation as well as the three meditative concentrations without recitation (abiding in fire, abiding in sound, and the ultimate sound that confers liberation). The siddhis cannot be attained without having done the approximation retreat with four daily sessions. However, to attain only trivial attainment, these practices aren't necessary.

The special actual attainments are of three types. If categorized from the viewpoint of their nature, they are the best, the intermediate, and the least. The best actual attainment is that of the knowledge-holder, the intermediate is that of extrasensory perception, and the least is complete knowledge of all the scriptural texts, sūtras, commentaries, and treatises.

- The *attainment of the knowledge-holder* is the awakened state of an omniscient buddha, which is accomplished in Kriyā and Cārya Tantra by extending one's lifetime through special practices. The attainment of a knowledge-holder includes having extrasensory powers such as seeing other worlds and the sentient beings in them, understanding and speaking many languages, knowing the past and future, being able to manifest many bodies, reading others' minds, knowing their level of realizations, and so forth. It also includes having complete knowledge of all the scriptural texts and the various types of wisdom, such as clear wisdom that understands the subtle and difficult points of the Dharma without confusion; quick wisdom that cuts off all ignorance, wrong conceptions, and doubt; great wisdom that has no resistance to understanding the meaning of the Buddha's extensive scriptures; and profound wisdom that understands the meaning of the scriptures in a profound, limitless way. In addition, a knowledge-holder has the wisdom to teach the Dharma, elucidating the definite, correct understanding of all the words and meanings of the scripture; the wisdom of debate, which confidently refutes the pernicious words expressing wrong views; and the wisdom of composition, which uses perfect words and grammar to express the meaning of clear wisdom that gives joy. All these wisdoms can be attained through the practices of Mañjuśrī. For this reason, upon awakening in the morning, monastics recite Mañjuśrī's mantra.

- The *intermediate type of actual attainment* is the extrasensory perception of invisibility; taking the essence (T. *bcud len*), which enables meditators to subsist solely on the essence of flowers without eating food; and quick legs that enable them to go somewhere quickly by rubbing certain substances on the legs.
- The *least actual attainment* includes the complete knowledge of all the scriptural texts, as well as the ability to dispel interference by putting others under one's power, or in extreme circumstances killing those who cause great harm to sentient beings or the Buddhadharma. It's important to understand the context of this attainment. These abilities don't mean you can kill or chase away people that you do not like. A practitioner must have the full development of bodhicitta and perform these actions with compassion in order to protect sentient beings from creating heavy destructive karma.

If the actual attainments are categorized according to signs of their attainment, those who have the power of long life can make longevity pills. Other signs of actual attainments are being able to fly, nectar overflowing (amrita, S. *amṛta*), smoke emitted from various substances, and flowers coming out of tormas.

When you do the close-approximation retreat, if your mind is riddled with doubts—Can I actually generate myself as a deity? Is this practice like imagining a fairy tale? When will I attain quick legs? Will I be famous when I have extrasensory perception?—your practice won't go very well. Rather, focus on cultivating a firm basis of the determination to be free from saṃsāra, great compassion and bodhicitta, and the correct view of emptiness. Don't concern yourself with attaining fantastic, strange signs of different attainments. If this is your aim, it's a very small one.

Great Kriyā Tantra masters, such as Buddhaguhya and Vajrabodhi, have slightly different explanations of how the actual attainment of a knowledge-holder—buddhahood—is achieved through this practice. You can learn more about these topics by studying Tsongkhapa's *Great Exposition of Secret Mantra*; and Khedrup Gelek Palzang's *General Exposition of Tantras*, where he says that there's no difference in the manner of attaining the buddhahood in Kriyā and Caryā Tantra and in the Pāramitāyāna.

Training in the Body, Speech, and Mind of a Buddha

Kriyā Tantra presents the path in terms of how to actualize the body, speech, and mind of a buddha. The method to actualize a buddha's body is to visualize yourself as the deity, the method to actualize a buddha's speech is mantra recitation, and the method to actualize a buddha's mind is the concentration of the ultimate sound that confers liberation, preceded by the concentration abiding in fire and the concentration abiding in sound.

The body of the deity. Ordinary practitioners of Kriyā Tantra do not generate themselves as the deity. They visualize the deity in front of them, whereas the principal practitioners of Kriyā Tantra visualize themselves as the deity by meditating on the sixfold self-generation practice of deity yoga. Self-generation as the deity (T. *bdag bskyed*) is not a generation by the mouth (*kha bskyed*) where you just recite the words of the sādhana; it is generating yourself as the deity.[32]

There are two ways of meditating on the six deities. The first is the meditation with meditative stability: meditate on the six deities in sequence and gradually generate yourself as the deity. Then remember and individually review the details of the deity's body, the color of each face, the position of each hand, and the implement it holds and cultivate concentration on that. The second way is with concentration, where you focus on a single object—the deity's body or the deity's main face—and remain single-pointedly on that.

The question arises: Is imagining that you have the deity's body—in this case, Avalokiteśvara's form—a mistaken consciousness since you are not a deity at present? The consciousness's mode of ascertainment understands emptiness—even though it doesn't directly perceive it, because the deity's body is appearing—so the consciousness is not mistaken with respect to its mode of ascertainment, because emptiness exists.

The purpose of the sixfold self-generation is to cultivate clear appearance of yourself as the deity and divine identity as the deity to counter ordinary appearance and ordinary grasping, which are impediments on the tantric path. Training in divine identity as a deity is on the level of mental consciousness, not your sense consciousnesses, so you won't see your body as Avalokiteśvara's body with your eyes. Although tantric practitioners cultivate the conviction that their wisdom manifests in the form of the deity in their meditation sessions, when their sessions conclude they don't expect to open their eyes and discover that they have eleven heads and a thousand arms!

The speech of the deity. The speech of the deity is actualized through the whispered and mental recitations of mantra as described above. The fourfold mantra recitations are done when your concentration is firm. These four are yourself as the deity, the front deity, mind, and sound.

The mind of the deity. From here, progress to the three meditative concentrations without recitation—the concentrations abiding in fire, abiding in sound, and conferring liberation at the end of sound. The deity's mind is actualized by these three concentrations without repetition, as explained above.

The meditative concentrations of abiding in fire and in sound are ways to cultivate serenity. Through the meditative concentration abiding in fire, practitioners gain physical and mental pliancy; and through the meditative concentration abiding in sound, they gain actual serenity. In the yoga without signs, after attaining serenity on the deity's body, meditate on emptiness in association with deity yoga. By alternating analytic and stabilizing meditation, attain the union of serenity and insight. In *Stages of Meditation*, Kamalaśīla spells out how to unify serenity and insight (DY 169):

> When, due to having cultivated insight, wisdom becomes too dominant, serenity is lessened. Thereby, like a butter lamp set in a breeze, the mind wavers, due to which suchness is not seen very clearly. Therefore, at that time you should cultivate serenity. Also, when serenity is predominant, you will, like a person asleep,

> not see suchness very clearly. Therefore, at that time, you should cultivate wisdom. When, like two oxen yoked as a pair, both are engaged equally, you should abide without application [of the antidotes] as long as body and mind do not become adversely affected.

Yoga with Signs and Yoga without Signs

The fourfold mantra repetition and the meditative concentrations abiding in fire and abiding in sound are called the *yoga with signs* because they still have the signs of inherent existence that accompany conventional appearances. The meditative concentration conferring liberation at the end of sound is the *yoga without signs* because it eradicates grasping inherent existence as well as the appearance of inherent existence. Here, practitioners meditate so that the deity's body and the mantra appear to the appearance factor of the mind and their emptiness appears to the ascertainment factor of that mind. This is meditation on the union of the two truths in Kriyā Tantra.

6 | The Paths of Caryā Tantra and Yoga Tantra

Caryā (Performance) Tantra

When we think of Tantra in terms of two types of yogas—external and internal—Caryā Tantra has equal emphasis on the two. Caryā Tantra practitioners undertake the external activities and rituals found in Kriyā Tantra involving cleanliness, and in addition, practice the inner yogas. The explanation of Caryā Tantra contains the same four outlines as Kriyā Tantra: how to become a proper vessel, the ethical restraints (samaya) and commitments to keep purely, how the close approximation or retreat is done, and how to achieve the actual attainments.

The principal tantras in Caryā Tantra are the *Vairocanābhisaṃbodhi Tantra* (*Mahāvairocana Tantra*, J. *Dainichikyō*) of the tathāgata lineage or family. Two others are the *Vajrapāṇi Empowerment Tantra* of the vajra lineage, and the *Extensive Tantra of Hayagrīva* of the lotus lineage. The *Ārya Mañjuśrī Root Tantra* is also a Caryā Tantra text.

Becoming a Suitable Vessel

Prior to receiving the empowerment, study and practice Sūtrayāna so that you have a firm foundation in the common preliminaries of the path—the determination to be free from saṃsāra, bodhicitta, and the correct view of emptiness. Then receive from a fully qualified tantric master a proper empowerment into a maṇḍala of a Caryā Tantra deity such as Vairocana Abhisaṃbodhi. Whereas Kriyā Tantra has only two empowerments—the water empowerment and the crown empowerment—Caryā Tantra has all five empowerments of the five buddha families. Aside from that, the remaining procedures and meditative techniques are similar to those in Kriyā Tantra.

Keeping the Ethical Restraints and Commitments Purely

Having received empowerment, keep the samaya and ethical restraints purely. The principal ethical restraints to keep are the bodhisattva precepts, so safeguard yourself from committing any of the eighteen major downfalls or forty-six minor transgressions. The practice of Vairocana Abhisaṃbodhi instructs us not to abandon the pure Dharma or bodhicitta even at the cost of our lives. Great emphasis is placed on this. Likewise, it says to abandon acting with miserliness, holding a malicious intention, or harming any sentient being. It is important to anchor yourself in the foundation of the practice: abandoning the ten nonvirtuous actions. The ethical restraints held in Kriyā Tantra are also held in Caryā Tantra.

Practicing the Close Approximation

The close approximation is divided into two: the yoga with signs and the yoga without signs. The division into these two yogas is found in the three lower classes of Tantra—Kriyā, Caryā, and Yoga, whereas the generation and completion stages are found exclusively in Highest Yoga Tantra. The yoga with signs includes the outer fourfold mantra recitation and the inner fourfold mantra recitation. For each of these, there are four undegenerating branches of whispered recitation and mental recitation. When doing the mental recitation, do the wind yoga (*prāṇāyāma*) of binding the breath as explained in Kriyā Tantra. As in Kriyā Tantra, the yoga with signs includes the concentrations abiding in fire and abiding in sound, whereas the yoga without signs is the ultimate sound conferring liberation.

As in Kriyā Tantra, before generating yourself as a deity, meditate on emptiness. Your body, mind, and self lack any inherent essence. Likewise, the four great elements composing your body are empty of inherent existence. Your aggregates and self are empty and the same is true of a buddha's aggregates and self. Meditate until you have conviction that neither you nor a buddha exists inherently, and likewise that the aggregates lack an inherent nature. The I that appears as the deity and the deity's body appear falsely.

Like a reflection in a mirror, they don't exist in the way they appear. On the ultimate level they are empty like space, yet conventionally they appear falsely, like a hologram or the people on a TV screen.

Then contemplate the inseparability of these two truths: because persons and phenomena depend on many other factors—ordinary beings arise due to the twelve links of dependent origination and various other causes and circumstances—they lack true existence. Because they are empty of true existence, they arise dependently.[33] Meditating in this way, you will understand that generating the deity within emptiness is suitable.

On this basis, think that the wisdom mind that realizes emptiness arises in the form of the deity and holds the divine identity of being the deity. Without understanding emptiness, reciting the mantra *oṃ svabhāva-śuddhāḥ sarva-dharmāḥ svabhāva-śuddho 'ham* and saying "everything becomes empty" won't mean anything to you. Don't think that emptiness is just a matter of all appearances disappearing and there is nothing. Rather, understand emptiness properly—that emptiness and dependent arising are complementary; the two both exist on one object.

The meditation on emptiness is done employing the various lines of reasoning found in the Pāramitāyāna: Nāgārjuna's four- and five-point refutations; Candrakīrti's seven-point refutation; the analysis of one and many; the refutation of the four extremes of existence, nonexistence, both, or neither; diamond slivers refuting inherently existent arising; the four essential points; and dependent arising. Here we again see the importance of having a firm background in the practice of the Pāramitāyāna to meditate on Tantra.

The yoga with signs is defined as the meditative technique of deity yoga that is *separate* from meditation on emptiness. The yoga without signs is defined as the meditative techniques of deity yoga that are together with meditation on emptiness.

Some scholars assert that deity yoga with signs is not held by a mind understanding emptiness, while deity yoga without signs is held by a mind understanding emptiness. However, according to our tradition, this is not correct because there is yoga with signs that is held by a mind that understands emptiness. For example, the self-generation of the deity and the self-generation of the outer and inner fourfold recitation are done within a state of emptiness. When a practitioner has strong meditation on emptiness through any of the lines of reasoning mentioned above and does these practices, the generation of the deity is held by a mind that understands emptiness. Thus, being held or not held by a mind that understands emptiness cannot be the way to differentiate the yogas with and without signs. Here "held" means associated with or informed by a particular mental state.

According to Sūtrayāna, when there is the appearance of conventional objects, the mind cannot simultaneously realize emptiness nonconceptually, and when meditators are in nonconceptual meditative equipoise on emptiness, conventional objects do not appear to their minds; only emptiness appears.

However, in Tantrayāna the inseparability of method and wisdom isn't the same as in Sūtrayāna. Rather, one mind can have both the conventional appearance of the deity and the mind realizing the emptiness of the deity. How are method and wisdom united? Prior to generating the deity, meditators have a strong understanding of emptiness. Within that understanding (or out of this understanding) of emptiness, the wisdom mind then manifests as the appearance of the deity. The mind that understands emptiness itself appears in the form of a deity, so method and wisdom are inseparably together. The mind that has the appearance of the deity and the mind understanding the deity's emptiness are one nature but different isolates. While on the path, meditators cannot have both minds in one cognition—they only imagine that they do—but this ability is attained at buddhahood.

In Tantra, the causes for the appearance of the deity and the realization of the deity's emptiness are created together so that at buddhahood both method and wisdom are simultaneously together in one cognition. The *Great Exposition of Secret Mantra* explains that at the time of the result, the basis—a buddha's body adorned with the signs and marks—and the mind, which resides in that body and does not grasp true existence, coexist at the same time, inseparably and of one nature.

Similarly, at the time of the path, it is necessary to practice a skillful method in which method and wisdom are practiced inseparably in order to collect merit and wisdom simultaneously. In other words, to attain simultaneous method and wisdom in one cognition, yogis practice method—their body appearing in the form of the body of a buddha—and at the same time, their mind does not grasp the true existence of any phenomena. The discriminating awareness that understands the non-true existence of the appearance of the deity and the mind of deity yoga itself are one nature, even though they are different. They have different isolates, so although they are one nature, they are not completely the same. They are different aspects of the same thing. The pristine wisdom that realizes emptiness appears in the aspect of the deity. In this way, the appearance of the deity, which is a conventional truth and the method side of the path, and the pristine wisdom that apprehends the emptiness of all phenomena—including the emptiness of the appearance of the deity—are together in one mind. The pristine wisdom is the wisdom aspect of the path, and the emptiness of all phenomena that it perceives is the ultimate truth.

In the resultant stage, the wisdom and method are inseparable in one cognition. On the path these two are not simultaneous in the same cognition, but you imagine they are. This is the method followed on the Tantra path that leads to inseparable wisdom and method on the resultant stage.

Although the yoga without signs is a yoga of nondual profundity and clarity, it is not merely a deity yoga in which the appearance of the deity is held by a mind that understands emptiness, because that was present previously in the yoga with signs. That is, by meditating on emptiness, a meditator has a strong understanding of emptiness, so that when he comes out of that meditation and then does the self-generation as the deity—which is the yoga with signs—his meditation becomes a deity yoga *held* by a mind with the understanding of emptiness. That is, although the mind visualizing himself as a deity does not itself realize emptiness either conceptually or nonconceptually, it is influenced by the meditator's previous meditation on emptiness.

The yoga without signs differs from this in that the understanding of emptiness itself appears in the form of the deity. It is not merely a deity yoga held by a mind that understands emptiness, because such a mind is separate from meditation on emptiness. It does not analyze emptiness, nor does it become a single-minded concentration of signlessness. To be meditation on emptiness, that mind must analyze and gain an understanding of emptiness, and not merely be held by the force of the mind that understood emptiness prior to it. Even if a meditator has reached perfection in the meditative concentration of the yoga with signs, this is not a direct opponent that can cut the root of saṃsāra. Therefore, it is necessary to meditate on the yoga without signs that itself can cut the root of saṃsāra.

How is this meditation done? Practitioners skillfully meditate according to oral instructions from their spiritual mentor; they practice alternating analytical and stabilizing meditation on emptiness without meditating on the conventional aspect of the deity. The yoga without signs is a meditative concentration in which you continually familiarize yourself with the understanding of emptiness that you have gained by ascertaining emptiness with a reasoning negating true existence, such as the refutation of being one and many, dependent arising, and so on. The yoga without signs is the actual meditation on emptiness, employing both stabilizing and analytical meditations on emptiness.

Some scholars object to this. They say that if we consider the yoga without signs to be only meditation on emptiness, then that meditation is no longer deity yoga, because the body of the deity having faces and arms does not appear to that mind. The reason the deity's body doesn't appear is that the meditating mind directly understands emptiness, and to such a mind conventionalities such as the appearance of the deity's body do not appear.

We refute their assertion by saying there is no pervasion, because to a mind that understands emptiness conceptually by means of reasoning, the appearance of the basis of emptiness (the object whose emptiness you are meditating on) still appears. Tsongkhapa asserts this in *Ocean of Reasoning* (T. *Rtsa shes tik chen rigs pa'i rgya mtsho*), his commentary on Nāgārjuna's *Treatise on the Middle Way.*

That qualm concerns whether a mind that conceptually realizes emptiness is considered deity yoga. The next qualm concerns whether a mind that nonconceptually realizes emptiness in the yoga without signs is deity yoga. Someone says that it cannot be deity yoga because minds that nonconceptually realize emptiness do not have the appearance of any conventional phenomena, so the form of the deity with arms and legs does not appear, and thus it is not deity yoga.

The response is that whether it is a yoga with signs or without signs, it is not pervasive that the form of the body of the deity must appear to that mind. In the case of nonconceptual realization of emptiness, the mind is focused single-pointedly on emptiness. One aspect of this mind appears in the form of the deity's body or speech, and another aspect nonconceptually realizes its emptiness and acts as the antidote that cuts the ignorance that is the root of saṃsāra. This is the union of the two truths, explained by Losang

Chokyi Gyaltsen in his *A Discussion between Self-Grasping and the Wisdom Realizing Selflessness* (T. *Bden 'dzin shags 'debs*).

Achieving the Actual Attainments (Siddhi)

The attainments and the signs of attaining them are similar to those in Kriyā Tantra. By relying on external substances such as the sword, the stage of knowledge-holder of the sword is attained. By meditating on the places of the body and the maṇḍalas of earth, water, fire, and air, the four actions of pacification, increase, influence or control, and ferocity are attained. If you actualize Mañjuśrī and recite the mantra together with bodhicitta while visualizing Mañjuśrī, you will attain the samādhi of not forgetting bodhicitta.

Yoga Tantra

The tantric teachings that came to Tibet were mostly Kriyā Tantra and Highest Yoga Tantra; the transmission of Caryā Tantras and Yoga Tantras were not numerous. Yoga Tantra emphasizes the inner yogas over the outer activities, although it still relies on some external actions. Yoga Tantra relies on the *Compendium of Principles of All the Tathāgatas* (*Sarvatathāgatatattvasaṃgraha*, J. *Kongoucyoukyou*), which is the root Yoga Tantra, and the main explanatory tantra, *Vajraśekhara*, which concerns the vajra realm and Sarvavid Vairocana.[34] The three Indian sages known as experts on Yoga Tantra are Buddhaguhya, Ānandagarbha, and Śākyamitra.

Becoming a Suitable Vessel

A solid foundation in the stages of the common path and the three principal aspects of the path is essential for your practice of Tantra to be successful. Then, relying on a fully-qualified tantric master, receive empowerment into maṇḍalas such as the practice of Vajradhātu (*rdo rje dbyings*), Vajra Īśvarī (*rdo rje dbang phyug ma*), and Sarvavid Vairocana (*kun rig rnam par snang mdzad*). In addition to the five empowerments of the five buddha families, the vajra guru empowerment is given in Yoga Tantra.

Purely Keeping the Ethical Restraints and Commitments

Empowerment is taken on the basis of having taken refuge in the Three Jewels and keeping one of the seven sets of prātimokṣa precepts. The bodhisattva precepts are given, and the tantric ethical restraints and commitments of the five buddha families are received with the vajra guru empowerment. The tantric samaya are explained in the first chapter of *Glorious Supreme Primal Tantra Paramādhyā* (*Śrīparamādi Tantra*) and in the *Compendium of Principles of All the Tathāgatas* (*Sarvatathāgatatattvasaṃgraha*). All three sets of ethical restraints are to be kept purely. The ethical restraints and commitments guide and train our mental, verbal, and physical actions, making the mind conducive for cultivating the path.

Practicing the Close Approximation

This section has two parts: the yoga with signs and the yoga without signs. The yoga with signs, in turn, has two parts: the yoga with signs with a coarse visualization of the deity and the yoga with signs with the visualization of the subtle hand implements or mudrās.

The Yoga with Signs

1. The *yoga with signs with a coarse visualization* of the deity has three levels in which the close approximation can be done:

- The most extensive is to do the single yoga of the deity with whom you have an affiliation, as determined at the time of the disciple empowerments, the five empowerments of the five buddha families. During these, you toss a flower into the maṇḍala and depending on where it lands in the maṇḍala, it indicates an affiliation with a specific meditational deity. You then do the single yoga of that particular deity. In the great yoga of self-completion, you meditate to gain three samādhis—the initial preparation, supreme royal maṇḍala, and supreme royal activities—which are done in accordance with the vajra guru empowerment. This is the most complete or extensive way of doing the close approximation.

- The intermediate is engaging in the supreme triumphant victory maṇḍala generation.
- The least is reciting the mantra of each deity one hundred thousand times.

These particular teachings and practices are contained in the root tantra *Tattvasaṃgraha,* which is divided into four chapters. The five buddha families are complete in these four chapters. The first chapter, "Vajra Sphere" (*vajradhātu*), concerns Vairocana; the second, "Victory over the Three Realms," concerns Akṣobhya; the third, "Taming Sentient Beings," pertains to Amitābha; and the fourth, "Accomplishing Purposes," includes both Ratnasambhava and Amoghasiddhi. Here, Ratnasambhava is considered the agent and Amoghasiddhi the action.

Details about the single yoga and the samādhis of the great yoga of the self-completion are found in Tsongkhapa's *Great Exposition of Secret Mantra*. Also study the sādhanas of these practices written by Buton Rinpoche.

The practice of Sarvavid (Kunrig) contains the application of the four seals to four specific areas: the application of the great seal to the body, the application of the Dharma seal to speech, the application of the pledge seal to the mind, and the application of the action seal to virtuous conduct. These are connected to the three practices in Yoga Tantra: the practices of the basis of purification, the purifying path, and the purified result, each of which has four aspects. The four aspects of the basis of purification are the practitioner's body, speech, mind, and activities. The path that purifies them are the practices of the great seal, phenomena seal, pledge seal, and wisdom or action seal. These bring about the four purified results: the body, speech, mind, and activities of a buddha.

BASIS OF PURIFICATION	PURIFYING PATH	PURIFIED RESULT
Body	Practice of the great seal (*mahāmudrā*)	Body of a buddha
Speech	Practice of the phenomena seal (*dharmamudrā*)	Speech of a buddha
Mind	Practice of the pledge seal (*samayamudrā*)	Mind of a buddha
Activities	Practice of the wisdom or action seal (*karmamudrā*)	Activities of a buddha

Regarding the particular applications of each mudrā, many visualizations and factors are involved to stabilize them. There are about three hundred mudrās to be applied during the actual close-approximation practice, and it is important to apply each one. If one mudrā is missing, the process is interrupted and is incomplete. Without a particular reference, such as a sādhana that you are familiar with, understanding this discussion in the *Great Exposition of Secret Mantra* is difficult. In this case, refer to your own sādhana practice. This completes discussion of the yoga with a coarse visualization of the deity.

2. The *yoga with signs with the visualization of the subtle hand implements or mudrās*. Having clearly visualized yourself as the deity, at the upper tip of the central channel—at the tip of the nose—imagine a very small five-spoked vajra, which is the color of the special deity that you have an affiliation with. The thinnest part of the vajra is the width of a hair, the largest is the size of a sesame seed. With practice, gradually train the mind to hold this image very clearly and very stably, by relying on the instructions in Kamalaśīla's *Stages of Meditation* and in Maitreya's instructions *Differentiation of the Middle and the Extremes* (*Madhyāntavibhāga*) and *Ornament of Mahāyāna Sūtras* (*Mahāyāna-sūtrālaṃkāra*).[35] Then, having very stable concentration on this, do the visualizations of emitting and recollecting. Through this practice, you develop serenity that is free from subtle laxity and subtle restlessness. This and the three samādhis of the great yoga of the self-completion are similar to the generation stage of Highest Yoga Tantra.

The Yoga without Signs

By using the various refutations of inherent existence, arrive at the certainty that you, the deity, and the mantra syllables lack true existence. Then alternate stabilizing and analytical meditation on this understanding, and in this way attain the union of serenity and insight that has a correct inferential understanding of emptiness. At that point, the second of the five paths, the path of preparation, is attained. After that, when you perceive emptiness nonconceptually, the path of seeing is attained, and with further familiarity with emptiness, the path of meditation and the path of no-more-learning are attained, as described above.

Achieving the Actual Attainments (Siddhi)

In Yoga Tantra, many actual attainments are discussed. They are achieved by three means: dhyāna (meditative concentration), recitation of mantra, and fire pūjā. One of the best actual attainments is the "state of a holder of knowledge mantra," in which, as a bodhisattva, you have the form of a buddha. Another best actual attainment is the form of the great mudrā of the body of your meditational deity. These two are considered the most excellent actual attainments in Yoga Tantra.

In the three lower tantras, the achievement of the supreme actual attainment—buddhahood—depends on previously accomplishing the worldly attainments. But in Highest Yoga Tantra, by meditating without break on the generation and completion stages, it is not necessary to first achieve the worldly actual attainments such as flying in the sky and clairvoyance. You can reach the supreme attainment directly. Other feats that can be attained through Yoga Tantra are discovering treasure, walking on water, and walking in space.

Unlike Pāramitāyāna, attaining awakening without having to accumulate merit for three countless great eons is a unique characteristic of Highest Yoga Tantra. When practicing the three lower tantric classes, it is necessary to eventually practice Highest Yoga Tantra to attain full awakening.

Concluding Comments on the Three Lower Tantras

The Perfection Vehicle (Pāramitāyāna) sets forth a variety of practices involving the six perfections and so forth. Some people assert that there is no difference in the number of practices that are used to collect merit and wisdom in the Tantrayāna and the Sūtrayāna. This is incorrect. Tantrayāna contains methods such as deity yoga and mantra recitations that enable practitioners to gain the worldly attainments, to invite the blessings and inspiration of the meditational deities, and to receive the protection of the buddhas and ārya bodhisattvas. Through these methods, it is possible to attain awakening more quickly through Tantra.

In both the Perfection Vehicle and the Tantra Vehicle, method practices such as bodhicitta, generosity, and the common attainments (supernormal powers) enhance the wisdom realizing emptiness, but they differ in the way awakening is attained. Ngawang Palden in his *Presentation of the Grounds and Paths of Mantra* says (DY 209):

> In Pāramitāyāna, the wisdom consciousness is caused to possess the capacity to abandon the cognitive obscurations through training for a limitless time in limitless varieties of generosity, and so forth. However, the three lower tantras do not say that one trains for a limitless time in limitless varieties of generosity and so forth, as in the Pāramitāyāna, nor do they set forth a means of generating a special subject (subtler consciousness) that realizes emptiness, as is done in Highest Yoga Tantra. Therefore, the realization of emptiness must be enhanced through skillful means, such as many common attainments and being blessed under the direct care of buddhas and higher bodhisattvas.

In short, bodhicitta and training in the six perfections are common to the Pāramitāyāna and Mantrayāna, but training in limitless varieties of generosity and so forth isn't shared with Mantrayāna, because Highest Yoga Tantra has other methods to increase the collection of merit.

Some people state, "We are told that in the Pāramitāyāna, practitioners must rely on accumulating merit for three countless great eons to attain awakening. Since the Tantra Vehicle is said to be quicker than the

Pāramitāyāna, the practice of any of the four tantric classes is quicker than the Pāramitāyāna." The implication is that by practicing the three lower tantric classes, practitioners would not have to rely on accumulating merit for three countless eons to attain awakening. This, too, is incorrect, because the attainment of buddhahood without having to accumulate merit over three countless eons is an exclusive characteristic of Highest Yoga Tantra and does not apply to the three lower classes of Tantra. To attain awakening through the three lower classes of Tantra, it is necessary to also rely on the two stages of Highest Yoga Tantra. In short, the ability to attain awakening in one lifetime in the time of five degenerations is not pervasive to all four tantric classes; it is a unique quality of Highest Yoga Tantra.

Vajrayāna and the Five Paths and Ten Grounds

How do the tantric paths fit into the schema of the five paths and the ten grounds found in the Pāramitāyāna? Kriyā Tantra is divided into the five paths found in the Pāramitāyāna: the paths of accumulation, preparation, seeing, meditation, and no-more-learning of Kriyā Tantra. After attaining nonconceptual perception of emptiness, practitioners put effort into abandoning the afflictive obscurations and the cognitive obscurations by traversing the ten bodhisattva grounds. The details of how to generate the various antidotes and at what path they overcome the various obscurations in the three lower tantras are very similar to the Pāramitāyāna. Since we have studied this extensively, it is not necessary to go into it in detail now.[36]

The three great masters of Yoga Tantra—Buddhaguhya, Śākyamitra, and Ānandagarbha—explain the Buddha's awakening through the practice of Yoga Tantra in slightly different ways. Śākyamitra and Buddhaguhya assert that he was a tenth-ground bodhisattva when he took birth. After he did ascetic practice near the Nairanjana River, he entered the samādhi called the "great fourth dhyāna of bringing everything to an end." The buddhas of the ten directions came together and roused him from the dhyāna with the sound of their fingers snapping and said that he cannot completely purify himself through only that samādhi. The bodhisattva asked how to do this, and the buddhas led him to Akaniṣṭha (T. *'og-min*), the highest pure land. Leaving his ordinary body at the riverbank, he went to Akaniṣṭha with a mental body. The buddhas conferred the crown empowerment on him and directed him in cultivating the five manifest awakenings in sequence. These five come about through reciting and contemplating the meaning of a mantra and realizing subtle emptiness. The bodhisattva attained buddhahood as the complete enjoyment body, Mahāvairocana. Afterward he performed four types of miracles, went to the peak of Mount Meru to set forth the Yoga Tantras, and returned to India where he reentered his old body. He then manifested overcoming the demons and attaining full awakening.

Ānandagarbha asserts as follows: the bodhisattva, after accumulating merit for three countless eons, was a tenth-ground bodhisattva. In Akaniṣṭha he entered meditative equipoise on the concentration pervading space. The buddhas of the ten directions roused him from that concentration with the sound of their fingers snapping and said that he cannot completely purify himself through only that concentration. The bodhisattva inquired how to do this, so the buddhas gave him the crown empowerment and led him to cultivate the five manifest awakenings. Having attained full awakening as a complete enjoyment body of Mahāvairocana, he performed the four types of miracles and set forth the Yoga Tantras at the peak of Mount Meru. He then displayed the twelve deeds of a buddha, beginning with taking birth in Kapilavastu.

REFLECTION

1. What are yoga with signs and yoga without signs? What is the purpose of meditating on each one?
2. What are some of the qualities of the three lower tantras?

7 | Highest Yoga Tantra

Before delving into Highest Yoga Tantra teachings, it's good to reinforce our bodhicitta motivation. The lama is fortunate to have the opportunity to teach bodhicitta, and disciples are extremely fortunate to hear teachings on bodhicitta, the altruistic intention cherishing others more than yourself. Whoever generates this altruistic intention will set out on the path to true happiness. If you wish for genuine peace and harmony, there is nothing more you could ask for than reflecting on bodhicitta. Please read and reread chapter 1 in Śāntideva's *Engaging in the Bodhisattvas' Deeds* so you will always remember the benefits of bodhicitta and will practice it diligently.

Bodhicitta is not taught to everyone, and there's no expectation that everyone can practice bodhicitta. I teach bodhicitta and the thought-training methods that stem from it widely to implant seeds on people's minds. If it's not in your capacity to generate bodhicitta now, aspire to it in the future and rejoice at the seeds in your mind that come from listening to teachings on generating bodhicitta. At least avoid wrong views, such as saying that aspiring to become a buddha and leading all sentient beings to awakening is impossible or just wishful thinking. Similarly, if you cannot generate tantric realizations now, make sure to plant seeds of doing so and rejoice at hearing tantric teachings. This will enable you to meet the Tantrayāna and engage in the practice in future lives. Bodhisattvas benefit others joyfully, not through suffering and austerity. Even if a practice is difficult, rejoice at aspiring to do it in the future.

Levels of Meaning

In Highest Yoga Tantra, one word may have several levels of meaning, just as in the Perfection of Wisdom there are explicit and implicit meanings. In Highest Yoga Tantra, the multiplicity of meanings is even more pronounced. One word may have four modes of explanation:

1. The literal meaning
2. The general meaning, an explanation in common with Sūtrayāna and the three lower tantras
3. The hidden meaning, which is of three types:
   - that which conceals the method for taking desire into the path
   - that which conceals appearance
   - that which conceals the conventional truth, the illusory body
4. The ultimate meaning, relating to the realization of clear light and illusory body

There is also a mode of interpretation called the "six boundaries": the definitive and the interpretable (1, 2), the intentional and the nonintentional (3, 4), and the literal and nonliteral (5, 6) meanings.

In approaching Tantra, it is important to keep in mind that there are two styles of presentation. The first is the public presentation where many people listen to the teaching. The second is the private explanation, which is designed for the needs of a specific practitioner. This distinction is particularly pronounced in the Sakya teachings on the path and result.

Distinguishing the Four Classes of Tantra

Highest Yoga Tantra is widespread in the Tibetan and Mongolian Buddhist communities, and some of its texts are also found in Chinese and Japanese. Some of the prominent Highest Yoga Tantra practices found in Tibetan Buddhism are those of Guhyasamāja, Cakrasaṃvara (Heruka), Yamāntaka, Kālacakra, Hevajra, Guhyagarbha, Vajrakīlaya, and Vajrayoginī. Each of these names may refer to a deity, a tantric text, or a system of tantric practice. These tantric systems often have their own terminology and description of the stages of the path of practice of that deity, who represents the perfect awakened state.

The four tantric classes can be differentiated in two ways: one is by its emphasis on either external activities or internal yogas. To review, Kriyā Tantra mainly emphasizes external activities; Caryā Tantra places equal emphasis on both external activities and internal yogas; Yoga Tantra mainly emphasizes internal yogas, although it includes some external activities; and Highest Yoga Tantra emphasizes special methods of internal yoga.

There is no difference between the understanding of emptiness in the Pāramitāyāna and Tantrayāna. However, there is a difference in the consciousness perceiving emptiness; in Highest Yoga Tantra, that consciousness is great bliss. The second way to differentiate the four tantric classes is in terms of the bliss used as the method. In Kriyā Tantra, it is the bliss of seeing the partner; in Caryā Tantra, it is the bliss of exchanging smiles with the partner; in Yoga Tantra, it is the bliss of holding hands with the partner; and in Highest Yoga Tantra, it is the bliss of the joining of the two organs.

Differences also exist in the manner of cultivating serenity. In Yoga Tantra it is done by focusing on the visualization of the subtle vajra at the tip of the nose and the three samādhis of the great yoga of self-completion. These are similar to meditations found in the generation stage of Highest Yoga Tantra. The three lower tantras, on the other hand, have only the yoga with signs and the yoga without signs; they don't speak of the generation and completion stages.

In general, the method to cultivate samādhi and serenity in Sūtrayāna and the three lower tantras is similar. When meditators can maintain concentration on the chosen meditation object for four hours, it's said they have attained single-pointed concentration (*samādhi*). Continuing to practice, when their concentration induces the bliss of mental and physical pliancy, they have attained serenity. In the lower tantras, the process is similar, but the meditation object is the appearance and divine identity as the deity. After gaining serenity, meditators continue practicing and attain the first dhyāna. As their concentration becomes subtler, they attain the second, third, and fourth dhyānas and the four formless meditative absorptions. Although the fourth formless absorption, the peak of saṃsāra, is very subtle according to Sūtra and the lower tantras, according to Tantra it lacks intensity and clarity.

In Sūtra and the three lower tantras, concentration functions on a comparatively coarse level, so strong mindfulness and introspective awareness are necessary to prevent distractions disturbing concentration. However, in Highest Yoga Tantra the way to attain serenity differs. It contains techniques to withdraw and dissolve the coarser states of mind, bringing the mind to an extremely subtle state in which these coarse distractions cannot arise. This serenity is especially deep and firm. And when the subtlety of the concentration is due to great bliss, the power of the mind to cognize the object increases, as do the clarity and vividness of the mind.

According to explanations in the sūtras and three lower tantras, the cultivation of serenity involves only stabilizing meditation, not analytical meditation. However, in Highest Yoga Tantra these two types of meditation, which are usually cultivated separately, are cultivated together. This is due to the unique method of penetrating the vital points of the body, which enables insight to be developed through stabilizing meditation. Whereas serenity and insight are attained sequentially in Sūtra and the three lower tantras, in Highest Yoga Tantra the most astute practitioners attain them simultaneously. In addition, Highest Yoga Tantra contains special methods to attain the truth and form bodies of a buddha by having the winds enter, abide, and dissolve in the central channel. These techniques are not found in the lower tantras. Here we see why the meditative techniques of Highest Yoga Tantra surpass those of Sūtrayāna and the lower tantras.

How Vajrayāna Brings Awakening

Let's pause to summarize and review the way to progress on the path. Since all sentient beings have the potential to become fully awakened buddhas, it is said that eventually even śrāvaka and solitary-realizer arhats will enter the Mahāyāna. Although they have already realized emptiness nonconceptually, when they enter the bodhisattva path they must still complete training in the perfections and proceed through all Mahāyāna paths and grounds. Even a tenth-ground bodhisattva following the Pāramitāyāna must ultimately enter the Vajrayāna to overcome all cognitive obscurations. Thus both Sūtra and Tantra practices are necessary to become a buddha.

Why is this? Our three doors of body, speech, and mind have coarse and subtle defilements that must be purified and removed. The coarse faults of body and speech are the seven destructive actions,[37] which are overcome by engaging in the higher training in ethical conduct, especially by living with monastic precepts. Coarse mental faults are pacified through the meditations on the kindness of others, love, compassion, and so forth in the higher training in concentration. The ignorance grasping true existence is overcome by the wisdom realizing emptiness, which is cultivated in the higher training of wisdom.

Subtle defilements of body, speech, and mind are eliminated through the practice of Highest Yoga Tantra. The practices of clear appearance and divine identity on the generation stage subdue faults regarding the body, especially grasping the body as ordinary. The practice of illusory body subdues subtle faults of speech, especially conceiving our speech and subtle winds to be different natures. The practice of clear light overcomes subtle faults of mind, specifically the obscurations preventing the attainment of all awakened qualities.

As discussed before, to liberate ourselves from saṃsāra and attain buddhahood to benefit all sentient beings, both afflictive obscurations and cognitive obscurations must be completely removed from our mindstream. Only the direct, nonconceptual realization of the emptiness of inherent existence can remove the fundamental ignorance, indicative conceptions, and other afflictions from the mind so that they can never arise again. Because the clear-light mind is so subtle, when it realizes emptiness, it becomes a powerful tool to eliminate all obscurations quickly. Therefore, sincere yogis train in meditations to make manifest the subtlest mind during their lives by practicing the completion stage. Through this, without dying they dissolve the winds into the indestructible drop at the heart and meditate on emptiness with the subtlest mind of clear light.

To develop this ability, tantric practitioners must practice the generation stage on the basis of a firm understanding of the four truths, the three higher trainings, the six perfections, and so on to prepare their minds. Unless we have practiced in previous lives, gaining all these realizations in this life is difficult. If a skilled practitioner cannot make manifest the stage of actual clear light while alive, the natural dissolution of the winds into the indestructible drop at the heart cakra at the time of death affords the opportunity to access the subtlest clear-light mind and use it to meditate on emptiness.

After a person experiences the stages of dissolution of the winds and coarser minds, the fundamental innate clear-light mind becomes manifest. In Sūtra, the last moment of consciousness of a dying person is said to be neutral.[38] In Tantra, methods exist to transform this mind into virtue. It is not possible for the fundamental innate clear-light mind to be transformed into nonvirtue, because all indicative conceptions have ceased during the dissolution process.

The clear light of death of an ordinary person is said to be "conceptual," which in this context means that the mind is obscured. When ordinary beings experience the fundamental innate clear-light mind of death, they are not aware of the mind having an object. Some scholars assert that emptiness appears to the clear light of death but is not ascertained. Others say its object is a form of voidness that is similar to emptiness but is not the emptiness of inherent existence. In either case, any absence of manifest ignorance at the time of the clear light of death is temporary, and the eighty indicative conceptions and other afflictions reemerge in the bardo and the next rebirth. However, a person who has trained diligently in tantric methods can use this natural absence of ignorance during the clear light to meditate on emptiness. Ordinary beings who lack training miss this opportunity. For them, it is as if their mind were in a faint when the clear light dawns. They are neither aware of its presence nor able to utilize it for meditation.

Some highly realized practitioners meditate in the clear light at death for days after the breath has stopped. Some attain realizations, even full awakening. However, staying in the clear light at death time is not necessarily indicative of having yogic realizations. A few people who do not seem to be yogis—although they may have had the experience of some form of clear light while alive—stay in the clear light due to other circumstances. Most likely, this is related to the power of their virtue. Although this is the case, if they lack the wisdom realizing emptiness, they do not receive great benefit from staying in the clear light.

All the great masters stress the importance of understanding the nature of the mind. This refers to manifesting the example clear light and the actual clear light—states of mind that realize emptiness—on the completion stage. Yogis who can do this are close to buddhahood. These states of mind are much subtler than those used in the Pāramitāyāna. The actual clear light is the fundamental innate mind of clear light that realizes emptiness and is made manifest by dissolving all winds in the central channel at the heart. In addition, the basis of emptiness is special: it is not an impure object such as our ordinary five aggregates, but the subtlest mind that has been purified. In short, at high levels of the completion stage the fundamental innate mind of clear light realizes its own empty nature, which gives it special power to eliminate defilements from the mind. Both the subject, the subtlest mind, and its object, emptiness, are purified.

This is the meaning of realizing the nature of the mind in Tantra; such a realization leads quickly to full awakening, our final goal. When Gampopa first met Milarepa, Gampopa boasted about his strong single-pointed concentration. Milarepa responded, "That's nice, but I know the nature of my mind."

Meditational Deities and the Ultimate Nature of Desire

The true nature of the afflictions can be understood in two ways. In the way common to all vehicles, the ultimate nature of the afflictions is their emptiness of inherent existence, which in Nyingma terminology is also referred to as *kadag*, "primordial purity." The second way of understanding the nature of afflictions is based on knowing that all minds and mental factors—be they coarse minds such as a sensory consciousness, discursive thought, or afflictions—are permeated by the essential nature, the innate mind of clear light, *rigpa*. In Nyingma practice, meditators do not follow the objects of their perceptions because focusing on external objects stimulates afflictions that catch us in the subjectivity of the experience. Clinging and grasping ensue, and karma is created. Instead, practitioners observe the nature of the afflictions when they arise, and release clinging and grasping to the object by placing the mind on the nature of the affliction itself. This produces what is known as the "self-liberation of afflictions."

In Tsongkhapa's commentary on Ghaṇṭāpa's *Five Stages of Cakrasaṃvara* (*Śricakrasaṃvarapañcakrama*), entitled *Opening the Eyes to View the Hidden Meaning* (*Sbas don lta ba'i mig 'byed*), he comments on the phrase "although born from desire, yet not soiled by the defects of desire." This does not mean that desire does not arise. Desire arises, but practitioners avoid being negatively affected by its destructive aspects. Because afflictions such as sexual desire are emotional states, the mind is not as discursive as usual and conceptual thought diminishes. At this time, practitioners can use the affliction like a key by focusing on that state of mind and directing it into realization of emptiness. This is similar to Nyingma practice. Both Nyingma and the Highest Yoga Tantra seek to make manifest the subtlest, nonconceptual mind and use it to meditate on emptiness.

A text on the Guhyasamāja completion stage states that there are occasions in our ordinary mental states when comparatively subtle minds arise—for example, when sneezing, fainting, yawning, deep sleep, or in sexual union. Since it is difficult to catch the subtle mind during these experiences, another method is to utilize sexual union to dissolve the coarser states of mind and access the subtlest clear-light mind. To do this, generation-stage practitioners meditate on the divine appearance and divine identity of being the deity in union with a consort. Although this is at the level of imagination, they consciously and intentionally try to generate states of bliss by melting the drops within the central channel. They also practice reversing the drops so no fluid is emitted. In this way, yogis induce states of bliss that automatically bring progressively clearer and subtler states of mind that focus on emptiness.

Because this is a method for accessing the subtlest mind, it is suitable to depict some meditational deities in sexual union. However, it would clearly be inappropriate to visualize Buddha Śākyamuni in his monastic form like this. To enable meditators to engage in these practices, the meditation deity that is visualized and meditated on assumes the form of a couple, symbolizing the union of method and wisdom. This presents a path where the bliss arising from desire is utilized on the path to make manifest the clear-light mind and use it to understand the nature of reality.

Understanding the significance of meditational deities appearing in such erotic forms is critical. Without it, we risk confusion concerning the Buddha's teachings. In the sūtras and the Vinaya, the Buddha instructed lay followers in ethical conduct regarding sexual relationships: unwise or unkind relations are to be abandoned. For monastics, celibacy is essential. For practitioners of Highest Yoga Tantra, orgasmic emission constitutes a transgression of a root tantric precept. This is clear, but when we encounter images of Yamāntaka and other meditational deities in sexual union, we may become confused. What is the Buddha advising? In the non-Buddhist Indian tantric tradition, Śiva and his consort Pārvatī are portrayed side by side, not in union like Buddhist tantric deities. It seems that Hindu Tantra respects conventional norms, whereas Buddhist Tantra defies them. However, this is not the case at all. For this reason, I advise Tibetan monasteries in India not to publicly display images of deities in union in temples that are visited by pilgrims and tourists who could easily misunderstand their meaning. These images are meant for people who know their significance and appreciate and properly understand their meaning.

Excellent Features of Highest Yoga Tantra

The great masters praise Highest Yoga Tantra for its wonderful qualities. Practicing it enables us to begin to understand the ultimate meaning of buddha nature. Although the *Sublime Continuum* reveals the unpolluted awareness, its real meaning is found only in Highest Yoga Tantra with the explanation of the fundamental innate mind of clear light. When this subtlest consciousness is transformed into the path—that is, when it is used to realize emptiness directly—practitioners are equipped with a very powerful instrument that can quickly purify the two obscurations and bring to completion all magnificent qualities of a buddha.

Our coarse body and mind are different entities, whereas a buddha's body and mind—the form body and truth body—are two aspects of one entity. They are the continuity of causes that are also one nature—the subtlest body and subtlest mind—that can be transformed into the two buddha bodies.

In Sūtrayāna, three types of nirvāṇa—nirvāṇa with remainder, nirvāṇa without remainder, and nonabiding nirvāṇa—are possible because of natural nirvāṇa, the empty nature of all phenomena. So too, in Highest Yoga Tantra, the resultant body and mind of a buddha are possible because on the level of the basis, there are the subtlest mind and wind. By understanding this subtlest level according to Highest Yoga Tantra, we will gain true confidence in the tantric method's ability to bring full awakening.

Highest Yoga Tantra presents the way to transform the fundamental innate mind of clear light and its accompanying wind into the path by first dissolving the coarser levels of mind and wind that propel them. This can be done by cultivating three main methods: (1) wind yoga, which is the principal approach of Guhyasamāja, (2) four types of bliss, which is the principal approach of mother tantras, and (3) nonconceptuality, which is the principal approach of mahāmudrā and dzogchen. All of these methods can bring the same resultant buddhahood.

Utilizing Afflictions in the Path

Another unique quality of Highest Yoga Tantra is that afflictions can be utilized on the path. Tantric texts describe the method metaphorically. Just as an insect that is born in wood eats the wood and completely consumes it, likewise with desire as its cause, a blissful mind arises, which cognizes the emptiness of phenomena and cuts ignorance, the root of desire. Desire itself is not transformed into the path but is utilized to generate the great bliss that meditates on emptiness.

This is not a case of desire being transformed or transmuted into the blissful mind realizing emptiness. Afflictions are to be destroyed on the path; they are wrong consciousnesses that are counter to path consciousnesses. Although we sometimes hear "the five afflictions become the five wisdoms," this should not be understood literally. Attachment and anger may be used in the path, but that doesn't mean those afflictions become the path. Rather, in particular cases, with particular yogis, a mind with affliction can support the path.

In the Pāramitāyāna, afflictions are eradicated by applying a mind that is an antidote, a mind that cognizes things in the opposite way: instead of being jealous of someone, practitioners rejoice in that person's good qualities and good fortune. However, in addition to the Pāramitāyāna method, in Tantrayāna, yogis may utilize the afflictions to enhance their practice of the path and in that way destroy the afflictions. When afflictions are used in this way, they are automatically reduced and overcome, without making special effort to eradicate them. In the same way as an insect born in wood consumes the wood, the clear-light mind born from desire can consume and eradicate the afflictive mind. Desire does this by supporting the generation of great bliss that is used to realize emptiness directly. This cannot be done in the Pāramitāyāna.

In short, the bliss that is a by-product of attachment is used to generate the blissful wisdom that realizes the ultimate nature. Just as wind extinguishes a small flame but fans a huge fire, attachment destroys ordinary beings but can be used to increase wisdom by a skillful Tantra practitioner. However, desire never becomes a path. When the bodhicitta—the subtle drop in the crown cakra—melts, the experience of bliss in the channels arises. That great bliss is derived from desire, but it is not polluted by ordinary desire and instead is used to meditate on emptiness. Over time, meditation on emptiness completely uproots desire and other afflictions.

How can anger be utilized on the path? Just as excrement is filthy on a street but is useful fertilizer on a field, anger is a hindrance to awakening and must be eliminated, but in particular circumstances it can be used to benefit others, provided the motivation is pure.

Anger cannot be transformed into compassion, but it can be used to create a forceful attitude that is directed to destroying anger and other afflictions. When anger has decreased and the mind is in a neutral state, compassion can arise. The anger itself has not become or been transformed into compassion, because compassion is a mind of a different nature—it is virtuous, whereas anger is nonvirtuous, and one cannot become the other. But the force of anger can be directed toward eliminating anger so that compassion can arise. When bodhisattvas use anger for a positive purpose, their fundamental motivation must be bodhicitta. It is in this light that we can understand wrathful deities. Yamāntaka appears ferocious, but his wrathful countenance is directed toward the afflictions. He has compassion for sentient beings and wants to destroy their afflictions and defilements that keep them bound in saṃsāra.

Can an afflictive mental state be the substantial cause of an undefiled mind? It seems that the continuity of a doubt tending toward the wrong conclusion is the substantial cause for doubt that is equal toward both conclusions. Equal doubt can become doubt tending toward the correct conclusion, which becomes a correct assumption. This becomes inference, and the continuity of inference becomes a direct reliable cognizer. Thinking like this, it appears that the continuity of the mind grasping true existence can become the mind realizing selflessness and eventually the omniscient mind.

We can accept that the continuity of the inference realizing the aggregates as impermanent can become a yogic direct perceiver of impermanence. This is one reliable cognizer being the cause for another reliable cognizer. But it is dubious that the true-grasping mind can become the omniscient mind. The doubt thinking that sound is permanent is not a reliable cognizer. When someone who has this doubt gradually comes to realize that sound is impermanent, this realization is a correct consciousness that can proceed to become omniscient mind. The original doubt thinking sound is permanent, however, is not a substantial cause for omniscient mind. In the same way, when attachment is utilized in the path, attachment is not a substantial cause for awakening, although it is a cooperative condition. It cannot be the substantial cause, because the nine levels of attachment are abandoned by the path of meditation.

This point can be tricky. The mental afflictions can never be the substantial cause of omniscience, but in the context of following the progression of the three levels of doubt, it seems that there could be continuity from affliction to omniscience. What forms this continuity? The clear and cognizant nature of the mind. It continues, but the afflictions that obscure and pollute it do not continue and must be abandoned.

In short, afflictions must be eradicated for wisdom to arise. The expression in Tantra that the five afflictions become or are transformed into the five wisdoms should not be taken literally. However, afflictions can be used to support a path. Desire is an afflictive mind. In Sūtrayāna it is eradicated by an antidote that is its opposite, such as contemplating the disadvantages of attachment and the impermanence of the object of attachment. But in Tantra, attachment is not counteracted directly like that. Instead, it is used to create bliss, and without directly fighting that attachment, yogis use the blissful mind to make manifest the subtlest clear-light mind and use it to realize emptiness. The realization of emptiness overcomes attachment by abolishing the ignorance on which attachment depends. In this way attachment is employed to enhance yogis' practice of the path, and that naturally leads to the reduction and eradication of attachment without having to employ effort to eliminate attachment directly.

REFLECTION

1. What is the meaning of primordial purity?
2. What is the purpose of making manifest the subtlest mind in Highest Yoga Tantra?
3. How can some afflictions be utilized on the path? Are afflictions trans-

formed into the path or utilized on the path? What is the difference between them?

4. How is the metaphor of an insect born in wood used?

Cultivating Serenity and Insight in Highest Yoga Tantra

If practitioners did not attain serenity prior to entering Vajrayāna, they may do so during the generation stage. The methods for attaining it in the three lower tantras are the same as in Sūtrayāna—eliminating the five faults by applying the eight antidotes and practicing the six powers and four types of attention while progressively accomplishing the nine mental abidings.[39] Highest Yoga Tantra contains special techniques involving concentration on subtle objects such as syllables or drops of light at certain points within a meditator's body imagined as the deity's body.

In Sūtrayāna, meditation objects such as a kasiṇa, the four immeasurables, the conventional nature of the mind, and the image of the Buddha are used. In the coarse generation stage of Vajrayāna, the object of meditation is the clear appearance of yourself as the deity, the maṇḍala, or a subtle syllable visualized in your deity body. Using such an object to cultivate serenity brings special results. Through self-generation as the deity, practitioners cultivate clear appearance and divine identity. Analytical meditation goes over the details of the deity's body so that it clearly appears to the meditator's mind; then stabilizing meditation is done to develop serenity on that. Stabilizing meditation is also done when cultivating divine identity.

Clear appearance as the deity must be influenced by the understanding of emptiness. If the mind is tinged with self-grasping when meditating on clear appearance and divine identity, those will vanish and ordinary appearance and ordinary grasping will arise in their stead. At that time meditators' meditation does not constitute generation-stage practice. But when it is done properly, serenity and insight are attained simultaneously.

In Sūtrayāna, serenity and insight are attained separately, whereas in Tantra they are cultivated together. In the coarse generation stage, practitioners primarily employ analysis to cultivate the clear appearance of themselves as the deity and use stabilizing meditation to cultivate divine identity of being the deity who is empty of inherent existence. The coarse generation stage is completed when meditators can maintain concentration on the entire maṇḍala and its deities as well as the subtle deities on the sense organs for four hours.

Continuing to practice, during the refined generation stage they imagine the entire maṇḍala and the deities in it in a tiny drop the size of a sesame seed at the upper or lower openings of the central channel. Visualizing the entire maṇḍala in a subtle drop the size of a sesame seed in the meditator's deity body increases the sharpness of analysis and concentration—qualities that are necessary in order to visualize many figures in fine detail. Here analysis aids stability, enabling meditators to attain serenity without forgoing analysis and to quickly attain the union of serenity and insight. They attain the union of serenity and insight by visualizing the maṇḍala deities emanating from and reabsorbing into the maṇḍala deities in this subtle drop. Emanating the deities involves analytical meditation; their reabsorption involves stabilizing meditation. In this way, analytical and stabilizing meditation are practiced at the same time with one consciousness, not alternately as in Pāramitāyāna. This unique quality of Highest Yoga Tantra enables meditators to attain serenity and insight simultaneously in a united manner.

Meditators may develop great bliss during the refined generation stage by melting the drop at the crown of the head or by concentrating on a subtle object such as a white bodhicitta drop at the lower end of the central channel. Bliss is also cultivated through practice with a mudrā, who is usually, but not always, an imagined consort on the generation stage. On the completion stage, the mudrā may be imagined or actual, although only lay yogis may have an actual karmamudrā. Monastics must have an imagined or wisdom mudrā.

When meditators can maintain concentration on this for four hours, it marks the completion of the refined generation stage. The union of serenity and insight is attained on the generation stage, prior to entering the completion stage. This is the case in mahāmudrā, dzogchen, the Sakya practice of the equality of saṃsāra and nirvāṇa, and the Gelug practice of the union of bliss and emptiness. All of these are single-pointed absorptions without discursive analysis.

After the union of serenity and insight has been attained on the generation stage by using special tantric methods, practitioners principally do stabilizing meditation when they meditate on emptiness.

On the completion stage, meditators develop the wisdom of great bliss by melting the drops at the crown cakra. As they flow down, great bliss arises. The more intense the bliss, the subtler the mind becomes. The subtler the mind, the greater is the ability to gain certainty of emptiness. Both stabilizing and analytical meditation are encompassed within this meditation. In this way meditators gain serenity and insight simultaneously with a subtle mind of great bliss. Similarly, the subtler the meditation object, the subtler the mind concentrating on it becomes. When this refined state of concentration is focused on emptiness, the realization of emptiness becomes very subtle.

Meditation on Emptiness in Vajrayāna

The understanding of emptiness is at the core of Vajrayāna. Disregarding emptiness and thinking that we ordinary beings are now buddhas because we visualized ourselves as such misses the point of Vajrayāna. Rather, we have to eradicate the mind grasping inherent existence with a wisdom mind knowing that phenomena lack inherent existence. If phenomena existed inherently as they appear to us and as we ignorant beings hold them to exist, we would already perceive ultimate reality. There would be no way to change our perceptions and thoughts to make them more realistic. Freeing ourselves from afflictions would be impossible, as would liberation and buddhahood. To avoid this, we must have the correct view of emptiness and meditate on it repeatedly.

Not everyone enters Tantra with the same background. For example, some people hold the Yogācāra view of emptiness until they have attained the stage of slight falling of wisdom on the generation stage. To continue on the path, they must generate the Prāsaṅgika view. As those who have the Prāsaṅgika view progress in their understanding of emptiness, so do their understandings of karma and its effects and of conventional objects; and as their conviction in karma and its effects and conventional objects grows, so does their conviction in emptiness.

The phrase "everything becomes emptiness" occurs frequently in tantric sādhanas. At this point, practitioners are to stop and meditate on the lack of inherent existence.[40] Following this is the phrase "from within emptiness appears . . ." and a description of the maṇḍala, the deity, offering substances, and so forth follows. By frequently dissolving things into emptiness, followed by having them appear as dependently arisen, illusion-like phenomena, practitioners are reminded that everything occurs within emptiness, the ultimate nature of all phenomena.

When meditating on emptiness after saying "everything becomes emptiness," don't think that everything disappears into nothingness—this is falling to the extreme of nihilism. Do not think that things were inherently existent before but now you have made them empty of inherent existence. They have always been and will always be empty of inherent existence. The difference is that now you realize that emptiness.

Two features must be complete in the meditation on emptiness. First is the dissolution of all appearances. That includes both the appearance of phenomena as ordinary and the appearance of them as inherently existent. At the level of appearance, these two (phenomena and the appearance of their inherent existence) no longer appear to the mind. At the level of apprehension, the mind apprehends the emptiness of inherent existence. Emptiness is the object of this mind, so there is the combination of an emptiness that is the dissolution of appearances and the emptiness of inherent existence of all phenomena.

In his sādhana *The Means of Attainment Called "All Good"* (*Samantabhadranama-sādhana*), Buddhajñāna raises these questions: "Generation-stage meditation primarily consists of visualizing the deity, without any explicit meditation on emptiness. How can this deity yoga practice become an antidote to eliminate the root of saṃsāra, the grasping at true existence? Isn't the mind imagining a deity opposite to the wisdom realizing emptiness where only emptiness appears?"

Buddhajñāna then responds, saying that meditation on emptiness is embedded in the generation-stage practice. First, meditate on the emptiness of your self and your body and mind. Then meditate that the mind understanding emptiness takes the form of the deity. That is, the deity's body is nothing other than the wisdom realizing emptiness. Thus, meditating on emptiness is important because afterward you meditate that the wisdom realizing emptiness becomes the "substance" of your deity body. Dissolving ordinary appearances is also essential, because without dissolving ordinary appearances and the appearance of inherent existence, arising in the form of a deity is not possible.

After arising as the deity, meditate on the emptiness of the deity, which is a manifestation of your wisdom realizing emptiness. The I that is merely designated in dependence on the deity's aggregates is empty of inherent existence. Thus, within the generation-stage practice, focusing on emptiness is primary and visualization of the deity is secondary.

Kamalaśīla recommends contemplating emptiness when distraction arises in meditation (DY 200):

> The *Cloud of Jewels Sūtra* says, "Those who are skilled in this way about faults take as their yoga the meditation on emptiness in order to become free from all elaborations. Through much meditation on emptiness, when they thoroughly examine the nature of those places where their minds scatter and which they like, they realize them as empty. When they analyze what the mind is, they realize it as empty. When they examine by what mind that is realized, they realize it as empty. Through realizing such, they enter the yoga of signlessness." This indicates that whoever does not analyze in this way will not enter signlessness.

After imagining your wisdom consciousness vividly appearing as the deity's divine body, be aware that simultaneously that wisdom ascertains the noninherent existence of the divine body. These two—the mind of deity yoga and the wisdom realizing noninherent existence—are one entity, but nominally different. Some scholars say that the appearance of a mind ascertaining emptiness in the form of a deity means that this mind has emptiness as its conceived object and a divine body of the deity as its appearing object. Thus, the mind of deity yoga has a factor of ascertainment—the understanding of the lack of inherent existence—and a factor of appearance—the vivid appearance of a divine body. In this way, one aspect of the meditation on divine identity observes the ultimate—emptiness—and the other observes the conventional—a divine body. This mind of deity yoga has the mode of apprehension of a nonaffirming negative, since it ascertains only emptiness although the deity appears to it. This occurs due to special training in the Vajrayāna.

But is this really unique to Vajrayāna? Among sūtra interpretations, there appear to be two views regarding whether a phenomenon qualified by emptiness appears to a mind that inferentially cognizes that emptiness. Some people say that in Sūtrayāna, the sprout—the object qualified by emptiness—*appears* to an inferential cognizer realizing its emptiness, although that consciousness *ascertains* only emptiness. That is, the object qualified by emptiness appears during inferential cognition of its emptiness. However, others say that the phenomenon qualified by emptiness does not appear to an inferential consciousness cognizing emptiness.

To sustain their understanding of the view subsequent to meditative equipoise on the generation and completion stages, yogis do analytical meditation on emptiness. On the completion stage they focus on subtle essential points in the body. This makes manifest a subtler mind and also generates great bliss. In this way, the subtle wisdom mind of great bliss sustains the view of emptiness within meditative equipoise. At this time, yogis do not engage in analytical meditation.

Bliss and Emptiness

The minds that meditate on emptiness in Sūtra and Tantra are not the same. In the Pāramitāyāna, bodhisattvas meditate on emptiness with an ordinary mind, whereas in Highest Yoga Tantra, they awaken the subtlest mind. Furthermore, that subtlest mind is not ordinary; it is in the nature of bliss, and this blissful mind is used to realize emptiness.

To yogis meditating on the completion stage, all phenomena in the maṇḍala appear as manifestations of the subtlest wind and blissful wisdom. At the stage of buddhahood, all appearances—maṇḍalas, deities, offerings, and so forth—are manifestations of the wisdom of inseparable bliss and emptiness from the Buddha's perspective.

What does it mean to unite bliss and emptiness? In Highest Yoga Tantra practice, yogis transform their minds into the nature of bliss, and that blissful mind is used to perceive emptiness. This occurs through the melting of the drops within the central channel and by reversing the drops so they are not emitted. In this way, yogis induce states of bliss that automatically bring subtler states of mind. This blissful mind then focuses on emptiness. When yogis concentrate on emptiness, they do not know that their minds are experiencing bliss. There is no thought "I'm experiencing bliss," but the mind itself is in the nature of bliss—bliss is not an object that the mind perceives. Without losing that experience of bliss, the mind meditates on emptiness with either an inferential or direct realization of emptiness. Because emptiness is perceived by a blissful mind, the understanding of emptiness is much more powerful. This is the real essence of Tantra—how tantric practice can hasten the attainment of buddhahood

Meditation Sessions in the Generation Stage

The main practitioners of Highest Yoga Tantra in our world are human beings whose bodies comprise six substances, three from their mother and three from their father. In addition, these practitioners are properly prepared and qualified as described above.

At this point, it would be helpful to have a general overview of the generation stage in the Highest Yoga Tantra. Highest Yoga Tantra has several unique presentations that call for new vocabulary. It will require study to learn and remember these and to connect the various ideas. Take your time and know that your effort will bring good results.

The generation stage is a yoga that (1) is a meditation that newly and mentally imagines an aspect similar to death, bardo, or rebirth and (2) does not arise from causing the winds to enter, abide, and dissolve in the central channel through the power of meditation but ripens the continuum so that one can progress to the completion stage in which that is done. The meaning of this will become clearer as we continue.

Deity yoga is not simply the visualization of the deity. It includes meditating on the emptiness of the deity while retaining the visualized appearance of yourself as the deity. In this way, deity yoga has two aspects, one focused on conventional truth—the appearance of the deity—the other focused on ultimate truth—the emptiness of the deity. The purpose of this is to be able to apprehend the two truths with one consciousness at the time of attaining full awakening.

In the generation stage of deity yoga, practitioners meditate on the emptiness of themselves and the deity to counteract the self-grasping ignorance that is the root of saṃsāra. Here the object that is realized is the empty nature of the mind and the subject realizing it is the mind. In this way, the subject and object are nondual. After dissolving all appearances of the ordinary self and ordinary environment into emptiness, practitioners meditate that this wisdom realizing emptiness appears in the form of the deity and the maṇḍala. Without meditating on emptiness, if you maintain your ordinary view of an inherently existent self, the mind that visualizes yourself as the deity is a wrong consciousness.

Some generation-stage sādhanas describe generating yourself as the deity first as a causal vajra-holder and then as the resultant vajra-holder. While meditating on the sādhana during the initial phase of the self-generation practice of cultivating the identity of the deity, meditators visualize their wisdom realizing emptiness appearing in the form of a light, syllable, implement, or deity that is the causal vajra-holder. This is found in the meditation of taking the bardo into the path to the enjoyment body. The process of self-generation continues with other visualizations until the meditator arises in the full form of the deity, known as the resultant vajra-holder. This is the meditation of taking rebirth into the path to the emanation body.

In other cases, meditators generate themselves as a deity through a process called the "five clarifications" in which the appearance of their wisdom as the deity evolves and becomes clearer in five steps: (1) the mind principle where meditators meditate on emptiness and then meditate on a moon disc with the sixteen Sanskrit vowels, (2) the sattva principle where they meditate on a moon disc with the thirty-six Sanskrit consonants, (3) the concentration principle where they meditate on a vajra on top of the moon disc, (4) the vajra principle where the vajra transforms into a hand implement, and (5) the Vajradhara principle where this transforms into the full body of the deity. A more concise explanation is clarification through: (1) suchness, (2) moon, (3) seed syllable, (4) implement or symbol, and (5) full emergence as the deity (YT 36). Although the self-generation as the deity may be done in several ways, the most important part is to meditate on the vast and the profound by cultivating the clear appearance of yourself as the deity and holding the divine identity of being an awakened being.

Serious practitioners do these meditations by relating them to their own mental state and level of realization. They will also ensure that their concentration is free from laxity and restlessness. The methods to counteract these two hindrances are the same as in Sūtrayāna.[41] Practitioners should judge for themselves whether their mind is too tight or too relaxed.

Being able to single-pointedly hold a clear image of yourself as the deity for a long period of time obstructs the usual sense of ordinariness that thinks, "I am an ordinary, limited being with afflictions in saṃsāra." It also leads to a sense of divine identity of being the deity in which, referring to the conventional I, you think, "I am the deity." As the clear appearance as the deity and the sense of being the deity through cultivating divine identity increase, you will come to a point such that when you think of yourself, you will feel "I am the deity." Although you are not yet the actual deity, this thought eliminates many obstacles, such as the low self-esteem thinking you are incapable, and stimulates you to practice more intensely.

In all these steps of the meditation, it is crucial to constantly reaffirm your awareness of emptiness. Without this, you could easily slip into thinking you are an inherently existent deity and thus generate many afflictions and wrong views.

But the question arises: Isn't imagining ourselves as deities and holding divine identity of being deities a wrong consciousness? After all, other persons' reliable cognizers negate that I am the deity. In his *The Way to Practice the Two Stages of Kālacakra*, Gyaltsab says no, this is a factually concordant awareness. It is unsuitable to meditate on your flesh and bone body as a divine body. Your ordinary body is not a buddha's body; you are a sentient being, not a buddha, and believing that you are a buddha would be a wrong consciousness. However, there is a buddha that you will become. You will be awakened in the form of, for example, Tārā. There is a person Tārā that you will become. If you now think, "I am Tārā," this I is not limited to the specific I of the present. It is the general I, not the specific I that you are now.[42] When you say, "When I was a little child," the I you're referring to is the general I that can refer to all the persons you have been in the past and will be in the future. Even though the I of you as a child and the I of today are not the same, there is the general I that is held in common. So when you imagine yourself as a deity and hold that identity, that is not a non-factually concordant consciousness.

After practicing properly in this way, meditators will have a clear visualization of the entire maṇḍala and all the deities in it. At first they can establish clarity on the visualization slowly, by remembering each part of the maṇḍala individually. As their concentration improves, they will reach a point where they can establish clarity on the maṇḍala and the deities in it—the supporting and supported maṇḍala—instantaneously. This appearance is so vivid that it is as if they can see and touch the deities. When they can hold this visualization single-pointedly for one-sixth of a day—that is, for four hours—they have realized the coarse generation stage.

Continuing to practice, they now imagine the entire maṇḍala and the deities in it in a tiny drop at the upper or lower opening of the central channel. At first they can do this gradually, in stages, and with more practice they can instantaneously have a clear vision of all this with stability and clarity. When they can maintain this for four hours, they have completed the refined generation stage.

Once generation-stage practitioners have firm meditative stability, they engage in various meditations to deepen meditative stability, such as emanating deities from their heart and dissolving them back into the heart. These meditations include visualizations of subtle hand implements or subtle syllables at the upper end of the central channel and subtle drops or syllables at its lower end. When they feel tired after engaging in these meditations, they refresh their minds through reciting mantra. There are several types of mantra recitation—for example, commitment mantra recitation, mantra recitation gathered up like a heap, and wrathful mantra recitation.

REFLECTION

1. What is the role of generation-stage practice?
2. How are serenity and insight generated and united in Highest Yoga Tantra?
3. What is the role of bliss in realizing emptiness? How is bliss generated in Highest Yoga Tantra and how does it differ from the bliss of ordinary sexual relations and the bliss of serenity?

Post-Meditation Time

Since tantric practitioners must lead a life that is never separated from the practice of method and wisdom, what they do in the break times between formal meditation sessions is very important. In this regard, they engage in various yogas, such as the yogas of sleeping, waking up, eating, washing, and blessing the speech. There are even practices to be done while relieving oneself.

The great tantric masters instruct that what you accomplish in meditation sessions should complement and reinforce the practice during the break time, and what you do in the break time should complement and reinforce the practice during meditation sessions. It is during the post-meditation period that practitioners can evaluate whether their practice during the meditation sessions has been successful or not. If they find that despite having meditated for years, their way of thinking, behaving, and living during post-meditation time remains unchanged, that is not a good sign. You don't take medicine to look at its color or taste it but to improve your health. After taking a medicine for a long time, if it does not affect your health positively, you should act to correct the situation. Similarly, whether your practices are elaborate or concise, they should bring about some transformation and change for the better. For this to occur you must maintain a good motivation, listen to the meditation instructions carefully, and put them into practice correctly in both meditation sessions and break times.

To sustain the understanding of emptiness they gained in meditation sessions on the generation and completion stages, in the time subsequent to meditative equipoise, yogis do analytical meditation on emptiness and contemplate bodhicitta, the six perfections, and so on.

In the times between meditation sessions, generation-stage practitioners regard all appearances as the deity and the maṇḍala, all sounds as mantra, and all thoughts as the deity's mind. Completion-stage practitioners regard all appearances as the manifestation of bliss and emptiness.

Meditation Sessions in the Completion Stage

The main practitioners of Highest Yoga Tantra in our world are human beings whose bodies comprise six substances, three from their mother and three from their father. In addition, these practitioners are properly prepared and qualified as described above. This is especially important to engage in the completion stage.

The definition of completion stage is a yoga in the continuum of a trainee that arises from causing the winds to enter, abide, and dissolve in the central channel by the power of meditation. The completion stage begins when a practitioner who has completed the refined generation stage by meditating on the entire maṇḍala in a subtle drop at the lower opening of the central channel can make the winds enter, abide, and dissolve in the central channel by the power of meditation. During the completion stage, practitioners cultivate the ability to control the various elements of the subtle body in order to make manifest the subtlest clear-light mind and use it to realize emptiness directly. They also develop the ability to use the subtle winds to produce a subtle illusory body.

There are many types of completion-stage practices, such as the yoga of *tummo* (inner heat), wind yoga, the yoga of the four joys, and so forth. Wind yoga makes use of the currents of wind in the body and includes techniques such as vase breathing, technically referred to as "vajra recitation."

In addition to having received the empowerment and meditation instructions from a qualified tantric master, keeping the tantric ethical restraints and commitments, and accomplishing the generation-stage practice, to engage in the completion-stage practices meditators must have a thorough understanding of the structure of the subtle body. This includes the stationary channels, the flowing winds, and the drops that reside in certain parts of the body. Based on correct knowledge of the physical structure of the body, when meditators focus on and penetrate certain vital points, they can withdraw and dissolve the coarser levels of wind and mind. This leads to manifesting the subtlest clear light, like that at death, and transforming it into the entity of the path—that is, into the wisdom realizing emptiness. This is the key to all higher realizations, and once meditators have this key, they can attain buddhahood through the path of Guhyasamāja by actualizing the illusory body, through the path of Kālacakra through generating an empty form, or through the rainbow body as explained in the *Magical Net Tantra* (*Māyājāla Tantra*) and the dzogchen texts, and so forth. These three are methods to actualize the form body of a buddha are unique to Tantrayāna.

Through these means, sharp-faculty yogis of Highest Yoga Tantra can attain full awakening in this very lifetime. Those with middle faculties—those who attain the example clear light in this life—can attain awakening in the bardo. Those of lower faculties will attain awakening in a future life, possibly after a series of lives. Practices such as the transference of consciousness (*saṃkrānti*, *'phowa*) are explained for these people. The accomplishments of all three levels of practitioners depend on their keeping the tantric ethical restraints and commitments purely, and sincerely purifying any transgressions.

8 | The Tantric Perspective of Body and Mind

Tantrayāna is also called Mantrayāna. *Man* refers to the mind, and *tra* means "to protect." Thus, Mantrayāna is a method to protect the mind from ordinary appearances and ordinary grasping as well as from the dangers of saṃsāra. The biggest danger of saṃsāra is its root, grasping inherent or true existence, and the antidote to this is the wisdom realizing emptiness. According to Mantrayāna, the source of saṃsāra is not only grasping true existence but also the wind that is its mount. Each of the eighty conceptions that obscure the mind has a wind that is its vehicle. When we remember an object of attachment, the wind makes the mind "go" to the object—that is, to cling to that object—and through clinging, polluted karma is created.

Because these winds are subtle, a coarse mind that realizes emptiness is not sufficient to eradicate true-grasping. By having the winds enter, abide, and dissolve in the central channel, innate bliss arises, and the primordial clear-light mind manifests. Practitioners use this blissful, extremely subtle mind to realize emptiness directly, and through this, they are able to eradicate true-grasping and the winds that are its mount. This is one of the unique and outstanding qualities of Highest Yoga Tantra.

To access this subtlest mind, a meditator must be able to make the winds enter, abide, and dissolve into the heart cakra. Although this is actually done on the completion stage, meditation on taking death, bardo, and rebirth into the path on the generation stage is an excellent preparation. Doing this meditation necessitates an understanding of the tantric view of body and mind and their relationship. But before we turn to this topic, let's review scientific and Buddhist perspectives on the body, brain, and their relationship to the mind.

The Tantric View of Body and Mind

I have enjoyed many discussions with scientists and have visited several of their laboratories. Scientific research on meditators is useful, though some proficient meditators in the Tibetan community do not wish to take part in it.[43] To remedy this, I encourage scientists to take up meditation and do research on their own internal states to see if they can identify the levels of consciousness and wind.

Buddhism views the body and mind as different things. The body is made of material substances and its functions can be measured by scientific instruments. Mind or consciousness is not physical in nature, so although some scientific instruments can measure some changes in the body that occur due to changes in the mind, they cannot measure the mind itself, which is in the nature of clarity and cognizance.

Scientists consider the brain a vital organ and study it in an attempt to understand the mind. Although Buddhist texts speak extensively about the mind, they make little mention of the brain. Nowadays we cannot help but wonder why that is. Although we do not know for sure why previous yogis did not speak about the brain and neurological system, one theory is that they chose not to discuss them because they were not directly related to the path to awakening. Transforming the mind is foremost for liberation and awakening, and physiological changes in the body do not necessarily affect the subtle levels of consciousness. Manipulating the subtle winds, on the other hand, directly influences the mind and enables access to subtler levels of consciousness. For this reason these are discussed in depth in scriptures.

Modern science investigates the neurons, synapses, and chemical and electrical interactions associated with the brain. Although these differ from the inner winds, I think they could possibly form a basis for common analysis and a way for scientists and Buddhists to work together to understand the relationship between the mind, the brain, and the inner winds.

Scientists have yet to determine whether consciousness occurs in response to stimulation in the brain or if consciousness is the cause for brain activity. Looking at it from a Buddhist viewpoint, if we focus on the winds (*vāyu* or *prāṇa*), channels (*nāḍī*), drops (*bindu*), and cakras (energy centers) in the body, we can say the body and mind mutually influence each other. Speaking in terms of the coarse body and mind, when emotions such as anger, rage, and jealousy arise in the mind, the winds become agitated, producing physiological changes. An imbalance of the inner winds ensues, and this produces emotional turbulence. The situation with the subtlest body and mind differs: in ordinary circumstances, the clear-light mind does not manifest while the brain is functioning; in fact, it can exist and function independent of the brain and the physical body.

What is the process by which the body and mind influence each other? In the second chapter of the *Commentary on (Dignāga's) "Compendium of Reliable Cognition,"* Dharmakīrti discusses how an internal state called "contact"—which is the coming together of the object, sense faculty, and mind—serves as the condition for the physical experiences of pain or pleasure. This experience becomes the object of the mental consciousness that in turn serves as the basis of mental happiness or unhappiness. This is the Sūtrayāna explanation of the causal relationship of the body and mind.

From the Tantrayāna viewpoint, the winds in the body are the medium through which cognitive processes and consciousness function. Physical processes—such as bodily sensations, brain chemistry, and the physical nervous system—affect the winds, which are the support of the minds' cognitions, feelings, and mental factors. The winds are the vehicle through which the changes at the physical level affect the mind and mental processes. Similarly, changes in our mental state—such as thoughts, conceptions, attitudes, emotions, and so forth—can affect our body. This process is again mediated by the winds. That is, our moods, emotions, attitudes, and thoughts affect the inner winds, which then affect the physical body—for example, by stimulating or dampening the adrenal system and influencing our physical health.

The fundamental innate clear-light mind is accompanied by the subtlest wind, which in Vajrayāna texts is said to be endowed with five-colored radiance. The subtle wind is connected with the internal elements of the body, which, in turn, are connected to the five coarse physical elements of earth, fire, water, air, and space. Thus, there is a relationship that begins with the fundamental innate clear-light mind, which is one nature with the subtlest wind. This gives rise to subtle winds, which influence the five internal elements of earth, water, fire, wind, and space that constitute our physical body. This could be the mechanism through which the mind and body influence each other.

Certain physical exercises done by yogis and yoginīs affect the flow of the winds and thus influence the mind. Concentrating on specific places in the body where the cakras are located likewise affects the winds, and thus the mind and emotions. Because of the interrelationship between body and mind, by the mind engaging in certain meditation techniques, the body's ability to produce heat and to breathe can be significantly affected.

On the other hand, many of the transformations that occur in the mind can also be understood in terms of the seeds and latencies of mental afflictions (wrong views, distorted conceptions, and disturbing emotions) and karma (the physical, verbal, and mental actions they motivate). These seeds and latencies are carried by the continuum of the mental consciousness—and ultimately by the mere I—and are produced by previous thoughts, emotions, feelings, and actions.

Sūtra and Tantra share a common explanation for the process of entering saṃsāra—the twelve links of dependent arising. Understanding this, practitioners seek the correct view of emptiness, since this realization of the ultimate nature cuts the root of our saṃsāra, self-grasping ignorance. Understanding the uncommon explanation in Mantrayāna of how we enter saṃsāra will stimulate us to learn about the subtlest mind and wind and how to dissolve the coarse winds and make manifest the fundamental innate clear-light mind. Once the subtlest mind has realized emptiness, it can eliminate all conceptual elaborations stemming from self-grasping ignorance.

Regarding the Tantric description of the body and levels of mind, Aku Sherab Gyatso (1803–75) in the *Sacred Words of Akṣobhya*, a commentary on the *Guhyasamāja Tantra*, clarifies:

1. The coarse body is our ordinary body composed of flesh, bones, blood, and so forth that is the ripening result of karma.
2. The subtle body is the abode (the channels), the moving (the winds), and the arranged (the red and white and drops, also called bodhicittas).
3. The extremely subtle body is the winds that are the mounts of the three empties (the white appearance, red increase, and black near-attainment).

4. The subtlest body is the wind that accompanies the fundamental innate clear-light mind.

Regarding the mind and its levels:

1. The coarse mind comprises the five sense consciousnesses and the mental consciousness when we are awake.
2. The subtle mind comprises the mental consciousnesses of sleep and dream.
3. The extremely subtle mind consists of the minds of the white appearance, red increase, and black near-attainment.
4. The subtlest mind is the fundamental innate clear-light mind.[44]

According to tantric physiology, the winds in the body are not moving air, they are vital energies that cause all movement by and within the body, such as breathing, the circulation of blood and other fluids, muscular movement, defecation, urination, and so on. Other winds are instrumental in the functioning of the six consciousnesses (the five sense consciousnesses and the conceptualizing mental consciousness). These consciousnesses could not operate without the winds to provide a medium for their "movement." For this reason, the winds are described as mounts on which the mind "rides," like a rider on a horse.

The winds may be coarse or subtle. The coarse winds operate in the ordinary waking state, whereas the subtle winds operate during sleep, fainting, sneezing, orgasm, and dying. The subtlest wind also serves as the mount of subtlest awareness, the innate clear-light mind.

Like the winds, consciousnesses can be coarse or subtle; the five sense consciousnesses are coarse awarenesses that ride on the coarse winds. The subtlest mind is the fundamental innate mind of clear light, which is one nature with the subtlest wind. Their being one nature means the innate clear-light mind and the subtlest wind exist together and are inseparable. They are one nature and different isolates; they exist together but are nominally different.

The clear-light mind functions to cognize its object,[45] and its wind functions to move the clear-light mind. The clear-light mind is not manifest during the ordinary waking state. In the case of an ordinary person, it manifests naturally only at the time of death, sleep, fainting, sneezing, and orgasm. During the process of dying, our sense consciousnesses and coarse mental consciousnesses gradually dissolve into the clear-light mind, while the coarse winds dissolve into the subtlest wind. When the dissolution of both is complete, the clear-light mind manifests. Thereafter, the clear-light mind and the subtlest wind leave the physical body, give way to the slightly coarser body and mind of the bardo, and then go on to the next life, in which the coarse consciousnesses and winds reappear and operate again.

The Body

The main practitioners of Highest Yoga Tantra in our world are human beings whose bodies comprise six substances, three from their mother and three from their father. In addition, these practitioners are properly prepared and qualified as described above. Whereas the Sūtrayāna approach primarily speaks of the coarse mind and coarse body that scientists also study, the Tantrayāna describes subtle states of mind and their relationship to the subtle body consisting of channels, cakras, winds, and drops. These channels, cakras, winds, and drops cannot be seen by our eyes and are not found when a body is dissected. Tantras describe how to manipulate these aspects of the body to make manifest the subtlest mind and use it to gain deep and stable Dharma realizations.

The human body has three main *channels*: the central (*suṣumṇā nāḍī*), right (*piṅgalā nāḍī*), and left (*iḍā nāḍī*) channels. The central channel runs from the mid-brow to the crown, where it curves and goes down the center of the body in front of the spine, ending at the tip of the sexual organ. The right and left channels are on their respective sides of the central channel, running parallel to it and extending from the nostrils to the crown and then downward, hooking into the central channel about four fingerwidths below the navel. The two side channels encircle the central channel at the cakras, preventing the winds from entering the central channel. Many smaller channels branch out from the three main channels, and even smaller channels branch out from them. According to tantric texts, there are 72,000 such channels in the human body.

A series of *cakras* exist at various points along the central channel. The five main cakras are (1) crown cakra with thirty-two petals, (2) throat cakra with sixteen petals, (3) heart cakra with eight petals, (4) navel cakra with sixty-four petals, and (5) secret cakra at the base of the spine with thirty-two petals. There are also cakras at the forehead and at the tip of the sexual organ.

There are ten flowing *winds*—five major and five minor—that run through the system of channels. The coarser winds govern bodily functions such as digestion and movement. The ten winds are the life-supporting wind, equalizing wind, upward-moving wind, all-pervasive wind, nāga wind, turtle wind, chameleon wind, Devadatta wind, wealth wind, and the downward-voiding wind. Other winds are the mounts on which the various types of consciousnesses ride. Some of these facilitate perception by our five physical senses. There are also subtler winds that are associated with subtler levels of mind.

The *drops* are white and red elements in the channels or particular cakras of all human bodies. The indestructible drop at the heart is the union of the red and white drops received at the time of conception from our mother and father, respectively. Further red and white drops evolve from the indestructible drop and are in channels throughout the body. The white drop is more prominent at the top of the head, the red drop at the navel cakra just below the physical navel. The drops can be neither seen by the eye nor touched by the hand.

There are two indestructible drops at the heart. One is the subtlest wind-mind that is eternal. The continuum of this drop goes until full awakening. The other is a subtle substance that endures until the person dies. It is outside the eternal drop and covers it. At the time of ordinary death, all the winds gather at the indestructible drop. The white drop located at the crown cakra and the red drop at the navel cakra also gather there. The outer indestructible drop opens and releases the inner one. This is the moment of death.

Meditation on subtle drops at the upper and lower tips of the central channel draws the winds into the central channel, which causes the drops to melt. For yogis, the drops descending and ascending in the central channel bring a mind of great bliss, which is then used to meditate on emptiness. Meditation on *tummo* (inner fire) is one meditation that causes the drops to melt.

The *Kālacakra Tantra* refers to four types of drops: (1) the drop between the eyebrows, which is manifest during the waking period, (2) the drop at the throat, which is manifest during the dream state, (3) the drop at the heart, which is manifest at the time of deep sleep, and (4) the drop at the navel, which is manifest at the fourth stage (death).

The winds, channels, and cakras are described differently in various contexts. Tibetan medical texts differ from tantric texts. Even within tantric systems, the presentations of the winds and how they dissolve at the time of death differ somewhat in Kālacakra and Guhyasamāja systems. The structure of the system of channels and cakras also varies in some tantras of the Old Translation school and New Translation school. These variations accord with differences in the bodies of practitioners.

Areas of commonality between Buddhism and science interest me.[46] In addition to the correlation of space particles with physics, the tantric description of subtle channels, winds, and drops in the body may be related to neuroscience and to the immune system. The four drops spoken of in the *Kālacakra Tantra* may have correlations with certain chemicals in the brain or with hormones. Their strength or weakness may also affect the immune system and the body's ability to prevent and counteract disease. However, we must not jump to quick conclusions or make artificial analogies. More research, conducted by both scientists and skilled meditators, is needed.[47]

The Mind

Sūtras and tantras both speak of clear light, but the meaning in each differs. In the sūtras, clear light refers to emptiness, the lack of inherent existence, which is a permanent phenomenon and a nonaffirming negative. In texts such as Maitreya's *Sublime Continuum*, clear light refers to the clear and cognizant nature of all consciousnesses. The unique meaning of clear light in the tantras is the subtlest mind (T. *shin tu phra ba'i sems*). This mind may be referred to as "the auspiciousness that resides in the heart of all sentient beings," because saṃsāra and nirvāṇa both depend on this subtlest clear-light mind. The coarser levels of mind and the elements such as earth that form the bodies of sentient beings arise from their clear-light minds.

In *Completing the Five Stages in a Single Sitting* (*Rim lnga gdan rdzogs kyi dmar khrid*), Tsongkhapa explains the coarse, subtle, and subtlest levels of mind from the Tantric perspective. This division of mind into various levels is not done in terms of the basic entity of mind—its clarity (luminosity) and cognizance. Rather, it is made in terms of the wind on which each mind rides. Coarse minds arise through interaction with the brain, sense faculties, and coarse winds. Subtle levels of mind depend on subtle winds.

The subtle mind includes the eighty indicative conceptions and the afflictions. The subtlest wind and the subtlest mind of clear light that depends on it are inseparable. One cannot exist without the other one simultaneously existing. From the viewpoint of its function, this unity is called "subtlest body"; from the viewpoint of its clarity and cognizance, it is called "subtlest mind." The inseparable subtlest wind-mind is the ultimate basis of designation of the person. It is also the basis of both saṃsāra and nirvāṇa. Here we see that the basis for becoming a buddha is already in us; it simply needs to be purified and developed.

Each level of mind has winds that are its mount. Although they are called "winds," these are not like the external wind that blows through the trees. Rather, they are a type of energy that courses through the body and connects the mind to the physical body.

As mentioned above, the winds influence the mind. When our winds are unbalanced, we feel stressed or anxious; when they are balanced, the mind is calmer. The mind also influences the winds. An intention in the mind affects the winds, which then cause the body to act and speech to occur, and thus physical and verbal actions come about.

The coarse and subtle winds function differently. From the point of view of going and coming, the name "wind" is given. From the point of view of apprehending an object, the name "mind" is given. In the case of coarse consciousnesses such as our sense consciousnesses, the coarse winds accompany the consciousnesses and enable the perception of objects to occur. These winds "move" the mind to the object. That is, they energize the mind, enabling it to perceive the object. Sometimes it is said that the winds "go" to the objects we apprehend. The wind and the mind don't literally leave the body and go to the external object. Rather, "go" indicates that the wind and mind are focused on that object. It is analogous to using binoculars to see something far away. The binoculars stay here; they don't go to where the object is. Similarly, the coarse winds and minds of our visual and auditory consciousnesses don't go to the external location of their objects.

In āryas' meditative equipoise on emptiness, there is no appearance of duality, so at that time the wind is not "moving" the mind toward its object.

Here the wind is the cooperative condition for the next moment of the mind directly realizing emptiness.

Mental Consciousness

The mental consciousness itself has various levels. The mind planning what we will do today is coarser than the mind that is dreaming, and that in turn is coarser than the mind that is in deep sleep. Levels of single-pointed concentration developed through the methods described in sūtras are subtler than our everyday mind, while some of them are coarser than the mind directly realizing emptiness according to Sūtrayāna. This mind, in turn, is coarser than the fundamental innate mind of clear-light.[48]

From the viewpoint of the Guhyasamāja system, the subtlest level of consciousness consists of the four "empties." These empties do not refer to the emptiness of inherent existence. They are levels of consciousness that are empty or devoid of the coarser wind that serves as the mount of the coarser levels of mind that precede it. The four empties are called "empty," "great empty," "very empty," and "all empty," referring respectively to the vivid white appearance, the red increase, the black near-attainment, and the all-empty clear light that arises when all the winds have dissolved in the central channel. Although the term "subtlest mind" pertains to all four empties, it especially refers to the all-empty clear light that is the subtlest mind.

When the eighty indicative conceptions that are subtle levels of conceptuality cease, the four empties arise sequentially, the latter ones being subtler than the earlier ones. The subtlest is the all empty, which is so-called because all the previous levels of subtle consciousness have ceased. It is also called the fundamental innate clear-light mind. This mind is innate in that it abides perpetually, whereas all other levels of mind are adventitious because they are linked to the physical body with its sensory faculties and coarser winds. When the physical body and the coarser winds do not function, neither can these adventitious conceptions.

It is difficult to ascertain the consciousnesses of the four empties in our experience. Doing so requires firm concentration and yogic meditation. Sometimes we may have a glimpse of these minds during a severe illness or accident when the coarser consciousnesses temporarily dissolve. It is said that while falling asleep, yawning, sneezing, fainting, or experiencing orgasm, we may also be able to have a brief experience of these subtler minds. They also appear during the process of dying, but in general only an experienced meditator can recognize them at that time.

In ordinary sentient beings, these subtler states of wind-mind arise and cease naturally, without any spiritual significance. By practicing special yogic methods on the path, the subtlest levels of wind-mind can be made manifest and then transformed into the actual clear light and pure illusory body—two realizations of the completion stage. When the union of the actual clear light and pure illusory body is attained, the result—the truth body and form bodies of a buddha—are actualized.

Some dzogchen and mahāmudrā texts refer to the clear-light mind as the ultimate reality. Using terminology in this way makes it seem that a person actually manifests the ultimate reality during the death process. However, for ordinary beings this is not the case. There can be two kinds of ultimate reality: ultimate reality in the context of the subject—the clear-light mind—and in the context of the object—the clear light that is emptiness. The latter is the actual ultimate reality. This exposition is found in the *Guhyasamāja Tantra*.

Knowing an Object

Do all consciousnesses know an object? The answer varies according to the presentation. The initial presentation of mind that we learn usually comes from the mind and awareness texts (T. *blo rig*) and accords with the Sautrāntika view of the mind. Gen Lobsang Gyatso, the former principal of the Institute of Buddhist Dialectics, wrote a mind and awareness text from the Prāsaṅgika viewpoint. In both the Sautrāntika and Prāsaṅgika systems, the mind is defined as that which is clear and cognizant (T. *gsal zhing rig pa*). "Clear" refers to assuming the aspect of the object or being generated in the aspect of the object, and "cognizant" means to experience or engage with the object. Here we are speaking of the general meaning of "clear and cognizant," not of the clear-light mind of tantra.

What does it mean, then, to speak of a nonconceptual mind that has no object, or of a consciousness that does "not realize anything"? It is said that "not realizing anything is to realize the true nature," and dzogchen speaks of "setting the mind vividly." Perhaps, in these cases, the quality of being cognizant or knowing could be spoken of in terms of the potential or capacity to know the object. However, considering that the word "mind" (*vijñāna*, T. *shes pa*) means "to know," that presupposes the mind knowing something. How do we reconcile the mind being something that knows an object with these dzogchen practices that speak of a mind that seems not to engage or realize anything? Are there consciousnesses that have no object?

From the Prāsaṅgika viewpoint, every mind, be it correct or erroneous, is said to be a direct reliable cognizer with respect to its own appearing object. That is, it is reliable with respect to its own experience. It notices and can induce a memory of its appearing object.[49] Seen from this perspective, every consciousness must have an object, and there cannot be a consciousness that has no object. Still, although there could be minds without an engaged object (*pravṛtti-viṣaya*)—the object with which the mind actually engages—there could not be a mind without an appearing object. So the fact that after meditating in a nonconceptual state a person can recall that experience indicates that there was some awareness of it. The question is whether that is the engaged object of that mind.

How does this pertain to the fundamental innate clear-light mind? It's difficult to attribute an active cognizant component to that mind. We can speak of it more as a capacity or potential to know, because when our coarse consciousnesses are functioning, the fundamental innate clear-light mind is dormant and does not apprehend an object. Only when the coarse consciousnesses have dissolved—that is, they have ceased to function—can this subtlest mind manifest and apprehend objects. In the absorption process, the fundamental innate clear-light mind arises after the mind of black near-attainment, which has two phases: the first phase has mindfulness, while the second does not. The second phase is similar to being unconscious in that the person has no mindfulness and later is unable to recall that experience. In dzogchen, there is the notion of "innate mindfulness" (T. *lhan cig skyes pa'i dran pa*),[50] which is said to be present and inseparable from the experience of clear light. It is a quality of mind that has a reflexive quality, so that that mind realizes its own nature.

The fundamental innate clear-light mind may arise in two ways. The *first is a natural process* in an ordinary being and occurs after the coarse winds and the consciousnesses they support dissolve. When the clear light arises in this way, it has no quality of knowing. We can only speak of its capacity to know. Alternatively, some people say it has the quality of knowing, but the knowing is so weak that the person cannot recall what was known. In either case, an ordinary person is not aware that the fundamental innate clear-light mind is manifest at that time.

The *second is through yogic practices* found in Vajrayāna, in which the coarse winds and minds are deliberately dissolved. As the dissolution occurs, the mind becomes increasingly subtle until the fundamental innate clear-light mind becomes manifest. Completely free from the clutter of the coarse afflictive mental states, this subtlest mind of clear light is luminous[51] and can clearly know and ascertain an object—in this case the emptiness of inherent existence.

While analytical meditation is essential when meditating with the coarser levels of mind, in the completion stage of the Highest Yoga Tantra it is discouraged because it has the adverse effect of obstructing the dissolution of the winds and thus interferes with the ceasing of the coarse consciousnesses and the arising of the luminous fundamental innate clear-light mind. In Sūtrayāna, analytical meditation is done to intensify the experience of emptiness, making it clearer and more spontaneous, whereas in Tantrayāna the same purpose is accomplished to an even greater extent by using stabilizing meditation to dissolve the coarser winds. Thus, in Highest Yoga Tantra, the vibrant clarity of the mind is brought about by stabilizing meditation, which facilitates the absorption of the winds and thus the arising of the fundamental innate clear-light mind.[52]

Supersensory Perception and Karmic Winds

Due to the role winds play in the perception of sights, sounds, odors, and so forth, supersensory perception of the five senses can be developed by training the winds through wind yoga. Interestingly, according to Abhidharma texts and the Pāramitāyāna perspective, only the visual and auditory consciousnesses can experience supersensory perception because direct contact with the object is not necessary for ordinary seeing and hearing. Supersensory perception through the olfactory, gustatory, and tactile senses cannot be developed, because to perceive the object, the nose, tongue, and body faculties must directly contact the object. However, through the practice of wind yoga in Highest Yoga Tantra, the winds can be controlled and made sufficiently powerful to contact smells, tastes, and tactile objects so that supersensory perception of their respective objects can occur. The winds close the gap between the mind and its object.

The *Kālacakra Tantra* discusses "karmic winds"—winds that operate when various mental states arise in us. Their power can provoke anger or other destructive emotions to arise. Since the winds and mind are intricately related, purification of the winds is done in tantric practice to reduce and eventually eliminate defilements from the subtlest wind-mind.

Death, Bardo, and Rebirth

Highest Yoga Tantra contains a detailed description of the minds and winds during death, bardo, and rebirth.[53] It also presents a way of taking these natural events into the path to awakening.

In a natural death, the dying process occurs in eight stages, during which several events gradually occur. In the case of a sudden death due to an accident, these eight events happen very quickly. In the first four stages, the body becomes weaker and gradually loses its ability to support consciousness. At this time, the earth, water, fire, and wind elements successively lose their strength, and the coarse winds gradually dissolve. As a result, the five sense consciousnesses—visual, auditory, olfactory, gustatory, and tactile—successively dissolve and lose their ability to function, and the dying person becomes less involved with the five sense objects of the external world—sights, sounds, smells, tastes, and tactile objects. Each of the basic wisdoms an individual has also sequentially dissolve.

As each of the elements loses its strength, an outer sign noticeable by other people occurs. In addition, the person experiences an internal vision: first a mirage-like vision, then a vision of being enveloped in incense smoke, a vision like sparks or fireflies in dark space, and a vision of the glow of a light that is about to go out. After that, the breath stops, the coarse consciousnesses have dissolved, and the karmic links between the coarse consciousnesses and the physical body are severed. The physical body can no longer function as a support for the coarse levels of mind, and clinically speaking, the person is dead.

However, from the view of tantric Buddhism, the subtle mind is still conjoined with the body, and the body will not begin to decompose until that mind has departed. After the breath has stopped, the extremely subtle minds—the white appearance, red increase, and black near-attainment—successively arise. These subtle consciousnesses are associated with eighty indicative conceptions that cease as the white appearance occurs. Although all eighty conceptions dissolve at this time, thirty-three conceptions are associated with the white appearance, forty with the red increase appearance, and seven with the black near-attainment appearance. These eighty conceptions are called "indicative conceptions" because they indicate various levels of the wind. They differ in the force of the winds that are associated with them; for example, emotions such as strong desire and aversion depend on the more forceful winds of the white appearance. The indicative conceptions associated with the black near-attainment are more neutral states. The eighty conceptions cease when the winds that support them dissolve. That gives rise to the subtler minds of the white appearance, red increase, and black near-attainment.

After the four elements have dissolved, the white bodhicitta (drop) received from the father at the time of conception descends from the crown of the head to the heart, and the person experiences the white-appearance consciousness. Then the red bodhicitta (drop) received at the time of conception from the mother rises from the navel cakra to the heart, and the person experiences the red-increase consciousness. When the two drops join at the heart and the consciousness is inside, there is the experience of the black near-attainment consciousness. This has two phases: initially the mind is conscious, then it goes into an unconscious phase. The longer the unconscious phase, the more vivid is the clear light that follows.

The dissolution or absorption of the minds of white appearance, red increase, and black near-attainment means that those consciousnesses no longer manifest and have become latent. They don't dissolve one into the other, rather one dissolves and the next one arises: the mind of white appearance ceases and the mind of red increase appears, and so on. At the end of the dissolution process, all the winds gather at the indestructible drop inside the central channel at the heart.

The coarse indestructible drop was formed at the time of conception from the red and white substances—the blood (egg) and sperm—from our mother and father, respectively. It is indestructible until the time of death. Inside it is the indestructible drop that is the subtlest wind-mind.[54] All winds ultimately dissolve into the indestructible drop at the time of death. At this time the clear light of death—the subtlest mind—dawns. This is the actual moment of death. When the consciousness leaves the coarse body, signs may appear, such as a drop of blood appearing from the nose or a white substance coming from the end of the sexual organ.

The charts below detail these eight stages, showing the factor dissolving, the external sign, and the internal sign for each of the first four stages, and the factor dissolving, the cause of the vision, and the internal vision for each of the last four stages.

STAGE 1

FACTOR DISSOLVING	EXTERNAL SIGN	INTERNAL VISION
Earth element (water element becomes prominent)	Body becomes thin, limbs lose their power, body feels heavy as if it were sinking into the earth. Person may grab at something as if they were falling.	Trembling silver-blue mirage in the distance, feeling like one's whole existence is water
Form aggregate	Body loses power, limbs shrink	
Basic mirror-like wisdom that clearly perceives many objects at the same time	Unclear and darkening sight	
Eye faculty	Cannot control or move eyes, cannot open or close eyes, movement of eyeballs ceases, cannot clearly recognize people or things	
Form source: objects of sight—colors and shapes—disintegrate	Body radiance and color fade, cheeks become sunken, body becomes hollow looking	

STAGE 2

FACTOR DISSOLVING	EXTERNAL SIGN	INTERNAL VISION
Water element (fire element becomes prominent)	Bodily fluids—saliva, urine, blood, perspiration, semen—dry up. Throat and lips are dry, cannot swallow or take food.	Smoke filling space, feel there is fire and heat around
Feeling aggregate	Body consciousness no longer experiences pleasure, pain, or neutral feelings.	
Basic wisdom of equality that is mindful of pleasurable, painful, and neutral feelings	No longer experience pleasurable, painful, or neutral mental feelings	
Ear faculty	Hearing of external sounds ceases.	
Sound source (various types of sounds)	Cannot hear subtle humming in ears	

STAGE 3

FACTOR DISSOLVING	EXTERNAL SIGN	INTERNAL VISION
Fire element (air element becomes prominent)	Cannot digest food, body becomes cold as bodily heat disappears.	Many sparks or fireflies in space
Discrimination aggregate	Are not aware of things around oneself, cannot recognize the surrounding people or discern the purpose of what they say	
Basic wisdom of discrimination that knows names, purposes, and distinguishes among things, and that identifies and remembers friends and relatives	Cannot remember the names of or recognize people	
Nose faculty	Breathing in is more difficult and weaker; breathing out is longer and stronger.	
Odor source (various types of smells)	Cannot smell	

STAGE 4

FACTOR DISSOLVING	EXTERNAL SIGN	INTERNAL VISION
Air element	Breath stops, the ten internal winds dissolve into the heart cakra.	A very dim light about to go out, like a faint light in the bottom of a well
Aggregate of miscellaneous factors	The body cannot move.	
Basic wisdom of accomplishment that knows external activities, purposes, and so forth	Are not aware of activities, purposes, and surrounding people; no sense of the necessity and purpose of external plans and work	
Tongue faculty	Tongue thickens and contracts, its root becomes blue.	
Taste source (various tastes)	Cannot taste anything	
Tactile faculty	Tactile faculty ceases to function.	
Tactile source	Cannot experience smooth and rough, soft and hard, hunger or thirst	

At this point, a doctor would pronounce the person dead because they show no signs of life. From a tantric viewpoint, the person's lack of responsiveness is due to the dissolution of the coarse levels of consciousness that have ceased to function.

It is important for the dying person to generate a virtuous state of mind before the coarse consciousness has completely dissolved, because their mental state at that time influences the karma that will ripen and influence their next birth.

STAGE 5

FACTOR DISSOLVING	CAUSE OF VISION	INTERNAL VISION
80 indicative conceptions	Winds in the body enter the right and left channels. The winds above the heart open the crown cakra and enter the central channel at the top of the head, releasing the white seed received from the father at the time of conception. It goes down to the heart cakra.	Clear vacuity filled with white light, like a clear autumn sky full of bright moonlight. This is the mind of white appearance.

STAGE 6

FACTOR DISSOLVING	CAUSE OF VISION	INTERNAL VISION
Mind of white appearance	Winds in right and left channels below the heart enter the central channel at the secret cakra. They rise, opening the navel cakra and releasing the red seed received from the mother, which was at the navel cakra. It flows upward to the heart cakra.	Clear vacuity filled with red light, like a copper-red reflection in the sky when the sun is about to set. This is the mind of red increase.

STAGE 7

FACTOR DISSOLVING	CAUSE OF VISION	INTERNAL VISION
Mind of red increase	Upper and lower winds go to the heart cakra and enter the coarse indestructible drop at the heart.	At first, vacuity filled with darkness; then not mindful of any object, as if in an unconscious swoon. This is the mind of black near-attainment.

STAGE 8

FACTOR DISSOLVING	CAUSE OF VISION	INTERNAL VISION
Mind of black near-attainment	All winds dissolve into the indestructible drop at the heart.	Clear vacuity free from white, red, and black visions. Completely clear space, like sky of an autumn dawn. This is the mind of clear light of death.

In Highest Yoga Tantra, meditators train to recognize the eight visions first by imagining them in the generation stage and then by actually dissolving the winds in the completion stage. They can recognize the eight visions while dying and meditate on emptiness throughout the dissolution process, especially while the clear light of death is manifest. For such meditators, the clear light of death (the "mother clear light") and the clear light that realizes emptiness (the "child clear light") are united. However, people who have not trained to recognize the visions, who did not accumulate great merit, and who do have the strong aspiration to recognize the eight visions are unable to recognize them while they are dying. The opportunity to know emptiness with the innate clear-light mind slips by them.

In his commentary on the *Kālacakra Tantra*, Khedrup Norsang Gyatso (1423–1513) said that during the death process, when one awakens the clear light of death, emptiness appears because all the other visions have ceased. My senior tutor, Kyabje Ling Rinpoche, said that Gyuto Tantric College maintains that when one experiences the clear-light mind at death, there is the appearance of emptiness, but ordinary beings do not ascertain it. However, other scholars assert that even at the point of death, what appears to the ordinary person's clear-light mind is not the emptiness of inherent existence.

If we accept that emptiness can appear to the clear light of death, then when someone who has had some experience of emptiness reaches the early part of the black near-attainment when memory is still present, they should remember the emptiness of inherent existence. Then, after they pass through the second part of the black near-attainment, which is an "unconscious" state, they arrive at the clear light of death, and due to that intention to remember emptiness, they will remember emptiness and remain absorbed in emptiness—a profound realization. At this time they will engage in stabilizing meditation without analysis.

The moment the subtlest wind-mind is manifest is the actual moment of death. After that, the clear light of death ceases and the other seven stages occur in reverse order—going from clear light to black near-attainment, to red increase, and so forth up to the mirage-like vision—as the consciousness takes a bardo body. The bardo being exists until the time of birth in a suitable body in one of the six realms (except the formless god realm). Just before taking rebirth in another coarse physical body, the bardo being again experiences the eight visions ending in clear light. After again going through reverse process out of the clear light, rebirth into the new body is complete. In the case of a human being, this occurs at the time of conception.

Taking Death, Bardo, and Rebirth into the Path to the Three Buddha Bodies

The best method to dispel defilements and cultivate excellent qualities is to apply our coarse, subtle, and subtlest bodies and minds to Dharma practice. In this way we skillfully use what we already have—this human body composed of six elements—to attain awakening.

Death, bardo, and rebirth characterize our existence as sentient beings; we have beginninglessly and repeatedly experienced these three. Tantra contains a skillful method in which death, bardo, and rebirth are correlated with the three bodies (*kāya*) of a buddha: the truth body, enjoyment body, and emanation body. In their tantric writings, Nāgārjuna and Āryadeva have described unique techniques whereby instead of helplessly going through these three experiences, we can gain control of them and use them to attain the three buddha bodies. This can occur due to features shared in common between these three ordinary experiences and the three buddha bodies.

The truth body consists of a buddha's wisdom truth body (the omniscient mind) and the nature truth body (true cessations in which all defilements have been forever eliminated, and the emptiness of inherent existence of this mind). Death is similar to the truth body: all coarser consciousnesses have dissolved, the subtlest clear light mind has manifested, and the appearance of coarser phenomena has vanished into emptiness.

The enjoyment body is the subtle form in which a buddha appears to ārya bodhisattvas in the pure land. The enjoyment body arises from the truth body and is the link between a buddha's mind and emanation bodies in which a buddha teaches in the world. The bardo body is similar to the enjoyment body. From the clear light of death, a form made of subtle wind that is together with the subtle mind arises in the bardo. It is the link between the subtlest wind-mind of death and the coarse body and mind of rebirth into a physical body.

The emanation body is a coarser appearance, for example the historical Śākyamuni Buddha, in which a buddha manifests in a form to communicate with and guide ordinary sentient beings. A buddha may make many emanation bodies, according to the needs of various sentient beings. An emanation body arises from the subtler enjoyment body just as the coarser state of rebirth follows the subtler bardo state.

In Highest Yoga Tantra, meditation on taking death into the path to the truth body transforms ordinary death so that it becomes conducive for the attainment of a buddha's truth body. On the generation stage, practitioners imagine going through the eight absorptions of the death process and making manifest the subtlest clear light. At this point, they imagine employing the clear-light mind to meditate on emptiness as the path to the truth body. During the completion stage, practitioners' experience is more profound because the winds actually dissolve into the central channel at the heart and come closer to making manifest the innate clear-light mind. They meditate on emptiness with the subtlest wind-mind and attain the example or actual clear light.

To take the bardo into the path to the enjoyment body, upon arising from meditative equipoise on emptiness after death, generation-stage practitioners imagine assuming a subtle body—often in the form of a syllable or implement. This is similar to an ordinary person assuming a subtle bardo body after death. During the completion stage, a practitioner takes the bardo into the path to the enjoyment body by using the subtle winds to generate an impure and then a pure illusory body.

Just as an ordinary person leaves the bardo and takes rebirth into the coarse body of a new life, to take rebirth into the path to the emanation body, generation-stage practitioners imagine arising as the full form of the deity. On the completion stage, their illusory body reenters the coarse physical form, taking birth into an impure and then a pure emanation body.

In brief, at the time of death, meditators who are well trained will be able to recognize the signs of death and put them to good use, maintaining their awareness without being overwhelmed by the various sensations and visions that appear to the mind. Ordinary people may remain in the clear light of death for up to three days, but some experienced meditators can abide in it for a week or more. Although the person may externally appear to be dead—the breath, heart, and brain waves have stopped—the body does not decompose, indicating that they are meditating in the innate clear light. My senior tutor, Kyabje Ling Rinpoche meditated in the clear light for thirteen days after clinical death.

After the clear light, yogis at an advanced level of the completion stage will arise in the illusory body instead of the bardo and continue to practice until attaining full awakening, while others will make their illusory body reenter their coarse body.

BASIS	GENERATION-STAGE PATH	COMPLETION-STAGE PATH	RESULT
Death	Meditate on emptiness.	Example clear light and actual clear light	Truth body
Bardo	Imagine arising as a shaft of light, seed syllable, or hand implement.	Impure and pure illusory bodies	Enjoyment body
Rebirth	Imagine arising as the deity.	Illusory body reenters the body. At the end of the path, the wind-mind manifests as a deity.	Emanation body

Nyingma texts describe the process of taking death, bardo, and rebirth into the path to the three buddha bodies differently. Instead of referring to meditation on the three bodies, they speak of three concentrations: the concentration of suchness, the concentration of arising appearances, and the causal concentration. These three concentrations are equivalent to the generation-stage practices explained in Highest Yoga Tantra: (1) the concentration of the initial application involves a condensed deity practice—

for example, meditating only on the central deity instead of the complete maṇḍala; (2) the concentration of the supreme conqueror maṇḍala involves meditation on the entire maṇḍala and its deities; and (3) the concentration of the supreme conqueror activities includes visualizing the activities of the deities.

Purifying the Basis of Purification

From a tantric viewpoint, what is the basis to be purified? In meditation, we can see that all our wandering in saṃsāra—all the duḥkha of rebirth in the three lower realms and in the upper realms as well—is due to being under the power of afflictions and karma. All of this arises through our winds and minds, which in tantra are the bases to be purified to stop wandering in saṃsāra. Death, bardo, and rebirth under the power of afflictions and karma will happen to all ordinary beings, so these also need to be purified.

How does death come about? It occurs when the coarser winds are no longer able to function and support the mind. First, the coarse winds of the sense consciousnesses start to collect and dissolve, the body gets weaker, and the sense consciousnesses lose their ability to perceive objects. Only the subtler winds and minds remain. When all the winds dissolve into the indestructible drop at the heart—which is the subtlest wind-mind of the actual indestructible drop—and the substance indestructible drop opens, death occurs and the subtlest wind-mind leaves the coarse body.

When entering the bardo, the reverse sequence of the dissolution of the winds occurs. The arising of the black near-attainment marks the beginning of the bardo. The subtle wind-mind becomes coarser as the black near-attainment, red increase, and then white appearance arise in reverse order. The subtlest wind becomes the substantial cause for the bardo body and the subtlest consciousness is its cooperative condition.

When the bardo being arises from the subtlest wind and mind due to the disturbance of afflictions and karma, a saṃsāric rebirth will occur. In this way, under the influence of afflictions and karma and due to the dissolution and reappearance of the levels of winds and consciousness, saṃsāra continues.

The paths that can eliminate or purify ordinary death, bardo, and rebirth under the force of afflictions and karma are the paths of the completion stage, principally the paths of the example and actual clear light, the impure and pure illusory bodies, and the impure and pure emanation bodies. To attain those levels of realization, it is necessary to first practice the common path, receive empowerment, keep the tantric ethical restraints and commitments, complete the meditations on the generation stage, and enter the completion stage.

REFLECTION

1. What is the tantric description of the body? Of the mind?
2. Describe the death process in terms of the absorptions of elements and winds and the visions that appear to the dying person.
3. How are important levels of the completion stage similar to death, bardo, and rebirth? How are these similar to a buddha's three resultant bodies?
4. How are the above sets of three analogous to the states of sleep, dream, and waking?

Near-Death Experiences and the Illusory Body

Attaining an illusory body is an important completion-stage practice. On high levels of training in the illusory body, yogis practice separating the illusory body from the coarse body and then having it reenter the coarse body.

Aside from the illusory-body practice and other profound trainings on the completion stage, I do not believe it is possible to separate the subtlest body from the coarse body and later bring it back. Once people have reached the bardo, they cannot come back into their present body, although it could be possible to resuscitate them during the dying process while the various dissolutions are occurring. The four later signs—the vivid white appearance, red increase, black near-attainment, and clear light—occur after the breath has stopped. Health-care professionals say that someone may be resuscitated within a half an hour after breathing has stopped. But once the clear-light mind has left the body and entered the bardo, resuscitation is virtually impossible.

How, then, do we account for near-death experiences? For example, a person arises from a coma and reports the procedures the doctors performed while he was unconscious. He may have seen his body on the operating table as he looked down at it from the ceiling or seen a tunnel with relatives who tell him to return to his life. This is compelling, no doubt. Such events could be an instance of suprasensory awareness or an out-of-body experience that resembles a coarse dream body. However, I do not think the extremely subtle wind-mind leaves the body, adopts the body and mind of a bardo being, and then reenters the body of the previous person who becomes conscious again. The bardo body is connected to the body of the future life, not the body of the life that ended.

Similarly, when a person experiences visions and so forth as part of a near-death experience, these are not necessarily the eight signs that occur at death. These could be similitudes of the eight signs that occur as coarse winds dissolve, just as similitudes occur when falling asleep and during orgasm. But unless one can control the elements through meditation, returning from the clear light of death itself is extremely difficult.

The first step of the completion stage in the Guhyasamāja practice is isolated body. Here practitioners practice dissolving the winds into the central channel. As the winds and elements dissolve, the eight signs occur. While a practitioner is becoming familiar with this practice there is no certainty as to the order of the visions or their intensity. Sometimes one is stronger, another time another is. As a practitioner becomes more proficient in the practice, the order of the visions becomes more certain.

The practice of dissolving the winds in the central channel and then into the indestructible drop at the heart occurs at the end of the stage of isolated mind and brings the example clear light. Only at this time does one experience the actual dissolution of the elements and the eight visions exactly as during the death process. At that point the six knots at the heart cakra loosen and do not tighten again. Arising from the final example clear light, practitioners assume an impure illusory body. With such bodies, yogis can engage in supernormal feats such as flying in space or passing through walls. Because the dissolution of the winds has been attained through diligent, exacting practice and by the force of strong bodhicitta conjoined with the realization of emptiness, such experiences are very different from those of ordinary beings who have unusual experiences. Having actualized the impure illusory body, with continuous and diligent practice yogis will be able to attain full awakening before too long.

In short, while ordinary beings have experiences that may resemble those of tantric yogis, it is important that they do not become enraptured with such experiences, mistakenly thinking that now they are realized tantric yogis. Such arrogance is a trap: you become more interested in preserving your image of a realized practitioner than of actually accomplishing all the steps of the path from the beginning. Such phony practitioners do not progress on the path and their "teachings" may be harmful to others. It is always better for yourself and others to be humble and to present as an ordinary being.

Preserving Good Qualities from Life to Life

Because great changes occur to the body and mind at death and during the bardo, and given the strong power of our habitual afflictions, a beginner may have difficulty maintaining the same level of good qualities developed in this life in the next life. Only when a practitioner has attained meditative stability, strong virtuous qualities, and potent counterforces to afflictions do these remain firmly intact from one life to the next.

In general, all practices done in relation to the subtlest mind are more reliable and stable because the continuity of this mind goes from one life to the next. Since the coarse levels of mind are dependent on the physical body and the brain, when these cease functioning at the time of death, the coarser levels of consciousness also stop functioning. This makes virtuous qualities developed only with the coarse level of mind less stable. However, the familiarity you have gained with virtuous qualities has left latencies on your mindstream, and in the next life you will experience the results of this habituation. In this way, your life has been meaningful, your practice has served its purpose, and you will continue to progress on the path to buddhahood.

9 | The Path of Highest Yoga Tantra

THE EXPLANATION OF Highest Yoga Tantra (Anuttarayoga Tantra) has two sections: the general tradition of Highest Yoga Tantra and the tradition of Kālacakra. Since many books have already been written about the Kālacakra system, we will leave it to the reader to look into these. Some recommendations are in the Recommended Reading section at the end of this book.

As with the explanations of the three previous tantric classes, the general tradition of Highest Yoga Tantra has four major topics: (1) how to become a proper vessel for meditating on the path, (2) the close bonds (samaya) and precepts to be kept purely, (3) the path to follow, and (4) how the actual attainments or siddhis are attained.

Becoming a Suitable Vessel

The main practitioners of Highest Yoga Tantra are human beings whose bodies comprise six substances, three from our mother and three from our father. These practitioners must be properly prepared and qualified as described earlier, with a correct understanding of the defects of saṃsāra, the four truths, bodhicitta, and the emptiness of inherent existence. Without a firm foundation in these topics, we may spend a lot of time visualizing deities and doing meditations on the cakras, winds, and drops without changing our situation of being confused sentient beings.

The doorway to enter Highest Yoga Tantra is receiving a proper empowerment derived from a tantric text that comes from a reliable source and has been followed by fully qualified masters or practitioners. The empowerment must be given by a fully qualified tantric master.

The empowerment of a specific deity contains four empowerments: the vase empowerment, secret empowerment, wisdom empowerment, and word empowerment. To follow both stages of the Highest Yoga Tantra path—the generation stage and the completion stage—all four empowerments must be received. The vase empowerment must be received from either a maṇḍala drawn on cloth, a maṇḍala made of powdered sand, or a body maṇḍala. It is said that some special disciples may be able to receive the vase empowerment from a maṇḍala of meditative concentration, which is a visualized maṇḍala that appears both to the lama and the disciple as a result of their individual concentrations. Regarding the conferral of empowerment from the body maṇḍala, this is found, for example, in Tilbupa's five-deity tradition of Cakrasaṃvara (*dril-bu lha-nga*) where there is both a body maṇḍala and conferral of the empowerment from the body maṇḍala. The Guhyasamāja system also has a body maṇḍala, but empowerment is not conferred from it.

The three higher empowerments—the secret, wisdom, and word empowerments—are received from the maṇḍala of relative bodhicitta, the maṇḍala of the womb, and the maṇḍala of ultimate bodhicitta, respectively.

Keeping the Ethical Restraints and Commitments Purely

Merely receiving an empowerment is not sufficient to engage in the practice. It is necessary to receive teachings on the practice from a qualified tantric guru and to keep the ethical restraints (*samaya*) and precepts, particularly the fourteen root tantric precepts and the eight secondary tantric precepts. It is said that even if you don't do an extensive practice in four meditative sessions daily, if you keep all the ethical restraints and commitments purely, it is possible to attain the highest supreme attainment within seven or sixteen lifetimes. If you follow the teachings on the generation and completion stages received from a fully qualified tantric master and practice these intensively, it is possible to attain awakening in one lifetime, in one body, in this time of the five degenerations. This is a specific characteristic of Highest Yoga Tantra.

To learn what to practice and what to abandon to keep the ethical restraints and precepts, refer to these texts: Tsongkhapa's *Commentary to the Fifty Verses on the Guru* (*Bla ma lnga bcu pa'i rnam bshas*) and his *Explanation of the Root Downfalls in Tantra* (*Snags kyi rtsa ltung gi rnam bshad*). Also read the *Clear Differentiation of the Three Ethical Codes* (*Sdom gsum rab dbye*) by Sakya Paṇḍita, and *Lamp for Clarifying the Samaya* (*Dam tshig gsal ba'i sgron me*) by Khedrup Norsang Gyatso.

Tantric masters usually give practice commitments that everyone who took the empowerment must fulfill. In Highest Yoga Tantra, practitioners must do the Six-Session Guru Yoga daily. There may also be a commitment to meditate on the sādhana every day and to do a retreat during which the deity's mantra is recited a certain number of times. Keeping these commitments given by the tantric masters is very important. After all, we took the empowerment because we wanted to do the practice; we didn't take it to collect empowerments or to put on airs that we are now a great practitioner.

Tantra is to be kept secret. There is a reason for this. If people do sādhana and its visualizations without proper preparation, they could become very confused. If they read a book and start doing completion-stage practices without the empowerment, without keeping the ethical restraints, and without correct instructions, they could disrupt the normal flow of the winds, causing mental imbalance and physical illness.

The Path to Follow—Generation Stage

The path to follow has two subdivisions: the method for meditating on the two stages and the actions that enhance or increase these two. The method for meditating on the two stages also has two divisions: how to meditate on the generation stage and how to meditate on the completion stage. The generation stage is defined as a yoga that (1) is a meditation newly and mentally imagining an aspect similar to any of the three—death, intermediate state, and rebirth, and (2) does not arise from causing the winds to enter, abide, and dissolve in the central channel through the power of meditation but ripens the continuum so that one can progress to the completion stage in which that is done.[55] The meaning of this will become clearer as we continue. However, whatever is included in the generation stage is not necessarily a meditation in analogy with death, bardo, or rebirth. For example, meditation on the protection wheel in the practice of the thirteen-deity Yamāntaka is not analogous to any of those three.

Uncommon Factors to Be Abandoned by the Generation Stage

The purpose of the generation stage isn't only to perfect our concentration and skill at visualization. Most important, the purpose is to abandon ordinary appearance and ordinary grasping. *Ordinary appearance* is the appearance of ourselves as ordinary sentient beings with saṃsāric bodies made of unclean substances that age, fall ill, and die. *Ordinary grasping* is holding ourselves to be inherently existent persons as well as thinking of ourselves as ordinary beings who are inept, unappreciated, full of faults, and have no hope of becoming fully awakened. Ordinary appearance and ordinary grasping are reversed by dissolving our old self into emptiness and then imagining that wisdom realizing emptiness arising as the deity with a body made of light and a compassionate mind that knows phenomena are empty and arise dependently.

Thus, deity yoga is not simply the visualization of the deity or mantra recitation. It includes meditating on the emptiness of the deity while retaining the visualized appearance of yourself as the deity. In this way deity yoga has two aspects: one focused on conventional truth—the appearance of the deity; the other focused on ultimate truth—the emptiness of the deity. The purpose of this is to plant seeds to apprehend both truths with one consciousness when you attain awakening.

In the generation stage of deity yoga, before generating themselves as deities, practitioners meditate on the emptiness of both themselves and of the deity to counteract the ignorance that is the root of saṃsāra. In a sādhana this follows the recitation of the mantras *oṃ svabhāva śuddhāḥ sarva dharmāḥ svabhāva śuddho 'haṃ,* and *oṃ śūnyatā jñāna vajra svabhāvātmako 'haṃ.*[56] In this meditation on emptiness, the object that is realized is the (ultimate) nature of the mind, and the subject that is realizing it is the mind. The subject and object are nondual in that the mind is realizing its own ultimate nature. Although you may not have realized emptiness, at this point meditate on the understanding that you have, either by recalling it or by reflecting on one of the refutations negating inherent existence.

After dissolving all appearances of the self and environment into emptiness, meditate that this wisdom realizing emptiness appears in the form of the deity and the maṇḍala. If you maintain the ordinary view of an inherently existent self without meditating on emptiness, the mind that then visualizes yourself as the deity is a wrong consciousness because an inherently existent saṃsāric self does not exist, and thus it can't be a deity.

Some generation-stage sādhanas describe generating yourself first as the causal vajra-holder and then as the resultant vajra-holder.[57] In other cases, you generate yourself as a deity through the five clarifications—five stages in the process of generating yourself as the deity.[58] Although there are various ways that the self-generation as the deity may be done in the generation stage, the most important part of the meditation is to meditate on the vast and the profound by cultivating the clear appearance of yourself as the deity and the divine identity of being an awakened being.

The main practice to do after generating yourself as the deity and before reciting the mantra is meditation on the clear appearance of yourself as the deity and having the identity as the deity. To develop clear appearance, after meditating on emptiness, slowly go through the stages of appearing as the deity. Then cultivate concentration on the image of yourself as the deity, first having a general image, then reviewing the details, and focusing single-pointedly on the image of being the deity. Having done that for a while, then focus on the thought "I am the deity." Think about how you as the deity would view people and interpret the events happening around you. With the generosity, fortitude, kindheartedness, compassion, and wisdom of the deity, imagine relating to people and events in the world.

Serious practitioners always relate these meditations to their own mental state and level of realization. They ensure that their meditation is free from laxity and restlessness. The methods to counteract these are the same as in Sūtrayāna.[59] When meditating to develop single-pointedness, practitioners should judge for themselves whether their focus on the meditation object is too tight or too relaxed. By continuously assessing the state of your mind, cultivate concentration correctly.

The opponent for ordinary appearance is the appearance of the complete and pure supporting and supported maṇḍala. The opponent for grasping at the ordinary is to identify as the deity and think of your environment as that of the deity. Meditation on the identity of the deity is the main point, and meditation on the appearance as the deity is auxiliary.

Although the generation stage alone is not capable of abandoning the ordinary appearances of environment and beings that appear to sensory cognitions, it can block the appearance of the ordinary environment and beings to mental cognitions. Although people and things may look the same as usual to your sense consciousnesses, your mental consciousness will see them as the supporting and supported maṇḍala—the deity's environment and the deity.

After practicing properly in this way, you will be able to have a clear visualization of the entire maṇḍala and all the deities in it. At first you can establish clarity on the visualization gradually, by remembering each deity and object in the maṇḍala. As your concentration improves, you can establish clarity on the maṇḍala and all the deities in it—the supporting and supported maṇḍala—instantaneously. This appearance becomes so vivid that it is as if you could see and touch them. When you can hold this visualization single-pointedly for one-sixth of a day—that is, for four hours—you have realized the coarse generation stage.

Continuing to practice, now imagine the entire maṇḍala and the deities in it in a tiny drop at the upper or lower openings of the central channel. At first, you will be able to do this gradually in stages, and with more practice, you will do this instantaneously with stability and clarity of the visualization. Being able to maintain this for four hours marks the completion of the refined generation stage. These stages are explained more below.

Being able to single-pointedly hold a clear image of yourself as the deity for a long period of time obstructs the usual sense of ordinariness that thinks, "I am an ordinary, limited being with afflictions in saṃsāra." This opens the door to the divine identity of being the deity in which, referring to the conventional I, you think, "I am the deity." As your clear appearance as the deity and your sense of being the deity through cultivating divine identity increase, you come to a point when thinking about yourself, you will feel "I am the deity." Although you are not yet the actual deity, this thought eliminates many obstacles such as self-pity and a lack of self-confidence and stimulates you to practice more intensely.

In all these stages of meditation, it is crucial to frequently reaffirm your awareness of emptiness. Without this, you could easily slip into thinking you are an inherently existent deity and thus generate more egregious afflictions.

Once generation-stage practitioners have firm meditative stability, different meditations such as emanating deities from the heart and dissolving them back into the heart are done to increase meditative stability. These meditations also include visualizations of subtle hand implements or subtle syllables at the upper end of the central channel and subtle drops and syllables at its lower end. When practitioners feel tired after doing these meditations, they recite the deity's mantras to refresh the mind. There are several types of mantra recitation that are explained in the sādhana of each deity.

As beginners doing your first deity yoga retreats, you may think reciting mantras is the most important part of the sādhana; however, this is not the case. You recite many mantras during the approximation retreat because this gives you the ability to do the concluding fire pūjā. Completing both the retreat and the fire pūjā, you then have permission to do the self-empowerment ritual, which enables you to renew your tantric ethical restraints and commitments.

REFLECTION

1. What is ordinary appearance? What are its disadvantages?
2. What is ordinary grasping? How does it hinder us on the path?
3. Describe the practice of divine appearance and how it functions as an antidote to ordinary appearance.
4. Describe divine identity and how it counteracts ordinary grasping.

The Coarse and Refined Yogas of Single Mindfulness

The generation stage has two parts: the coarse yoga of single mindfulness and the refined conceptual yoga.

Single mindfulness of the deity doesn't mean just being mindful of the deity once, nor does it mean being mindful of only one deity. It means to continually maintain mindfulness of the deity and mindfulness of yourself as the deity. Although this meaning can be applied to both the coarse and refined generation stage, here it specifically refers to the coarse deity yoga of the generation stage that concerns both the supporting and supported maṇḍala. The supporting maṇḍala is the deity's environment, the supported maṇḍala includes the deities in the maṇḍala. At this point in the sādhana—

just before reciting the mantra(s)—work on developing single-pointed concentration on the clear appearance of being the deity and on holding the identity of being the deity.

After the coarse generation stage is perfected, proceed to the refined generation stage, which is also called the refined generation stage of conceptual yoga. In general, there are four stages to generate the path in your mindstream: (1) a beginner, (2) the slight falling of pristine wisdom, (3) attaining a little power over pristine wisdom, and (4) attaining complete power over pristine wisdom. The first two stages and part of the third stage are included in the generation stage. The other part of the third stage and the fourth stage are in the completion stage.

(1) In the stage of a *beginner*, your aim is to gain clarity on the maṇḍala. Cultivate the visualization of the complete coarse maṇḍala slowly, in stages, and with effort. Like a small child walking slowly, establish clarity of the complete maṇḍala. This stage goes from the beginning of the practice until you are able to visualize the coarse maṇḍala gradually, but not instantaneously. However, you are not yet able to visualize the small deities on the sense organs.

(2) During the stage of *slight falling of pristine wisdom* you develop the ability to clearly visualize the complete coarse maṇḍala all at once, instantaneously. You are also able to clearly visualize the small deities on the sense organs of the principal deities gradually—Kṣitigarbha on the eyes, Vajrapāṇi on the ears, and so forth. Although you cannot visualize the small deities instantaneously, you can do so gradually and gain clarity on them slowly and in order.

The difference between the first two stages is that at the stage of the beginner, you gain the ability to clearly establish the visualization of the coarse maṇḍala slowly and in stages, whereas at the stage of the slight falling of pristine wisdom, you are able to clearly establish the entire coarse maṇḍala all at once, but you still must establish the clarity of the small deities on the sense organs slowly and in stages.

When you have familiarity with the self-generation and are single-pointedly meditating on clear appearance and divine identity, extraneous appearances—such as the sounds, sights, and so forth in the room—do not arise to the sense consciousnesses. At the time when the mental consciousness is single-pointedly focused on a specific object, its ability to act as an immediately preceding condition for the arising of a sense consciousness is blocked and the perception of extraneous objects is limited. This does not cease extraneous appearances forever but ceases distractions to sense objects during our meditation.

(3) The stage of *a little power over pristine wisdom* occurs when, in addition to being able to clearly visualize the maṇḍala's principal deities all at once, you can also clearly and instantaneously visualize the small deities on the sense organs with all their implements. The third stage has periods of both generation-stage and completion-stage practice and lasts until you gain full power over pristine wisdom (the fourth stage). In addition, at this stage there is no separation between meditation sessions and break times—you can maintain the visualization of the supporting and supported maṇḍala throughout the day, so doing the self-generation once a day is sufficient.

To review, the coarse generation stage is practiced from the beginning of the self-generation up to the actual mantra recitation. This includes the self-generation, meditation on clear appearance, divine identity, other visualization, and meditation on a small drop at the tip of the nose to counteract laxity and restlessness.

Practitioners on the first two stages—the stage of a beginner and the stage of the slight falling of pristine wisdom—may visualize a small drop at either the upper or lower end of the central channel to eliminate mental laxity and restlessness, two of the main obstacles to gaining serenity and single-pointed concentration. However, they do not yet visualize the entire maṇḍala or a hand implement inside this drop. The ability to firmly and stably place the mind on that drop occurs on the third stage, the stage of a little power over pristine wisdom.

Although practitioners haven't established serenity during the first two stages, by using special methods to develop concentration—for example, by focusing on a subtle drop, syllable, or hand implement at the upper and lower ends of the central channel or at the navel (and later at the heart), which are essential points of meditation—they begin to tame the winds. They do a lot of analytical meditation to cultivate clear appearance and divine identity in the first two stages. The meditations on the drops facilitate the winds entering the central channel at later stages of the path. Then at the time of meditating on the concentration of the supreme conqueror maṇḍala, for example,[60] they will be able to quickly eliminate mental laxity and restlessness. In this sense the method to attain single-pointed concentration in Highest Yoga Tantra is very different from that in the Pāramitāyāna and the three lower classes of Tantra.

For practitioners who have attained perfect serenity through the Pāramitāyāna method, too much analytic meditation can adversely affect stability on the meditation object. However, in Highest Yoga Tantra, doing a lot of analytical meditation when cultivating serenity isn't an interference; in fact, the analysis makes the stability firmer. This is a special characteristic of Highest Yoga Tantra that distinguishes it from other methods.

Attaining *perfection of the coarse generation stage* occurs when you can all at once establish the clarity of the entire coarse maṇḍala of deities as well as the deities on the sense organs and maintain single-pointed concentration on this for one-sixth of a day (four hours). The *practice of the refined generation stage* occurs while practitioners cultivate total clarity of the visualization of the complete supporting and supported maṇḍala with all the deities without confusing any details, in a tiny drop at the tip of your nose or at the lower end of the central channel. This also has two stages: (1) establishing clarity of all figures in the drop in stages, and (2) doing this all at once.

When you can meditate with clarity and stability on the complete supporting and supported maṇḍala inside a drop of clear light at the tip of the nose (the upper end of the central channel), a drop of clear light at the heart, or a drop of substance at the lower tip of the channel and are able to maintain this for four hours, you have attained *perfection of the refined generation stage*. The clarity of your concentration is such that you can distinguish the black and white parts of the deities' eyes within this fine drop.

The special objects of abandonment of the generation stage are the appearance of and grasping at ordinariness. Ordinary appearance is not the environment and beings that appear to sense consciousnesses but their appearance to the mental consciousness. The appearance to your mental consciousness of the pure maṇḍala, the deities in it, and yourself as a deity counteracts ordinary appearance; divine identity is the antidote to grasping yourself and the environment as ordinary. When your mental consciousness is very familiar with these, your visual consciousness does not *apprehend* objects as impure. However, the generation stage does not stop *appearances* to sense consciousnesses, so you can still make a cup of tea and drive a car.

Developing clarity of the clear appearance involves analytical meditation because you repeatedly visualize the maṇḍala and note all its details. Then generate divine identity, thinking "I am the actual deity; this is the actual maṇḍala." Use stabilizing meditation to make your concentration firm.

Serenity is attained when you have stability on the subtle drop at the upper end of the central channel. Then meditate on repeatedly emitting and reabsorbing the object with discriminating wisdom, and through this unite serenity and insight. The generation stage is complete when this yoga becomes stable. In all parts of the generation stage, maintain awareness of emptiness as much as possible.

The stages of beginner, slight falling of pristine wisdom, and a little power over pristine wisdom are parts of the generation stage. The first two occur during the coarse generation stage, and the third during the time of the refined generation stage and the beginning of the completion stage.

(4) The *stage of complete power over pristine wisdom* is part of the completion stage. To review, in the first two stages, meditate on the coarse supporting and supported maṇḍalas. Meditate on the drops at the upper or lower tips of the central channel to eliminate laxity and restlessness, although the primary meditation is on clear appearance, divine identity, and other visualizations. When, in the third stage, you have attained stability on the small drop, then meditate on the entire maṇḍala within the drop.

To aid your understanding and practice of Highest Yoga Tantra, study such texts as Tsongkhapa's *Explanation of the Systematic Stages [of Guhyasamāja]* (*Rnam-bzhag rim-pa'i rnam-bshad*) and Khedrup Gelek Palzang's *Ocean of Attainments of the Generation Stage* (*Bskyed-rim dngos grub rgya-mtsho*). It's also helpful to study the ārya tradition of Guhyasamāja in texts by Nāgārjuna and those by Nāgabodhi.

Furthermore, study the three bases to be purified—ordinary death, bardo, and rebirth—and the three factors that purify them—example and actual clear lights and illusory body, and the three resultant buddha bodies that are attained through this process. By contemplating these, you will understand how all these fit together in your practice.

Generation Stage and Completion Stage

Definition of the generation stage: a yoga that (1) is a meditation newly and mentally imagining an aspect similar to any of the three—death, bardo, and rebirth—and (2) does not arise from causing the winds to enter, abide, and dissolve in the central channel through the power of meditation but ripens the continuum so that one can progress to the completion stage in which that is done.

STAGE OF ATTAINMENT	STARTING POINT	MAIN PRACTICE[61]
Stage of a beginner (coarse generation stage)	Have uncontrived bodhicitta. Received empowerment and teachings on the practice, and are keeping the precepts and commitments. Know the sādhana well and can do self-generation.	Establish visualization of coarse supported and supporting maṇḍala using the five clarifications. Cultivate clear appearance and divine identity. Meditate on small drop at tip of nose to counteract laxity and restlessness.
Stage of slight falling of pristine wisdom (coarse generation stage)	Can visualize complete coarse maṇḍala and deities in it all at once, but lack clarity on small deities on sense organs.	Visualize complete coarse maṇḍala and deities in it all at once. Develop clarity on small deities on sense organs. Increase and stabilize clear appearance and divine identity.
Stage of a little power over pristine wisdom (refined generation stage)[62]	Have clear visualization of subtle deities on sense organs all at once. Have stability on small drop at upper or lower tip of central channel.	Meditate on maṇḍala inside small drop at the upper or lower ends of the central channel. Can establish all figures in the drop in stages.
Stage of complete power over pristine wisdom (completion stage)	Can meditate with stability on maṇḍala in small drop of clear light at upper or lower tip of central channel or at the heart.	Meditate on the practices of isolated body, speech, and mind, and on the illusory body to attain the stage of the actual clear light.

REFLECTION

1. What is the main practice on the stage of a beginner?
2. What does the practice on the stage of a little power over pristine wisdom add to this?
3. What is the purpose of meditating on a small drop at the upper or lower ends of the central channel? How does this prepare you for the completion stage?

10 | Introduction to the Completion Stage

THE DEMARCATION BETWEEN the generation stage and completion stage of Highest Yoga Tantra is the ability to make the winds enter, abide, and dissolve in the central channel in the same manner as at the time of death. Practitioners who are able to do this before death can attain the highest realizations in this life.

Putting Together the Elements of the Path

Tantric realizations are attained by practicing the entire path, from the Fundamental Vehicle teachings to the Mahāyāna and the Vajrayāna. To understand this, let's review how all the various elements of the path fit together to bring full awakening.

To attain the insights of the completion stage, you must have previously trained your mind in the common paths of renunciation, bodhicitta, and the correct view of emptiness. Without these as a proper foundation, the uncommon realizations of Vajrayāna cannot blossom in your mindstream. The mind of renunciation arises by contemplating the three types of duḥkha in saṃsāra and cultivating the determination to be free from these. Great compassion, the root of developing bodhicitta, arises by considering that others experience the same duḥkha in saṃsāra as you do and aspiring to relieve them from it. The most effective way to do this is to have the qualities of a buddha, and thus bodhicitta is born in your mind.

To develop these virtuous attributes, you must hear extensive teachings, think about and discuss them repeatedly to ensure you understand them correctly, and repeatedly meditate on them to integrate them with your mind. Don't think that hearing teachings and meditating on them are unrelated activities, that you leave aside the teachings you have heard and studied and meditate on something else. Rather, whenever you learn about a topic, try to meditate on it that very day. In addition, meditate on the teachings you have previously heard and studied.

If you haven't developed serenity before entering Tantra, do so as outlined in the coarse and refined generation stages. Attain a state of serenity in which you have completely eliminated all mental wandering. When you have accomplished this, you will have a tool that is like an airplane: if you park it somewhere, it stays there; if you need to go somewhere, it will take you there quickly and steadily. Serenity can be applied to any virtuous object of meditation that you learn, enabling you to integrate the Dharma into your life.

In addition to generating serenity, the purpose of the coarse and refined generation stage is to cease ordinary appearance and grasping ordinary appearance. Meditating on the clear appearance of being the deity is the antidote to ordinary appearance, and holding the identity of being the deity ceases grasping the ordinary. These practices begin to purify the bases—ordinary death, ordinary bardo, and ordinary rebirth—and ripen into the ability to attain the actual opponents to purify these—the example and actual clear lights and the impure and pure illusory bodies on the completion stage.

Some people wonder: I am not an actual deity, so isn't imagining myself to be one deceptive? Dharmakīrti gave a helpful reasoning to dispel this doubt: There is purpose to a mind that holds the rays of light reflected by a precious gem and takes them to be a jewel, but taking the light of a lamp as a jewel is distorted and lacks a good purpose. The purpose of visualizing yourself as a deity and holding the identity of being an awakened being is not to deceive yourself or others, it is to purify your mind and dispel obstacles to practicing the path leading to buddhahood.

Take the example of practitioners who have a clear understanding of renunciation and bodhicitta, crowned with the correct understanding of emptiness. On this basis, they imagine dissolving into emptiness, arising as the deity, and holding the divine identity of the three buddha bodies—the truth body, enjoyment body, and emanation body. This has meaning and purpose, like the mind holding the light rays of a jewel to be the jewel. Holding the identity of a fully awakened being in your meditation encourages you to imagine acting the way a buddha does in the break times by imagining having the qualities of the three buddha bodies, such as radiating light to purify sentient beings, manifesting as whatever benefits those sentient beings at that time, or appearing as food for the hungry, or as a doctor and medicine for the ill, and so on. It helps you to think of how you can be of greater benefit to the people and animals you encounter in your life.

Imagining yourself as a deity and acting as one leaves a strong impression on your mind, and this seed will ripen into the ability to become a buddha and engage in a buddha's awakened activities. Thinking in this way influences you to act according to the identity you hold. If a well-educated official holds the dignity of being an official but doesn't act properly, that won't do. He should act in accordance with what he is. Likewise, if you hold the identity of having the body, speech, and mind of a buddha, acting in a foolish or self-centered manner won't do.

Attaining completion-stage realizations depends on being able to induce the winds to enter the central channel. At present, the winds stay in the branch channels. Through meditative practices, you must stop the winds from moving in the branch channels and collect them into the central channel. Since the winds and the mind are inseparable, when the mind is focused on a particular object, the winds collect there too. During the refined generation stage, when meditators focus on a certain point in the central channel, the winds collect there and begin to enter the central channel, which causes meditators to experience some bliss. Therefore at the stage of a little power over pristine wisdom—the third of the four coarse and refined yogas of single mindfulness—they experience a part of the completion stage while doing the generation-stage practice.

When, through the practices of the completion stage, you can collect the winds in the central channel, you have the method to attain buddhahood in one lifetime. However, meditation on the channels, winds, and drops is also done by non-Buddhist meditators who do not attain awakening. As Jetsun Milarepa said, "Just collecting the winds—without the basis of renunciation, bodhicitta, and realization of emptiness, and without receiving proper empowerments and purely keeping the tantric ethical restraints and commitments—is not so surprising; even a bellows is filled with air." In contrast, Milarepa relied on his guru, the great translator Marpa. He purified his negative karma, created extensive merit, and received all the preliminary trainings and proper empowerments from Marpa. He then followed the Vajrayāna instructions and procedures and attained awakening in his lifetime.

REFLECTION

1. Why is it important to dissolve your ordinary body and self into emptiness before doing the self-generation as the deity? What are the faults and dangers of not doing this?
2. Is imagining yourself to be a deity a wrong consciousness? Why or why not? What are the purposes of doing so?

The Vast and Profound

In Sūtrayāna, "vast" refers to the teachings and practices of the method aspect of the path: the determination to be free from saṃsāra, bodhicitta, and the practices associated with them, such as generosity, ethical conduct, and fortitude. "Profound" refers to the wisdom aspect of the path, specifically to the wisdoms of conventional truth and ultimate truth, especially the wisdom realizing the emptiness of inherent existence. In Highest Yoga Tantra, these and other terms have different meanings that develop from and go beyond the meaning in Sūtrayāna and the lower tantras. For example, unlike in Sūtrayāna, the "nonconceptuality" (T. *rnam par mi rtog pa*) spoken of in Highest Yoga Tantra occurs with the dissolution of the coarse winds and coarse mind with its diverse thoughts, especially the eighty conceptual thoughts. This brings about a profound state of thoughtlessness free from manifest afflictions.

The dissolution of these coarse winds and conceptions may occur in two ways. One is natural, during the death process. This happens automatically due to karma. Another is through yogic practice where meditators employ special techniques to dissolve the coarse minds and winds and allow the subtlest clear-light mind to manifest. The latter is a special state of thoughtlessness: it is not a state of blank-mindedness but an alert and bright mind that is free from all discursive thought. If practitioners use the subtlest clear-light mind to focus nondually on emptiness, the *actual clear light* of the completion stage, a profound state of thoughtlessness, can be realized. Thereafter, when a slightly coarser wind and mind arise, the pure illusory body arises. This pure illusory body is called the "vast."

The illusory body is of two types: one polluted by afflictions, the other unpolluted by afflictions. Similarly, the clear-light mind that acts as a cause of an illusory body is of two types: one having afflictive obscurations and the other that is freed from them. When practitioners can dissolve the coarse winds into the heart cakra, the *example clear light* manifests. This subtle mind realizes emptiness inferentially, through the medium of a conceptual appearance. When meditators emerge from this meditative equipoise, they attain an *impure illusory body*, formed by the subtle winds. When they later completely dissolve the coarse winds—this time into the indestructible drop at the heart—and all conditions are ready, they realize the *actual clear light*. This subtlest mind realizes emptiness directly and nonconceptually. Due to its power, the afflictive obscurations will forever cease when meditators arise from this state in a *pure illusory body*. The pure illusory body is a path, although unlike other paths, it is not a consciousness. Through more practice, when meditators again dissolve the winds and manifest the subtlest clear light, they attain the *union of the vast and profound*. Through more training, when all factors necessary to attain the highest union—the clear light and illusory body of the path of no-more-learning—then full awakening is actualized and the truth body and form body of a buddha are present.

Levels of Completion-Stage Practice

After practitioners have attained the perfection of the coarse and refined generation stages, they proceed to the completion stage. The manner of practicing the completion stage may vary according to the Highest Yoga Tantra deity. Here, we will focus on the Ārya Parent and Child tradition of Guhyasamāja.[63]

The definition of completion stage is: the uncontrived yoga in the mindstream of a trainee that is generated by entering, abiding, and dissolving the winds into the central channel by the power of meditation. The completion stage of the Ārya tradition has six stages: isolated body, isolated speech, isolated mind, illusory body, clear light, and state of learners' union, which in turn has two branches, the state of union with abandonment and the state of union with realization. This same material can also be spoken of in five stages where isolated body is included in isolated speech. In that case, the actual clear light is called fourth-stage clear light. This material can also be expressed in four stages, or in the six branches of application. These various divisions are only different ways of condensing the material into various classification schemes. They are not contradictory. The six stages can also be abbreviated into two: (1) the samādhis (single-minded concentrations) of the three isolated states, and (2) the samādhis on the two truths. The samādhis of the three isolated states are: the samādhi on the vajra body, which is the isolated body; the samādhi on the vajra speech, which is the isolated speech; and the samādhi on the vajra mind, which is the isolated mind. A brief overview of the stages of completion-stage practice follows:

- In the stages of *isolated body, speech, and mind,* your body, speech, and mind are isolated from ordinary appearances and ordinary grasping, including the appearance of and grasping at inherent existence. The body appears in the aspect of the deity and the maṇḍala. Meditators don't see what is dirty as pure, nor do they think unpleasant feelings are pleasant ones. Rather, their ordinary body, feelings, mind, and so forth are dissolved into emptiness, and having been removed from true-grasping, they are designated "I." Divine identity is cultivated based on this merely designated I appearing as the deity.

  At the conclusion of the isolated body, practitioners can dissolve the winds into the central channel and meditate on the wisdom of bliss and emptiness. Beginning at this stage and continuing through the rest of the completion stage, meditators focus on subtle drops and may meditate on tummo.
- At *isolated speech,* ordinary wind or breath, which is the basis of our speech, is isolated from ordinary appearance and ordinary grasping, and meditators contemplate that the flow of the winds is naturally the sounds of the syllables *om ah hum* or *hum hoh.* This yoga loosens the knots in the central channel above and below the heart cakra.
- At *isolated mind,* by relying on practice with a qualified partner

(*mudrā*), the knots around the heart cakra are untied and the winds enter, abide, and dissolve into the indestructible drop in the heart cakra. This leads to the example clear light, when the subtlest mind realizes emptiness conceptually. Here "conceptual" does not mean coarse conceptuality, such as when we think about what we will do today. This is a very fine level of conceptuality that prevents seeing emptiness directly.

- At the conclusion of meditating on the final example clear light, the winds appear in the form of an *impure illusory body* in the shape of the deity. This is impure because the mind is not yet free from the impurity of the afflictive obscurations.
- The *actual clear light* manifests when all the winds enter, abide, and dissolve in the indestructible drop at the heart cakra. The subtlest mind now realizes emptiness nonconceptually. This realization comes about either through dissolving the winds through practice with a mudrā or by the natural dissolution of winds that occurs at the time of death. This is the realization of nondual bliss and emptiness, the ultimate clear light, which is the direct antidote that will forever eradicate the afflictive obscurations. When these yogis arise in a pure illusory body, ignorance is totally eliminated and they become arhats. Contemplating this gives them a sense of anticipatory happiness—because this is the fulfillment of their human intelligence and potential.
- The state of *learners' union*—so-called because yogis must still complete the path—occurs after meditators arise from meditation on the actual clear light into a *pure illusory body*. It is pure in that the mind accompanying it is forever and completely free from afflictive obscurations. This is the state of *union with abandonment* (T. *spangs pa zung 'jug*), so-called because the pure illusory body and the abandonment of the afflictive obscurations have come together within the meditator.
- Meditators now repeatedly enter meditative equipoise on the actual clear light, familiarizing themselves with it until the spontaneous wisdom of the actual clear light brings forth the pure illusory body. This is the *union with realization* (T. *rtogs pa zung 'jug*), the union of body (pure illusory body) and mind (actual clear light) as one entity.
- By continuing to practice, when all cognitive obscurations have been completely eradicated from this union of actual clear light and pure

> illusory body, yogis attain the state of *union with no-more-learning* (*nonlearners' union*), buddhahood, the state of Vajradhara.

This union of the subtlest clear-light mind and subtlest illusory body is not owned by an external agent or person. It was not given to the meditator by an external being or force. Rather, the potential to attain it has been within us since beginningless time. When the potential of the innate clear-light mind becomes manifest in its full form, that is Buddha, the ultimate union of the subtlest body and mind that spontaneously appears in manifold forms to benefit sentient beings.

In the Pāramitāyāna, the antidote to grasping true existence is the realization of emptiness by the coarse mind. After collecting merit for two countless great eons, Pāramitāyāna bodhisattvas overcome afflictive obscurations at the eighth ground. In contrast, by using the subtlest clear-light mind, bodhisattvas can overcome afflictions quickly in Highest Yoga Tantra. When all winds have been dissolved in the indestructible drop and the subtlest clear-light mind manifests and realizes emptiness, grasping states of mind cannot function, and the mind is an extremely powerful tool to eliminate all cognitive obscurations and attain peerless awakening.

However, actualizing the subtlest clear-light mind alone is not sufficient. Studying Madhyamaka philosophy and understanding the subtle distinctions concerning self-grasping according to the different philosophical systems is essential because this fine-tunes your recognition of the object of negation according to the Prāsaṅgikas.

When you understand the possibility of eliminating afflictive obscurations through this process, you will truly appreciate your precious human life. A human body born from the womb with six elements is special in Tantra. Even bodhisattvas in Sukhāvatī make prayers to be born into this world with such a body that can be used to practice Highest Yoga Tantra. The Buddha gave teachings on the Highest Yoga Tantra especially to human beings with such a body. It may not be suitable for others who lack this type of body.

In the *Treasury of Knowledge*, Vasubandhu said that karma created earlier in this life can ripen later in the same life. If you use your body to gain realizations of the completion stage, you will have the ability to create great merit by employing the illusory body. The merit of unifying the subtlest clear-light mind realizing emptiness with the pure illusory body can bring full awakening in this life.

REFLECTION

1. What is the demarcation of attaining the union with abandonment? What has been abandoned?
2. How does the union with realization differ from the union with abandonment?
3. What is the union with no-more-learning and how does it differ from the union with realization?

Paths That Overcome Ordinary Death, Bardo, and Rebirth

The actual paths that eliminate ordinary death, bardo, and rebirth under the power of afflictions and karma are on the completion stage, mainly the example and actual clear lights and the impure and pure illusory bodies.

Having achieved perfection in the coarse and refined generation stage, practitioners practice the completion stage. In the case of Guhyasamāja, yogis visualize themselves as Vajradhara with consort and focus on a bright-red sun disc the size of a mustard seed in the central channel at the cakra in the sexual organ. Focusing on it over time, they collect the winds in the right and left channels there and direct them into the central channel. The stage of isolated body begins when meditators are first able to draw the winds into the central channel at this cakra, which loosens the knots around the central channel. Isolated body is so-called because it is different and removed from the ordinary body.

It is also necessary to loosen the knots around the central channel at all cakras. To do this, yogis engage in the practice of vajra recitation (*rdthe-rje'i I bzlas-pa*, also called vajra breathing) on the stage of isolated speech, and use it to collect the winds and loosen the knots at the throat cakra.

The most important and most difficult knots to loosen are those at the heart cakra. To do this, practitioners continue to practice vajra recitation, now focusing at the heart cakra. By doing this, the winds enter the central channel and dissolve at the heart cakra.

Of the ten major and auxiliary winds in the body, the most difficult to gather and dissolve is the all-pervading wind. Yogis continue practicing until they can—through the internal conditions of vajra recitation or the external condition of union with a qualified seal—gather and dissolve all the winds, including the all-pervading wind, at the heart cakra, similar to what occurs at the time of death. The ability to do this before they die marks the attainment of the example clear light and the realization of the isolated mind.

The example clear light (*dpe'i 'od-gsal*) is a subtle consciousness that blissfully cognizes emptiness conceptually. It is attained when the subtle winds are dissolved in the indestructible drop in the central channel at the heart. When yogis leave that concentration, they manifest an impure illusory body and will definitely attain buddhahood in that lifetime. Those who manifest an impure illusory body after leaving the example clear light do not need to practice with an actual karmamudrā (action consort) to attain awakening. At the time of death, some yogis attain the example clear light instead of experiencing the clear light of death. From the example clear light, they manifest an illusory body similar to an enjoyment body instead of entering the bardo under the control of afflictions and karma.

At Tsongkhapa's time, some people did not practice the prātimokṣa precepts well and some thought they were unnecessary to attain awakening. To demonstrate that the root of attaining awakening is strictly keeping the prātimokṣa precepts of monks and nuns, Tsongkhapa did not attain awakening during his lifetime. He kept his monastic precepts purely while alive and died as a monk with pure precepts. At the time of death, he manifested the actual clear light and then attained awakening in the bardo by manifesting an enjoyment body.

How is an illusory body manifested from the clear light? The example clear light is one of the subtlest levels of consciousness. To achieve an illusory body instead of the bardo, this subtle consciousness of the example clear light acts as a cooperative condition, and the subtlest wind that is inseparable from it acts as the substantial cause. By means of the example clear light and the subtle wind, yogis manifest the impure illusory body.

When yogis arise from the example clear light in the form of the meditational deity, this is an actual deity—it fulfills the definition of an actual deity. Prior to this, the various deities meditators visualized during isolated body, speech, and mind were imagined deities; they were not deities that fulfilled the definition of a deity. Although the impure illusory body that looks like a deity is known as the body of a deity by definition, it is not a vajra body (T. *rdo rje sku*). Being impure due to its being together with a mind that still has afflictive obscurations, the impure illusory body cannot go to buddhahood and must be abandoned on the path. According to the layout of the five bodhisattva paths in the context of Highest Yoga Tantra, the attainment of the impure illusory body marks the beginning of the second path, the path of preparation. At this point the yogi does not have a direct nonconceptual perception of emptiness and thus has not abandoned the afflictive obscurations that bind beings to saṃsāra.

To attain the next stage, the actual clear light (T. *don gyi 'od gsal*), yogis practice the two types of dissolution: the taken-all-together dissolution (T. *ril 'sdzin*) and the subsequent dissolution (T. *rjes ghig*). In the taken-all-together dissolution, only yourself as the deity dissolves from your head, feet, and two sides into the heart and enters the clear light. In the subsequent dissolution, yogis first dissolve the environment and the maṇḍala deities in stages into themselves. Then their deity body dissolves into clear light as above. By practicing dissolution using these two methods—in which yogis manifest the signs of the dissolution of the winds in the same way as in the process of death—they attain the fourth stage, actual clear light. Their subtlest mind, the innate clear light, becomes the blissful awareness inseparable from the nonconceptual cognition of emptiness. This subtlest wind-mind has the power to eradicate the afflictive obscurations preventing liberation.

Subsequent to manifesting the actual clear light, when the subtlest mind becomes slightly coarser, yogis immediately manifest the pure illusory body. This is the transformation of the ordinary process of death and bardo under the control of afflictions and karma into the path. Instead of the innate clear light taking a bardo body, the actual clear light manifests as a pure illusory body. The actual clear light is the uninterrupted path, and the pure illusory body is the liberated path that immediately follows it. This illusory body is pure in that the afflictive obscurations have been eradicated. With this attainment, the uninterrupted path of the actual clear light has ceased.

Although the pure mind of the actual clear light is not manifest at this moment, this attainment is known as the attainment of unity.

What, then, has been unified in this stage of unity? It is the unity of the pure illusory body and the abandonment of the afflictive obscurations. This is not a unity with the actual clear light, because that has ceased with the attainment of the pure illusory body.

Attainment of the fourth-stage actual clear light marks the beginning of the path of seeing in Highest Yoga Tantra. Of the ten bodhisattva grounds, it is the first. When the liberated path that follows the actual clear light is attained, this is the beginning of the path of meditation and the second bodhisattva ground. This differs from the Pāramitāyāna and three lower tantras.

All afflictive obscurations have now been abandoned, and the only remaining obscurations are the cognitive obscurations. Removing these is now the meditator's focus. After attaining the pure illusory body, some yogis make it go back into the old aggregates, whereas others do not. In either case, yogis continue their single-pointed meditative absorption on emptiness. Through this, they eventually attain an actual state of union. Now both the actual clear light and pure illusory body are together simultaneously in the actual *state of learners' union*. With further meditation, yogis gain the *state of union without learning*, at which time the actual clear light and pure illusory body are together *and* all subtlest cognitive obscurations have been eradicated. This is buddhahood, which has the seven kisses of perfection.

To review, isolated body, speech, and mind practices have ripened from generation-stage practices. The difference is that in the three isolated practices, the winds actually enter, abide, and dissolve in the central channel at the various cakras. Signs appear that the winds have entered into the navel cakra: Yogis put a hair in front of their nose; if the hair doesn't move from one side to the other, that indicates there is equal movement of the breath through both nostrils. This is a sign of the winds *entering* the central channel at the navel. Normally, the breath (winds) doesn't pass in and out of the nose with equal force.

The sign that the winds *abide* in the central channel is that breath ceases completely; there is no flow of breath through the nostrils. If the yogis are in an unfamiliar place, the people there might think they are dead and take the body away, so they must be careful! Another danger is that when their breath stops, they may not be aware that this is due to subtle mental laxity, not the abiding of the winds in the central channel. Subtle mental laxity is not a great achievement at all! They need to continue their meditation to eliminate this fault. They have succeeded in doing so when not only has the breath through their nostrils stopped but also their lower abdomen doesn't move.

The sign of the actual dissolution of the winds into the central channel are the signs of the dissolution sequence of the elements. When earth dissolves into water, there is the mirage-like appearance. When water dissolves into fire, there is the smoke-like appearance; when fire dissolves into wind, there's the appearance of tiny sparks of light, and when wind dissolves into consciousness, there's the appearance of a tiny butter lamp in a dark well. After that comes the white appearance, the red increasing appearance, and the black near-attainment, followed by the clear light.

All the important points of the practice of Highest Yoga Tantra are abbreviated into the above practices. If you have a good understanding of these essential points, it will increase your aspiration to actualize them. But attaining these realizations is not easy. It is important to read and study extensively and to practice diligently. But the end result is the ability to benefit all sentient beings effectively and simultaneously abide in meditative equipoise on the ultimate nature of reality, and this is definitely worthwhile and meaningful.

The Nine Mixings

The nine mixings follow from the practices of taking death, bardo, and rebirth into the path to the three buddha bodies. One presentation is explained in Tsongkhapa's *Lamp Illuminating the Five Stages,* which explained the *Guhyasamāja Tantra.* Another presentation comes from Marpa. Both presentations contain the same factors and come to the same point. Tsongkhapa's presentation goes like this:

1. The three that mix *death with the truth body,* the buddha's mind, are ordinary death, dreamless sleep, and the four empties in the completion stage.

2. The three that mix the *bardo with the enjoyment body* are the bardo of the waking state existence, the dream state, and the path (illusory body).
3. The three that mix *birth with the emanation body* are birth in the womb, birth of arising from the dream state into the waking state, and birth when the illusory body reenters the coarse aggregates.

The first two factors in each set are events in ordinary life, the last relates to the path to awakening.

THE MIXING	BASIS IN LIFE	SIMILITUDE IN LIFE	CORRESPONDING BUDDHA BODY
Mixing death with the truth body	Death	Deep sleep	Four empties on the completion stage
Mixing the bardo with the enjoyment body	Bardo that occurs immediately after death	Dreaming	Illusory body
Mixing birth with the emanation body	Birth in a new body	Arising from the dream state into the waking state	Illusory body reenters the coarse aggregates

At the time of the clear light of death, the subtlest mind is manifest; in the bardo, the subtle mind is active; and in the next rebirth, the coarse mind manifests when the sense faculties and sense consciousnesses of the fetus become active, and the being of the new life interacts with its environment.

What happens when we ordinary beings fall asleep, dream, and wake up? In our daily lives, we rely on our five senses, but as we fall asleep our sensory perceptions cease. The winds in our bodies dissolve to some extent, but not completely, making the mind subtler during deep sleep. Deep sleep in particular presents an opportunity for yogis to access the innate clear-light mind, which, when used correctly, can be brought into the path to the truth body.

When going from deep sleep to dreaming, the winds and consciousness become slightly coarser and various appearances arise in the dreaming mind. The dream state is similar to assuming a subtle body in the bardo and corresponds to the enjoyment body, a subtle body in which a buddha teaches ārya bodhisattvas in a pure land.

In the state of waking up that follows the dream state, both the winds and the consciousnesses become even coarser like they do when a being is reborn in another body. This corresponds to the emanation body as it acts and engages with sentient beings in our world.

To be able to meditate on emptiness at the time of death, yogis train to contemplate emptiness during deep sleep. To do that, they must first master meditation on emptiness while awake. In the generation stage, practitioners visualize the eight signs of dissolution as if they were occurring. After they become familiar with this meditation, they train to detect a similitude of the eight dissolutions while falling asleep and to recognize sleep as sleep.

Then on the completion stage, these yogis engage in wind yoga, vase-like meditation, and other techniques to actually dissolve the winds into the heart cakra. Through this they will experience the actual eight signs as well as the various levels of mind up to the fundamental innate clear-light mind in meditation and at death.

During their waking hours, generation-stage practitioners meditate and imagine arising in a subtle body in the form of an implement or syllable. After they are familiar with this when awake, then while dreaming they practice recognizing the dream as a dream. One way to do this is by wind yoga. If practitioners have not reached that level of practice, they may do it by the power of intention. That is, before falling asleep, they set a strong intention to recognize their dreams as dreams. Recognizing dreams as dreams is easier than recognizing sleep as sleep by the power of intention.

The purpose of dream yoga in Vajrayāna practice is to access the clear-light mind. Once practitioners recognize that they are dreaming, they focus on the heart cakra of the dream body and try to dissolve the winds there. This leads to the experience of the clear light of sleep when the dream ends. Although this clear light is not as subtle as when all the winds dissolve, practitioners can make it subtler, prolong its duration, and use it to enhance their realization of emptiness. Just as dream objects do not exist as they appear, so too after emerging from meditative equipoise on emptiness, in the time of subsequent attainment all phenomena appear to meditators as like illusions—they appear inherently existent but do not exist in that way.

There are two types of dream bodies: one is an ordinary dream body that ordinary people have when they dream. The other is a special dream body cultivated through tantric practice for the purpose of being able to continue one's Dharma practice while asleep, and on the completion stage to actualize an illusory body.

An ordinary dream body remains inside the coarse physical body when we dream. A few ordinary people, due to either previous training or karmic predispositions, may experience lucid dreams or out-of-body experiences when the dream body goes outside during the dream. However, their subtlest body does not leave at this time. That only occurs at the time of death. These rare individuals have the ability to go to other places in their dreams without having trained in a specific practice. I heard of an elderly Tibetan mother who cautioned her relatives, "I'll be immobile, do not touch my body." Then, for a week her body lay there. When she awoke, she related the places she had visited.

Initially, tantric practitioners may visualize that within the clear light of sleep the subtle body departs the coarse body, goes to different places to do virtuous activities, and reenters the coarse body before waking up. Later, completion-stage yogis train to generate a special dream body through manipulating the winds. With this body, they engage in many virtuous activities that enhance their practice.

On high levels of the path, tantric trainees cultivate a special dream body as a means to attain the enjoyment body of a buddha. Two techniques are used to generate the special dream body: the power of intention and aspiration, or manipulating the winds in the practices of wind yoga. Created from subtle winds, this special dream body can separate from the ordinary body, enabling yogis to create vast amounts of merit by serving sentient beings and making offerings to the Three Jewels while their physical body rests. Although the special dream body may leave the physical body and go places, the people in those places cannot see it.

To generate a special dream body, a tantric practitioner must first be able to recognize sleep as sleep and dream as dream. To have lucid dreams, your diet must be compatible with your metabolism and bring the phlegm, bile, and wind elements into balance. If sleep is too deep, the dream will not be clear. In this case, practitioners are advised to eat less and to place their attention at the mid-brow while falling asleep. Sleeping too lightly is also an obstacle. To remedy it, one should eat oily and heavy food and concentrate on the navel cakra or secret cakra while falling asleep. If the dream is not clear, one should focus at the throat while falling asleep. When a practitioner is dreaming, a friend nearby saying, "Now you're dreaming," may help the practitioner recognize the dream as dream. After learning to lucid dream through effort and practice, practitioners can gain control over their dreams and their contents.

Some people can recognize a dream as dream by the power of karma without meditative practice. But to ascertain the clear light without any meditation practice is extremely rare. Some people can do general dream yoga without a great deal of foundation. In fact, dream yoga is common to Buddhists and non-Buddhists, and by following these techniques, some non-Buddhists experience results. However, Buddhists have a special motivation and aim when doing dream yoga: to realize emptiness and attain awakening for the benefit of all sentient beings.

Pāramitāyāna also stresses the importance of transforming sleep, but in a slightly different way. Sleep is considered a changeable mental factor—that is, it may be virtuous or nonvirtuous depending on its accompanying motivation. Before falling asleep, practitioners develop virtuous attitudes such as bodhicitta, and awareness of impermanence or emptiness. By continuing these into the period of sleep, sleep becomes virtuous, and practitioners wake up with a positive attitude to begin the new day. The Pāramitāyāna does not seem to have techniques to alter dreams so that they become virtuous, although it does mention certain signs in dreams that indicate purification or spiritual realizations if the dreams occur repeatedly. In addition, other factors are taken into account to determine if these dreams are worthy of notice.

The coarse forms of clear light arise in deep sleep as well as when yawning, sneezing, fainting, or experiencing orgasm. Of these, the clear light at the time of orgasm is the strongest. This is a natural process, like the arising of the clear light of death when an ordinary being dies. It is not the result of deliberate effort. In contrast, advanced tantric practice involves deliberately developing the ability to dissolve the winds into the central channel and thus make manifest the subtlest clear light. Since orgasm is the strongest of the natural experiences—aside from dying—it can be used in meditation to extend the experience of clear light and make it more vivid. When the clear light is manifest longer in meditation, practitioners' meditation on emptiness will be stronger and longer. In this way, these natural occurrences of the winds dissolving can be used in the path.

Managing the shifts in the winds during sexual union is a special form of practice; it is not ordinary sexual activity. Vajrayāna ethical restraints govern how and when this practice is done. Qualified practitioners must have renunciation of saṃsāra, bodhicitta, and the correct view of emptiness. They must also have received the proper empowerments and instructions for this practice, and keep ethical restraints and commitments purely. They must be able to control the regenerative fluid, prevent its emission, and draw the subtle drops from the lower part of the central channel up to the crown. Practitioners' realization of emptiness at this point is so deep that tasting excrement would be the same as tasting chocolate. Thus, this practice is very different from what is popularized nowadays as "tantric sex."

People frequently ask if dreams are reliable indicators of the future. A person could have new understandings about themselves in a dream, but in general the content of dreams is not significant. Individuals must examine and conclude for themselves if a specific dream has value. I know one meditator who dreamed of a path through the mountains, and when he later escaped from Tibet, he saw that path and followed it. Some people dream that their guru gives them instructions. Here discretion is necessary. We need to consider if the appearance of the spiritual mentor is pleasant or not and if the instructions accord with the Dharma or not. A dream of our guru may or may not be influenced by the guru. People often like to think it is; this makes their mind happy and inspires them to practice. In that case, thinking like that is not harmful. But the guru who appears in a dream is not our actual guru. We must remember that dreams are dreams and not relate to them as if they were real and inherently existent.

More about the Nine Mixings

Another presentation of the nine mixings contains the same factors organized in a slightly different manner. Based on teachings by his guru Nāropa, Marpa gave instructions on the nine mixings: three in the waking state, three in the sleep state, and three at death. At each of these three times, yogis correlate these states with the three buddha bodies. Done on the completion stage, these practices make manifest the innate clear-light mind that can be used to meditate on emptiness. On the generation stage, practitioners visualize the mixings.

The waking state mixed with the three buddha bodies. Yogis meditate on specific practices to make the winds enter, abide, and dissolve in the central channel at the heart. This induces the eight signs—the mirage and so forth up to the clear light. They use this meditative equipoise to meditate on emptiness with the subtlest clear-light mind. This correlates with the truth body. From this state, yogis arise in the aspect of the enjoyment body Vajradhara, who is white, with one face and two arms. Having held the divine identity as the enjoyment body, like a wisdom being merging with the commitment being they reenter their coarse body. In a sādhana, the commitment being is the deity that meditators imagine being—for example, the principal deity in the Guhyasamāja maṇḍala. The wisdom beings are deities that are invoked from their natural abode and dissolve into the commitment being.[64] This visualization helps meditators hold the divine identity of being the emanation body of the deity instead of thinking, "I'm not a deity, I'm just pretending to be one."

The sleep state mixed with the three buddha bodies. To succeed in this, yogis must first be able to mix the waking state with the three buddha bodies. The process here is similar to that in the waking state: (1) causing the winds to enter, abide, and dissolve in the central channel at the heart, stimulating the eight signs—mirage, smoke, fireflies, dim light, white appearance, red increase, black near-attainment, and clear light, (2) arising from that in a dream body that is the form of the deity, and (3) reconnecting the dream body with the old body and holding the divine identity of being the deity. Here these three stages occur as yogis fall asleep and enter a period of deep sleep, dreaming, and waking up. In this way there are three sequential steps that mix the sleeping state with the truth body, the dream state with the enjoyment body, and the waking state with the emanation body.

Initially maintaining awareness during non-dreaming deep sleep is difficult. Most people have no awareness in this state. Practitioners access the state of deep sleep by first engaging with the dreaming state when the mind is comparatively grosser and they can recognize dreams as dreams. They practice dream yoga by deliberately maintaining conscious awareness while dreaming. They also learn to modify their dreams or even deliberately conjure certain dreams while in the dream state. When they are able to do that and have gained mastery in dream yoga, they can gradually approach meditating during deep sleep. To do this, when they are aware that they are dreaming, they focus their attention at the heart of the dream body and visualize dissolving into emptiness through the eight-stage dissolution process. In this nonconceptual state, they meditate on emptiness.

Mixing the death process with the three buddha bodies. To succeed in doing this, yogis need to be able to do the mixings in the waking state and sleep state. Ordinary beings usually have no awareness of the eight signs and no aspiration to attain the three buddha bodies. But yogis who have strong mindfulness and introspective awareness and who have at least an inferential realization of emptiness and the ability to control the winds, actually manifest the innate clear light and meditate on emptiness at death. They do not enter the bardo under the control of afflictions and karma. After their meditative equipoise on emptiness with the example clear light or actual clear light, they arise as the actual deity in an impure or pure illusory body, respectively. They will attain awakening without being born again in a saṃsāric body. Following this, they enter the heart of future parents visualized as the couple Vajradhara. When conception occurs, they arise in the form of the emanation body Vajradhara, white with three faces and six arms, and meditate with divine identity. With the enjoyment body of a buddha, they teach ārya bodhisattvas in a pure land; with the emanation body of a buddha they manifest many forms to benefit sentient beings. Although this is explained as if the three buddha bodies are attained sequentially, in fact they are attained simultaneously, the moment the cognitive obscurations have been forever ceased.

Meditators on the generation stage practice the nine mixings in the waking state by imagining the environment dissolving into them, themselves dissolving into the syllable hum at the heart, the hum gradually dissolving from the bottom up into emptiness. They imagine the winds entering, abiding, and dissolving in the central channel at the heart, manifesting the subtlest clear light, meditating on emptiness, arising as the enjoyment body, and then as the emanation body of Vajradhara. They imagine as described above when in deep sleep, the dream state, and waking up. They aspire to develop the similitude of the nine mixings and then continue the practice on the completion stage to the point where they can actually manifest the three buddha bodies at death. If they cannot do it at the end of that life, they aspire to have a fortunate rebirth in all future lives until they can bring this practice to fruition and attain the actual three buddha bodies.

THE NINE MIXINGS

	IN THE WAKING STATE	DURING SLEEP	AT DEATH
MIXING WITH THE TRUTH BODY	Through meditation, the winds enter, abide, and dissolve in the central channel, bringing the eight signs. With the mind of clear light, one meditates on emptiness.	By meditating while falling asleep, the winds enter, abide, and dissolve in the central channel, giving rise to the eight signs. When the mind of clear light of sleep manifests, one meditates on emptiness.	At the time of death when the winds are naturally entering, abiding, and dissolving in the central channel, the eight signs arise. By recognizing the innate clear-light mind—a mind of great bliss united with the subtlest mind that nonconceptually perceives emptiness—the mind is purified of defilements.
MIXING WITH THE ENJOYMENT BODY	When the black near-attainment of the reverse order dawns, the enjoyment body Vajradhara arises and one holds the divine identity of being Vajradhara.	From the clear light of sleep, when one begins to dream, the enjoyment body Vajradhara arises and one holds the divine identity of being that.	From the clear light of death, when the black near-attainment of the reverse order arises, one arises as the actual deity Vajradhara with a vajra body.
MIXING WITH THE EMANATION BODY	Arising from this meditation, the mind reenters the old body like a wisdom being merging with the commitment being, and one holds the divine identity of being the emanation body.	Upon waking up, the mind arises from the dream and enters the heart of the old body visualized as the commitment being, and one holds the divine identity of being the emanation body.	After leaving this state, the mind enters the hearts of their future parents visualized as the couple Vajradhara. Upon conception, one arises in the aspect of the emanation body Vajradhara.

Advice

I'd like to share some advice so that your tantric practice will bear fruit. To practice the generation and completion stages, in addition to especially strong bodhicitta that cannot bear sentient beings living with duḥkha for a fraction of a moment longer, you need a good understanding of both the Sūtra path and the Tantra path. I recommend that you begin with the paths and grounds (T. *sa lam*) texts that cover how practitioners progress through the stages and paths of Tantrayāna, and then study texts such as *Lamp Illuminating the Five Stages of the Completion Stage* (*Rdzogs rim rim lnga gsal sgron*),[65] which explains the tantric paths clearly and in an easy to understand way, and Losang Chokyi Gyaltsen's *Essence of the Five Stages* (*Rim lnga snying po*).[66] In this way, you'll learn about these practices extensively, completely, and clearly. Furthermore, study the *Guhyasamāja Root Tantra* together with its six explanatory tantras and the texts of the Ārya tradition stemming from Nāgārjuna and Āryadeva. If you practice everything explained in these texts on the basis of firm renunciation, bodhicitta, and wisdom realizing emptiness, the path to buddhahood will become very clear to you, as when you go to a familiar place.

By studying such texts, you will gain a full understanding of the points to practice. We should be like Tsongkhapa, who followed the tradition of Go Lotsawa for the explanation of the tantras and Marpa Lotsawa's explanation of the guidelines. If you do this, all the tantric texts of the Gelug, Sakya, Nyingma, and Kagyu traditions will appear as actual personal instructions.

Study the above texts through the system known as the six alternatives and the four modes of meaning and explanation as described in other texts. By studying in these ways, the meaning of the texts will become clear. Read and study these texts and hear teachings on them not just once or twice, but many times. Then think about the meaning of what you have studied and heard so that your understanding grows. From the three—view, meditation, and action—this is the life force of the correct view.

Likewise, to do the practices that activate the subtle body, you need to have a clear idea of the channels and winds in the body; here the power of mindfulness is important. Be mindful—that is, keep in mind—the methods to overcome obstacles when working with the channels and winds. You need not only mindfulness regarding the faults and the good aspects of the channels and winds but also introspective awareness to apply antidotes to the faults. This is the life force of meditation.

To do these practices and accomplish their purpose, familiarity is needed. Familiarity is the life force of action and is attained by practicing in four sessions daily. In short, the powers of hearing and thinking are the life force of the correct view, the powers of mindfulness and introspective awareness are the life force of meditation, and the power of familiarity is the life force of action. By training in this way your practice will bring good results.

11 | Going Deeper into the Completion Stage

THE TOPIC OF the six levels of the completion stage, though briefly mentioned above, is extensive and difficult to understand when explored in detail. We need to approach it gradually and build a solid foundation based on the four truths and other Sūtrayāna teachings. The great lama Phagmo Drupa (1110–70) said, "To attain awakening in one life, in one body, is a great quality of the tantric path." I agree that this is a preeminent quality of Tantra, but we should proceed on this path with progressive development. First, tantric aspirants must put energy into understanding the three principal aspects of the path—the determination to be free from saṃsāra, bodhicitta, and the correct view of emptiness—which are the basic practices in common with the Pāramitāyāna.

On this basis, you can enter Vajrayāna and engage in the practices of the coarse and refined generation stage. Having completed those, practice the various wind yogas to activate the subtle body. The *Subsequent Tantra of Guhyasamāja* explains six *accompanying yogas* of the completion stage: individual withdrawal, meditative stabilization, vitality-exertion, retention, subsequent mindfulness, and concentration. The first two are included in isolated body, vitality-exertion in isolated speech, retention in clear light, and subsequent mindfulness and concentration in the state of union.

Isolated Body

The six stages of the completion stage commence with isolated body. Isolated body begins when, having completed the refined generation stage, yogis' meditation on the entire maṇḍala in a subtle drop at the lower tip of the central channel produces pristine wisdom realizing emptiness that arises from the winds entering, abiding, and dissolving in the central channel. This stage goes until just before yogis can generate pristine wisdom that arises from the lower and upper winds dissolving in the central channel at the heart.

The *basis to be purified* by isolated body is our state as sentient beings circling in saṃsāra; the *purifying path* refers to learning āryas' nonconceptual realization of emptiness. Some learning āryas have already abolished their afflictive obscurations and others have not. The *purified result* is buddhahood.

Isolated body can be divided into the isolated-body practice of one hundred pure buddha families, which can be condensed into five buddha families, three secret families, or one buddha family of the greatest secret. The hundred buddha families correspond to the hundred polluted factors of our saṃsāric existence.

On the stage of isolated body, the basis consists of twenty coarse factors: the five aggregates; four elements; six sensory faculties such as the eye and ear; and the five sense objects of sights, sounds, and so forth. Each of these is polluted, but in isolated body they are generated in the pure aspect of twenty deities. The twenty coarse phenomena are the basis of isolated body and the twenty deities are what they transform into.

The way in which the twenty coarse phenomena are generated as the twenty deities is as follows: Each of the five aggregates is associated with a particular tathāgata, thus the five buddha families.[67] The four elements—earth and so on—are meditated on as the four mothers or consorts.[68] The six sensory faculties are meditated on as the six bodhisattvas.[69] The five sense objects are meditated on as the five vajra goddesses.[70] Since each of these twenty factors is present in each of the five buddha families, there are one hundred pure buddha families.[71] Or, put another way, each of the twenty deities incorporates the five buddha families, so there are one hundred deities altogether.

When the five buddha families are abbreviated into three, they represent the vajra body, speech, and mind—Vairocana symbolizes the body, Amitābha speech, and Akṣobhya mind. The other two are abbreviated into these three by including Ratnasambhava with Vairocana for body, and Amoghasiddhi with Amitābha for speech. These three can be further

THE FIVE BUDDHA FAMILIES AND THEIR CORRELATES[72]

	VAIROCANA	RATNASAMBHAVA	AMITĀBHA	AMOGASIDDHI	AKṢOBHYA
AGGREGATE	Form	Feeling	Discrimination	Miscellaneous factors	Consciousness
ELEMENT	Earth	Water	Fire	Wind	Space
MOTHER, CONSORT	Locanā	Māmakī	Pāṇḍaravāsinī	Tārā	
SENSE FACULTY AND BODHISATTVA	Eye Kṣitigarbha	Ear Vajrapāṇi	Nose Khagarbha	Tongue Lokeśvara	Tactile Sarvanivāraṇa-Viṣkambhini
SENSE OBJECT AND GODDESS	Rūpavajra (form)	Śabdavajra (sound)	Gandhavajra (smell)	Rasāvajra (taste)	Sparśavajra (tangibles)
INNER VISION	Mirage	Smoke	Fireflies	Dim light at end of tunnel	
WISDOM	Mirror-like = pristine wisdom in the continuum of an ārya buddha that realizes all phenomena of the three times and their ultimate and conventional natures without any gap or obstruction.	Equality = pristine wisdom in the continuum of an ārya buddha that engages in working for others without partiality.	Discriminating = pristine wisdom in the continuum of an ārya buddha that views sentient beings' thoughts individually, without mixing.	All-accomplishing = pristine wisdom in the continuum of an ārya buddha that can enact actions for sentient beings' different purposes.	Sphere of reality = pristine wisdom in the continuum of an ārya buddha who has eliminated the two obscurations.
AFFLICTION	Ignorance	Miserliness, arrogance	Attachment	Jealousy	Anger

abbreviated into one buddha family when all of them are included in Vajradhara, who constitutes the sixth buddha family. That is known as the one great secret buddha family.

All the correlations above are applicable to the absorptions of the elements during the death process and during completion stage. After the absorptions of the earth, water, fire, and wind elements, the three extremely subtle minds dissolve. When the eighty indicative conceptions dissolve, the white appearance arises. This is the appearance like moonlight in a clear sky. When the white appearance dissolves, the red increase arises; it is the appearance of sunlight, like sunrise in a clear sky. When the red increase dissolves, the black near-attainment arises; it is the appearance of thick darkness, as if fainting and losing consciousness. When the black near-attainment dissolves, the clear light arises and there is the clear appearance like the autumn sky at dawn.

The procedure for meditating on the absorptions can be found in the ritual texts and sādhana practices of Guhyasamāja and other deities, particularly during the imagined dissolution of the aggregates and so forth culminating in the clear light. At that time, of the five aggregates that dissolve, Vairocana signifies the aggregate of form. At the same time Locanā (earth), Kṣitigarbha (eye faculty), and Rūpavajra (sights) dissolve. When these absorptions occur on the completion stage due to dissolution of winds, they are analogous to the first dissolution in the death process. With each successive dissolution in the death process, one of the body's elements loses the ability to act as the basis for its corresponding aggregate, sense faculty, and sense object, which then weaken and cease to function. "Earth dissolves into water" means that the earth element can no longer act as the support for the body. The body weakens and the dying person has the sensation of being pressed down or buried by earth. They may even reach up to grab something. The person cannot see very clearly, and they experience an internal sight like a mirage; the glistening appearance of water arises as the earth element dissolves and the water element becomes prominent.

With each successive dissolution, an element ceases to act as the support for consciousness, and the person withdraws from the world of the senses and approaches death. In the Guhyasamāja practice, this process is duplicated first through imagination in the generation stage, then through actually dissolving the winds in the completion stage.

When meditators have perfected the coarse and refined generation stages by meditating on a very subtle drop at the lower tip of the central channel, the winds start to enter, abide, and dissolve into the central channel. Because the mind and the winds are related, when the mind focuses there single-pointedly, the winds also collect at that point and start to dissolve. When the winds enter, abide, and dissolve in the central channel, the various signs of the dissolution of the elements occur. Together with that, yogis experience the *four empties*—the empty, the very empty, the great empty, and the all-empty. These are the extremely subtle consciousnesses that are used to realize emptiness—the mind of the radiant white appearance, the mind of the radiant red increase, the mind of the black near-attainment, and the subtlest clear-light mind that manifests when all winds have entered, abided, and dissolved in the indestructible drop in the central channel. These four minds lack gross conceptuality, although the first three are said to be conceptual because they still have subject-object duality and the appearance of inherent existence. The last empty is the subtlest clear light that is inseparable from the subtlest wind; it lacks all elaborations.[73]

At this time on the path, yogis also experience the four joys or blisses—four blissful consciousnesses that arise due to the melting of the bodhicitta (subtle drops in the central channel) and its movement through the various cakras. Some scholars say the four empties and four joys are the same; others say they are not identical. When the white drop melts and descends from the crown cakra to the throat cakra, there is joy; when it goes from the throat cakra to the heart cakra, there is supreme joy; when it goes from the heart cakra to the navel cakra, there is special joy; and when it goes from the navel cakra to the bottom of the central channel at the secret place, there is innate bliss and emptiness. When the red drop ascends the central channel going to the navel, heart, throat, and crown, the four joys again arise. These four are more intense because the drop is ascending the central channel.

Why is this stage called isolated body? The basis from which things are to be isolated or removed is the body with its twenty coarse factors of the five aggregates, four elements, six sensory faculties, and five sense objects. What they are to be isolated from is ordinary appearances and grasping or conceiving the ordinary. The counterforces that remove these are the clear appearance of yourself as the deity to remove ordinary appearance, and holding the divine identity of the deity to overcome grasping the ordinary.

The purpose of meditation on the stage of isolated body is for the basis—the ordinary body—to be separated from ordinary appearance by appearing as the deity in the maṇḍala that is the manifestation of bliss and emptiness and to generate a blissful consciousness that meditates on emptiness. This is accomplished by dissolving the winds into the central channel and meditating on the wisdom of bliss and emptiness. Emerging from this meditation in which the body was isolated from ordinary appearance and grasping, everyone and everything now appear to the yogi to be sealed by bliss and emptiness and to arise in the aspect of the deity and the maṇḍala.

Isolated Speech

The stage of isolated speech begins when yogis generate the pristine wisdom of the white appearance that arises when the winds at the top and bottom tips of the central channel enter, abide, and dissolve in the central channel at the heart due to meditating on a mantra drop at the heart. It continues until the knots at the heart are completely loosened by the power of meditation, enabling the winds to enter, abide, and dissolve into the indestructible drop at the heart, which generates the pristine wisdom of the white appearance. Everything before that—starting from when yogis can make the winds enter, abide, and dissolve into the central channel at the heart up to the point just before they can loosen the knots and make the winds dissolve into the indestructible drop at the heart—is the stage of isolated speech.

The speech that is the basis from which impurities are to be removed isn't our ordinary communication, but the sound of breath when inhaled, the sound at the pause when the breath abides in the central channel at the heart, and its sound when exhaled. What is to be removed is grasping the sound of the wind being inhaled, abiding, and exhaled as different from the sound of the three syllables *om ah hum*. This is accomplished through the practice of vajra recitation of the isolated speech, which isolates the wind from ordinary appearance and ordinary grasping by seeing its natural vibration as the "sound" or vibration of *om ah hum*. Through this practice, yogis recognize the natural vibration of the breath during inhalation as the tone *om*, the vibration when it dissolves and abides in the central channel at the heart as the tone *ah*, and the sound during exhalation as the tone *hum*. This practice gathers the winds at the throat cakra and loosens the knots around the central channel there.

The practice of vajra recitation (T. *rdo rje'i bzlas pa*) is a type of breath/wind yoga (*prāṇāyāma*, T. *srog rtsol*), which is called vitality-exertion.[74] It covers a range of meditations on drops, syllables, and so forth that stop the movement of the winds in the right and left channels so that they enter the central channel. Breath-control meditation is done at three points along the central channel: (1) at the mantra drop at the heart cakra in the central channel, (2) at the light drop at the upper end of the central channel, and (3) at the substance drop at the lower tip of the central channel. Only the practice done with the light drop at the upper end of the central channel is actual vajra recitation and isolated speech; the other two types of wind yogas are not actual vajra recitation or isolated speech but are still included in isolated speech and are practiced during that level.

Initially, yogis meditate on the first wind yoga, the mantra drop at the heart. The nature of this drop is the syllable *hum* imagined at the heart cakra. By focusing on it, winds from the upper and lower parts of the body enter the central channel and go to the area of the heart. As the winds enter and dissolve there, yogis experience the white appearance, like brilliant moon light. This experience marks the beginning of isolated speech.

The second yoga focuses on a light drop visualized at the upper tip of the central channel at the base of the nose, between the eyebrows. Yogis observe that as the breath passes by the light drop during inhalation, when it abides at the heart, and when it is exhaled, it vibrates with the "tone" of *om*, *ah*, *hum*, respectively. This practice is actual vajra recitation; it causes the winds in the central channel to move back and forth and slightly loosens the knots at the heart. Due to this, the winds start to enter, abide, and dissolve in the indestructible drop.

The third yoga is meditation on a substance drop and is done to enhance the process of the winds entering the indestructible drop. This yoga involves practicing with a consort—either a wisdom mudrā (visualized consort) or an action mudrā (*karmamudrā*) who is an actual consort that has accomplished the same stage of spiritual development as the yogi. The substance drop is composed of the white and red drops and is imagined at the point where the lower tips of the central channel of each partner meet. The substance drop is not emitted. This yoga further loosens the knots around the central channel at the heart and facilitates the dissolution of some of the winds in the indestructible drop.

There are two ways to do the vajra recitation: with the five major winds and with the branch winds. The practice of the vajra recitation with the five major winds is done to attain the four types of actions: pacifying, increasing, power, and ferocity. It is done with the five auxiliary winds when yogis wish to attain extrasensory perceptions with the eye, ear, nose, tongue, and body. Another way of doing vajra recitation employs the ascending and descending winds.

Vajra recitation with the all-pervasive wind is the most difficult. The method and instructions for causing the all-pervasive wind to dissolve through vajra recitation is extremely secret. It is only taught to one disciple at a time, or it is not explained clearly, but hints about it are given when explaining other topics.

Vajra recitation is not simple and the great texts explain it in many ways. Practitioners of this meditation must have stable and definite realization of the three principal aspects of the path. In addition, they must have completed the coarse and refined generation stages. Practitioners who are properly prepared can do the practices of the isolated body and the vajra recitation of the isolated speech and realize the clear light at the end of the third stage, isolated mind.

Isolated Mind

Just as there are various signs of progressing from isolated body to isolated speech, signs occur when transitioning from isolated speech to isolated mind. Isolated mind begins when meditators have fully released the knots at the heart by employing *inner conditions* such as vajra recitation and the dissolutions of the two meditative concentrations that withdraw the winds into the central channel and by employing the *outer condition* of a mudrā (consort).

Of the two meditative concentrations—subsequent dissolution and taken-all-together dissolution—*subsequent dissolution* begins by visualizing the buddhas in a splendid pure land. Light from the *hum* at the yogis' heart radiates and dissolves the pure land and buddhas in it; the light then dissolves into their body and coalesces at the heart. All appearances cease and they meditate on emptiness. In a slightly different description of the subsequent dissolution, yogis visualize the elaborate maṇḍala with the celestial mansion, the main deity couple, and the entourage of other deities. Yogis imagine the celestial mansion dissolving into the entourage, which dissolves into the main deity couple. The consort dissolves into the main deity, who dissolves into the hum at the heart. Sequentially, the vowel beneath the main part of the *hum* dissolves into the root letter, this dissolves into the top line of the *hum*, this into the drop, the drop into the squiggle. The squiggle dissolves completely, and they meditate on emptiness.

In the *taken-all-together dissolution*, light from the *hum* at the yogis' heart dissolves their entire body into light; appearances cease and they meditate on emptiness. In short, everything dissolves into emptiness all at once. Through the *subsequent* and *taken-all-together* meditative concentrations, the winds enter and dissolve in the central channel at the heart and loosen the knots around the central channel, further contracting the winds.

The *outer condition* is an action mudrā, a living human being. An imagined wisdom mudrā is also considered an outer condition, even though such a partner is not made of external matter. Through union with the mudrā, the winds dissolve in the indestructible drop at the heart, and this generates the pristine wisdom of the white appearance. Isolated mind goes from this point up to just before the attainment of the impure illusory body.

There are two types of isolated mind: A *mere isolated mind* is attained when, in reliance on a wisdom mudrā, *some* winds dissolve into the indestructible drop. A *final isolated mind* is attained only by relying on an action mudrā or at death when *all* winds dissolve into the indestructible drop. Isolated mind is so-called because the mind is isolated from conceptuality by becoming the nature of inseparable bliss and emptiness.

The purpose of isolated mind is to dissolve all the winds into the indestructible drop in the central channel at the heart after loosening the knots around that channel. It is extremely difficult to bring all the winds, particularly the all-pervasive wind, into the central channel and have them dissolve in the indestructible drop at the heart. The methods for doing this can be learned in authoritative texts. Meditators need to be able to differentiate bringing the winds in the vicinity of the central channel at the heart from actually dissolving them in the very center of the central channel at the heart. There are many methods for doing this that vary according to yogis' inclinations; these include the six yogas of Nāropā and tummo (inner heat) meditation. When all the winds have dissolved into the indestructible drop in the central channel at the heart, the signs of the dissolution manifest similar to the time of death. After meditating on emptiness with the example clear light, which arises at the end of isolated mind, yogis attain the impure illusory body. It is now definite that they will attain awakening in that very lifetime.

Many important and critical points arise in the discussion of isolated mind. Scholars and yogis debate these points. If you haven't studied the great texts extensively, these points could be confusing. You can explore these later as you learn more about the completion stage.

REFLECTION

1. What is the basis of isolated body and what is the body to be isolated from?
2. What is the basis of isolated speech and what is to be isolated from what?
3. What are the two types of isolated mind? Why is the final isolated mind so special?

Practice with a Mudrā

Ceasing all coarser winds and minds and dissolving them in the indestructible drop at the heart is essential for the innate clear-light mind to fully manifest. Generating the experience of great bliss is a method to do this. To generate a blissful awareness that is sufficiently intense and powerful to dissolve the coarse winds and minds, many yogis rely on a mudrā, often called a "seal" or "sealing" physical partner.

In paintings of maṇḍalas, the central deity is often depicted as a "father and mother" couple in union. Some people mistake this as an ordinary sexual relationship, but there is a huge difference between ordinary sexual relations and the practices of a qualified yogi relying on a qualified partner for the purpose of developing a mind of great bliss that realizes emptiness. The former perpetuates saṃsāra, while the latter can eradicate the two obscurations and lead to full awakening. Therefore, only especially qualified, advanced practitioners on the completion stage of Highest Yoga Tantra who have successfully trained in the practices of the subtle channels and winds are permitted to practice with an actual physical karmamudrā partner. Such yogis have full mastery of the winds and channels and are never in danger of experiencing the ordinary bliss of orgasmic emission that would prevent or destroy their generation of a mind of great bliss. They are merely using their external body as a mechanical device to intensify the blissful wisdom of emptiness that they have already attained.

Before reaching this advanced level of accomplishment, practitioners may use only a visualized wisdom mudrā or partner (*jñānamudrā*). In Khedrup Norsang Gyatso's commentary on the *Abbreviated Kālacakra Tantra* entitled *An Ornament for "The Stainless Light,"* he explains that for practitioners with especially sharp faculties, relying on a visualized wisdom partner can also generate a mind of great bliss strong enough to dissolve all the winds in the center of the heart cakra so that the clear-light mind completely manifests. Thus it's not mandatory or necessary to rely on a physical partner. However, once yogis have attained isolated mind by relying on a wisdom mudrā, the dangers and disadvantages of having an action mudrā do not arise and yogis can use one.

Whether qualified yogis practice with a visualized wisdom partner or a physical karma partner, it is essential that they keep the purpose of this practice in mind and consistently maintain the three recognitions: while in union both partners recognize or visualize (1) their bodies in the form of the two deities in union; (2) their speech as the expression of the clear-light mind of inseparable bliss and emptiness, symbolized by syllables that transform into their sexual organs visualized as a vajra and bell; and (3) their minds as the fundamental innate clear-light mind that is inseparable from the wisdom realizing emptiness. When yogis hold these three recognitions in mind, reliance on a visualized or a physical partner becomes a skillful method on the path to eliminate the two obscurations. People who rely on a karma partner without these three recognitions transgress a tantric precept.

The various systems of Highest Yoga Tantra use different techniques to make manifest the clear-light mind. One of these is to use blissful orgasm—but without emission—to withdraw the coarser levels of consciousness and make manifest the subtle mind. For this reason, sexual desire may initially be used when practicing with a wisdom or karma partner. This generates a very powerful blissful mind that is then used to realize the emptiness of inherent existence, strengthening the power of this realization to overcome the afflictive obscurations and cognitive obscurations.

In the final stages of the path, the advanced yoga methods for drawing the winds into the central channel entail male and female yogis sitting in a posture of union. Both partners must have reached the same advanced level of spiritual development; both must have the ability to control their subtle winds and minds so that even though the bottom tips of their central channels touch, they avoid orgasmic release.

Sitting in such a yogic posture while engaging in complex visualizations and meditating on emptiness is done to enhance the practice only on the most advanced levels. It is not done as the main practice or engaged in regularly, and it is certainly not a practice for people on earlier stages of the path. The difficulty of practicing with such a blissful consciousness makes it clear that only special advanced practitioners are capable of engaging in the practice. They must be guided by a teacher in the proper methods and keep the tantric ethical restraints and commitments. Many tantric precepts regarding consort practice must be followed while in union; transgressing them creates great negative karma. If such practice is done without the proper understanding of how sexual union is used on the path, there is the danger that yogis transgress tantric commitments and that people nearby misinterpret their actions and lose faith in the Vajrayāna. Needless to say, consort practice must be done skillfully and with great care.

There has been and still is much misunderstanding and confusion about practicing with a mudrā. In certain sādhanas, the deity is visualized as a couple in union. This symbolizes the unity of method and wisdom on the path, the unity of compassion and wisdom, and the unity of the blissful mind and the wisdom realizing emptiness. In the generation stage, the self-generation practice involves imagining oneself being a deity in union. The purpose of this is to prepare meditators to practice with an actual mudrā when they become suitable vehicles. This is not an excuse to pursue or enjoy ordinary sexual relationships.

Consort practice is limited to a very few highly realized practitioners on the completion stage. I know of very few—maybe just a handful—of people qualified to do this practice now. They are very discreet, and others don't know what they practice. Both partners must have the same level of realization. They must receive teachings on this complex practice from a qualified teacher. If the male's realization is more advanced, he is able to assist the female in gaining higher realizations, and if the female's realization is more advanced, she is able to assist him in gaining higher realizations. On the other hand, if neither is a qualified tantric practitioner although they may mistakenly believe themselves to be, then serious consequences arise because they are deceiving themselves and others.

If either partner is a monastic, they must disrobe to prevent scandals and misinterpretations by the public. If a monastic engages in sexual relationships, they have committed a defeat and are no longer a monastic. If a lama or monk coerces or sweet-talks a woman into having sex, saying that she is a ḍākinī and that she will experience a great blessing by doing "consort" practice with him, that is abuse.

Someone once asked me, "Since we don't know who has high realizations and who doesn't, who are we to say if a monk or lama has abused or exploited a woman?" My response was that highly realized women who are suitable karmamudrās do not cry out "Abuse!"

Unfortunately, some lamas and monks do not behave properly and scandals arise. This causes much confusion in the minds of people and ruins the reputation of Tibetan Buddhism among both Buddhists and non-Buddhists. Such abuse and inappropriate behavior must stop. People ask me why I don't reprimand or punish these people. My thinking is that if they don't listen to what I say during teachings, they also won't listen if I call them out publicly. It is more suitable for their teacher or the head of their tradition to speak to them, or for their monastery to deal with this according to Vinaya.

REFLECTION

1. What are the two types of mudrās? What are the qualifications of a yogi who can use them?
2. What are the faults and dangers of unqualified people thinking their ordinary sexual relationships are "tantric sex"?

3. How does this practice with a consort help a qualified yogi to attain realizations on the path?

4. How does sexual union with an action mudrā differ from ordinary sexual relations?

5. What are the three recognitions both partners must hold while in union?

The Inseparability of Bliss and Emptiness

In Tantra, the unique meaning of the inseparability of compassion and emptiness is the inseparability of great bliss and the pristine wisdom realizing emptiness. Here compassion refers to bliss and bodhicitta refers to the subtle drops in the central channel whose movement generates bliss. The bliss cultivated in Tantra differs from the bliss developed in serenity where meditators experience the physical and mental bliss that comes from pliancy. Bliss in Tantra is not the unpolluted bliss of the realization of emptiness, because that is experienced by all āryas, not just tantric yogis. Nor is it a state of blank-minded nonconceptuality, because it arises through analysis. It is not the bliss that arises when the white bodhicitta melts but does not enter, abide, and dissolve in the central channel, because generation-stage practitioners experience that. It's not the bliss from ordinary sexual union, because it's experienced only by tantric āryas on the completion stage. The great bliss generated in Highest Yoga Tantra is the innate bliss generated by the winds entering, abiding, and dissolving in the central channel and the drops melting and moving in the central channel. It exists only on the completion stage, after mastery of the generation stage. The experience of great bliss is generated simultaneously with the realization of emptiness, and the subject and object of great bliss are inseparable, like water mixed with water.

Great bliss is called "compassion" because etymologically it means "stopping joy." In the understanding of compassion common to Pāramitāyāna and Tantrayāna, compassion is a form of the kind heart. When we generate compassion for others' duḥkha, we may initially feel a sense of unease or despair, which stops the joy of loving others. However, in the unique context of Tantrayāna, great bliss is called compassion because the experience of this bliss involves stopping the bliss of emission. Ordinary compassion cannot completely eradicate duḥkha; this is accomplished by the wisdom realizing emptiness. Here in Highest Yoga Tantra, the mind of great bliss itself is generated into the wisdom realizing emptiness, and in this way it becomes the supreme mind realizing emptiness that can actually protect sentient beings and overcome their duḥkha. In this sense great bliss is called compassion. This is the best example of the inseparability of method and wisdom because the two minds—the mind of great bliss and the wisdom realizing emptiness—are integrated and become one entity.

There are different ways of presenting the inseparability of wisdom and method. In another way, the mind of great bliss is the apprehending subject, the consciousness, and the apprehended object is emptiness. They become inseparable when a practitioner generates the mind of great bliss and at that moment remembers the view. In this way bliss and emptiness—as subject and object—are integrated, whereas in the previous example, the inseparability derives from integrating two minds that then become the same entity.

The inseparability of compassion and emptiness in Highest Yoga Tantra can also refer to the inseparability of the pure illusory body and the actual clear light.

The Completion-Stage Practice of the Two Truths

There are two ways to progress from isolated mind to illusory body: one is to practice with an action mudrā, the other is to practice vajra recitation while dying. Both methods lead to the dissolution of all winds in the indestructible drop and the manifestation of the innate clear light. From the clear light yogis then arise in an illusory body instead of entering the bardo. Both methods involve the practice of the two truths. The two truths may be practiced individually and then inseparably. Practicing them individually is of two kinds: the completion-stage practices of (1) the illusory body, which is the conventional level of truth; and (2) the clear light, which is the ultimate truth.

Illusory Body

At the level of the basis, what is to be purified is the subtlest wind and subtlest consciousness that manifest at the time of the clear light of death. How does this come about? The generation-stage practice of taking death as the path to the dharmakāya prepares meditators to actualize the example clear light. By meditating on the generation stage in analogy with the death process, later, on the completion stage, meditators will experience the example clear light. In this generation-stage practice, meditators imagine the winds gathering in the central channel and imagine experiencing the inner signs that occur as the elements dissolve, such as the mirage, smoke, fireflies, and so on. Then on the completion stage, they actualize the example clear light that overcomes the ordinary clear light of death and puts an end to ordinary death. The example clear light is so-called because it's an example or metaphor for the actual clear light. It is not a mind of actual clear light, because it is polluted by subtle dualistic appearances, whereas the actual clear light that follows is a nonconceptual, nondualistic realization of emptiness by a mind of great bliss.

Just as the example and actual clear lights differ, so do the impure and pure illusory bodies that they respectively produce. Because the example clear light is polluted by the afflictive obscurations, the impure illusory body is under the influence of the polluted karma that projected it. Because the actual clear light is purified of all afflictive obscurations, the pure illusory body that emerges from it is not under the influence of afflictions and polluted karma.

There are several ways to advance from example clear light to illusory body. All of them entail the subtle mind separating from the coarse body, which temporarily ceases to operate. Only if this occurs can the illusory body appear.

One way that the body and mind separate occurs naturally after death. In the dissolution process at death, when the white appearance manifests, the eighty conceptual consciousnesses cease. After they cease, the red increase, the black near-attainment, and the subtlest clear light manifest sequentially, arriving at the last moment of that life. Then the reverse sequence of eight visions of the dying process occur, beginning with the black near-attainment, red increase, and so on. When the subtlest wind becomes slightly coarser, it leaves the old body and arises in another place in the form of a bardo being. The wind-mind first leaves from the heart, and then departs the body through any of the orifices—the crown of the head, the eyes, the ears, or the lower orifices. When ordinary human beings will take birth in an unfortunate realm, the mind departs from the lower orifices. When they will be reborn in a fortunate realm, it leaves through the crown of the head.

Yogis who have attained isolated mind and are capable of practicing vajra recitation and the two stages of withdrawal—instantaneous and gradual—while actively dying can transform this ordinary process of death, bardo, and rebirth into the path to awakening. They can control the winds and cause them to dissolve into the indestructible drop. Being familiar with the death process, they can follow what is happening to them as they die and then meditate in the clear light of death. Then, instead of arising in the ordinary bardo, when the mind and winds become slightly coarser and the black near-attainment arises, simultaneously the impure illusory body appears. With the five-colored subtlest wind acting as the substantial cause, and the subtlest mind as the cooperative condition, the impure illusory body automatically appears together with the supporting and supported maṇḍala, like a fish jumping out of water.

Although it is a body of a deity by definition, it is not a vajra body, because it must be abandoned before attaining full awakening. Nevertheless, this illusory body is an actual deity with the signs and marks of a buddha, and the yogis who attain it can advance through the remaining stages of Highest Yoga Tantra without being born in a coarse body again. Tsongkhapa used this method to attain awakening.

There are two viewpoints about whether the illusory body is attained within the coarse body or outside of it. The Upper and Lower Tantric Colleges assert that it initially arises only outside the coarse body, while Khedrup Norsang Gyatso and Gyalwa Ensapa say it initially arises in the heart cakra in the coarse body. Others say it could arise either way. Although there is a lot of discussion on this point, this issue is not of great importance. Once you have the experience yourself, you will understand how it happens. Even having a conceptual understanding of the illusory body is very helpful and creates great merit.

The illusory body may also arise apart from the old aggregates of the yogi's coarse body. How and why does this happen? Using the example of what happens at death helps us to understand. After the clear light of death manifests, ordinary people attain the bardo. At that time, the subtlest wind-mind separates from the coarse body and arises in the form of the bardo being that abides in a place separate from the old aggregates. Likewise at the time of the path, as the example clear light ends, the subtlest wind-mind becomes slightly coarser and, instead of arising as a bardo body, it arises as an illusory body that can be known in a place separate from the old aggregates.

The illusory body can travel to many places—to pure lands and to polluted realms. Milarepa and others who have attained it emanated many forms, taught in many places, and made offerings in many places simultaneously. In this way, they created great merit that supported their attaining future realizations. The ability to do these actions is a sign of having attained an illusory body. In recent times some monks from the tantric college who were in prayer sessions were also seen walking on the street at the same time. There are also stories of a few monks from the tantric college spending the night sleeping in an alms bowl.

The illusory body is a subtle form made of subtle illusory wind; it is not a coarse material body, even though it has shape and color.[75] When the illusory body leaves the coarse body, it's not a vague material object floating out of the coarse body, like in the movies. Rather, think of an image of the moon reflected in water. The moon in the reflection did not leave the moon, descend, settle and stay on the lake. Likewise, after the clear light, the illusory body instantaneously arises in a place in the form of the deity. It doesn't leave the heart, travel to the crown of the head, come out, and then stand up in front of you!

The other way to separate the subtle mind from the coarse body is through meditation. One way of doing this is through the transference of consciousness (T. *'pho-ba)*.[76] Here meditators expel the subtlest wind-mind in the form of a deity through the crown of the head and transfer the consciousness to a pure land such as Vajrayoginī's pure land. It could also be transferred to the body of a recently deceased person; however, the lineage for the latter practice has been discontinued. Both of these transferences are found in the six yogas of Nāropā. However, neither directly leads to attaining an illusory body.

Another method to generate an illusory body is to practice with an action mudrā at the end of isolated mind. With the aid of an action mudrā, all winds are dissolved into the indestructible drop. When this occurs, the coarse body ceases to function and the example clear light dawns. After meditating with the example clear light, the winds become slightly coarser and the black near-attainment arises. Simultaneous with the mind of the black near-attainment, the impure illusory body is attained instead of the bardo body. The subtlest wind is its substantial cause, and the subtlest mind is its cooperative condition. The impure illusory body appears as a deity and is the actual body of a deity. Yogis who have attained this have overcome death. Because they have control over the winds and appear as a deity, they are not propelled to take a bardo body and another saṃsāric life under the power of afflictions and karma.

The impure illusory body may stay outside the coarse body as long as yogis remain in the meditative equipoise of the final isolated mind in which everything appears like an illusion. As that meditation comes to a close, the illusory body reenters the coarse body. The coarse body can't be completely abandoned at this point because the force of the polluted karma that caused it hasn't been destroyed—this happens later, at the attainment of the actual clear light. Even when meditators attain the actual clear light followed by the pure illusory body, they don't necessarily completely abandon the coarse body. To benefit certain disciples, they may find it useful to maintain this body as one of their emanation bodies.

Twelve similes give us hints about the qualities of the illusory body. Like the *moon reflected in the water* of many ponds at the same time, the illusory body can appear anywhere and as many things simultaneously. Like a *shadow*, it's the appearance of a body without flesh, bones, or organs. Like a *water bubble* that appears suddenly out of water, the *illusory body* arises all at once from emptiness. Like a *mirror image of Vajradhara*, all the limbs of the illusory body are complete.[77]

The stage of the impure illusory body is known as the stage of self-blessing. Here *self* refers to the person. *Blessing or inspiration* (T. *byin gyis rlabs*) has the connotation of improving, enhancing the radiance, or transforming into magnificence. Practitioners become more radiant and eliminate whatever impurities they previously had. To do the illusory-body practice or the self-blessing practice, yogis must have received the secret empowerment. If someone tries to meditate on the illusory body without receiving the secret empowerment, they will not have realizations or insights.

Just before Milarepa was going to leave Marpa, they did the circle of offering (*tshogs kyi 'khor lo*). At this time, Marpa manifested the complete Hevajra maṇḍala from his heart. Such things as this were seen. Milarepa vowed to Marpa, "I will meditate according to the proper procedures and in the correct way, just like you have done, until I gain all the realizations and attainments that you have." With this thought he departed from his guru. He went into retreat in caves in the snowy mountains, and practicing astutely and diligently, he actualized attainments similar to those of his guru, Marpa. This is the connotation of "self-blessing." In Milarepa's case, it was a transformation of the self from a previous state into one with many more great qualities.

Correlations between the Basis, Path, and Result

Previously we discussed the nine mixings. To review, we will now focus on the correlation of our ordinary states of death, bardo, and rebirth with realizations on the tantric path and the fully awakened state of buddhahood. In doing this, Tantrayāna's skillful methods become very apparent. Daily activities such as sleeping, dreaming, and waking up can be conducive to understanding certain aspects of the path and later to bringing forth the resultant buddha bodies. Deep sleep is similar to death in that the mind is in a subtler state and isn't involved with sense objects. There are visualizations and practices on the tantric path to purify deep sleep and the clear light of death so that on the path they become the actual clear light, and at the resultant time the dharmakāya of a buddha.

The dreaming state and bardo are similar in that they both have bodies made of the winds, not flesh and bones, and they can move around. On the path these become the impure and pure illusory bodies, the latter becoming a buddha's resultant enjoyment body.

The waking state resembles rebirth because the mind is associated with a coarse body and again relates to external sense objects. On the path, this is correlated with the illusory body reentering the coarse body, and at buddhahood with a buddha's emanation body.

If we think about the similarities between these sets of correlates, we see that right now at the time of the basis, we have the factors that can be purified and transformed into aspects of the path and into the resultant three bodies of a buddha. The scene is set. Now we need to hear and study teachings and engage in the work of purification and developing excellent new qualities.

Contemplate the correlations between the ordinary state of the basis, the path of transformation, and the resultant three buddha bodies.

Correlations between the Basis, Path, and Result

BASIS	ORDINARY STATES	PATH	RESULT: BODY OF A BUDDHA
Deep sleep	Clear light of death	Actual clear light	Truth body (dharmakāya)
Dreaming	Bardo	Impure and pure illusory bodies	Enjoyment body (pure illusory body in pure lands)
Waking up	Rebirth	Reenter coarse body	Emanation body (body manifested to benefit ordinary beings)

Conduct Enhancing the Path

Vajrayāna contains techniques to enhance the practice of the completion stage. Some of these can be done by generation-stage practitioners, others only by completion-stage yogis. Some of them may be practiced at the time of the empowerment, others at the time of meditation on the path. Among the special behaviors to be done at the time of the path, some are for the purpose of attaining stages that haven't yet been attained, and others are to enhance those that have already been attained.

In general, there are four occasions when yogis engage in conduct to enhance their practice of the path. One is on the generation stage and three are on the completion stage. (1) When, having perfected the coarse and refined generation stages, they seek to enhance the wisdom of bliss and emptiness. Never mind the refined generation stage, even to practice the coarse generation stage is difficult. The great Ra Lotsawa, who attained many inconceivable realizations, had only achieved perfection in the coarse generation stage. Thus practitioners should practice at their own level. (2) On isolated mind, when they seek to accomplish the impure illusory body. (3) When, having an impure illusory body, they aim to attain the actual clear light or learners' union. (4) On the learners' union when they want to attain the union without learning.

At each of these occasions, three conducts (T. *spyod pa gsum*) may be done to enhance yogis' practice of the path. These three conducts are those with, without, and completely without elaboration. Each conduct is a method that give extra power to hasten yogis' practice enhancing the concentration of bliss and emptiness by enjoying sensual pleasures in general and those with a mudrā in particular through understanding their ultimate nature. These conducts must be done by qualified yogis with the correct understanding of emptiness and for the purpose of advancing on the path to awakening.

The *conduct with elaboration* is held in a three-storied house that is analogous to the inestimable mansion of the deity. On the top floor, yogis and yoginīs gather. All of them have equal completion-stage realizations. If they practice Guhyasamāja, thirty-two yogis and yoginīs corresponding to the thirty-two deities in the Guhyasamāja maṇḍala attend. Everyone wears costumes and masks resembling the faces of the deities.

Together they perform the tsog offering (*gaṇacakra,* T. *tshogs kyi 'khor lo*) and sport with desirable objects. They engage in music, song, dance, and gestures as explained in the ritual texts, and in this way generate the concentration of bliss and emptiness. While engaged in these conducts, they train in seeing whatever appears as being empty, that emptiness is bliss, and the bliss dawns as the body of the deity. It is said that King Indrabhūti did this in his palace and succeeded in increasing his realizations.

For generation-stage meditators to engage in conduct with elaboration to attain the common supernormal powers,[78] they must be fully confident in their ability to maintain clear appearance and divine identity as the deity. Furthermore, they must have received special detailed oral instructions about the proper way to practice this conduct. To enter into union while on the generation stage, they bless the space and the secrets (the two organs called the vajra and lotus) and then join them. They block the holes with the syllable *phat* and hold the bodhicitta without emission. During the completion stage, four positions must be practiced according to instructions. The difficulty in understanding and enacting the instructions points to the fact that mudrā practice is not ordinary intercourse and the consort cannot be just anyone but must be someone who keeps their ethical restraints well and is knowledgeable in this practice.

When practitioners reach a stage of pure insight, they are allowed to engage in all these elaborate actions, including some unconventional ones, such as hunting. A sign that they can engage in such conduct is the ability to cause fruit to fall from a tree by the power of their single-pointed samādhi and then cause the fruit to go back up onto the tree by the power of their concentration. Another example is they can kill a deer, eat its flesh, and snap their fingers to cause the parts of the deer to reassemble and become a live deer again. Also, they can destroy an enemy or a harmful being and then transfer its consciousness to a pure land. People who are capable of doing these things have reached the stage where they are allowed to engage in actions with elaboration.

Conduct without elaboration is similar to conduct with elaboration in that there is a tsog gathering with yogis and yoginīs. It differs in that they do not engage in so many actions; for example, they do not respond to songs and dances, or perform certain gestures and responses to them. This conduct is of three types, depending on the number of mudrās involved.

Conduct completely free from elaboration is done without any external activities. It involves meditation on the wisdom of indivisible bliss and emptiness together with a wisdom mudrā. The bliss of experiencing the five sensual qualities of a partner—especially touch—is combined with the wisdom ascertaining the mudrā's ultimate nature, emptiness. This increases the bliss, which enhances the concentration of bliss and emptiness.

In the conduct completely without elaboration, yogis do only necessary external actions, such as eating, sleeping, and defecating, and they engage in meditative equipoise on emptiness with the clear-light mind as much as possible. This increases the bliss, which in turn increases the power of the clear light. This practice is done only with a wisdom mudrā abiding at the heart, not with an actual karmamudrā. Meditation on emptiness serves the same function as engaging with a mudrā. This is one reason why emptiness is called the "mother of the conquerors" and "mahāmudrā."

Why do yogis engage in these conducts that serious spiritual practitioners usually abandon? In general, meditators who have mastered the coarse and refined generation stages perform the three types of conduct to attain the common supernormal powers, such as the four actions (purification, increase, power or control, and ferocity), as well as other supernormal feats. Completion-stage meditators do the three types of conduct to enhance their meditation on emptiness.

Many of you may have heard stories of the strange behavior of some realized tantric practitioners. It is easy to misunderstand these stories, or to overlook their deeper meanings. To give you a sense of how these great yogis practiced, I'd like to share a few stories about them.

The great translator Marpa Lotsawa had four disciples who specialized in meditating on the channels and tummo. Marpa taught and guided them, but ignored Milarepa, showing him a fierce demeanor and giving Mila only a few teachings.

Motivated by compassion for Milarepa, Marpa's wife gave Milarepa a letter to deliver to another lama and told Mila to request him for teachings. When Mila arrived, he saw many people acting in harmful ways around that lama's monastery. Prior to finding his guru Marpa, Mila had studied black magic. He could cause hailstorms, a skill he had learned previously from a non-Buddhist teacher. The lama asked Mila to cause a hailstorm to disperse the harmful beings. The hailstones were very large and killed many birds.

Mila collected all the dead birds in a big sack and brought them back to the lama's monastery. Feeling great regret for having killed these birds by causing a hailstorm, he lamented, "In the past I accumulated so much negative karma, and now look, although I've been trying to practice the Dharma, I have accumulated so much negative karma from killing these birds. What shall I do?"

The lama consoled him, "Don't worry. In the future when you become a buddha, all these birds will be your disciples." He snapped his fingers, and the birds flew away. That is one story about the great yogi Milarepa.

Another story occurred when Milarepa met his disciple Rechungpa coming back from India. They saw a yak horn on the road, and Mila asked Rechungpa to pick it up. Rechungpa refused, saying that it was of no use, "We cannot eat or drink this, so there is no use carrying a yak horn with us." Milarepa replied, "You must take it because there will be a time when we need it."

Later they came to an open plain, and Mila caused large hailstones to rain down. Lacking shelter, Rechungpa covered his head with a blanket. When the hail stopped and the sun came out, Rechungpa removed the blanket and looked around. He heard Milarepa singing, but he couldn't see him. After trying to locate Mila, Rechungpa saw the yak horn and looked inside. There sat Mila, singing. Mila said, "Since I am an older man I'd rather stay in the inner part of the horn, and since you are a young man you should stay in the lower part of the horn." Rechungpa bent down and tried to go inside the yak horn, but even his fist couldn't fit in, let alone his whole body. Yogis such as Mila who have attained the illusory body can do these sorts of miraculous feats. This horn was later kept in the sacred Jokhang temple in Lhasa.

The Gelugpa lama Jamyang Dewai Dorje, who lived at the time of the seventh Dalai Lama, had very high realizations and engaged in elaborate actions. He once put honey on a board and many flies got stuck in the honey. He then ate the flies by licking the board.

Meditators can engage in such activities only if they have attained very high realizations. At that time there are no limits to what they can and cannot do. Whoever sees the face of a yogi who has attained the impure illusory body through this practice will definitely not fall into the unfortunate realms. Although the activities of such yogis may seem like the activities of a madman, if you possess excellent discriminating awareness, you will be able to understand and to distinguish a yogi from someone suffering from mental illness.

REFLECTION

1. What are the two types of illusory body? How do they differ?
2. How is the process of dying and death similar to the dissolution that tantric yogis practice to gain realization? How do they differ?
3. Describe the three conducts, their purpose, and their desired outcomes.

Meanings of "Clear Light"

Before explaining the next stage, the actual clear light or fourth-stage clear light, it's helpful to know the meaning of the term "clear light" in varying contexts.

In Pāramitāyāna the *object clear light* refers to the cognized object, emptiness, the ultimate nature of all phenomena. *Subjective clear light* refers to the subject, the wisdom nonconceptually realizing emptiness. *Clear-light nature* refers to the conventional nature of the mind in which the afflictions are adventitious and do not abide in the clear and cognizant conventional nature of the mind.

In Vajrayana, the *example clear light* comes at the end of isolated mind when all the winds have dissolved into the indestructible drop in the central channel at the heart. The example clear lights of isolated body, speech, and mind and the impure illusory body realize emptiness conceptually—that is, by means of an image created by the mental consciousness. Thus they are considered dualistic in that regard.

The fourth-stage clear light is the *actual clear light* that directly and nonconceptually realizes emptiness after all the winds have completely dissolved into the indestructible drop at the heart. Whereas the example clear light imagines bliss and emptiness to be combined, the actual clear light nondually combines bliss and emptiness as the single taste of the ultimate nature. The actual clear light of the uninterrupted path is the direct antidote to the afflictive obscurations, and the actual clear light of the liberated path has abandoned these obscurations. The actual clear light that is the direct antidote to the cognitive obscurations and the actual clear light of the liberated path that has abandoned those obscurations realize emptiness directly, without any conceptual appearance. Uninterrupted paths are wisdom consciousnesses that cease afflictions. Liberated paths are wisdom consciousnesses that prevent them from ever returning. Uninterrupted paths kick a thief out of your home, whereas liberated paths lock the door behind them so they can never return.

Clear light also refers to the subtlest mind that naturally manifests at death and is one nature with the subtlest wind. In ordinary beings this clear light is obscured by defilements. It manifests temporarily at the culmination of the death process. Present in all saṃsāric beings, it is the clear light that is the basis of purification in Vajrayāna. The *mother clear light* (T. *ma'i 'od gsal*)—the subtlest mind that is naturally empty of inherent existence—arises naturally during death, while the *child clear light* (T. *bu'i 'od gsal*) is the subtlest mind that realizes emptiness and arises only when the winds have dissolved in the central channel through the force of meditation. The mother and child clear lights come together like two close friends and blend inseparably when the wisdom mind realizes its own ultimate nature.

The clear light of the completion stage can also be spoken of in terms of its literal, general, hidden, and ultimate meaning. There are two *general meanings* of "clear light," neither of which is unique to the completion stage. The first is a coarse mental consciousness realizing emptiness; this can be experienced in the Pāramitāyāna, the three lower tantras, and Highest Yoga Tantra. The second is a blissful mind that realizes emptiness. This is experienced in both the generation and completion stages of Highest Yoga Tantra when the drops in the central channel melt.

The *hidden meaning* of clear light is the example clear light of isolated mind that conceptually realizes emptiness. It is called "hidden" because it manifests only when the winds dissolve into the central channel. Although the example clear lights of isolated body, isolated speech, and mere isolated mind are not fully qualified example clear lights, they are called example clear lights and understood as the hidden meaning of clear light.

The *ultimate meaning* of clear light is the actual clear light, the blissful clear-light mind that directly realizes emptiness. It is ultimate in the sense that it is the best clear light and occurs on the levels of actual clear light, learners' union, and nonlearners' union.

Actual Clear Light

To do the practices of clear light and thus attain the fourth stage actual clear light, it is necessary to receive the third empowerment, the wisdom empowerment. The impure illusory body arises subsequent to the example clear light. It exists without interruption until the actual clear light is attained, at which time the impure illusory body ceases. The pure illusory body later manifests from the actual clear light.

After the impure illusory body has reentered the old body, yogis continue their practice in meditation sessions as well as in break times. In some meditation sessions they again dissolve the winds into the indestructible drop at the heart and meditate on the emptiness of all phenomena. In other sessions, they meditate on the defects of saṃsāra, compassion, bodhicitta, various concentrations, and emptiness. Post-session, they manifest diverse bodies and forms with the impure illusory body to benefit sentient beings. They also practice the three conducts. When signs appear that they are close to attaining the actual clear light, they engage in union with a karmamudrā. While in union, they maintain mindfulness of the empty nature of sense objects and diligently meditate on the instantaneous and gradual dissolution processes. Through this, the minds of white appearance, red increase, black near-attainment, and clear light dawn. When all the winds have dissolved into the indestructible drop at the heart and that blissful clear light realizes emptiness directly without any dualistic appearance, the impure illusory body ceases, and the clear light becomes the uninterrupted path of the path of seeing that is a direct antidote to the afflictive obscurations. The moment the fourth-stage *actual clear light* arises, all afflictive obscurations have been forever ceased. This marks the first ground in Highest Yoga Tantra. The yogis become āryas and are forever free from saṃsāra.

The actual clear light is attained at dawn when the sky is free from moonlight, sunlight, and darkness and the clear light is free from the faults of the white appearance, red increase, and black near-attainment—minds that perceive emptiness conceptually.[79] The actual clear light is a mind of great bliss that nonconceptually and directly realizes emptiness after all the winds have completely dissolved into the indestructible drop at the heart. The bliss and the dissolution of the winds increase the power of this mind.

Some practitioners attain full awakening in the bardo. Having completed the generation stage, they practice the completion stage and reach the level of isolated mind. Generating a strong motivation to attain the actual clear light, at death they meditate on the absorption of the elements and winds, and after the clear light of death and child clear light "recognize" each other, they arise in an illusory body instead of a bardo body.

Learners' Union—the Inseparability of the Two Truths

Why is it important to enter the path of Highest Yoga Tantra to become a buddha? The latencies of grasping the dualistic appearance of the minds of white appearance, red increase, and black near-attainment as well as all other cognitive obscurations must be forever cleansed for the dharmakāya to be attained. To attain a buddha's omniscient mind requires first attaining the actual clear light that integrates bliss and emptiness. This blissful wisdom clear-light mind perceives emptiness nonconceptually and nondualistically. To generate the form bodies of a buddha, it is necessary to manifest the pure illusory body that arises from the subtlest wind as its substantial cause and the actual clear light as its cooperative condition. The methods to purify and activate the wisdom of great bliss realizing emptiness and its mount, the extremely subtle wind, are discussed only in Highest Yoga Tantra.

The paths of the Pāramitāyāna and the three lower tantras do not have the power to cleanse the latencies of the dualistic appearances of the white appearance, red increase, and black near-attainment. They do not tap into and utilize the subtlest winds and subtlest mind that are one nature and develop them so that a buddha's truth body and form body arise. Only the path of the Highest Yoga Tantra has the techniques and ability to do this. It explains two ways to access the subtlest wind-mind: (1) by entering into union with a karmamudrā—this facilitates the winds dissolving into the central channel and indestructible drop just as they do at death—and (2) through meditation practice to dissolve the winds into the indestructible drop at the heart.

Having attained the actual clear light, yogis now seek to actualize the learners' union. They "wake up" from the actual clear light when the wind that is its mount begins to move slightly. Simultaneously this wind, which has five-colored rays of light, acts as the substantial cause and the mind of clear light acts as the cooperative condition for the pure illusory body to arise. This marks the beginning of the *union with abandonment* (T. *spangs pa zung 'jug*). This is not a union of the pure illusory body and the actual clear light—that union is attained later. Rather, it is a union of the abandonment of all afflictive obscurations and the pure illusory body. Simultaneous with this, the mind of black near-attainment of the reverse sequence arises, the actual clear light ceases, the liberated path of having eradicated the afflictive obscurations is attained, yogis become arhats, and the path of meditation of Highest Yoga Tantra is attained.

Now, yogis emphasize doing virtuous deeds to advance the collection of merit. From their illusory bodies, they emanate many forms that go throughout the universe to benefit sentient beings. In this way they quickly create great merit and can bring many sentient beings to the Buddhadharma. Since the pure illusory body is a different entity than the coarse body and can leave and reenter the coarse body as it pleases, yogis may also reenter their old, coarse bodies to engage in virtuous actions to benefit sentient beings.

Having attained the *union with abandonment*, yogis do not take up new paths but familiarize themselves with their previous trainings. Seeking to abandon all cognitive obscurations, they may abide in the coarse body and repeatedly meditate on the two concentrated modes of dissolution—gradual and taken-all-together—and meditate with the actual clear light. They also engage in any of the three types of conduct to advance their practice.

From the union with abandonment, yogis advance to the *union with realization* (T. *rtogs pa zung 'jug*) comparatively quickly. They reenter meditative equipoise on emptiness with the mind of actual clear light. When this is actualized, they attain the union of the pure illusory body and the actual clear light, which are of one nature. This is referred to as the union of body and mind or the union with realization.

Due to practicing in this way, after some time they will experience signs of attaining the nonlearners' union. When their collections of merit and wisdom are complete, the remaining cognitive obscurations are vanquished and buddhahood is attained.

Twenty-one or twenty-three states of union are included in the nonlearners' union of buddhahood. These include the union of saṃsāra and nirvāṇa, the union of the perceiver and the object perceived, the union of method and wisdom, the union of the two truths, and so on. Having a mere general understanding of the nonlearners' union brings great benefit by planting virtuous seeds in our mindstreams and strengthening our aspirations to follow the path of Highest Yoga Tantra and attain full awakening.

Starting Points of the Stages within the Completion Stage

Just as a building is constructed from the ground level up, this chart is to be read from the bottom up, showing a practitioner's advancement on the completion stage.

Definition of completion stage: a yoga in the continuum of a trainee that arises from causing the winds to enter, abide, and dissolve in the central channel by the power of meditation.

STAGES	LEVELS OF STAGES	STARTING POINT	PATHS
Nonlearners' union (buddhahood)	n/a	All cognitive obscurations have been eradicated.	No-more-learning
Learners' union	Union with realization	Reenter meditative equipoise on emptiness with the mind of actual clear light. Attain the union of the pure illusory body and the actual clear light, which are one nature. This is the union of body and mind.	Meditation
	Pure illusory body Union with abandonment (union of the abandonment of afflictive obscurations and the pure illusory body)	Arise in a pure illusory body that is simultaneous with the mind of black near-attainment of the reverse sequence that occurs when the winds move slightly from the actual clear light. At the same time, one attains: • the liberated path that has abandoned the afflictive obscurations • the second bodhisattva ground and the path of meditation of Highest Yoga Tantra • the state of an arhat • an actual vajra body	
Clear light	Actual clear light	Attained when all winds are dissolved in the indestructible drop at the heart and the blissful wisdom of clear light ascertains emptiness nonconceptually and nondualistically. At the same time: • the impure illusory body ceases • the first ground and path of seeing of Highest Yoga Tantra are attained • the uninterrupted path that is the direct antidote to the acquired and innate afflictive obscurations is attained	Seeing

STAGES	LEVELS OF STAGES	STARTING POINT	PATHS
Illusory body	Impure illusory body	The actual attainment of a deity body that is simultaneous with the mind of near-attainment of the reverse sequence that occurs when the winds move slightly from the example clear light of the final isolated mind. The example clear light is the cooperative condition and the fundamental wind in the indestructible drop that is its mount is the substantial cause.	Preparation
Isolated mind	Final isolation of mind (example clear light)	Attained with the dissolution of all winds into the indestructible drop, inducing the fully qualified pristine wisdom of (white) appearance.	
	Mere isolated mind	Having fully untied the channel knots at the heart, one generates the pristine wisdom of (white) appearance that has arisen due to the dissolution of the four root winds (excluding the pervasive wind) in the indestructible drop at the heart.	
Isolated speech (isolated body included)	Isolated speech	Engage in vajra recitation to loosen the knots above and below the heart. When the upper and lower winds enter, abide, and dissolve in the central channel at the heart (but not in the indestructible drop), the pristine wisdom of (white) appearance arises.	
	Isolated body	After culminating refined generation stage, one generates the pristine wisdom realizing emptiness that arises by the winds entering, abiding, and dissolving in the central channel by meditating on the entire maṇḍala in a subtle drop at the lower tip of the central channel.	
Generation stage	n/a	Attained with the experience of the clear appearance of the coarse maṇḍala without omissions or additions to the visualization, together with uncontrived divine identity.	Accumulation

Main Practices of the Completion Stage

Read from the bottom upward.

STAGES	LEVELS OF STAGES	MAIN PRACTICES	DISSOLUTION OF WINDS IN CENTRAL CHANNEL
Resultant, buddhahood	Nonlearners' union	Engaging in the awakening activities of a buddha to benefit sentient beings	At the indestructible drop at the heart (all winds)
Learners' union	Union with realization	• Engage in any of the three conducts • Meditate repeatedly on the two types of withdrawal • Repeatedly familiarize with actual clear light	
	Union with abandonment (union of the abandonment of afflictive obscurations and the pure illusory body)		
Clear light	Actual clear light	Continue to meditate with mind of bliss and wisdom that nonconceptually realizes emptiness	
Illusory body	Impure illusory body	• Engage in any of the three conducts • Meditate repeatedly on the two stages of withdrawal • Repeatedly meditate on emptiness with example clear light until realizing emptiness nonconceptually with the mind of clear light • Manifest diverse bodies and forms to benefit sentient beings	
Isolated mind	Final isolated mind (example clear light)	Internal conditions: • Vajra recitation observing the pervasive wind • Meditation on the yoga of the two stages of withdrawal External condition: union with an action (actual) mudrā and doing vajra recitation	
	Mere isolated mind	Internal conditions: • Vajra recitation observing the pervasive wind • Meditation on the two stages of withdrawal of the two concentrations External condition: union with a wisdom (imagined) mudrā	At the indestructible drop at the heart (four root winds, excluding pervasive wind)

STAGES	LEVELS OF STAGES	MAIN PRACTICES	DISSOLUTION OF WINDS IN CENTRAL CHANNEL
Isolated speech (isolated body included)	Isolated speech	3 vajra recitations (vitality-exertion): 1. meditate on mantra drop at heart 2. meditate on light drop at tip of nose (the actual vajra recitation) 3. meditate on substance drop at tip of secret place	At the heart
	Isolated body	• Meditation on subtle drops, tummo • Meditation on emptiness with blissful mind, 4 empties, 4 joys • Individual withdrawal: viewing all sense objects that appear as manifestation of bliss and emptiness • Concentration: yoga that views objects and so forth as manifestations of bliss and emptiness in the aspect of deities	At the lower tip of the central channel
Generation stage	n/a	Refined generation stage: meditates on the entire supporting and supported maṇḍala the size of a mustard seed. Coarse generation stage: meditates the entire coarse supporting and supported maṇḍala.	Imaginary dissolution

The Union of the Two Truths

Like many other terms, the meaning of "union" differs according to the context; there are the union of bliss and emptiness and the union of the two truths. When speaking of the union of the two truths in Highest Yoga Tantra, the union of bliss and emptiness is one part of the pair (ultimate truth) and the illusory body is the other (conventional truth). When these two are inseparably joined, they form the union of the two truths.

The *union of bliss and emptiness* is an indivisible union of the mind of great bliss and the wisdom realizing emptiness. Here wisdom realizing emptiness and bliss are experienced as the entity of one consciousness. This may come about in two ways. In the first, practitioners have previously realized emptiness, and the wisdom realizing emptiness is then conjoined with bliss. That is, wisdom is generated in the aspect of bliss, so that wisdom and bliss become one nature. This sequence in which the realization of emptiness precedes the actual experience of great bliss is the way most practitioners of Highest Yoga Tantra generate the union of bliss and emptiness. However, another way is possible in which yogis melt the drops in the channels generating bliss, and this blissful mind is then used to newly realize emptiness.

Some tantric practitioners may initially follow the Yogācāra view of emptiness. Although this view is helpful to some people, it is an incomplete understanding of emptiness. By applying tantric meditative techniques, such as igniting the tummo or penetrating the vital points of the body through wind yoga, meditators generate an experience of bliss. This leads to a state where the coarser levels of mind and wind dissolve. Such a deep experience may lead practitioners to a subtler understanding of emptiness—that phenomena are mere designations imputed in dependence on their bases of designation; they are empty of inherent existence.[80]

Practitioners with sharp faculties—who are the main practitioners of Highest Yoga Tantra—have realized emptiness before they receive a Highest Yoga Tantra empowerment. In this case, the realization of emptiness precedes the experience of bliss.

When engaging in tantric meditation, sharp-faculty meditators employ methods such as deity yoga, igniting tummo, and penetrating the vital points of the body by wind yoga. Through the force of desire, these meditation methods melt the drops in the channels. When these drops of bodhicitta melt, yogis experience a physical sensation within the central channel that gives rise to a powerful experience of bliss. This bliss, in turn, induces a subtle mental bliss, which leads to the experience of subtler states of mind. When meditators then recollect their realization of emptiness, the experience of mental bliss is conjoined with the mind realizing emptiness. This is the union of bliss and emptiness. The experience of bliss is the same for both male and female meditators.

The Five Paths according to Vajrayāna

In *Courageous Compassion*, we discussed the paths and grounds for śrāvakas, solitary realizers, and bodhisattvas from the viewpoint of the Pāli tradition and the Mahāyāna. This included the step-by-step process as presented in the Pāramitāyāna through which bodhisattvas gradually abandon layers of afflictions and defilements and develop levels of spiritual realizations.[81] Bodhisattvas who follow the Vajrayāna progress through the paths and grounds as presented in Highest Yoga Tantra. Although the names of the paths and grounds in both systems are the same, due to the unique qualities of Vajrayāna—especially the activation and transformation of the subtlest wind and mind—the meanings in the two systems differ.

In *Lamp Illuminating the Five Stages*, Tsongkhapa explains the paths and grounds according to Highest Yoga Tantra in general.[82] The path of accumulation follows the common paths of learning the four truths, having some experience of the determination to be free from saṃsāra, bodhicitta, and the correct view of emptiness. It ranges from generating bodhicitta according to the common paths up to but not including the ability to induce the four empties by causing the winds to enter, abide, and dissolve in the central channel. The tantric path of accumulation concludes just before yogis can induce the wisdom realizing emptiness by dissolving the winds into the central channel by the power of meditation.

The path of preparation begins with inducing the wisdom realizing emptiness by the winds entering, abiding, and dissolving in the central channel due to the power of meditation at the beginning of the completion stage—that is, when the refined generation stage ceases and the isolated body of the completion stage begins. The path of preparation extends through generating the impure illusory body and concludes just before yogis' subtlest mind perceives emptiness nonconceptually for the first time.

The path of seeing and the first ground called Very Joyful begin with the first moment of the actual clear light—the subtlest mind that realizes emptiness nonconceptually due to the entering, abiding, and dissolving of the winds in the indestructible drop at the heart. It extends until just before the pure illusory body is realized.

The path of meditation begins with the first moment after the actual clear light arises into the pure illusory body. This also marks the learners' union with abandonment, which is the union of the pure illusory body and the abandonment of all afflictive obscurations. Yogis again enter the actual clear light and emerge in a pure illusory body. This time the actual clear light and pure illusory body are united, and the union with realization is attained.

The path of meditation encompasses the remaining nine bodhisattva grounds and extends until just before the attainment of the union with no-more-learning. The path of no-more learning begins when all cognitive obscurations have been completely abandoned. This is full awakening, buddhahood, the union of a nonlearner.

The Completion Stage according to Other Highest Yoga Tantras

Highest Yoga Tantra includes the practices of many deities. Previously, we spoke of the Guhyasamāja Ārya tradition and the structure of its completion stage. In this section, I'll introduce you to some more Highest Yoga Tantra deities. Some of these are practiced in several of the four Tibetan traditions; others are practiced more by one tradition or another.

The Guhyasamāja system has two major traditions, the Ārya tradition and the tradition of Jñanapada. The completion stage of the latter tradition is divided into four parts known as the four blisses or the four drops. These four drops are the indestructible drop at the heart, the secret drop at the jewel (the lower tip of the central channel), the emanation drop at the upper tip of the central channel at the nose, and the special indestructible drop at the heart. The state of union is achieved by meditation involving these factors. Although the nomenclature in this tradition is different, the attainments are the same as in the Ārya tradition.

There are three major traditions of Cakrasaṃvara (Heruka): those of Luipa, Tilbupa or Gandhapada, and Kṛṣṇācārya. Of these, the completion stage of Luipa's tradition is known as the great yoga. The completion stage of Tilbupa's tradition consists of five stages: the stages of self-blessing, the multicolored vajra, filling the jewel, Jālandhara, and the inconceivable.

The completion stage of Mahācakra or the Great Wheel of Vajrapāṇi (*phyag rdor 'khor lo chen po*) contains the stages of four blessings—the blessings of the body, speech, mind, and thusness. As with other tantras mentioned above, the meaning of this fits in with the six-level completion stage of Guhyasamāja.

There are three traditions of Yamāntaka: red Yamāntaka, black Yamāntaka, and Vajrabhairava forms of Yamāntaka. In these three traditions, the completion stage consists of four yogas: the yogas of shape, mantra, commitment (*samaya*), and pure pristine wisdom.

According to Gampopa, the six yogas of Nāropā, also called the oral instruction transmission for achieving liberation in the bardo, are: tummo (*caṇḍālī*), clear light (*prabhāsvara*), dream state (*svapnadarśana*), illusory body (*māyādeha*), bardo (*antarābhava*), and transference of consciousness (*saṃkrānti*). Following Phagmo Drupa, Tsongkhapa classifies the six yogas as: tummo, illusory body (including dream yoga), clear light, transference of consciousness, forceful projection (*parakāya-praveśa*), and bardo.[83]

The Kālacakra Tantra's completion stage has six levels: individual withdrawal, meditative stabilization, vitality-exertion, retention, subsequent mindfulness, and concentration. The completion stage of Hevajra is called "including the three empowerments in the path." It has two presentations of the completion stage, one by the mahāsiddha Dombipa called "spring-like drop" and the other by Mithupdawa called "stages of dissipation of colors."

Other mahāsiddhas who attained great accomplishments spoke of the completion stages of more tantras. All of these share common features: practitioners have stable training in the common preliminary path, have received the full and proper empowerments that are the gateway to enter Highest Yoga Tantra, are safeguarding all the ethical restraints and commitments, perfecting the coarse and refined generation-stage practices, and engaging in the completion-stage practices to attain awakening. All of them are the same in these features, although they may differ in their techniques to make the channels, winds, and drops usable. Nevertheless, all these techniques to work with the channels, winds, and drops cause the winds to enter, abide, and dissolve into the central channel. This causes the flaming of tummo, which melts the bodhicitta drops. As a result, the pristine wisdoms of the four joys and the four emptinesses arise. By continuously cultivating this pristine wisdom of the simultaneous joy or the clear light, yogis attain the substantial cause for the truth body of a buddha. Then they attain the mind of clear light and the illusory body, which is made of the subtlest wind. This is similar to what occurs in the ordinary bardo in the stages that occur after death. The illusory body is the substantial cause for the form body of the buddha and the clear light becomes the substantial cause of a buddha's truth body. In this way, through their diligent and compassionate practice, yogis attain full awakening.

The system that differs the most from this general mode of practice is Kālacakra, which has unique methods for creating similitudes of a buddha's body and mind. Instead of teaching methods to separate the subtlest body and mind from the coarse body and mind, it teaches a method to make the coarse body and the subtle body of winds and drops vanish.

When you have studied and found certainty in all the major texts, you will see that even though all of these tantras may not have the same terms or mention exactly the same points in their explanations, their meaning is not contradictory and they all lead to the same goal.

How to Manifest the Results

The results of Vajrayāna are said to be three, depending on the aspirations of the practitioners and the realizations they cultivate and attain on the path: (1) the supreme result is attaining the fully awakened state of Vajradhara, the supreme actual attainment; (2) the middle result is attaining the eight great siddhis; and (3) the least result is attaining the actions of pacifying, increasing, power or control, and ferocity. The last results are the common actual attainments that are shared by highly realized yogis who are not yet fully awakened.

There are three ways of attaining the fully awakened state: in this lifetime, in the bardo, and after a series of lifetimes. Attaining awakening *in this lifetime* refers to attaining buddhahood in one lifetime and in one body during the time of five degenerations. In general, practitioners can attain awakening in one lifetime through the tantric path. In the three lower tantras it is accomplished by extending the lifespan through long-life practices, whereas in Highest Yoga Tantra, once a practitioner has attained the illusory body, it is certain they will attain full awakening in that life.

To attain awakening *in the bardo*, practitioners must have already achieved the state of isolated mind. Then at the time of death, instead of experiencing the clear light of death under the control of afflictions and karma, they meditate with the example clear light, and in the bardo they manifest the illusory body. They continue from there to eradicate both the afflictive and cognitive obscurations and attain awakening in the bardo.

Practitioners who have achieved isolated body or isolated speech but haven't yet attained isolated mind attain awakening *after a series of lifetimes*.

Practitioners who have the potential to attain awakening in this lifetime with one body during this time of the five degenerations are diligent in receiving and understanding all instructions on that Tantra from their tantric guru. Examples of such practitioners are Nāgārjuna in India and Milarepa in Tibet. Although this is called "awakening in one lifetime with one body," that is merely a convention. In fact, awakening cannot be attained with only one body. The reason is that the impure illusory body that manifested from the example clear light cannot go to the state of awakening and must be abandoned because it is not free from afflictive obscurations and is still connected to the coarse body of that lifetime, which was produced under the control of afflictions and karma. It must be relinquished, and with further practice awakening is attained with a pure illusory body. Only the pure illusory body is a vajra body that can continue to the awakened state of Vajradhara.

According to ancient Indian and Tibetan culture, the five degenerations of our time are:

1. Decreased duration of a lifetime. The first humans in our world system lived for an incalculable amount of time. It is said that the Buddha appeared when the lifespan was one hundred. Now, if we consider all the people in the world, not just those in places with good health care, very few live to be eighty or ninety. New diseases have appeared that destroy the lives of humans and animals.

2. Degenerated material resources, in quality and quantity. There were unplowed harvests at the beginning of the eon. Crops grew wild and there was no need to plant seeds. Now farmers must plant crops or cultivate orchards, and these are subject to human-made and natural disasters. Furthermore, natural resources are being exhausted. Treasures from the ocean and valuable minerals in the ground are being depleted. The amount of arable land has decreased, so people clear forests to plant crops. Wars are fought over oil and other natural resources.
3. Decrease in human beings' body size. In earlier times, animals were very large and humans were also big. Now bodies are getting smaller.
4. Degeneration of people's views. Previously people had strong conviction in the laws of karma, in rebirth and the possibility of being reborn in unfortunate realms. Nowadays people are no longer very interested in engaging in virtuous actions or purifying their negativities. Apologizing to others for our harmful actions and forgiving them for theirs is often seen as being either weak or unnecessary.
5. Decrease in the strength of people's virtuous mental states and actions and increase in the power of their afflictions. Even monastics have strong afflictions and poisons in their mindstream, and it is rare to find people who are practicing the Dharma properly.

REFLECTION

1. Describe the union of the two truths, the union of bliss and emptiness, and the union of body and mind.
2. What are the four activities of pacification, increase, control, and ferocity? Make examples of how they can be used to benefit sentient beings.
3. We live in the time of the five degenerations. How can we use them to energize our Dharma practice? How can we help to slow them down?

Knowing how much the five degenerations harm sentient beings and interfere with the existence of the Buddha's teachings in the future, let's conduct ourselves with a virtuous motivation, keep our precepts, and study and practice the Dharma diligently now when we have the opportunity. The instructions for attaining awakening exist, and if sincere meditators make effort and follow the precious instructions of Highest Yoga Tantra, then in individual cases they still have the possibility to attain full awakening in this life.

12 | The Path of Kālacakra Tantra

TRADITION HAS IT that on the full-moon day of the third month in the year after his awakening, Śākyamuni Buddha taught the *Perfection of Wisdom Sūtra in One Hundred Thousand Verses* at Vultures' Peak and simultaneously spoke the *Kālacakra Root Tantra* in the maṇḍala created at Dhānyakaṭaka in South India[84] to the king of Śambhala, Sucandra, together with a great assembly of other monarchs, bodhisattvas, and so on. The teachings passed from King Sucandra to a line of twenty-five lineage holders (T. *rigs ldan*) who held authority over the Kālacakra teachings. The first of these, Jampel Drakpa, wrote a great commentary to the Kālacakra teachings. Padma Karpo, a later lineage holder who is considered an emanation of Avalokiteśvara, wrote a famous commentary to the Kālacakra Tantra. These teachings are most widespread in the country of Śambhala. Śambhala belongs to this world, but it cannot easily be seen in the ordinary way. However, when dedicated disciples do the practices and purify themselves through this tradition, they can see Śambhala.

The *Kālacakra Tantra* appeared in our world later than most tantras. Its teachings concern not only the spiritual progress of individual practitioners but also the safety and prosperity of society in general. Like the other tantras, following the path according to the Kālacakra tradition has four parts: (1) how to become a proper vessel for the path, (2) the ethical restraints and commitments to keep purely, (3) how to meditate on the path, and (4) how to manifest the result. It is not necessary to go into much detail about these four here. Many books have been written about the Kālacakra practice that you can read.

Becoming a Proper Vessel

As in other tantras, receiving the suitable empowerments is crucial for engaging in Kālacakra practice. Kālacakra Tantra has more empowerments than other tantras. First, aspirants must receive the seven empowerments of entering like a child[85] from a Kālacakra maṇḍala of powdered stone. Then they receive the four higher empowerments, the four highest empowerments, and the supreme Vajra Guru empowerment. A few masters who are lineage holders and have authority in matters concerning Kālacakra are exceptions; they may receive empowerment from another type of maṇḍala.

The Ethical Restraints and Commitments to Keep Purely

Those who have received the empowerment should keep the fourteen root tantric precepts common to all Highest Yoga Tantras. There are also special uncommon precepts to keep in Kālacakra, the first of these being to abandon scorning or deriding your vajra masters. To learn more about these precepts, those who have the empowerment should read *Explanation of the Root Downfalls in Tantra* by Tsongkhapa, *Clear Differentiation of the Three Ethical Codes* by Sakya Paṇḍita, and *Lamp for Clarifying the Samaya* by Khedrup Norsang Gyatso.

Kālacakra also has twenty-five rules of ethical conduct: five sets of five rules. The first set is to abandon five nonvirtuous actions: taking life, taking what is not freely given, unwise or unkind sexual conduct, lying, and taking intoxicants. Ethical conduct means to subdue previous bad actions and to enter into proper conduct.

The second set is to abandon five auxiliary destructive actions: (1) gambling, playing dice, and a game with many stones that the Japanese call "Go"; (2) eating meat with the three impurities (meat from animals that you killed, meat from animals that you asked someone to kill, meat you know was killed for you); (3) idle gossip or meaningless talk; (4) ancestor-worship practices or worshipping dead parents; and (5) making blood offerings or sacrifices.

The third set is to abandon the five types of killing: the killing of cows (cattle), children, women, men, and destroying statues or representations of the Buddha's body, speech and mind.

The fourth set is to avoid five types of contempt: not having faith in the Buddha or the Dharma, having hostility or anger toward friends, being angry at your spiritual teacher, holding anger toward the saṅgha, and deceiving those who trust you.

The fifth set is to abandon five desires: attachment for sights, sounds, smells, tastes, and tactile sensations.

Practicing the Path of Kālacakra: The Generation Stage

On the basis of having received the empowerment, being familiar with the path common to all Buddhists, and keeping the ethical restraints and commitments purely, practitioners are now properly prepared to engage in the Kālacakra practice. There are several traditions that explain Kālacakra practice. In all of them, the practice has two parts: meditation on the generation stage and the completion stage.

In Kālacakra, the basis to be purified is death and rebirth. This differs from other Highest Yoga Tantras where the base to be purified is death, bardo, and rebirth.

In the generation stage the basis to be purified is the external Kālacakra (Wheel of Time) and the internal Kālacakra. The *external Kālacakra* is the world, our environment; the *internal Kālacakra* is the channels, winds, and drops in a human body. What purifies these two is the third wheel of Kālacakra, the alternative Kālacakra. What actually purifies them is the completion stage of Kālacakra, which has six branches, and what ripens into the ability to attain the six-branch completion stage is the generation stage. The generation stage is discussed either in terms of the complete body, speech, and mind of the alternative Kālacakra, or the outer and inner mind maṇḍalas (mind spheres). These are parts of the generation stage that will ripen into the six-branch completion stage, which will actually purify the basis, ordinary death and rebirth.

To have the complete body, speech, and mind of the generation stage that will later ripen into the completion-stage practice, the maṇḍala must have at least five deities. If you practice and perfect the yoga of a single deity, you will not gain the full development of the actions of pacifying, increase, power, and ferocity on the completion stage. The practices of the single deity Vajrabhairava and of Vajrayoginī initially appear as having only one deity.

However, this is not the case. All the hand implements and animals under the feet of the single Yamāntaka represent deities. When these are included in the count, there are forty-nine deities. Likewise, Vajrayoginī has many deities in her body maṇḍala, so this practice too has the required number of deities to ripen into the completion stage.

The generation stage of Kālacakra is divided into four branches of approximation and attainment: the approximation of vajra body, the close attainment of vajra speech, the attainment of vajra mind, and the great attainment of vajra pristine wisdom. Furthermore, there is a division of four perfections from examples that are mentioned in *Chanting the Names of Mañjuśrī* (*Mañjuśrīnāmasaṃgīti*): the perfections from the examples of one momentary stage, five aspects, twenty aspects, and the net of illusions.

Practicing the Path of Kālacakra: The Completion Stage

The completion stage of Kālacakra has two parts: (1) the vajra body, which is to be activated, and (2) the six branches of the completion stage that activate it (discussed in the next section).

The vajra body to be activated has three aspects: the channels, winds, and drops. The description of these differs from that in Guhyasamāja in several aspects. The right and left channels are parallel to the central channel from their top ends but cross over the central channel at the navel. Instead of the usual names of right, left, and central channels, in Kālacakra they are known as the sun channel, moon channel, and Rahula channel.[86] They're also called the fire, water, and space constituent elements, and their colors are red, white, and green. Blood, semen, and wind, respectively, are found in them.

Channels. The continuations of these three channels beneath the navel are called, respectively, "the orange one," "sheep," and "the fire of time" channels, and the constituent elements that are involved with them are the earth sphere, wind sphere, and sphere of pristine wisdom. Their colors are, in turn, yellow, black, and blue. What primarily flows through them are, in turn, feces, urine, and semen. These six are the six major channels.

There are six channel wheels or cakras. The one at the crown of the head has four channels branching out from it, at the forehead there are sixteen channels, at the throat there are thirty-two, at the heart there are eight, at the navel there are sixty-four, and at the secret place there are thirty-two channels.

Winds. In Kālacakra, there are ten winds. Whereas in Guhyasamāja it is said that in our ordinary state, no wind flows in the central channel, in Kālacakra the winds move in the central channel before beginning tantric practice and at the time of death. The all-pervasive wind may move through the body at other times as well. In addition, the winds can move from the central channel.

Drops. There are four drops about the size of mustard seeds that are made from red and white drops and are placed where the subtlest mind and wisdom abide. The drops are located at seven places in the body and are the basis for implanting various latencies or predispositions: (1) body drops are located at the crown and navel and have latencies involved with the time of being awake, (2) speech drops are located at the throat and secret place and have latencies involved in dreaming, (3) mind drops are located at the heart and the center of the sexual organ and have latencies involved in deep sleep, and (4) pristine wisdom drops are located at the navel and tip of the sexual organ and have latencies involved in absorption or sexual pleasure.[87]

As the bases for implanting karmic seeds and other latencies, these four drops have impure and pure aspects; they contain all spiritual obstacles as well. When winds collect at the locations of the drops, they activate the latencies there. In waking times, the winds gather at the crown of the head and at the navel; when dreaming, the winds gather at the throat and secret place, and so on. Certain seeds and latencies are activated when the winds are at each place, producing pure or impure appearances. For example, when awake, pure (the maṇḍala) or impure (a robbery) appearances arise. When dreaming, pure sound (mantra) or impure sound (harmful speech) appears. In deep sleep, pure nonconceptuality (direct realization of emptiness) or impure unclarity arise. When in sexual union, pure bliss (a blissful mind realizing emptiness) or impure emission of semen are produced. As ordinary saṃsāric beings, we experience only impure objects because we're unable to activate the latencies that produce pure objects. Through the practice of method and wisdom, these latencies are purified, giving the possibility for pure objects to arise.

By purifying the drops completely, only pure objects (pure appearances, pure sounds, nonconceptuality, and bliss) remain, and impure objects (frightening appearances, harmful speech, mental unclarity, and emission of semen) are prevented. Then, on the path, potencies in the body drops are purified and become empty forms (nonmaterial deity bodies) that will ripen into a buddha's body. Potencies in the speech drops are purified and become the sounds of mantra (indestructible sound) that will ripen as a buddha's speech. Potencies in the mind drops are purified into the nonconceptual realization of emptiness, and potencies in the pristine wisdom drops are purified into the immutable great bliss realizing emptiness. These last two will ripen as a buddha's mind. Potencies in the body drops become a buddha's emanation body, potencies in the speech drops become the enjoyment body, and potencies in the mind and pristine wisdom drops become the truth body. In short, by purifying and enhancing the drops, yogis will attain the body, speech, mind, and pristine wisdom of a buddha.

THE FOUR DROPS

DROP	PRIMARY LOCATION	LATENCIES	ORDINARY PRODUCT	PURIFIED PRODUCT	BUDDHA BODY
Body drop	Crown and navel	Waking	Impure appearances	Pure appearances	Emanation body
Speech drop	Throat and secret place	Dreaming	Erroneous or harmful speech	Pure sound, mantra	Enjoyment body
Mind drop	Heart and center of sexual organ	Deep sleep	Mental unclarity	Nonconceptual realization of emptiness	Truth body
Pristine wisdom drop	Navel and tip of sexual organ	Sexual union	Emission of semen	Immutable great bliss realizing emptiness	Truth body

Six Branches of the Completion Stage

Within Highest Yoga Tantra, in general there are two ways to attain full awakening. One is accomplished within the old, coarse body that arose due to afflictions and karma. Here yogis abandon the old body and actualize a pure illusory body that later becomes a buddha's emanation body. This is the method in the non-Kālacakra tantras. The second is found in the Kālacakra Tantra by transforming the old body into the "great seal of empty form" in union with the consort. This brings the union of supreme immutable bliss and empty form, which is comparable to nondual bliss and emptiness in the other tantras.

The six branches of the Kālacakra completion stage have the same names as in Guhyasamāja but differ in terms of the practices done on each branch. The six branches are individual withdrawal, meditative stabilization, vitality-exertion, retention, subsequent mindfulness, and concentration.

1. *Individual withdrawal* collects the winds back from the doors of the senses by focusing on a drop at the upper opening of the central channel. This meditation is done in the dark. Khedrup Gelek Palzang practiced this meditation in a completely black and dark room in Gaden Monastery in Tibet. As yogis make progress in this meditation, eleven objects called "night signs" and "day signs" sequentially appear to the mind. The four night signs are appearance like smoke, shimmering appearance like a mirage, appearance of the twinkling lights of fireflies, and appearance like the flame of a butter lamp that is about to go out. These are the same appearances that appear to the mind during the death process due to the dissolution of the four elements of earth, water, fire, and wind. One difference is that the sequence of the appearance of smoke and of the mirage are reversed at death.

   Then the six day signs arise: the planet Kālāgni (destructive fire at the end of an eon), the sun, the moon, the planet Rāhu (eclipse), lightning, and the blue drop. Sharp-faculty disciples can experience the appearance of the six daytime signs during the nighttime yogas. The eleventh sign is the appearance of the outline of Kālacakra and Viśvamātā (consort) in union inside the blue drop. They are the size of the width of a hair and are in the form of an enjoyment body having five certainties.[88] This is a precursor of the empty forms that will actually appear in the fifth branch. Although some of the signs appearing during individual withdrawal are similar to the ones occurring when the elements and winds dissolve at death, they aren't signs preceding the four empties, because they occur due to stopping the winds from going outside the sense doors, not due to the dissolution of winds in the central channel.

2. *Meditative stabilization* continues the yoga of individual withdrawal and is done to stabilize the night and day signs. Their becoming firm and clear indicates that the central channel has been purified, so the winds in the two side channels naturally begin to enter. The first two branches facilitate attaining a buddha's vajra body by making steady the empty form that has not been attained, that which is being attained, and that which has already been attained.
3. *Vitality-exertion* (breath control) has two phases. The first is vajra recitation and the second is vase breathing, which draws the life-supporting wind and downward-voiding wind into the central channel. Here, yogis visualize the winds from the lower part of the body are held in the shape of a vase below the navel. These two practices cause winds from the right and left channels to enter the central channel. Yogis gain power over the wind that is the root of speech, and through that they attain a buddha's speech.
4. *Retention* is holding the winds inside the central channel. After the winds have gathered in the central channel by vitality-exertion, yogis hold the breath to stabilize the winds in the central channel. This causes the generation of tummo. Vitality-exertion and retention facilitate attaining a buddha's vajra speech.
5. *Subsequent mindfulness* involves practicing with an imaginary (wisdom) seal or an actual (action) seal and engaging in the three conducts. This causes the tummo to blaze, melting the white drops at the top of the head. They descend one by one to the tip of the sexual organ, forming a column of white drops. This also causes innate immutable bliss. The drops are not emitted because these yogis have control over the winds that would normally cause emission. Yogis also cause red drops to rise one at a time to the top of the central channel, forming a parallel column of red drops going downward. Repeating this process, yogis stack more drops, forming a white column going upward from the bottom of the central channel and a column of red drops going down from the top of the central channel. When 1,800 white drops and 1,800 red drops have been stacked, and due to this 1,800 portions of the material body and karmic winds have been dissipated, yogis

have attained the first bodhisattva ground and the path of seeing. By repeating this process of stacking drops and experiencing bliss each time another drop is added to the stack until 21,600 red and white drops have been stacked, yogis eliminate obscurations and traverse the bodhisattva grounds and the path of meditation.

6. *Concentration* is the continuation of subsequent mindfulness, except now yogis practice with a great seal of empty form instead of a wisdom or action seal, in order to finish consuming the material aggregate, including the stacked drops. With the stacking of more and more drops, the material body and karmic winds are consumed and yogis experience supreme immutable bliss. This bliss strengthens the wisdom that realizes emptiness, eradicating the afflictive obscurations and the cognitive obscurations.

   As the process of stacking drops continues, yogis begin to become deities that are actual empty forms, although they aren't fully qualified until the end of the level of concentration. As each drop is stacked up or down without any emission, one part of the material body and karmic winds is consumed and one immutable bliss is experienced. As meditation continues, the drops are also consumed. The material body doesn't become an empty body; rather, it is consumed and vanishes, enabling the empty form, which is in the nature of bliss, to appear. The empty form is held by a mind of immutable great bliss. When this blissful mind and the empty form are united, they can emanate numerous emanation bodies throughout space. Exhausting the corporeal body that is the ripened result of polluted karma and attaining an empty form that is like a rainbow is a unique distinguishing characteristic of Kālacakra.

   At the completion of this process, yogis have abandoned all obscurations and actualized a buddha's mirror-like wisdom and the body of empty form. By these six distinguished concentrations, yogis attain the three vajras of body, speech, and mind simultaneously.

In short, the way to attain inseparable emptiness and bliss in Kālacakra differs from other Highest Yoga Tantras. In Kālacakra, emptiness is the empty forms of the male and female deities and bliss is the supreme immutable great bliss. The sixth branch of single-minded concentration comes about by combining the appearance of being the male and female deities of empty form with a mind experiencing immutable bliss within the state of emptiness. This is the state of union in Kālacakra.

Heartfelt Advice

Please continue to practice the Dharma with great faith and confidence in our teacher, the Buddha, and with great enthusiasm for the practices. Candrakīrti says in his *Supplement* that there is nothing that cannot be accomplished if we have enthusiastic perseverance. Think long term; if you don't see any accomplishments after practicing for a month, don't throw up your hands and abandon your practice. Rather, practice steadily with enthusiastic perseverance; in this way, you will be able to attain awakening.

Worldly activities have no end; engaging in them is like walking in a circle, going round and round but never getting anywhere. It's like being locked in a room with no exit. The ceaseless activities of this life just bring more duḥkha. The only time they seem to end is at the time of death, which is the time of the greatest suffering. However difficult Dharma activities may initially be, if you continue doing them, rather than increasing your duḥkha, they will increase your bliss and happiness. Upon attaining the state of unchanging bliss, you will bring your saṃsāra to an end.

Although the Dharma path has an end, it is not necessarily an easy path. The Buddha accumulated merit over three countless great eons to create the causes for full awakening. All of us wish to experience great, stable, and lasting happiness, and this requires training our mind over a long time.

The path may also be difficult at times. We see examples of great Tibetan practitioners who often had to go for several days without food. They meditated in difficult circumstances, living in cold caves for years, sitting on the bare ground or on rocks. Those studying in the monasteries often had to suffice with poor food, but as a result of persevering through these difficulties, they achieved high insights and realizations. In comparison, all of us are very fortunate. We don't have to undergo these difficulties. That we can practice in comfortable circumstances is a result of our previous accumulation of merit. In this time of the five degenerations, practicing for even a few hours with the intention to benefit others is extremely beneficial. The merit accumulated from hearing, thinking, and meditating for even two or three hours is much greater than the merit śrāvakas created by gaining stable realizations during the time of the Buddha.

Those of you who are ordained and have turned your minds away from lay life with its wealth, status, and relationships should practice well. You have a wonderful opportunity. It is important that monastics live in harmony, with peace and a friendly attitude toward one another.

There are excellent Dharma teachers with whom you can study. This too is a result of your previous collection of merit. While these teachers are alive, take advantage of the opportunity to receive teachings from them. Having an intellectual understanding of the Dharma is not sufficient; you must apply it to your own life and put it into practice. When the Buddha gave his first teaching—the first turning of the Dharma Wheel—he said, "This is the truth of duḥkha, the truth of the cause of duḥkha, the truth of its cessation, and the truth of the path to cessation." Due to the listeners' practice in previous lives, they were able to put these few words into practice and gain the greatest realizations.

If you hear or study numerous teachings but don't put them into practice, it is a great loss. Immediately put into practice and meditate on whatever teachings you hear or learn. Don't think that meditation and study are two separate things, that you can put aside whatever you study and meditate on something else. This isn't the way to practice. Bring the powers of hearing and meditating together so that they reinforce each other. Your power of meditation should be as extensive as your power of hearing and studying the teachings. If you don't learn the Dharma, you won't know how to meditate or what to meditate on. Be like the realized practitioners of the past who practiced hearing, thinking, and meditating together and experienced the results of doing so.

As you practice, your good qualities will increase, but do not go around boasting or bragging about them. Praise others' good qualities and hide your own.

To have all conducive circumstances to practice the Dharma—without having too much or too little, only just what is needed—is rare and difficult. Śāriputra aspired, "May I not be born in a rich family or in a poor family, but in a family in the middle." We don't need to pray for this, because we have this situation now. Having such an excellent working basis is very difficult to obtain in the future, so we should make use of it now. Please reflect that in previous lives we have practiced diligently, often in difficult situations, to obtain our present circumstances. Therefore we now have to work diligently to advance to awakening. It's like we have climbed halfway up a mountain. Now we need to go the rest of the way and try not to slide down.

Benefactors who help us or support us materially accumulate great merit. Milarepa said, "The meditator meditating on the mountain and the benefactor in the valley will reach awakening at the same time." This is an auspicious symbol of our interdependent relationship. The essence of that relationship is the dedication. Thus we should dedicate our merit so that everybody who helps us will put the Dharma into practice and attain the wonderful results.

I often recall a quotation from the *Guhyasamāja Root Tantra*, taught by Buddha Vajradhara himself. To paraphrase, "Outwardly perfectly keep the practice of the śrāvakas, and inwardly always have great joy and pleasure in the practice of Guhyasamāja."

The *Kālacakra Tantra* says, "Although it is not necessary for householders to wear the three robes of a monastic, they should try to follow all the monastic precepts." As human beings, we have some idea of what is good and what is bad. All of us are the same in wanting what is good and distancing ourselves from what is harmful. Therefore, it is important to investigate and make the determination to abandon doing what is harmful and resolve to do beneficial actions. Continually be aware and analyze these things. The Buddha encouraged us to investigate and not believe blindly. The important elements to keep in mind and cultivate constantly are bodhicitta and the wisdom of emptiness. By practicing in this way, your life will be meaningful, you will die without fear or regret, and you will have good conditions to continue learning and practicing the Dharma in future lives until you become a buddha!

REFLECTION

1. Which points of the above advice are the most powerful and inspiring for you?
2. What obstacles do you have to overcome to follow these, and what are their antidotes?
3. What ideas do you have to gradually build up your ability to enhance the antidotes and subdue the obstacles?

13 | The Four Tibetan Traditions

Nālandā and the Four Tibetan Traditions

All spiritual traditions have multiple branches and Buddhism is no exception. This multiplicity may stem from different lineages of transmission—that is, who brought the teachings to a new geographical area or who was the chief explicator of the teachings in a particular place. They may also arise due to differences in the scriptures that are studied, the interpretations of the scriptures, the practices that are emphasized, local culture, history, climate, government, and so on. Such multiplicity of traditions is natural; the Buddha accepted this, as have the great majority of his followers. Diversity allows each person to follow a system that best fulfills their spiritual needs and aspirations.

In Tibetan Buddhism there are four principal traditions—Nyingma, Kagyu, Sakya, and Gelug—many of which have sub-traditions.[89] A smaller tradition in terms of adherents is the Jonang tradition, which is discussed in the next chapter. The traditions were not known by these names in India, although their teachings and lineages existed there. All five Tibetan traditions are rooted in Indian Buddhism but are differentiated by the lineage of masters who propounded the teachings in Tibet. The four principal traditions share Sūtra teachings, and all have tantric teachings. Before talking about some of the unique qualities of each tradition with regard to Tantra, it's important to stress how much they have in common.

Not everyone is aware of their common origin, however. An American woman once said to me, "My friend told me that the Kagyu tradition doesn't come from Nālandā but from *dohās*"—Vajrayāna adepts' devotional songs of spiritual experience. I explained to her that her friend's statement was not correct. There are also many misunderstandings among followers of the four principal traditions. After giving a talk at a Kagyu center, someone said to me (Chodron), "I heard that Gelugpas just studied and debated, they didn't meditate. But you couldn't have given that talk if you didn't meditate."

All five Tibetan Buddhist traditions can be traced back to Nālandā, the great monastic university that existed for centuries in India.[90] Padmasambhava, a great eighth-century Indian yogi who brought Buddhism to Tibet, is seen as the originator of the Nyingma tradition. I don't know if he was affiliated with Nālandā, but Śāntarakṣita, his compatriot and contemporary who also brought the Buddha's teachings to Tibet, was a great master and abbot at Nālandā.

After the repression and persecution of Buddhism in Tibet by the Tibetan King Langdarma (877–906), many Tibetans made an effort to either go to India to receive teachings and empowerments or to invite qualified Indian masters to Tibet. All of the lineages that were brought to Tibet at this time were later termed the New Translation (Sarma) traditions. Their transmission to Tibet began with the great Tibetan translator Rinchen Zangpo (954–1055) and his Indian teacher Atiśa (982–1054), as well as other Tibetan masters such as Marpa Lotsawa (1012–96) and Drokmi Lotsawa (992–1072/1074).

Virūpa (eighth–ninth century), the great master to whom the Sakya tradition traces its origin, was a learned scholar and an abbot of Nālandā. He later became a great mahāsiddha.

Marpa, Milarepa, and Gampopa are the three great founding fathers of the Kagyu tradition. Marpa's teacher, Nāropa, was a top scholar from Nālandā who mastered all the major texts before becoming a tantric yogi.

Many of the New Translation traditions stem from Atiśa, another great master from Nālandā who passed the lineage of teachings to Drom Tonpa, Potowa, Sharawa, and Chekawa. Later these teachings were passed to Tsongkhapa, who was seen as the main teacher of the Gelug tradition.

Some people say that in Nyingma, philosophical study is irrelevant. This is not true, as we can see from the example of the great master Śāntarakṣita, who brought the ordination lineage to Tibet and founded Tibet's first monastery, Samye Monastery. The lineage of Padmasambhava and Śāntarakṣita later became known as the Nyingma tradition or the Old Translation tradition. Originally a scholar and abbot at Nālandā, Śāntarakṣita was proficient in philosophical debate. Those who claim to follow his tradition cannot say that the study of his philosophical works is unnecessary. Recently I read Śāntarakṣita's great work, *Compendium of Principles* (*Tattvasaṃgraha*), which is an encyclopedia of classical Indian philosophy. It was very difficult and I had to read many commentaries to understand it well. But because I am a little lazy, I later wrapped up the text and put it on the shelf!

Śāntarakṣita could have insisted that everyone at Samye learn Sanskrit, but he didn't. Instead, he emphasized the need to translate Buddhist texts into Tibetan so that Tibetans could study Dharma in their own language. Therefore, one department at Samye was for translation, while other departments were for lay followers, monastics, and followers of Chinese Buddhism. Śāntarakṣita envisioned Samye's monastics translating many texts and studying a diversity of philosophical views. As a result of his efforts, Tibetans nowadays have the Buddhadharma in their own language, and the texts translated into Tibetan almost flawlessly communicate the teachings of the three baskets—Vinaya, Sūtra, and Abhidharma.

When we examine the evolution of the Tibetan lineages, we find the Nālandā tradition at their root. Buddhism in Tibet is a continuation of the stainless tradition of Nālandā. This is an important fact because some people say that Tibetan Buddhism is a mixture of Buddhist and non-Buddhist elements, and some even called it Lamaism. I believe that if Nāgārjuna were to look at the tenets and texts studied today by contemporary Tibetan masters, he would be delighted that they uphold the Buddha's teachings.

Nālandā Monastery flourished for many generations. At the beginning, Nāgārjuna was a key thinker. Then Asaṅga became popular, and later Śāntarakṣita. When I mention Nālandā to my friends who are Indian scholars, they instantly recognize it as a highly sophisticated learning center where philosophical ideas were developed and refined. It was a place where Buddhist ideas were challenged and monastics had to think deeply about the nature of reality. It was not a place where monks simply chanted and beat drums. In the challenges put forth by non-Buddhists and the responses given by Buddhists at Nālandā, we see a dynamic and stimulating process of exploring the nature of reality.

Both Pāli and Sanskrit literature were studied at Nālandā, although Sanskrit literature became predominant later because it was the language used by Indian philosophers. Dignāga and Dharmakīrti were supreme in

Buddhist epistemology. Non-Buddhists challenged Dignāga's views, which gave Dharmakīrti the opportunity to explain them in depth. This produced more debate between Buddhists and non-Buddhists, and Śāntarakṣita responded to those discussions.

Through this dynamic interchange, Buddhist ideas flowered. Buddhapālita (470–550) illuminated and refined Nāgārjuna's views. Bhāvaviveka responded to him, and later Candrakīrti clarified their debates. By understanding Buddhist history, we will appreciate this evolution of ideas. Similarly, in our personal practice, we should learn different tenet systems, understand why their proponents supported those views, and then relate these views to our life. In this way, we will cultivate deep understanding and faith that is based on conviction rather than on vague preferences or blind belief.

Because many different Indian and Tibetan masters brought the Buddha's teachings to Tibet, there is a diversity of ideas regarding topics such as the differentiation of definitive and interpretable sūtras. Those in the Nyingma tradition are generally direct followers of the Indian masters Śāntarakṣita and Kamalaśīla. Since they accepted the *Sūtra Unraveling the Thought* (*Saṃdhinirmocana Sūtra*) as authoritative, the Nyingma tradition does as well. On the other hand, Tsongkhapa holds the *Teaching of Akṣayamati Sūtra* as authoritative. Some people regard him as an innovator because he held this view, but he followed Candrakīrti, who asserted in his *Autocommentary on the "Supplement to 'Treatise on the Middle Way,'"* that the *Descent to Laṅka* (*Laṅkāvatāra Sūtra*) and the *Sūtra Unraveling the Thought* are interpretable.

When we study an explanation in any of the four main Tibetan traditions, understanding the teaching on an affiliated topic in each tradition enriches our comprehension. All Tibetan traditions are getting at the same points, and all four main traditions study the texts of the seventeen Nālandā masters from India.[91]

Buddhism has been characterized by lively debate in India as well as in Tibet. When discussing ideas together, a correct knowledge of each other's vocabulary, definitions, and concepts is crucial to prevent misunderstanding. Many unfortunate misunderstandings have arisen and some still persist due to the lack of correct understanding of others' systems and terminology. For example, not all Tibetan scholars use the terminology found in Indian texts. When a respected teacher gives a specific teaching from their own experience to practitioners with particular dispositions and interests, practitioners from another tradition may misunderstand the meaning. But when we look into the matter, we find that although the terminology differs, they can agree on the meaning.

It has long been my belief that when understood in depth, all four main Tibetan traditions are unions of Sūtra and Tantra and all four share the Prāsaṅgika view of emptiness. Although they may sometimes use different terminology or have different perspectives and emphases, they share the essence of the Prāsaṅgika view: (1) clarity regarding conventional truths being dependent arisings and (2) the lack of findability ultimately of all phenomena, even emptiness. Furthermore, they also study the eighteen classic texts that provide a firm grounding in Sūtrayāna practice and prepare the ground for entering the Tantrayāna.

The Texts Shared in Common in the Four Tibetan Traditions

The Nyingma, Sakya, Kagyu, and Gelug are like fingers that come from the same palm—the Nālandā tradition. All four traditions study these thirteen classic texts. The Nyingma tradition lists them:

1. *Prātimokṣa Sūtra*
2. *Vinayasūtra* by Guṇaprabha
3. *Treasury of Knowledge* (*Abhidharmakośa*) by Vasubandhu
4. *Compendium of Knowledge* (*Abhidharmasamuccaya*) by Asaṅga
5. *Treatise on the Middle Way* (*Mūlamadhyamakakārikā*) by Nāgārjuna
6. *Four Hundred* by Āryadeva
7. *Supplement to the "Treatise on the Middle Way"* (*Madhyamakāvatāra*), by Candrakīrti
8. *Engaging in the Bodhisattvas' Deeds* (*Bodhicaryāvatāra*) by Śāntideva

9–13. Maitreya's five treatises: *Ornament of Clear Realizations* (*Abhisamayālaṃkāra*), *Ornament of the Mahāyāna Sūtras* (*Mahāyānasūtrālaṃkāra*), *Distinguishing the Middle from the Extremes* (*Madhyāntavibhāga*), *Distinguishing Dharma and Dharmatā* (*Dharmadharmatāvibhāga*), and *Sublime Continuum* (*Uttaratantra Śāstra*)

Of these, the first two are concerned with the Vinaya Basket, the next two with the Abhidharma Basket. The rest belong to the Sūtra Basket; the following four with the Madhyamaka view, and the last five with the bodhisattva path, buddha nature, and Yogācāra view.

The Nyingma lama Khenpo Shenga (1871–1927) wrote annotated commentaries on these thirteen texts, and together with these classical texts, his writings now form the core curriculum in most Nyingma monastic universities (*shedra*). His emphasis on these texts brought many practitioners back to the Indian sources and away from the arguments of later Tibetan scholars. In this regard, he says:[92]

> [In Tibet] there have appeared highly accomplished adepts who were no different from the *vidyādharas* of India, the Land of the Āryas. Yet although there have been countless eminent scholars, none of them can be compared with the Six Ornaments and Two Supreme Ones of India in terms of wisdom and awakened activity. [. . . Some] Tibetan scholars took as their basis the excellent Indian treatises but then added explanations based on their own clever ideas, with the result that on occasions their statements no longer accord with scripture or valid reasoning.

I agree with him and direct people to study these thirteen magnificent Indian texts. That will give you firm grounding in Sūtrayāna practice, thus setting the stage for entering the Tantrayāna.

The Sakya tradition adds five more classics to the above list:

1. *Compendium of Reliable Cognition* (*Pramāṇasamuccaya*) by Dignāga
2. *Ascertainment of Reliable Cognizers* (*Pramāṇaviniścaya*) by Dharmakīrti
3. *Commentary on "Compendium of Reliable Cognition"* (*Pramāṇavārttika*) by Dharmakīrti
4. *Treasury of Reasoning on Valid Cognition* (T. *Tshad ma rigs pa'i gter*) by Sakya Paṇḍita
5. *Clear Differentiation of the Three Ethical Codes* (*Sdom gsum rab dbye*) by Sakya Paṇḍita

The first four are about reliable cognizers and reasoning, and the last concerns ethical conduct in the Vinaya, the bodhisattva path, and Tantra.

All four Tibetan traditions study almost all of these eighteen important texts. Each tradition has its own unique qualities when it comes to Tantra; that is wonderful. But we shouldn't lose sight of their commonality. Personally speaking, I feel the Nālandā tradition and the Nālandā masters are very precious, which is why I value the painting of the seventeen great Nālandā masters and wrote a supplication to them.[93]

How to Approach the Various Tibetan Buddhist Traditions

In seeking harmony among the views of the Tibetan Buddhist traditions, it isn't necessary to shun critical analysis and espouse a vague attitude of "they are all one," or to pretend that there are no differences among the Tibetan traditions. Instead, we can adopt a generous view that focuses on the points that unite the traditions, and we can respect the teachers that see them as distinct but equally valid ways to talk about ultimate reality—the experience of which cannot be understood by words and concepts.

In this way, we emphasize what we have in common, learn from the points where we differ, and work together for the common good of the Buddhadharma in the world. In this age where religious philosophy is so often used to create controversy and conflict, it is important for us to be open-minded, respect each other, and avoid being embroiled in contention or competition.

The material in this chapter may initially be challenging, but if we persevere, understanding will come because causes produce concordant effects. If we study and reflect on the teachings, the result of deep understanding will naturally arise.

Before engaging with difficult topics, I remember the Gandhara statue of the Buddha depicting the six-year period when the Buddha engaged in ascetic practices before sitting under the bodhi tree and attaining awakening. To me this statue speaks of the necessity to exert effort and patiently endure hardships on the path to full awakening. This is one of the most moving images of the Buddha because it shows that attaining full awakening involves hard work and perseverance over time. This inspires my mind with courage and fortitude. As the Buddha went through difficulties to attain the unsurpassable state for the sake of sentient beings, we can as well.

In the remainder of this chapter and in the next chapter, I will discuss the view of emptiness and Vajrayāna in the four main Tibetan traditions in order to dispel misunderstandings and to show that, when understood properly, they have a similar view of emptiness. In describing the views of each tradition, I will speak in general. Within each tradition, some teachers in the past and present may have different views. I will first give a general introduction to each tradition, then explain that each one holds the Prāsaṅgika view, and finally discuss their approaches to Tantra.

The Nyingma Tradition

The Nyingma tradition is based on the earliest Buddhist teachings that came to Tibet in the eighth and early ninth centuries. It classifies the Buddha's teachings into nine vehicles (*yāna*), which may also be taught as the stages of practice people traverse to attain full awakening. The nine are divided into three sets of three and together are a complete form of Buddhism.

1. Vehicles that focus on the causes of duḥkha: these encompass the Sūtrayāna teachings.
    - The Śrāvaka Vehicle focuses on the four truths of āryas.
    - The Solitary Realizer Vehicle emphasizes the twelve links, which expand on the causal relationships between true duḥkha and true origin on the one hand, and between true cessation and the true path on the other.
    - The Bodhisattva Vehicle includes the teachings on the generation of bodhicitta and the bodhisattva practice of the six perfections, including serenity and insight. When trained in these, the practitioner progresses to Tantra.
2. Vehicles that emphasize Vedic-like asceticism: the outer tantras.
    - Action Tantra (Kriyā)
    - Performance Tantra (Caryā)
    - Yoga Tantra

These three center on the practice of deity yoga, which may be front generation, where the deity imagined in front of us radiates light into us, bestowing blessings and inspiration. It may also be self-generation, where practitioners dissolve into emptiness and imagine their wisdom realizing emptiness appearing in the form of the deity that they identify with.

3. Vehicles that focus on the method of powerful transformation: the inner tantras.
   - Mahāyoga or great yoga entails perfecting the generation-stage practices of deity yoga.
   - Anuyoga or subsequent yoga involves working with the subtle winds and their flow within the channels of the body.
   - Atiyoga or ultimate yoga refers to dzogchen (great perfection), the practice that concerns realizing rigpa (primordial awareness).[94]

Rigpa is the primordial innate mind, which is contrasted with *sem* (ordinary mind). Rigpa is pristine wisdom, unlike the ordinary mental states of *sem* that are temporary and adventitious. Rigpa is ever-present, it doesn't fluctuate like *sem* does, and it is both beginningless and endless. Rigpa is a beginningless awakened state, a quality of buddhahood that everyone possesses. However, it is obscured by afflictions and conceptualizations that result in our saṃsāric state. When those adventitious obscurations are removed, we are said to be reawakened. This is similar to the Perfection of Wisdom teachings calling the ultimate nature of our present mind "natural nirvāṇa," indicating that our present mind has the same empty nature as the liberated mind. Natural nirvāṇa, the emptiness of our present mind, is the basis for attaining the nirvāṇa that is freedom from afflictive obscurations, and nonabiding nirvāṇa, which is full awakening. Just as natural nirvāṇa is the basis for attaining actual nirvāṇa, in dzogchen the primordial buddhahood of rigpa enables us to actualize the reawakening of actual buddhahood.[95]

Rigpa is symbolized by the Samantabhadra couple or "All Good." Samantabhadra is said to be the primordial buddha. However, the symbolic Samantabhadra couple is not an external person who has been a buddha beginninglessly but refers to the nature of the mind itself. Two prominent aspects of dzogchen practice are *kadag* (T. *ka dag*) and *trekcho* (T. *khregs chod*). *Kadag* means "pure from the beginning" and refers to the nature of the mind. *Ka*, the first letter of the Tibetan alphabet, indicates beginning, and *dag* means "pure." This is not a temporal beginning but an ontological one—that is, the nature of the mind has always been pure and defilements have never entered its nature. *Trekcho* and *thod rgal* are often translated as "leap-over," but knowing its etymology gives us a deeper sense of its meaning. *Trek* means "hardness" or "blockage" and refers to inherent existence—the appearance of and grasping at inherent existence obstructs or blocks us from seeing rigpa's natural purity. *Cho* means "to cut," so *trekcho* means to cut or break through the blockage and obstructions that prevent us from seeing the nature of the mind that is pure from the beginning.

Just as the nine vehicles set out stages of practice, the Seven Treasuries of Longchenpa (1308–63) present a systematic approach to the Nyingma tradition. In this regard, I recommend reading Longchenpa's texts in the following order: *Treasury of Philosophical Tenets*, *Treasury of the Wish-Fulfilling Jewel*, *Mind at Ease*, *Treasury of the Supreme Vehicle*, and *Treasury of the Ultimate Expanse.*

The Nyingma tradition propounds the view of emptiness taught by Śāntarakṣita, a Mādhyamika. At the time the Nyingma tradition began, Candrakīrti's *Supplement* had not yet been translated into Tibetan, so no clear distinction between Svātantrika Madhyamaka and Prāsaṅgika Madhyamaka had been made in Tibet. However, people were familiar with Nāgārjuna's *Treatise on the Middle Way* because both the root text and the commentary *Akutobhayā* (T. *Ga las 'jigs med*) were translated into Tibetan in the early ninth century.[96] Other Madhyamaka works were rendered into Tibetan as well. There's no doubt that the Nyingma view was Madhyamaka.

In the meantime, Guru Padmasambhava privately taught Highest Yoga Tantra in Tibet and composed *Instruction on the Jeweled Garland of Views* (T. *Man ngag lta ba'i phreng ba*),[97] which explains all the major views about emptiness. Although Śāntarakṣita's work was Yogācāra-Svātantrika Madhyamaka, because Padmasambhava's commentary dealt with the major theories of emptiness, I believe the original Nyingma view must have been closer to the Prāsaṅgika viewpoint, even though Prāsaṅgika had not yet emerged as a distinct school in Tibet.

Later, after Atiśa came to Tibet, Rongsom Paṇḍita (1012–88), a great Nyingma scholar and practitioner, spoke of the Prāsaṅgika view in one of his texts. In addition, there is the great Nyingma adept Longchen Rabjampa, who was a contemporary of Buton Rinpoche.[98] Longchenpa clearly speaks about the Prāsaṅgika. In the nineteenth century, Ju Mipham (1846–1912) also clearly stated that the Nyingma view is Prāsaṅgika. In explaining the Prāsaṅgika view, we should bear in mind that Mipham Rinpoche's presentation and terminology differ from other schools. When reading his works, try to understand the terms and concepts in the ways he means them rather than imposing our definitions on his words. In the following passage from his *Gateway to Knowledge* (T. *Mkhas 'jug*),[99] he clearly explains the Prāsaṅgika view of the unity of dependent arising and emptiness:

> All phenomena do not come into being through their own inherent identity, but as a result of the coming together of causes and conditions, and when there are no conditions they do not arise. Even at the time when they appear, they appear while lacking any inherent existence, since they are like reflections, brought about by causes and conditions. Free from any conceptual elaborations such as being permanent or nonexistent, going or coming, arising or ceasing or being one or many, they appear while lacking true reality.
>
> When evaluating in this way, using reasoning investigating the ultimate in accordance with the actual nature of things, they are found to be mere unfailing dependent arising. Otherwise, if they were truly established in any way, such as arising according to the four extremes or four alternatives, or being existent or nonexistent, or permanent or impermanent etc., that would be inappropriate as an explanation for the conventional, and would result in a deprecation of all conventions.
>
> According to the Middle Way tradition, for whom the unreal illusory appearances of dependent origination and emptiness arise in the same reality, all the conventions of mere appearance are extremely reasonable. This being so, the conventions of the world, as well as the supramundane conventions of the four truths, Three Jewels and so on, are all perfectly established.
>
> This king of reasonings, the great dependent arising, includes all the other types of ultimate logic, such as diamond slivers[100] and so on, because they are all concerned with the seemingly real,

> unexamined appearances of dependent origination. When analyzed, no causes, effects or essential identities whatsoever can be established. The extensive variations of this logic that investigates the meaning of dependent origination are to be found in *Treatise on the Middle Way* and elsewhere.

Furthermore, the writings of other Nyingma scholars and practitioners, such as Dodrup Jigme Tenpai Nyima (Dodrupchen, 1865–1926) and his disciple Tulku Tsullo (Tsultrim Zangpo, 1884–c.1957), clearly spoke of the Prāsaṅgika view. There is no doubt.

We can divide the Prāsaṅgika view into the view according to the subject clear light and the view according to the object clear light. From this perspective, these Nyingma scholars were definitely Prāsaṅgikas regarding the view of the object, the emptiness of inherent existence. The primary focus of the view of dzogchen is the view of the apprehending subject, the clear light. Here, the practice of the subject clear light is not spoken of in isolation but is based on understanding the emptiness of inherent existence. Some texts on dzogchen practice speak about only the subject clear-light mind. They do not comment specifically on the object clear light because dzogchen scholars have previously explained primordial purity, the view of the object clear light. The unique feature of dzogchen is its understanding of the subject clear light, not the clear light that is the object. This is because the understanding of the object clear light is common to both Sūtra and Tantra.

Completion-stage practitioners in the Kagyu and Gelug traditions engage in the six yogas of Nāropā, completion-stage practices that the great Indian yogi Nāropa extracted from various tantras. These meditations are also found in the Sakya path and result (T. *lamdre*) practices and the Nyingma practice of the heart's drop. Nyingma dzogchen practitioners engage in three categories of completion-stage practices: mind (T. *sems sde*), space (T. *klong sde*), and pith instructions (T. *me ngag sde*). Although there are many texts on these topics, perceiving their subtleties is difficult. The category of pith instructions is said to be the most profound, while the mind and space practices lay the foundations to practice breakthrough.

The view of emptiness explained in the mind and space categories differs from the view expounded in the other eight vehicles in some aspects, but explaining this is difficult. Pith instruction practices have the twin aims of actualizing the truth body and enjoyment body. The practices of break-through and leap-over are the paths by which these two are actualized.

Understanding this leads us to comprehend what is meant by the great perfection (dzogchen) of the base, path, and result, although a full understanding of these can be gained only through experience, not merely by words. However, we can appreciate their profundity and difficulty by reading Longchenpa's text on dzogchen practices, *Treasury of the Supreme Vehicle* (T. *Theg mchog mdzod*); the root text and its commentary are both lengthy and difficult to understand. Longchenpa's *Treasury of Reality* (T. *Chos dbyings mdzod*) also outlines dzogchen practices. Relying on these two texts, you can be assured to gain a good understanding of dzogchen. Studying Jigme Lingpa's dzogchen text the *Treasury of Virtue* (T. *Yon tan mdzod*) is also important. An explanation of dzogchen practices is found in its second half. For an explanation of the entire Sūtra and Tantra path, Longchenpa's three-volume *Resting the Mind in Peace* (T. *Sems nyid ngal gso*) is excellent, and meditating on the teachings in it is beneficial.

Several short and succinct texts have been composed by highly realized masters who have experienced dzogchen and extracted its essence, and they have been able to recount their experiences in a few words. However, it would be very difficult to understand the entire dzogchen view and practice by using only these short texts. For example, of the many Perfection of Wisdom sūtras, the shortest is the single syllable *ah*, which is said to encompass the entire meaning of all the *Perfection of Wisdom* sūtras. However, understanding the deep meaning of all these texts by simply saying *ah* would be very difficult indeed!

By studying Madhyamaka philosophy in all its complexity, we learn various reasonings that lead us to realize that all phenomena lack inherent existence. To appreciate all the subtleties of this view, it is necessary to understand the views of the lower philosophical tenet systems. The resulting conclusion is succinct: phenomena are empty of inherent existence because they arise dependently. However, if we didn't investigate from the start and only said, "All phenomena are empty of inherent existence because they are dependently arising," we would not understand all the meanings or implications of this short statement, and thus could not gain a full understanding of emptiness. Similarly, if we read a short text on dzogchen composed by an experienced master and conclude that the dzogchen view is very simple, it indicates that we have not understood it properly. It would be ironic if the highest of the nine vehicles were said to be the simplest!

The Kagyu Tradition

The New Translation (Sarma) traditions do not significantly differ in their explanations of the Pāramitāyāna, although they differ somewhat in their explanations of Vajrayāna. If we don't investigate these differences in terminology, we may assume there are big differences in their teachings. However, when we understand the New Translation traditions well, it's evident that the basic structure and meaning of their doctrines are the same.

The Kagyu lineage comes principally from Nāropa, a well-respected scholar at Nālandā before he embarked on a journey to meet a tantric master. He practiced under the guidance of the Indian yogi Tilopa (988–1069) and then passed the tantric lineage to Marpa, an eleventh-century Tibetan master. Marpa went to India, where he studied with many Indian masters and learned the Madhyamaka view from the mahāsiddha Maitrīpa (1007–85), who followed Candrakīrti's view.

One of the principal teachings of the Kagyu tradition is mahāmudrā (great seal), which has both a Sūtra and a Tantra form. Sūtra mahāmudrā involves meditation on the clear and cognizant conventional nature of the mind as well as on the emptiness of inherent existence according to the Madhyamaka view. Tantra mahāmudrā taps into the primordial mind of clear light through uncommon tantric techniques.

The mahāmudrā lineage went from Nāropa and Maitrīpa to Marpa to Milarepa, and then to Milarepa's disciple Gampopa (Dagpo Lhaje, 1079–1153), the founder of the Dagpo Kagyu tradition. In what is called the "confluence of the two streams," Gampopa combined mahāmudrā and the stages of the path from the Kadam tradition. The four thoughts that turn the mind to Dharma—precious human life, impermanence and death, karma and its effects, and the disadvantages of saṃsāra—came from the Kadam tradition, as did the view of emptiness common to Sūtra and Tantra. The six yogas of Nāropā, the inner yogic practices of mahāmudrā, were added to these, forming a complete path. The four thoughts and the six yogas are also found in the Gelug tradition.

Meditation on mahāmudrā is done after establishing the view of emptiness. In his writings on mahāmudrā, Gampopa clearly speaks about the lack of inherent existence, nonproduction, and so forth, which form the fundamental view of emptiness, although he does not elaborately explain them. The Kagyu tradition has many branches and sub-branches that practice slightly different versions of mahāmudrā based on the view of emptiness.

Mahāmudrā takes the mind as the object of meditation, and meditation is done on both its conventional and ultimate natures. A qualified mahāmudrā master first introduces disciples to the conventional nature of the mind. The mind is the meditation object, and one side of the meditators' mind focuses on the mind. While doing that, they use mindfulness to check if faults in the meditation arise. If concentration is lost, or if laxity or restlessness arise, introspective awareness catches and remedies it. However, saying that one side of the mind observes the other side is problematic, because for ordinary beings two different states of mind cannot arise at the same time. So this kind of meditation is difficult to explain logically.

Mahāmudrā meditation on the ultimate nature of the mind involves examining the mind's emptiness, its ultimate nature. In tantric mahāmudrā, the primordial pure mind is the meditation object. To access it, practitioners engage in the practice of tummo.

The Kagyu view of emptiness accords with the Prāsaṅgika view. Nāropa highly praised Maitrīpa's *Ten Stanzas on Suchness* (*Tattvadaśaka*) and clearly highlighted the Prāsaṅgika Madhyamaka viewpoint in accordance with Candrakīrti's explanation. Since both Nāropa and Maitrīpa were Marpa's gurus, Marpa also held this view.

In the Kadam text *Lamp for the Path*, Atiśa says that Candrakīrti is the lineage holder of Nāgārjuna's teachings and that both Candrakīrti and Nāgārjuna assert the correct Madhyamaka view. Many other Kadam masters, such as Drom Tonpa, also hold this view. In this way the Kagyu tradition received teachings on the Prāsaṅgika view from both the mahāmudrā and Kadam traditions.

In his "Song to the Five Long-Life Sisters" (T. *Tshe ring mched lnga*), Milarepa says that although the Buddha, the paths and grounds, and even emptiness do not exist ultimately, the Buddha stated that they exist for a conventional consciousness not involved in analysis (SM 325):

> But in [the realm of] ultimate truth, Buddha himself does not exist;
> there are no practices or practitioners, no path, no realization, and no grounds,
> no Buddha bodies and no wisdom.
> There is, then, no nirvāṇa, for these are merely names and thoughts.
>
> Matter and beings in the universe are nonexistent from the start;
> they have never come to be; there is no truth, no innate-born wisdom,
> no karma, and no effect therefrom; even saṃsāra has no name.
> Such is the ultimate truth.
>
> Yet, if there are no sentient beings, how could the buddhas of the three times come to be?
> For if there is no cause, there will be no effect. Therefore Buddha says,
> "In conventional truth, all phenomena of saṃsāra and nirvāṇa exist."

Dependent arising is phenomena's conventional nature and emptiness is their ultimate nature. These two are mutually complementary.

The Perfection of Wisdom sūtras speak of the many paths and grounds, while mahāmudrā texts say that only a foolish person would conceive of paths and grounds within the deep state of mahāmudrā. These statements are not contradictory; each has its own specific intention. In this case, the Perfection of Wisdom sūtras speak from the perspective of conventional truths and conventionally existing paths and grounds, while the mahāmudrā texts refer to meditative equipoise on emptiness in which no conventional phenomena are perceived or conceived.

Marpa's personal meditation deity was Guhyasamāja, and he received this practice from his guru Nāropa. In the Gelug tradition, three Highest Yoga Tantra deities are emphasized: Guhyasamāja, Cakrasaṃvara, and Yamāntaka. The Gelug teaching on the five stages of the completion stage of Highest Yoga Tantra comes from Marpa's transmission of Nāropa's quintessential instructions on the *Guhyasamāja Tantra*. The two traditions have many other lineages in common, such as those of Cakrasaṃvara, the six yogas of Nāropā, mahāmudrā, and Hevajra. Thus the Kagyu and Gelug traditions share the same basis and general structure of the Tantra path, although each one has more extensive and clearer explanations on particular points.

The Sakya Tradition

The Sakya lineage is traced back to the ninth-century Indian scholar and yogi Virūpa. In the early part of his life, he was the monk Dharmapāla at Nālandā Monastery. A follower of the Yogācāra school, he interpreted Āryadeva's *Four Hundred Stanzas* according to those tenets. Later in his life, Virūpa came to understand the deepest view of emptiness according to Nāgārjuna and became a great yogi and practitioner of Highest Yoga Tantra who spread the Buddhadharma.

One of the greatest Tibetan scholars, Sakya Paṇḍita, clearly stated in his works that the most accurate theory of emptiness is the Prāsaṅgika Madhyamaka, as clarified by Candrakīrti. Therefore, the Sakya tradition also follows the Madhyamaka, and particularly the Prāsaṅgika, view.

The principal instructions of the Sakya tradition are contained in the lamdre literature. As Highest Yoga Tantra teachings, lamdre is explained on the basis of the *Hevajra Tantra*. These instructions use the framework of the three appearances and the three continua. The three appearances are three levels of spiritual perception: *impure appearances* are those of sentient beings with afflictions; *experiential appearances* are appearances on the path that occur when yogis with meditative concentration perceive phenomena's impermanence, insubstantiality, and lack of inherent existence; and *pure appearances* are those experienced by sugatas with awakened body, speech, and mind.

The three continua are (1) the *causal continuum* of the universal ground; (2) the *method continuum* of the body of practice; and (3) the *resultant continuum* of the vajra body, speech, and mind. These correlate to the *Guhyasamāja Tantra's* explanation of the three meanings of *tantra* (T. *rgyud*) or continuum: (1) the *basic continuum* (T. *gzhi'i rgyud*) or *causal continuum* of the universal ground, which is our current state; (2) the *path* (T. *lam gyi rgyud*) or *method continuum* of the body of practice in which we use

Dharma methods to purify the mind; and (3) the *resultant continuum* (T. *'bras-bu'i rgyud*), which is the state of the completely purified mind. I have received the lamdre transmission, so I consider myself a Sakya practitioner and engage in the Hevajra practice.

All sentient beings have the causal or basic continuum, which is similar to rigpa or Samantabhadra in the Nyingma tradition. The *awakening of the cause* in Sakya is comparable to the *identification of rigpa* in Nyingma. In Sakya, the causal or basic continuum is called the foundation-of-all (*ālaya*, T. *kun gzhi*), in that it is the basis for both saṃsāra and nirvāṇa. Spoken of in the Sakya teachings on the inseparability of saṃsāra and nirvāṇa, this continuous consciousness refers to the primordial clear-light mind, the mind that is the root of both saṃsāra and nirvāṇa. When this mind is obscured, it is the basis of saṃsāra, but when all obscurations are purified, the mind transforms and becomes the basis of nirvāṇa. While there may be differences in how each tradition identifies or awakens this pure mind, their ultimate purpose is the same.

The mind is called "the universal ground" because it is the basis or ground of both saṃsāra and nirvāṇa. It is causal in the sense that it has the ability to produce the result. It is a continuum because the continuity of clarity and awareness is present from our being a sentient being to our becoming an awakened vajra holder with pure appearances.

The *causal continuum*, foundation-of-all, contains all the phenomena of saṃsāra in the form of characteristics—it causes the world to appear the way it does. It also contains all the realizations and qualities of the path because as we practice deity yoga and cultivate faith, compassion, wisdom, and so forth, more good qualities arise and flourish, transforming our mind in the process. The causal continuum contains all the resultant attainments in the form of potency in that it has the potential to generate all attainments of nirvāṇa. In this way, all of saṃsāra and nirvāṇa are contained in the causal continuum, the foundation-of-all, and thus it is said that saṃsāra and nirvāṇa are inseparable.

In this context, the Sakya tradition speaks of the inseparability of clarity and emptiness (T. *gsal stong dbyer med*). *Clarity* refers to the primordial clear-light mind as explained in Highest Yoga Tantra, and *emptiness* indicates the empty nature of that mind. The inseparability of these two is free from elaboration, ineffable, and beyond words. It is realized through deep meditation. Characterized by clarity and emptiness, this true mind emerges when all defilements and obscurations have been eliminated.

Among early Sakya scholars, there were many great thinkers, and this is also true for later ones such as Gorampa Sonam Senge (1429–89) and Sakya Chokden (1428–1507). Although I haven't seen Sakya Chokden's explanation of emptiness laid out in detail, it is commonly said that he was influenced by the Jonang tradition and held an incorrect form of the view of other-emptiness. However, I did see a text by the great scholar and practitioner Dezhung Azom (1906–87) in which he explains the unique, pure philosophical viewpoint of the past Sakya tradition. He speaks of Jamyang Khyentse Wangchug (1524–68) and Mangtho Lhudrup, disciples of Tsarchen Losel Gyatso (1502–66) who lived during the time of the Second and Third Dalai Lamas and was the founder and one of the most distinguished scholars of the Tsar lineage. Dezhung Rinpoche explains that the view of emptiness taught by Khyentse Wangchug and Mangtho Lhudrup was mixed with the incorrect view of other-emptiness because they followed the teaching of Sakya Chokden.

The great Sakya master Rendawa (1349–1412) was a teacher of Tsongkhapa. Khedrup Gelek Palzang, one of Tsongkhapa's two chief disciples, noted in his *Miscellaneous Works* that although sometimes these two masters expressed their view of emptiness differently in their writings, their basic thought was the same—the view as expressed by Prāsaṅgika Madhyamaka.

The Gelug Tradition

The Gelug philosophical view in the stages of the path (*lamrim*) literature stems from the Kadam tradition, while topics relating to Tantra come from the Sakya and Kagyu traditions. Tsongkhapa, the founder of the Gelug tradition, held the Prāsaṅgika Madhyamaka view of emptiness common to both Sūtra and Tantra. His writing style and vocabulary are similar to those of the Nālandā masters Buddhapālita and Candrakīrti, whom he often quotes.

In Highest Yoga Tantra, when the Gelug speak of the indivisibility of bliss and emptiness (T. *bde stong dbyer med*), *bliss* refers to the clear-light mind and *emptiness* is its ultimate nature. Simply making manifest the subtle clear-light mind is not sufficient. Meditators must use it to meditate on and realize the correct view of emptiness. Similarly, just saying that all phenomena are devoid of inherent existence is not sufficient. A practitioner must realize the emptiness of the primordial clear-light mind and use that clear-light mind to meditate on the emptiness of all phenomena.

The Gelug tradition speaks of four empties—empty, great empty, completely empty, and all-empty. Here *empty* refers to subtle levels of consciousness that can be used to realize emptiness. Each of the four empties is a subtler consciousness than the previous one. They are so-called because each subsequent empty is empty of the preceding one—that is, all-empty (the ultimate primordial clear-light mind) is empty of the consciousnesses of completely empty, great empty, and empty. This is a type of other-emptiness, but here we are talking about levels of consciousness, not the ultimate nature of all phenomena. When speaking of emptiness as the ultimate truth, all phenomena—including the four empties—have the ultimate nature of being empty of inherent existence.

All these explanations—dzogchen, mahāmudrā, the inseparability of saṃsāra and nirvāṇa, and the indivisibility of bliss and emptiness—are about meditating on the emptiness of inherent existence with the primordial clear light, although their terminology and meditation techniques may differ.

Similarities among Traditions

The causal continuum—the mind that is the foundation-of-all, mentioned in Sakya—is continuous no matter what types of thoughts pass through the mental consciousness. If we meditate with careful observation, we can identify the mind that is the causal continuum in the space between thoughts. This meditation is also found in the Kagyu-Gelug mahāmudrā teachings where the subtle mind is identified by ceasing thoughts of the past and hope and fear for the future. As soon as such thoughts begin to arise, practitioners stop them and remain in the present moment of consciousness, a fresh and uncontrived state of mind that is called *subtle thought*.

Identifying this subtle mind between thoughts is not the full identification of rigpa. Reaching the state of pure rigpa is called *apprehending the dharmakāya*. This rigpa is able to distinguish between the consciousness that is the foundation-of-all and pristine wisdom. Dza Patrul Rinpoche, in his *Three Keys Penetrating the Core*, says that by repeatedly dwelling at the level of subtle thought, a state of wonderment free from all thought arises. It is a peaceful resting in the present, uncontrived, self-arisen mind. On the basis of this mind, practitioners go on to actually identify rigpa. The full identification occurs while resting in the uncontrived state by receiving the special blessings of the guru. In Sakya lamdre the identification of the foundation-of-all, the causal continuum, is similarly subtle, and while this is not the actual fundamental innate mind of clear light (T. *gnyug ma lhan cig skyes pa'i 'od gsal*) spoken of in Gelug, it is related to it.

Dzogchen practitioners continue to meditate with rigpa, and when thoughts or afflictions arise, without allowing the mind to be affected by the object or content of the thought, they focus on the ultimate, clear-light nature of the afflictive thought, resting their attention in this state without abandoning the affliction. While this is not easy, with training over time it is possible to do. In lamdre, practitioners first identify the coarse form of the causal continuum—the subtle level of thought mentioned above. On that basis, they use yogic techniques that in general correspond to the method continuum—that is, practitioners use various techniques and methods to purify the mind in the Guhyasamāja system—and through the yogic practice of the path continuum, they attain the resultant continuum, the dharmakāya. Here we see parallels between the dzogchen and lamdre systems.

One difference is that in dzogchen, practitioners can access the subtlest level of consciousness while ordinary, coarser levels of mind are active. By making the ultimate nature of these coarser thoughts the object of meditation, it is possible to access pure rigpa, the subtlest mind. However, in the Sakya, Kagyu, and Gelug traditions, while the coarser levels of mind are active, the subtlest mind, the innate mind of clear light, cannot manifest. It can manifest only after the coarser winds and consciousnesses have ceased, which is done by dissolving the winds in the indestructible drop in the central channel at the heart.

Dzogchen says that awakening is not attained by a fabricated mind but by identifying rigpa, understanding that all phenomena are its sport, and sustaining meditation on this. Some texts go on to say that with this practice, we need not study texts, recite mantras, visualize a deity, learn the Madhyamaka view, or meditate on the four truths or bodhicitta, because the dzogchen meditation is supreme. They assert that those other practices are "fabricated" in that they require effort and are done by a coarser mind involved in conceptions, while abiding in a state of rigpa is spontaneous, free from effort, and nonconceptual.

It is important to understand such statements properly. They are not meant for beginners, but for those who have trained thoroughly, beginning with the first of the nine vehicles and progressing to dzogchen. If overly eager beginners mistakenly believe this applies to them, they will not progress. Practitioners need to put great effort into learning and meditating on the nine vehicles under the guidance of a qualified teacher. Dodrupchen emphasized completing the preparatory practices, being introduced to rigpa by a qualified meditation master, and meditating on it with complete renunciation of the distracting pleasures and activities of this life. He himself did this. Similarly, Jigme Lingpa (1729–98) meditated with great effort for years before rigpa manifested clearly. We should not think that attainments come quickly or easily.

Are Sentient Beings Already Awakened?

After hearing various citations that say we are already buddhas and that all phenomena are pure, people often ask how this can be. If it were true, then wouldn't we be ignorant buddhas and wouldn't nonvirtue be virtue?

We can start to resolve these doubts with the Sakya lamdre explanation of the tantric path. In lamdre the term "tantra," which also means continuum, is explained on three levels: (1) the causal tantra that is the basis, (2) the method tantra that is the path, and (3) the resultant tantra that is the effect. All three arise from the fundamental innate clear-light mind.

Within the causal tantra, the foundation-of-all, the maṇḍala and the deities in it arise and all phenomena of saṃsāra and nirvāṇa are complete. In this sense, the foundation-of-all is the fundamental innate mind of clear light. Regarding ordinary unawakened beings, all phenomena of saṃsāra, such as our basic faculties and other ordinary phenomena, are present in the form of their natural characteristics; all phenomena of the path are present in the form of their qualities; and all phenomena of the resultant state of buddhahood are present in the form of potential. For this reason it is called the causal continuum.

A similar idea is expressed in the Nyingma tradition when it speaks of the equality of the basis and result. The basis is equivalent to the causal continuum in the Sakya tradition, and the result is equivalent to the resultant state of buddhahood. Understanding these concepts correctly is important, otherwise we risk the danger of thinking like the non-Buddhist Sāṃkhyas, who assert that the result is present at the time of the cause. Sāṃkhyas say, for example, that the sprout (the result) is already present in an unmanifest form in the seed (its cause).

The correct understanding of this view will enable us to comprehend Maitreya's pronouncement in the first chapter of *Sublime Continuum*: "The pollutants are adventitious; the good qualities exist innately." He does not mean that all the qualities and realizations of a buddha are actually present within the mind of an ordinary being. Instead, we should understand his meaning to be that these exist in the form of potential in the fundamental innate clear-light mind. It is in this context that statements such as "Recognizing one's true nature is equivalent to becoming totally awakened" are to be understood.

Similarly, passages in the *Hevajra* and other tantras say, "Sentient beings are completely awakened, but they are obscured by mental stains." Taken literally, this passage is difficult to understand. These two phrases are contradictory; how can someone be completely awakened and obscured by mental stains at the same time? But if we understand the meaning of sentient beings "are completely awakened" to be that they have the potential to become completely awakened, then we can understand their having adventitious mental stains at this moment.

Nāgārjuna's *Five Stages*, which presents the completion stage of Guhyasamāja, says that practitioners abiding in meditation on the illusory body perceive all phenomena in the same light. This means that when yogis on the completion stage arise in an illusory body, which is the nature of the subtlest wind and mind, they extend this perception to all phenomena, perceiving them as manifestations of the fundamental innate clear-light mind.

Although we may be able to understand the idea of perceiving all sentient beings as manifestations of the fundamental innate clear-light mind because this clear light is the fundamental source from which they all arise, how can we logically understand statements saying that the environment is a manifestation of the fundamental innate clear-light mind? This is not to be understood according to the Yogācāra tenets, which maintain that a phenomenon and the mind perceiving it are the same nature in that they arise from the same substantial cause, a latency on the mind. Rather, it means that the environment and all external phenomena are creations, manifestations, or appearances of the fundamental innate clear-light mind.

But saying that phenomena are the creations or manifestations of the clear-light mind doesn't mean that the mind becomes trucks or mountains, for then those external objects would be consciousnesses and sentient beings. That is clearly not the case.

All four classes of Tantra encourage practitioners in the three attitudes of viewing all appearances as the form of deities, viewing all sounds as mantra, and viewing all thoughts as the deity's wisdom. Practitioners train in these for the specific purpose of abandoning ordinary appearance and ordinary grasping, which produce afflictions and continue our unawakened existence. Ordinary appearance is the appearance of ourselves as the ordinary saṃsāric beings we are now, with all our faults. Ordinary grasping is believing ourselves to be such inherently existent sentient beings. Pure appearance, which is the opposite of ordinary appearance, is done on the level of imagination. It doesn't mean that with our eyes we see the people around us in the physical form of deities or that we hear only mantra and cannot carry on a conversation about practical matters. It also does not mean that all our thoughts are in fact wisdom consciousnesses. Rather, we relate or respond to these three *as if* they were pure, and in that way distorted conceptions and afflictions do not arise.

Another explanation of seeing all appearances as the form of deities relates to the lamdre teachings of the Sakya tradition. Here, the causal tantra is the foundation-of-all, and practitioners train to understand the significance and meaning of the foundation-of-all in order to attain a perception of everything as pure and divine.

The dzogchen master Dodrup Jigme Tenpai Nyima (Dodrupchen), in his *General Exposition of the "Secret Essence Tantra"* (T. *Gsang snying spyi don*), explains the cultivation of pure appearance from the viewpoint that all phenomena in saṃsāra and nirvāṇa are in fact manifestations of or the play of the fundamental ground known as *rigpa*. Rigpa is the source of everything that exists and appears in the expanse of reality. Thus saṃsāra and nirvāṇa are both manifestations of rigpa, the subtlest clear-light mind.

This is similar to the Madhyamaka explanation that emptiness is the source or origin of all conventional phenomena in that all phenomena are manifestations arising within the ultimate nature, emptiness. When we speak of natural purity, we refer to phenomena being pure of existing by their own character; they are empty of this false way of existence. Everything is naturally pure; everything by nature is empty. Meditating on emptiness doesn't make inherently existent phenomena empty of inherent existence. Rather, it isolates the mind from ordinary appearance. From the perspective of emptiness, all persons and phenomena lack inherent existence and are pure. When we perceive persons and phenomena with this perspective, we can apprehend them as pure—they are pure of any inherent existence.

Highest Yoga Tantra focuses on overcoming ordinary impure perception. Śrāvakas meditate repeatedly on the foulness of the body to generate renunciation of saṃsāra. It is said that they are so habituated to seeing themselves as impure that they cannot see phenomena as pure, nor can they imagine themselves as pure. To cultivate pure appearance, we must realize emptiness and then ascertain emptiness dawning as phenomena. In other words, pure appearance isn't projecting purity that isn't there; it's not talking yourself into seeing impure as pure. Rather, pure emptiness *appears* as objects; objects exist within emptiness because emptiness is their ultimate nature. Tsongkhapa's *Lamp Illuminating the Five Stages* says (SV 54):

> When all phenomena, the bases of isolation [from ordinary appearance and grasping], are delineated as essences of natural purity primordially empty of establishment by their own character, that very emptiness of inherent existence is ascertained as dawning as those phenomena; this is the meaning of phenomena being manifestations of emptiness.

The Sakya explanation of the inseparability of saṃsāra and nirvāṇa and the Nyingma explanation that all phenomena within saṃsāra and nirvāṇa are manifestations of or the sport of rigpa have a similar meaning. The subtle clear-light mind, rigpa, is eternal and its nature is undefiled. Based on this, we can extend the view of purity to include all phenomena, which are the manifestations or the sport of the fundamental basis, rigpa.

REFLECTION

1. Review how each tradition speaks of sentient beings' buddha nature and how it links the buddha nature to the resultant buddhahood.
2. Contemplate that although these explanations may differ within the context of each tradition, they come to the same point.
3. What is pure appearance? For some people, it seems that cultivating pure appearance is tantamount to projecting the fiction of purity on things that are not pure. What would you say to correct this misconception?

Sūtra and Tantra Methods to Meditate on Emptiness

Before realizing emptiness in tantric practice, a meditator must engage in analytical meditation on emptiness as explained in the Sūtra system. On the basis of the correct view gained through analytical meditation, a meditator then engages in tantric meditation. In his texts, Tsongkhapa explains that in Highest Yoga Tantra ascertaining and realizing emptiness is not done by the analytical meditation, as in Sūtra. Rather, it is done by making the mind subtler and subtler (DC 168–74).

As the mind becomes more and more subtle, disturbances from restlessness and laxity, the two principal hindrances to single-pointed concentration, lessen. In tantric practice, the feeling of bliss removes laxity, and making the mind subtler decreases restlessness. Here, lessening and eventually eliminating these two hindrances are not accomplished through conscious effort, as in Sūtra practice, but through dissolving the coarser levels of wind and mind, making the subtler levels of mind manifest and generating bliss. The subtler the mind becomes, the clearer the perception of the object, emptiness, is.

In the Pāramitāyāna, the purpose of stabilizing and analytical meditation is to remove the hindrances of restlessness and laxity so that the object is ascertained and seen clearly. In Highest Yoga Tantra, this same purpose is achieved without engaging in analytical meditation, but through making manifest the subtlest mind and using it to meditate on emptiness. Here, analysis could become a hindrance to doing this.

Of course, as a preliminary practice to Highest Yoga Tantra or dzogchen, it is essential that practitioners have studied and meditated on the correct view of emptiness with analytical meditation. One preliminary practice for dzogchen is to search for the source of the mind, how the mind abides, from where it comes, and to where it goes. This entails meditating on the ultimate nature of the mind, so the correct view of emptiness gained through refuting the object of negation by means of analysis is necessary. In this preliminary dzogchen practice of examining where the mind comes from, where it abides, and where it goes, we are not searching for these conventionally, because conventionally the mind comes from its immediate cause, dominant cause, and objective cause. On the conventional level, the substantial cause and cooperative conditions bring about the arising of a particular consciousness. When we talk about where the mind goes, conventionally it becomes the next moment of its continuum or transforms into a latency.

But here as a preliminary to dzogchen, when searching for the source of the mind, it is its ultimate nature, not its conventional causes and effects, that we seek to realize. Through this analytical meditation, the emptiness of the mind—its lack of inherent existence—is realized and meditated on. Having ascertained the view of emptiness through analytical meditation in the preliminary practices, practitioners go on to practice dzogchen. At this time, when doing the breakthrough practice, only one-pointed, nonanalytical meditation is done.

Mahāmudrā practice entails four yogas—one-pointed, free from elaboration, one taste, and nonmeditation. (These terms may vary in different sources.) The first two are common to Sūtra practice and include both analytical and stabilizing meditation. *One-pointed yoga* refers to serenity, which is attained through stabilizing meditation, while *yoga free from elaboration* indicates insight and involves analytical meditation. The last two yogas are unique to Tantra and point to the primordial clear-light mind. In *one-taste yoga*, practitioners attain an extraordinary insight such that conventional phenomena are seen as being of one taste in the sphere of the primordial clear-light mind. The strengthening of this realization becomes the *yoga of nonmeditation*. Each of the four yogas are subdivided into three—small, medium, and large—and are correlated with the five paths.

In the Sakya tradition, emptiness is explained in the teachings on experiential appearances of the yogi—the second of three appearances spoken of above. Here practitioners engage in analytical meditation on emptiness. After developing the realization of emptiness, they go on to practice the three continua, which involves meditation on the inseparability of clarity and emptiness.

In Gelug practice, the view common to Sūtra and Tantra is developed first, before entering tantric practice. This is important because without this realization, certain tantric practices cannot be done properly, let alone accomplished. For example, during the completion stage, practitioners train to see that everything is empty, emptiness is bliss, and bliss is the sport of the deity. These meditations cannot be done correctly without having ascertained the view of emptiness, which is done through analytical meditation as taught in the Pāramitāyāna. Meditation on emptiness on the completion stage is only nonanalytical, stabilizing meditation. Through this explanation, we see that in all four Tibetan traditions, meditation on emptiness done in Tantra is only stabilizing meditation; analytical meditation on emptiness precedes this.

In speaking of the view in terms of the various traditions, we must be sure to compare apples to apples, not apples to oranges. Usually, when people think about the view in dzogchen or mahāmudrā, they immediately relate it to Highest Yoga Tantra. But when they talk about the Gelug view of emptiness, they see it as a view common to both Sūtra and Tantra. When seen in this way, there seems to be a difference between the various views of emptiness. However, when we talk about the view in dzogchen, mahāmudrā, the inseparability of saṃsāra and nirvāṇa, and the indivisibility of bliss and emptiness as explained in the Highest Yoga Tantra of the Gelug tradition, we understand that all these views come to the same point.

Saying that all the views come to the same point and that all four traditions hold the Prāsaṅgika view does not mean there are no differences whatsoever. As mentioned at the beginning of this chapter, it means that the view in all four Tibetan traditions centers around (1) the infallibility of dependent arisings in the context of conventional truths and (2) the nonfindability of even emptiness ultimately. Within their similarities regarding these major points, the four traditions may differ on other less important assertions pertaining to the view.

Dzogchen, Highest Yoga Tantra, and Madhyamaka

I would like to continue with a more in-depth exploration of the views and practices of dzogchen, Gelug, and Madhyamaka. I do this to assuage the doubts of people who have not deeply and extensively studied and investigated the common results of these practices in the various traditions. This lack of knowledge has led to misunderstandings over the centuries among Tibetan Buddhist practitioners of the multiple traditions. It would be unfortunate indeed if these misunderstandings were to spread to practitioners of Tibetan Buddhism in other countries.

Tsongkhapa, the founder of the Gelug tradition, received dzogchen teachings from the Nyingma yogi Lhodrak Drubchen Namkha Gyaltsen (1326–1401). As evident in his biography, Tsongkhapa had profound realization of the view of emptiness based on the teachings he received from this yogi. Throughout history, up to the present day, we know of highly realized practitioners who gained their insights and skills through practicing the path as taught in Nyingma. When the results of following certain teachings are evident in this way, it is clear that those teachings are authentic and reliable.

In the *Miscellaneous Works* of Khedrup Gelek Palzang, one of Tsongkhapa's foremost disciples, someone asks if dzogchen is a pure teaching. Khedrup Gelek Palzang replies, "Yes, it is," and says that any criticism of it that occurred in Tibet was mistaken. The criticism had arisen not due to the doctrine itself but to the behavior of some tantric practitioners after the repression of Buddhist teachings by the Tibetan king Langdarma. Misunderstanding the teachings, these "practitioners" engaged in sexual union and emitted semen. Khedrup Gelek Palzang said that Tibetan translators had seen the original Sanskrit texts of the *Secret Essence Tantra* (*Guhyagarbha*) in India, and that the Nyingma teachings were valid. He warned that those deprecating these Mahāyāna teachings were creating the cause for unfortunate rebirths.

Although some Kagyu, Sakya, and Gelug masters refuted certain points in dzogchen, some people later mistakenly took that as a refutation of

Nyingma as a whole. Masters of the various Tibetan traditions have debated specific points for centuries, but this does not indicate that they deprecate one another's systems. Rather, these debates kept students' minds active and questioning, so that they could penetrate the actual meaning of these topics. The First Panchen Lama, Lobsang Chokyi Gyaltsen (1567–1662), affirmed in *Root Verses for the Precious Gaden Oral Transmission of Mahāmudrā* (v 10–11):

> Joining the coemergent, the amulet box, the fivefold, equal taste, the four letters, pacification, severance,[101] dzogchen, and instructions in the Madhyamaka view: [these] and other teachings are called by many names individually, but when examined by a yogi who has mastered definitive-meaning scriptures and reasoning and possesses inner experience, they come down to the same thought.

I share this view. How can we establish that dzogchen and Madhyamaka come to the same point? This cannot be done by comparing them directly, for the Madhyamaka view is held not only by bodhisattvas practicing Sūtra and Tantra but also by śrāvaka and solitary-realizer āryas, whereas dzogchen is not found in the Sūtra path of śrāvakas, solitary realizers, or bodhisattvas, or in three lower tantras. In the Nyingma presentation of nine vehicles, dzogchen is found only at the peak of these nine, Atiyoga, whereas the Madhyamaka view is held in all nine vehicles. However, if we look at the way of cultivating the Madhyamaka view with a special mind—the innate wisdom of great bliss as taught in the Highest Yoga Tantra—we may compare them at the same level. Here we can see their similarities.

The New Translation traditions' explanation of Guhyasamāja speaks of the view in terms of the subject and the object. The view in terms of the object refers to the object of the view—the emptiness of inherent existence—and this object is the same in Guhyasamāja and in Nāgārjuna's explanation of Madhyamaka. The view in terms of the subject is the consciousness realizing emptiness, and here there is a big difference between Sūtra and Tantra. In Guhyasamāja, emptiness is realized by an extremely subtle mind—the fundamental innate mind of clear light—while in general in Madhyamaka, there is no talk of the innate clear-light mind, and emptiness is realized by a consciousness that is comparatively coarser.

Ripa Damtsig Dorje, a student of the Nyingma master Dodrupchen, says the view in dzogchen is also described as the view in terms of the subject and the object. The view in terms of the object is the object clear light, the object realized by subtle wisdom. The view in terms of the subject is a subtle consciousness. The view in dzogchen refers to the union of this subtle wisdom consciousness with its object, emptiness.

This way of speaking of both the object and subject as the view is similar to the Sūtra system, where Mādhyamikas call emptiness the "object-ultimate" and the wisdom consciousness directly realizing it a "concordant-ultimate."[102] In dzogchen, the mind realizing emptiness is not this comparatively coarse mind but rigpa—the basic pristine mind—which is the fundamental innate mind of clear light. This mind is also said to be the final reality (T. *gnas lugs*) of phenomena. In Madhyamaka, this mind would be considered a concordant-ultimate and a conventional truth because only emptinesses—objects found by a probing awareness analyzing the ultimate mode of existence—are ultimate truths. The Madhyamaka definition of the two truths differs from the unique identifications of the two truths in dzogchen and in Highest Yoga Tantra. In dzogchen and Highest Yoga Tantra, the subtlest mind realizing emptiness is an ultimate truth, whereas in Madhyamaka it is considered a conventional truth.

Dodrupchen, a Nyingma master whose explanations I respect, speaks of the mind-vajra that is the mere clarity and cognizance that is the basis of all phenomena of saṃsāra and nirvāṇa. Called "vajra" because it is indestructible and is the final root of all minds, it is said to be permanent and unproduced in that it exists eternally and is not newly produced. It is called the ultimate truth because it is beyond all temporary phenomena. Its manifestations in coarse forms are conventional truths and are the sport or play of the mind-vajra. It has the nature of being the truth body at buddhahood. Here, too, terms such as "unproduced" and "ultimate truth" are used in a different way than in the Sūtra system.

Rigpa is also considered the ultimate truth, and its appearances as impure and pure phenomena are called conventional truths. Conventional truths are temporary coarse phenomena, whereas ultimate truth is the mind-vajra, which always exists and is fundamental and innate.

In the New Translation systems of Highest Yoga Tantra, the mind-vajra is called the fundamental innate mind of clear light, which is the basis of everything in saṃsāra and nirvāṇa, and is given the name "ultimate truth." It is also called the nature of phenomena (*dharmatā*, T. *chos nyid*), clear light, and unconditioned (*asaṃskṛta*, T. *'dus ma byas*). The meanings of "permanent" in dzogchen and of "unconditioned' in Highest Yoga Tantra differ considerably from the meaning of these words in Madhyamaka, as do the words "ultimate" and "conventional." We must take care to understand the meaning of a word correctly in different contexts. Not doing this results in misunderstanding that can adversely affect our meditation practice and provoke unnecessary friction among Buddhists.

In the Sūtra system, "permanent" usually means it doesn't change moment by moment, but sometimes it has other meanings. In the *Ornament for Clear Realizations* (*Abhisamayālaṃkāra*), Maitreya says that a Buddha's activities are permanent, meaning that they are inexhaustible. In some contexts, "permanent" may mean eternal: unending even if it changes moment by moment.

The multiplicity of meanings of "ultimate" also occurs in Madhyamaka and in the Sūtra system. In *Discrimination of the Middle and the Extremes* (*Madhyāntavibhāga*), Maitreya speaks of the object-ultimate (emptiness), the practice-ultimate (wisdom of meditative equipoise), and the attainment-ultimate (nirvāṇa). Similarly, in the Highest Yoga Tantra of the New Translation traditions, the actual clear light, the fourth of the five stages of the Guhyasamāja completion stage, is called "ultimate truth," and the pure illusory body is called "conventional truth." Nevertheless, according to Madhyamaka definitions of ultimate and conventional truths, the actual clear light would be a conventional truth. Thus, we need to be aware of how terms are used in different contexts and not jump to conclusions when we encounter an unfamiliar usage.

The nature of the mind-vajra is pure (T. *ka dag*), meaning it is empty of inherent existence. Within the mind-vajra's nature of clarity and cognizance, all phenomena of saṃsāra and nirvāṇa appear as the manifestation or sport of its spontaneous nature (T. *lhun grub*). Due to the emphasis in dzogchen on the mind as the source of saṃsāra and nirvāṇa, practitioners strive to realize both the empty and the clear natures of the mind. This agrees with what Āryadeva says in *Lamp for Integrating the Practices* (*Caryāmelāpaka-*

pradīpa), a commentary on the completion stage of Guhyasamāja, where he stresses that if we do not know the nature of the mind, liberation is impossible.

The mind-vajra of sentient beings is not polluted by defilements, even though sentient beings' minds are full of afflictions. The afflictions are the sport of the mind-vajra; they arise from it but do not pollute it. They are not the nature of the mind-vajra and can be eliminated. It's like muddy water—it looks dirty but its nature is still clear; when the dirt settles, that unstained nature is visible.

A Buddha's qualities are present in the nature of the mind-vajra. Due to certain conditions, such as the presence of defilements, they are not manifest, so it is said that we are awakened from the beginning. Nevertheless, this does not mean we are presently buddhas, for we would then be ignorant buddhas! Rather, that awakened nature is present and ready to be revealed when the obscurations are removed.

In the process of recognizing the mind-vajra and determining that all phenomena of saṃsāra and nirvāṇa are its sport, practitioners understand that phenomena exist only nominally and have never been established in their own right although they appear in that way and we grasp that appearance as true. With practice, as yogis cause these phenomena to appear as the sport of rigpa and familiarize themselves with that understanding, they do not get caught up in judgments, wrong conceptions, and confusion. As a result, they cease to create the karma that causes saṃsāra.

Highest Yoga Tantra says that all conceptions that create karma are coarse consciousnesses. When these and the minds of white appearance, red increase, and black near-attainment dissolve, the subtlest mind of clear light manifests. Abiding in this subtlest clear light prevents the process of saṃsāra from continuing by inhibiting the conceptual consciousnesses that cause it.

Just as Madhyamaka holds that phenomena of saṃsāra are false because they appear one way but exist in another, dzogchen says that although the phenomena of saṃsāra and nirvāṇa are the sport of rigpa, they do not appear that way and thus are false. By realizing this, we automatically know that these phenomena exist only conventionally, through the power of concept and name, even though the object of negation has not been explained in detail in dzogchen texts. This understanding of emptiness and nominal existence comes about through seeing all phenomena as the sport of the mind, while at the same time being aware of the basic mind, rigpa.

In Madhyamaka the realization of reality involves focusing on a nonaffirming negative[103]—the absence of inherent existence—in meditative equipoise. This nonaffirming negative does not indicate or imply anything positive; it is simply the absence or emptiness of inherent existence, which has never existed. In dzogchen, however, practitioners focus on the mere clarity and cognizant nature of the mind, which is an affirmative phenomenon, not a nonaffirming negative. Prior to this in the breakthrough practice, they have analyzed from where the mind came, where it abides, and where it goes. This leads to the understanding that the mind is empty of the conceptual elaborations of inherent existence.[104] Thus the meditation on rigpa involves focusing on an affirming negative—the mind that is understood as empty of inherent existence.

In Nyingma there is not an extensive explanation of whether this combination of mind and its emptiness is an affirming or nonaffirming negative. A few Nyingma scholars have said it is an affirming negative, but the issue must be examined closely. Previously we discussed two types of meditation, one in which we try to perceive an object such as impermanence or emptiness, the other in which we try to generate our mind into a particular subjective experience, such as love or compassion.[105] Meditation on emptiness is the former type, meditation on rigpa is the latter. Prior to focusing on rigpa, meditators have ascertained its emptiness, so a mind qualified by emptiness appears as the object of meditation. Although this seems to be an affirming negative, it differs from the affirming negative that is a composite of appearance and emptiness that is the object when perceiving illusion-like appearances.[106] Rigpa is a much subtler state of mind; it is not the coarser mind realizing illusion-like appearances described in Madhyamaka.

According to the New Translation traditions, the emptiness of inherent existence appears when the clear light is manifest. The Gelug yogi and scholar Khedrup Norsang Gyatso said that when the mother clear light—the clear light at the time of death—manifests in an ordinary being, emptiness appears, although it is not ascertained. Emptiness appears due to the dissolution of the coarse conceptual minds, not due to having realized that the object of negation does not exist. That is, the object of negation has not been refuted, just temporarily suppressed.

In dzogchen, as yogis meditate on the composite of appearance and emptiness of rigpa, gradually all conceptual elaborations fall away and the subtlest clear light that realizes emptiness manifests. For practitioners who have meditated on emptiness and then identify rigpa itself, when dualistic appearances cease the mind becomes inseparable from emptiness. This process of meditation, therefore, contains all the elements of meditation on emptiness common to Sūtra and Tantra in the New Translation traditions.

In the New Translation traditions, the fundamental innate mind of clear light cannot manifest while the ordinary coarse consciousnesses—the sense consciousnesses and the coarse mental consciousness—are functioning. These coarse consciousnesses must first dissolve to access the subtlest mind; these two levels of mind cannot be operative at the same time.

However, in dzogchen, practitioners can initially be introduced to rigpa while the coarse consciousnesses are present. Since the mind-vajra's qualities are clarity and cognizance and these two qualities are shared by all consciousnesses—even those afflicted with attachment or hostility—qualities of the mind-vajra can be identified in all these consciousnesses. How is this done? Dzogchen teachings explain that just after a certain experience—for example, hearing a sound—a mind free from conceptuality occurs before a conceptual mind arises thinking about the sound. The nature of that mind free from conceptuality is clarity and cognizance. By catching and then lengthening this experience, a practitioner begins to identify rigpa.

The *Kālacakra Tantra* in the New Translation traditions speaks of generating an empty form, which is an appearance of the subtlest mind, without that mind being manifest. An empty form can be generated even when the coarse sense consciousnesses are functioning. This is similar to the dzogchen view that the qualities of rigpa can be manifest without ceasing the coarse consciousnesses. Still, highly accomplished yogis practicing either dzogchen or Kālacakra do stop the six coarse consciousnesses and make manifest the subtlest mind of clear light as is done in the other Highest Yoga Tantra practices. The difference is that in initial levels of practice, practitioners can be introduced to rigpa without first ceasing the coarse consciousnesses.

As practitioners become more familiar with rigpa, their conceptions and afflictions have less and less power because they are focused on the clarity and cognizance of rigpa instead. That is, the mind gradually ceases its false superimpositions and elaborations of inherent existence projected onto phenomena.

In short, dzogchen, Kālacakra, and the New Translation traditions have different modes of practice for meditating with the subtlest clear light. However, these all come to the same point when practiced and actualized by dedicated yogis. Nāgārjuna said in the *Five Stages* (*Pañcakrama*) (KCI 220): "Everything is like the concentration of illusion." This is a clue that all sentient beings and their environment are the sport or play of wind and mind. It is in accord with saying that all phenomena are the sport of rigpa.

When I researched and contemplated this topic, I had the sense that Dodrupchen was stroking my head in agreement. Although I cannot claim definite insight into this matter, I have come to this conclusion through studying the great works of Madhyamaka, the *Guhyasamāja Tantra, Kālacakra Tantra,* and *General Exposition of the "Secret Essence Tantra"* by the great Nyingma master Dodrupchen, who was a disciple of Jamyang Khyentse Wangpo. I hope others will further explore these texts and topics.

14 | Coming to the Same Point

EMPHASIZING THE COMMONALITIES in the four Tibetan traditions, Panchen Lobsang Chokyi Gyaltsen said in his *Root Verses for the Precious Gaden Oral Transmission of Mahāmudrā* that the great seal (mahāmudrā) of the Kagyu tradition, the great perfection (dzogchen) practices of the Nyingma tradition, the path and result (lamdre) of the Sakya tradition, and the indivisibility of bliss and emptiness (T. *bde stong dbyer med*) of the Gelug tradition all come to the same point: understanding the fundamental innate clear-light mind. We have discussed this in the Nyingma description of rigpa and mind-vajra, the Sakya explanation of the foundation-of-all and the three continuums, the Kagyu practice of tantric mahāmudrā, and the Gelug description of uniting bliss (the subtlest clear-light mind) and emptiness.

The question arises: "Dzogchen is presented as the peak of the nine vehicles because its practitioners utilize rigpa, whereas in the preceding vehicles, they used mind (T. *sems*). How, then, can the dzogchen practice lead to the realization of the fundamental innate clear-light mind (T. *gnyug sems*), which is a mind?" In dzogchen, "mind" (T. *sems*) refers to the ordinary mind with dualistic perceptions and distorted conceptions, as distinct from rigpa, which is pure awareness. Not all traditions use the word *sems* in this way. This is the source of the question.

The dzogchen master Dodrupchen responds that Highest Yoga Tantra emphasizes exploring and developing the fundamental innate clear-light mind. This is also a feature of dzogchen. The difference lies in their methods. In Highest Yoga Tantra, techniques for exploring and developing the fundamental innate clear-light mind are practiced in a gradual process, leading from the generation stage to the three isolates of the completion stage and eventually to the stage of actual clear light. For yogis who have trained well in the first eight vehicles leading to the actual practice of dzogchen, the development and enhancement of the fundamental innate clear-light mind is not explained as a gradual process but as directly grasping the mind of clear light itself right from the beginning, by activating rigpa.

Differences in Approach, Unity in Results

Tantrayāna must be practiced on the basis of having some experience in Sūtrayāna. While the Tantra perspective often differs from the Sūtra presentation, if understood properly they are not contradictory.

One area of discussion between Sūtra and Tantra is the relation of body and mind. In Sūtra, these two are different natures—the body is matter, the mind is clarity and cognizance—whereas in Tantra the subtlest wind and mind are one nature. In both, paths are usually considered consciousnesses, although some say that right speech, which is form, is also a path. The body is not considered a path in the Pāramitāyāna because it is true duḥkha to be abandoned. Yet in Guhyasamāja, the illusory body, a subtle body formed from the subtle winds, is considered a path. Furthermore, in Pāramitāyāna, removing afflictions takes two of the three countless great eons that bodhisattvas need to reach awakening. However, in Guhyasamāja, the actual clear light eradicates both acquired and innate afflictions in one meditation session. To understand these points, we need to know about the subtle winds and consciousnesses, topics discussed only in Vajrayāna, not Pāramitāyāna, which is concerned with the coarse physical body and coarse consciousnesses.

There are differences among the tantras as well. Someone who has studied only Guhyasamāja will find the description of the channels, winds, drops, and the generation of empty forms found in Kālacakra to be puzzling. Someone who has studied and practiced only the Nyingma or the New Translation traditions may misunderstand explanations of the other traditions. Each system has its own distinctive presentations due to the variety of practitioners' dispositions, interests, and the structure of their subtle bodies. In all these cases, the guidance of a learned and experienced teacher is required to explain the noncontradictory nature of these descriptions and practices. Otherwise, if we have studied only one system, we can easily jump to false conclusions when hearing a passage from another system.

All these tantric systems contain unique techniques to accomplish the same aim of making manifest the fundamental innate mind of clear light that realizes emptiness. Guhyasamāja does this through the yoga of inner winds, Cakrasaṃvara uses the four joys, Hevajra emphasizes the practice of tummo. Kālacakra generates an empty form. Dzogchen employs sustained meditation in a state of nonconceptuality together with other internal and external conditions. A similar practice is found in Kagyu mahāmudrā.

Each system speaks of attaining buddhahood—the truth body and form body of a buddha—in slightly different ways. Guhyasamāja speaks of uniting the pure illusory body and actual clear light. Kālacakra explains uniting empty form and supreme immutable bliss through stacking the drops in the central channel to overcome obscurations to awakening. Dzogchen talks of unifying view and meditation or breakthrough and leap-over (T. *thod rgal*).

Confusion Involving Terminology

I've mentioned the confusion involving terminology that can easily arise among tenet systems and among Tibetan traditions. Sometimes a Sūtra teaching, such as the Yogācāra view of no external objects, is referenced in the context of Tantra. A Western friend commented that when I taught Gampopa's *Jeweled Ornament of Liberation* (*Dam chos yid bzhin gyi nor bu thar pa rin po che'i rgyan*), the view presented in that text did not seem to be Prāsaṅgika. Recently I received the four volumes of Gampopa's *Collected Works*, and in it I found a clear statement indicating that the view is similar to that of the Yogācāra-Svātantrika Madhyamaka. By following the Yogācāra's reasoning, Gampopa refutes external objects, and from this perspective he is closer to the Yogācāra view. However, he also refutes the inherent existence of the mind, and from that perspective he adheres to the Madhyamaka view. I believe that although Gampopa uses terminology in ways similar to Yogācāra Madhyamaka, his meaning is different.

To give two examples of confusion regarding terminology in Tantra and Yogācāra, in some tantric texts we find quotations that seem to refute external objects, and the *Guhyasamāja Root Tantra* speaks of eight types of consciousness. Both of these are Yogācāra tenets. I think that there was a specific purpose for Gampopa using Yogācāra terminology of no external objects when discussing certain tantric practices. Just because there is discourse on no external objects, we shouldn't immediately think that the speaker is referring to a Yogācāra view.

In the context of Yogācāra, rejection of external objects occurs as an integral part of the explanation of ultimate reality. They say that if something exists, it must be findable when we analyze and search for it. If we analyze and can't find it—as is the case with external objects made of partless particles—then it doesn't exist. They then say that we experience our internal mind, so it must exist, and since it exists it must truly exist. Mādhyamikas refute the way of searching for things asserted by Yogācārins. They say that Yogācārins refute the conventional existence of an object because they cannot find it ultimately, which is incorrect to do. The Mādhyamikas also say that when ultimate analysis is done, no external objects can be found. However, that does not refute their conventional existence because ultimate analysis cannot negate conventional existence. Similarly, if we apply ultimate analysis to the mind itself, we won't find it either, but that doesn't mean the mind doesn't conventionally exist. There should be no difference between the subject—the mind—and external objects; they both exist conventionally, but neither exists ultimately.

In Vajrayāna, however, there is a purpose for saying there are no external objects and that everything is the nature of the internal mind. An aim of deity yoga is to eliminate ordinary appearance and ordinary grasping. If we see ourselves as a truly existent person, it's difficult to imagine ourselves transforming into a deity. Similarly, if we consider the surrounding environment as an external object, we won't be able to transform it into the maṇḍala, the deity's residence. To overcome this difficulty, some practitioners and scholars find it helpful to think there are no external objects.

Some Vajrayāna texts explicitly present the Yogācāra position that rejects the conventional existence of the external material world. For example, the Vajrayāna commentator and mahāsiddha Ratnākaraśānti[107] does not accept the reality of the external material world. In addition, I saw in Abhayākaragupta's commentary on Nāgārjuna's *Compendium of Sūtras* passages that present a convergence of the views of Nāgārjuna and Asaṅga.[108]

When highly accomplished yogis compose spiritual songs based on their own realizations and experiences, they may say there are no external objects and everything is the nature of mind. But they say this not from the perspective of realizing that external objects do not conventionally exist but from the view that they do not exist ultimately or inherently.

Mind as the Creator

Both Sūtra and Tantra speak of the mind as the creator, but they do so in different ways. According to Sūtra, ignorance produces afflictions, which create karma, and karma influences the development of the world and the sentient beings in it. Yogācārins say that all external phenomena are projections or extensions of the mind. Mādhyamikas assert that all phenomena exist by being merely designated by name and concept. The Vajrayāna understanding that all phenomena are the play or sport of the clear light is very different from the Yogācāra view that all phenomena are the nature of mind.

Prāsaṅgika texts trace all existence back to the mind; Candrakīrti's *Supplement* states that the mind itself creates the entire world of our experience. Similarly, Nāgārjuna's *Five Stages*, written from the Vajrayāna perspective, says, "Abiding in the illusion-like meditative absorption, view all [phenomena] in a like manner."

In commenting on these lines in *Clear Lamp* (*Pradīpodyotananāmaṭīkā*), a commentary on the *Guhyasamāja Tantra*, Candrakīrti explains that while abiding in the illusion-like meditative absorption—which here refers to the illusory body—yogis extend that experience to all phenomena. They cultivate the perspective of all phenomena being illusion-like and resembling the illusory body that they have attained. Here we see concordance between the *Supplement's* statement that mind itself creates the entire world and Vajrayāna's perspective that the mind creates the world of our experiences.

When we analyze and go deeper into the nature of the mind, we discover subtler levels of consciousness and ultimately the subtlest mind of clear light. From the Vajrayāna viewpoint, the external world of sentient beings is created by or has arisen from this clear light. In addition, the final basis of designation of all sentient beings who live in that external environment is the subtlest clear light. In this way, both the sentient beings and the environment in which they live are, in some sense, manifestations arising from the clear-light mind. It is in this sense that we understand the statement that, in a causal sense, it is the mind that creates the world.

The Sakya's explanation of the inseparability of saṃsāra and nirvāṇa on the basis of the causal continuum, the foundation-of-all, elucidates the reality of saṃsāric phenomena in terms of characteristics of the causal continuum. All phenomena of the path—the five paths and ten grounds, and so on—are explained in terms of the qualities of the causal continuum, and the aspects of the resultant state are explained in terms of the potency of that causal continuum. In this way, the mind is the basis or creator of saṃsāra and nirvāṇa.

Statements found in mahāmudrā and dzogchen agree that the mind is the creator of the world in this causal sense. Madhyamaka Prāsaṅgikas also see the mind as the primary basis for the arising of phenomena because all phenomena are mere designations and constructs of the mind.

You may have noticed that all tantric traditions emphasize the emptiness of the mind, not the emptiness of external objects or even of the person. This is because our mind is the creator and the basis of both saṃsāra and nirvāṇa. Candrakīrti says (MMA 6.89):

> It is the mind that constructed the vast diversity
> of both the domain of sentient beings and their universe.
> The Buddha said all beings are born of karma:
> there is no karma without the mind.

On the coarse level, our mind is important because our intentions create karma, which influences our rebirths, experiences in life, habitual actions, and the type of environment we live in. On the subtle level, activating the subtlest mind and using it to realize its own empty nature has tremendous power to swiftly and conclusively eradicate all obscurations. The quality of the agent—the subtlest mind that realizes the emptiness of the mind—is unique in its clarity because all coarser and all afflictive states of mind are not operable. This mind is perceiving its own ultimate nature in such a way that they are indivisible. In Tantra it is as if something's own nature is manifesting as its own realization. For this reason, realizing the ultimate nature of the mind is paramount.

In Sūtra, we begin by meditating on the emptiness of the person because it is said to be easier to realize than the emptiness of the mind. However, according to Highest Yoga Tantra, meditation on the ultimate nature of the mind is foremost. This is expressed in a mantra we often recite in tantric practice, *oṃ śūnyatā jñāna vajra svabhāva ātmako 'ham*, which literally means "om emptiness wisdom vajra nature is my self-nature." Here "nature" refers to the reality being meditated on (emptiness) being the very nature of the agent that is meditating (the fundamental innate clear-light mind).

Presentations from Different Perspectives

To understand that the presentations of the four Tibetan traditions come to the same point, remember that they sometimes speak from different perspectives. For example, the Sakya school's presentation of the inseparability of saṃsāra and nirvāṇa does not need to be understood only from the Vajrayāna perspective. It may also be understood from a Pāramitāyāna perspective similar to the presentation of the equality of saṃsāra and nirvāṇa in the *Ornament of Clear Realization*. In *Treatise on the Middle Way*, Nāgārjuna equates saṃsāra and nirvāṇa because they have the same ultimate nature—emptiness—and says that the emptiness of inherent existence itself is nirvāṇa. In these contexts, the equality of saṃsāra and nirvāṇa and their inseparability is explained from the Sūtrayāna perspective of the ultimate nature.

The mahāmudrā and dzogchen presentations incorporate the Highest Yoga Tantra perspective, whereas the presentation of emptiness in *Treatise on the Middle Way* and the *Supplement* is from the viewpoint of reality as it is, which is common to both Sūtra and Tantra. Both perspectives are necessary. The Sakya presentation of the inseparability of clarity and emptiness is usually taught from the Tantric perspective. Highest Yoga Tantra explains that "clarity" refers to the primordial clear-light mind—which is empty of true existence—and "emptiness" indicates the lack of inherent existence that is the ultimate nature of that mind. Inseparable, these two are free from elaboration. Characterized by clarity and emptiness, the true mind emerges when all defilements and obscurations have been eliminated. In the practices of dzogchen and the inseparability of clarity and emptiness, the primary perspective is that of the subject, the experience of the clear light, whereas the Prāsaṅgika presentation is primarily from the perspective of the object clear light, emptiness.

Dzogchen speaks of reality as primordially pure (T. *ka dag*) and its nature as spontaneous presence (T. *lhun grub*). Reality being primordially pure refers to the emptiness of the object. Its nature being spontaneous presence refers to the quality of the subjective experience. The unity of the two is then explained. Similarly, in Gelug Vajrayāna, and particularly in the Guhyasamāja completion stage, there is discussion of the ultimate actual clear light where the perspective is primarily from the experience of the subject, the clear-light mind.

In relation to this, Khenpo Rinchen, a nonsectarian scholar and a Sakya abbot, told me of a comment by the master Jamyang Khyentse Chokyi Lodro (1893–1959) that the Gelug view is presented in relationship to the basic state, our common experience as ordinary beings; the Sakya view is presented in relation to spiritual experience of the path; and the dzogchen or Nyingma view is from the perspective of the resultant state, buddhahood, because from the perspective of a buddha there are no impure experiences or impure phenomena. Jamyang Khyentse Chokyi Lodro's comment seems accurate to me.

Avoiding Misunderstandings

In general, scholars and masters who study the texts of the four Tibetan traditions and have a good understanding of their different philosophical views explain their views clearly and precisely. But those scholars who have studied only the texts of their own tradition and know only that view often make unclear and incomplete presentations of the views of other traditions. This is important to bear in mind because, both in the past and the present, some lectures and articles on the four Tibetan traditions have created confusion. Unfortunately, scholars and masters who have thoroughly learned and practiced all four Tibetan traditions are few in number.

Even great masters and scholars may believe they have understood another scholar's position and refuted it, when in fact they have only a cursory understanding of the other's view. For example, Bhāvaviveka (500–570) had an imprecise understanding of Buddhapālita's view and thus misinterpreted it. Nonetheless, he proceeded to refute Buddhapālita's view. This becomes clear when we read Candrakīrti's commentary on their debate, in which Candrakīrti defends Buddhapālita's view and criticizes Bhāvaviveka's.

As human beings, even great masters can fall prey to such misunderstandings. Initially I didn't believe this could happen. All of them are disciples of the same teacher, Śākyamuni Buddha. All follow Nāgārjuna's view. How could they make incorrect assumptions about each other's positions? In my opinion, this happens because people become overly confident and think they have understood something when in fact they haven't. It seems Bhāvaviveka might have been overconfident, and on the basis of a rough reading of Buddhapālita's text misunderstood the meaning and refuted it.

Such misunderstanding among traditions can easily occur. It seems to me that the great Nyingma scholar and master Ju Mipham did something similar with respect to Candrakīrti's view and Tsongkhapa's explanation of it. This is my opinion. I don't know if it's correct or not, because I too have limited knowledge. Mipham Rinpoche principally studied only the Nyingma tradition. He went through one of Tsongkhapa's texts quickly and got a sketchy idea of it but did not study it in depth. In reading Ju Mipham's criticisms of Tsongkhapa, I noticed that some of his refutations were based on misunderstanding Tsongkhapa's position. For example, in Tsongkhapa's writings on Madhyamaka, he says the having-ceased of an object is an impermanent, conditioned phenomenon. Mipham refutes this as if Tsongkhapa had made it up, whereas Candrakīrti himself mentions this. To fully understand another's position, we must study all their works, not just one text, because a scholar may clearly and extensively explain a topic in one book but cover it only briefly in another. We should avoid being presumptuous and thinking we know the totality of someone's view from reading one book.

Another example is the great master and scholar Karmapa Mikyo Dorje (1507–54), who wrote a refutation of Tsongkhapa's work and in another instance praised Tsongkhapa. I believe that, due to some misunderstanding, these sages did not properly understand Tsongkhapa's thought.

Likewise, the Sakya scholar Taktsang Lotsawa (1405–77) raised eighteen objections to Tsongkhapa's teachings. While listing these, Taktsang Lotsawa says, "Although on the one hand Tsongkhapa says that when we search for the basis of designation of a phenomenon we cannot find anything, on the other hand when Tsongkhapa searches for the basis of designation, he finds that a having-ceased is an impermanent, conditioned phenomenon." Because he was open-minded, he later came to see that he had not properly understood Tsongkhapa's meaning, and acknowledging his own errors, he praised Tsongkhapa's greatness. All of us should emulate his open-mindedness and strive to understand all schools from their own perspective and without bias.

Dzogchen masters Dodrup Jigme Tenpai Nyima and his disciple Tulku Tsullo properly and completely understood Tsongkhapa's view. One of them had even studied with a Gelug teacher. Tulku Tsullo had a full understanding of the Sūtrayāna and Tantrayāna according to both the Nyingma and the New Translation traditions.

Similarly, Nyengon Sungrab Tulku (Khewang Lozang Dongak, 1903–57) first studied in the Gelug tradition and then became a student of the Nyingma lama Jambel Rolway Dorje, as a result of which he came to have a full understanding of dzogchen. His explanation of rigpa is very clear because he knows the shared points in the Tibetan traditions. If we want to bring genuine harmony and appreciation between the Nyingma and Gelug traditions, the writings of Dodrupchen, Tulku Tsullo, and Nyengon Sungrab are excellent in this regard. In the future, some scholars will study these debates and hopefully write books that will clarify them and put them in proper perspective.

Self-Empty and Other-Empty

The terms "self-empty" (T. *rang stong*) and "other-empty" (T. *gzhan stong*) were coined in Tibet. In general, *self-empty* refers to an object being empty of inherent existence—it is empty of existing as a self-enclosed entity, it is not its own ultimate nature, and its ultimate nature is its emptiness of inherent existence. *Other-empty* refers to a phenomenon lacking conventionalities that are not it. For example, the self-emptiness of a table is its emptiness of inherent existence, and an example of its other-emptiness is its not being the things inside its drawers.

When explaining the meaning of the subject clear light, dzogchen says its nature is primordially pure and lacks inherent existence. This relates to its being self-empty. The subject clear light is also free from temporary or adventitious factors (T. *glo bur ba'i chos*). This is its other-emptiness.

The continuum of the clear light never ceases. It is always there, with no beginning and no end. From this perspective, it is said to be permanent.

It is the subtlest consciousness, and all other phenomena arise from and dissolve back into it, so they are temporary. Here, the word "temporary" does not refer to adventitious defilements to be abandoned. Rather, because phenomena arise and dissolve back into the clear light, the clear light is empty of these temporary phenomena. This is the meaning of other-empty.

In the past, the term "other-empty" has indicated two different views in Tibet—one correct, the other incorrect.[109] According to the late Dilgo Khyentse Rinpoche, the above explanation is the correct view of other-empty. The clear-light mind is empty of coarser states of consciousness such as the white appearance, red increase, and black near-attainment (RR 371). In that respect, it is other-empty. The clear-light mind being empty of its manifestations—which is its other-emptiness—is not contradictory with its emptiness of inherent existence, its self-emptiness. This is so because the fundamental innate clear-light mind, which is the basis or substratum of its emptiness, is not asserted to be inherently existent. This is understood in dzogchen during the practice of primordial purity.

When explaining the clear light, the *Guhyasamāja Tantra* speaks about the four empties. Each subsequent empty is empty of the preceding empty. The meaning of "empty" in this case comes to the same point as the above meaning of other-empty.[110]

Dzogchen states that things do not exist inherently and do not exist in the nature of the primordial mind. I think this relates to other-empty. This primordial mind, which is empty of adventitious phenomena (other-empty) is itself empty of inherent existence (self-empty).

The Jonang Tradition

The Jonang (*jo nang*) tradition traces its lineage back to India and Nālandā University. Tsen Kawoche (b. 1021) and the Kālacakra master Yumo Mikyo Dorje (b. 1027) were the forefathers of the school. By the early fourteenth century, with the presence of Dolpopa Sherab Gyaltsen (1292–1361), the Jonangpa community of hermits had formed a distinct identity with their own scholastic tradition and esoteric lineage transmission. After being suppressed for some time due to their controversial views, in recent years Dolpopa's writings are again being studied and debated among Tibetans.[111]

In most cases the views and practices of the various Tibetan traditions come to the same point. However, there are cases in which they do not. As noted above, some versions of the view of other-emptiness are valid, while others are not. The view presented in dzogchen as described above is the correct view of other-emptiness. Among some followers of the Jonang tradition, which began as a branch of the Sakya but subsequently became its own tradition, a wrong view of other-emptiness developed.

Sherab Gyaltsen, a learned scholar, meditator, and practitioner of the *Kālacakra Tantra*, was the originator of the view he called the Great Madhyamaka (T. *dbu ma chen po*), which became the view of the Jonang school (TW 445–511). This view is based on ten sūtras that Dolpopa collectively calls the "tathāgatagarbha sūtras," the most well-known of which are the *Tathāgata Essence Sūtra* (*Tathāgatagarbha Sūtra*) and the *Great Nirvāṇa Sūtra* (*Mahāparinirvāṇa Sūtra*).[112]

Dolpopa maintained that many of the scriptures that people thought expressed the Yogācāra view actually expounded the Great Madhyamaka view, a view he said was previously unknown in Tibet. According to this view, the second turning of the Dharma Wheel, which sets forth the emptiness of inherent existence as explained in the Perfection of Wisdom sūtras, is a lower teaching, and the third turning is the highest teaching. Jonang masters state that Buddhapālita and Candrakīrti's explanations are unacceptable. Dolpopa expounded a convergence of the views of Nāgārjuna and Asaṅga, citing Nāgārjuna's *Praise to the Ultimate Expanse* (*Dharmadhātustotra*) as Nāgārjuna's final view. This view they call the Great Madhyamaka.

Seeing the third turning of the Dharma Wheel as the last teachings the Buddha gave, Dolpopa said they must be the Buddha's final view and are therefore definitive. Dolpopa understood the teachings in the *Tathāgatagarbha Sūtra* and the *Nirvāṇa Sūtra* literally and stated that all sentient beings already have within them an inherent buddha possessing the thirty-two signs and eighty marks. This inherent buddha—which is an unchanging (T. *'gyur ba med pa*) and thoroughly established (T. *yongs su grub pa*) entity—is sentient beings' ultimate nature and has existed in each sentient being since beginningless time. Existing independent of all other factors, this inherent buddha was not created by causes and conditions. It non-erroneously realizes reality and is already perfectly awakened. This ultimate truth, which is an affirmative phenomenon,[113] is called "emptiness," which according to the Jonang view means that it is empty of conventional phenomena. Being empty of conventional phenomena that are impermanent, duḥkha in nature, impure, and non-self—the four qualities ascribed to conditioned phenomena that are true duḥkha—the ultimate truth is permanent, pure, blissful, and self. This view contradicts the Prāsaṅgika's understanding of Nāgārjuna that the ultimate truth is a nonaffirming negative and that all phenomena—including emptiness—lack an intrinsic essence and are empty of inherent existence.

According to the Jonang view, the causes of saṃsāra are conceptual minds and the winds that are their mounts (MD 420). Thus the path does not involve negating inherent existence but realizing another affirmative phenomenon that is unrelated to everything else (EOE 102–3). Important Tibetan masters, including Rendawa and Tsongkhapa, took great pains to refute this view, the latter in his seminal work, the *Essence of Eloquence*.

According to the Jonang view, ultimate truth itself is independent, truly existent, and exists under its own power. While conventional phenomena are self-empty, ultimate phenomena are other-empty—they are empty of conventional phenomena. Jonang followers do not interpret self-empty to mean that conventional phenomena are not their own ultimate nature. Rather, they say that because phenomena are empty of themselves, they do not exist. Since conventional phenomena are unfindable under analysis, they exist only for mistaken consciousnesses. They do not appear to wisdom consciousness and thus do not exist. Liberation, on the other hand, is not empty of its own entity.

The Jonang tradition asserts that the two truths are different natures. Conventional phenomena are not empty of an inherent nature but are empty of themselves, and the ultimate truth is empty of being a conventional truth. The ultimate is a truly existent, absolute, independent phenomenon that exists in its own right and is unrelated to anything else. Every dependent phenomenon is conditioned, but emptiness is unconditioned and therefore not dependently existent according to this view. Scholars from other Tibetan traditions refute this position, saying that if the two truths were different natures and unrelated, realizing the ultimate nature of phenomena would not overcome ignorance regarding phenomena. They also assert that emptiness itself also exists dependently; it is not an independent absolute.

Jonang followers assert that the clear-light mind is permanent, eternal, and independently existent, and is not empty of inherent existence. Turning the mind away from conventionalities to realize this absolute ultimate leads to liberation. Holders of this view of other-emptiness say they avoid nihilism because the ultimate is not empty of inherent existence and they avoid absolutism because conventional reality is empty of itself. I once read a text by Dharmashri, the son of Yumo Mikyo Dorje. He stated that Nāgārjuna's view of emptiness was nihilistic because Nāgārjuna denied the inherent existence of emptiness. However, from the viewpoint of the other Tibetan traditions, the Jonang view is nihilistic because it denies the existence of conventional phenomena, and it is absolutist because it asserts emptiness to be independent and absolute.

The Jonang view of other-empty is refuted by many scholars from all four Tibetan traditions, who say that it contradicts many sūtras, such as the *King of Concentrations Sūtra*, as well as Nāgārjuna's *Treatise on the Middle Way*. They say it also runs counter to the Perfection of Wisdom sūtras in which the Buddha explicitly explains that both conventional and ultimate phenomena are empty of inherent existence—all phenomena from form to omniscience are equally empty of inherent existence.

According to Nāgārjuna's view, whereas an ultimate truth is not a conventional truth and a conventional truth is not an ultimate truth, the absence of one in the other is not emptiness. All phenomena—including emptiness—lack self-nature; they are empty of true existence and lack an inherent self-nature that is independent of other phenomenon. Meditating on emptiness as something unrelated to other phenomena distracts us from the real work of liberating ourselves from saṃsāra. Candrakīrti in his *Supplement* compares this to telling someone who is afraid of a snake that there is no elephant. Needless to say, this does not dispel the person's fear of a snake. Similarly, meditating on emptiness by mistaking it to be an independent ultimate does nothing to free us from saṃsāra.

Self-emptiness means that phenomena are empty of having their own inherent nature or essence. If someone incorrectly assumes that form, for example, exists inherently, takes that inherent existence as true, and then negates something above and beyond that, he has not correctly identified the object of negation. Such persons are not meditating on self-emptiness. In other words, form is empty; it is not being emptied by emptiness. We focus on form as we perceive it—just as it appears to our senses as inherently existent—and negate that inherent existence. That is the correct meaning of self-emptiness.

The Nyingma dzogchen teachings do not disparage the teaching of the second Dharma Wheel because all phenomena are seen to have the same taste in the primordial purity of being free from inherent existence. Thus the way Nyingmapa use the term "other-emptiness" differs greatly from the Jonang meaning of the term.

Nevertheless, some masters who were proponents of the Jonang view—such as the Kālacakra masters Dolpopa and Kunga Drolchok—achieved some realizations of the generation and completion stages of Tantra. Similarly, proponents of the Yogācāra view can have tantric realizations, although that view is also not the final view. But to realize both example clear light and actual clear light, the correct understanding of emptiness according to the Prāsaṅgika view is required.

The Mind and I

In our study of Vajrayāna, we've briefly covered many topics—the tantric description of the body and mind, qualities that distinguish Highest Yoga Tantra from the Sūtra path and the paths of the three lower tantras, the four Tibetan traditions, and Kālacakra to mention a few. But there is still more to explore, which we'll do now.

We may diligently meditate on the generation and completion stages, but without the correct view of the ultimate nature of phenomena, tantric realizations are out of reach. The essence of the correct view is twofold: all phenomena are empty of any inherent essence, and all phenomena are dependently designated. These qualities are mutually compatible and noncontradictory, with each one dawning as the meaning of the other.[114] The previous volumes—*Searching for the Self*, *Realizing the Profound View*, and *Appearing and Empty*—go into depth on these topics. Below we'll cover a few new points.

If the I exists as we think it does—as a real person that sets itself up and exists independent of all other phenomena—then it's difficult to explain why we say the I changes when the body changes, because the two would be unrelated. But when our body is sick, we say, "I am sick," and as our body ages, we say, "I am aging." This indicates that the self depends on the aggregates, in this case, on the body. Being dependent means the self is empty of inherent existence. Like Sūtra practitioners, Tantra practitioners also cultivate the wisdom realizing emptiness, but they take it a step further and imagine the wisdom realizing emptiness manifesting in the form of a meditational deity. They then identify with the deity and have a sense of I in relation to the deity's body and mind.

The subtlest mind is the source of all coarse consciousnesses. In some Sakya tantric texts, it is called the "foundation-of-all" (*ālaya*, T. *kun gzhi*). Here the term does not have the same meaning as in Yogācāra philosophy, where it refers to the foundation consciousness, a separate, truly existent, neutral consciousness that is a repository for all karmic seeds and latencies. The Yogācārins also assert that the foundation-of-all is the true identity of the person. But if it were, then it, not the wisdom realizing emptiness, would arise in the form of the deity. But this would be strange, because it would mean that the neutral foundation consciousness, not the virtuous wisdom mind, would arise in the form of the deity.

In Vajrayāna, the subtlest mind is a type of mental consciousness; however, it is not identical to the general mental consciousness. Tantric practitioners holding the Prāsaṅgika Madhyamaka view often call the clear-light mind the "foundation-of-all" because it is the foundation or basis of saṃsāra and nirvāṇa. During the time that all coarser consciousnesses have dissolved, karmic seeds and latencies are associated with the fundamental innate clear-light mind. However, this subtlest mind is not the repository for all karmic seeds at all times because when coarse consciousnesses are functioning, it is latent. In addition, the Prāsaṅgikas say that the fundamental innate clear-light mind is not the person. It is not a permanent soul or an independent agent. It, too, changes moment by moment, depends on parts, and exists by being merely designated. Unlike the foundation consciousness described by Yogācārins, it is not necessarily a neutral mind and will be transformed into an awakened mind.

The I or self exists by being merely designated. In relation to the coarse and subtle levels of body and mind, we can speak of the coarse and subtle self. Does this mean that two separate selves exist, one coarse and one subtle? No, it doesn't. When the coarse body and mind function, the coarse self is designated in dependence on them. At that time, we cannot speak of the subtle self because when the coarse levels of mind are active, the subtlest mind is latent and does not function. At the time of the clear light of death, only the subtlest wind-mind is present, and in dependence on that, the subtle I is designated.

The I of one life and the I of the next are designated in dependence on different aggregates, so they are different. One I may be an animal and the other a human being. However, the general I can be designated in dependence on the continuity of mind because the continuity includes both coarse and subtle levels of mind and the continuity of impermanent moments of mind goes from one life to the next. The I being designated in dependence on the mental continuum, for example, does not mean the mental continuum *is* the I or the person.

Some interesting questions arise. If Losang has a heart transplant, we still call him Losang even though he has a different heart. From a tantric viewpoint, he is still the same person because the eternal indestructible drop, the subtlest wind-mind at the heart cakra, is the same before and after the heart transplant. Suppose Dechen has a brain transplant. Would she still be the same person? From a Buddhist view, is she still Dechen because the indestructible drop is the same, or does the eternal indestructible drop from the brain donor come into Dechen's body when the brain is transplanted?

Vajrayāna contains the practice of transference of consciousness into a dead body. This lends an intriguing perspective to this discussion. In this practice, a highly realized yogi transfers his mind into the body of a recently deceased person—someone who died in an accident, not by disease. He does this to continue Dharma practice despite the malfunction of his body. Although the lineage for this practice is broken and the practice is no longer done, centuries ago a few exceptional yogis did this.

In that case, although the yogi's mind now resides in a different body, the person designated in dependence on that mind is still considered the same person in the same life. He has not gone through the death process and the clear light of death has not occurred, so he retains all the knowledge gained in his previous body, although now he has a different body and brain. Marpa's son, Dharmadodhe, did this practice and transferred his mind first into the dead body of a pigeon, which came to life and flew to India. There he transferred his mind from the pigeon's body into the body of a recently deceased boy and continued his Dharma practice. This seems to indicate that, at least for highly realized yogis, memory is not dependent on the brain. In addition, his Dharma attainments and virtuous qualities remained the same, even when he had a pigeon's brain. Such things are quite mysterious, but they give us an idea about how the various levels of mind function.

Different Perspectives on the Clear-Light Mind

Because sentient beings have different dispositions and interests, the Buddha taught different perspectives on one topic. The clear-light mind is one example of this. The New Translation traditions of Tantra—the Gelug, Kagyu, and Sakya—speak of the fundamental innate clear-light mind, the subtlest mind that arises through the cessation of all coarser levels of mind. However, this does not mean that the clear-light mind exists only when the coarser levels of mind have dissolved and become latent. The clear-light mind has been present from beginningless time. It existed in previous lives, at the time of conception of this life, and in the future it will continue into our next rebirth and eventually to buddhahood. It always exists, irrespective of the coarse consciousnesses being present or not.

The subtlest mind is the basis or foundation of the coarse levels of mind, which are emergent properties of the subtlest clear light. Both coarse and subtlest minds have the nature of clarity and cognizance, and both are present in our daily life, but the subtlest mind is latent when the coarse minds are active. The subtlest mind indirectly influences the coarse consciousnesses, although this is not an immediate causal moment-to-moment interaction. That is, the subtlest mind is not operative in the specific momentary functions of the coarse consciousnesses; however, the fact that the coarse consciousnesses have the basic nature of clarity and cognizance is due to the presence of the subtlest mind of clear light. In the absence of the subtlest clear-light mind, the coarse minds would lack those fundamental qualities of clarity and awareness and could not exist.

The Sakya tradition teaches that all coarse and subtle levels of mind are contained in the clear light in the form of seeds or latencies. Thus it speaks of the subtlest mind containing all resultant virtuous qualities and realizations of a buddha in the form of potentials, all the realizations of the path as qualities, and all attributes of ordinary levels of saṃsāra in the form of characteristics.

In dzogchen, the clear-light nature of mind, which continues without interruption, is an essential quality of consciousness. The clarity of the coarse mind is like the radiance of the clear-light mind. The primordial clear-light mind pervades all minds, even afflictive states of mind. Just as every part of a sesame seed is permeated by oil, all mental states, even afflictive minds, are permeated by the clear-light nature. Although the afflictive part of a mental state must be subdued, its nature of clear light is unpolluted and can be brought into the path. The afflictions cannot become a buddha's mind, but the clear-light nature that pervades them can. In the gaps between thoughts, the clear-light mind, also called *rigpa*, exists continuously.

Dzogchen describes how to bring the clear-light aspect of afflictive minds into the path while afflictions are manifest. For example, so long as there is water in a pond, the clear nature of that water remains. But when we stir the water, it becomes muddy, and we cannot see its essential clarity. To perceive its clear nature, we must stop agitating it and let it be still; then it will regain its clear nature, which is not something outside the muddy water. In the same way, afflictive mental states have the nature of clear light. We'll be able to see this clear-light nature when we allow the mind to settle.

Coarse consciousnesses, such as manifest afflictions, focus on external objects. Being object-oriented, they chase after their objects and arise in the aspect of their objects. That aspect covers or prevents the essential nature of clarity from being seen. Through practice, meditators learn to separate the clear-light aspect of those mental states from the aspect directed to the object. When the coarse mind withdraws from external objects, the aspects of those objects no longer appear to the mind. This allows the essential nature of clarity to become more apparent. For example, if a crystal is put on colored cloth, the clarity of the crystal cannot be seen very well. But if we look at the crystal itself, without any background, we can see it. Dzogchen meditation is nonconceptual; at first meditators focus on the lack of mental objects, but as they become familiar with the clarity of the mind, they vividly experience it.

The mind is pervaded by the clear-light nature even when thoughts arise. From the viewpoint of practice, these thoughts—be they virtuous or nonvirtuous—are obstructions to experiencing the clear-light mind. Therefore, dzogchen practitioners place emphasis on trying to still their minds, on stopping both virtuous and nonvirtuous thoughts, for only then will they experience the clear light. We can see many parallels between these teachings and those of the sudden, simultaneous approach taught in Chan Buddhism.

To experience instantaneous realizations in dzogchen requires completing a preliminary practice called "seeking the true face of mind." Practitioners do this by analyzing the mind's arising, abiding, and passing away. This analysis is similar to the logic of the Madhyamaka tetralemma, or fourfold analysis.

While on the path to awakening, the coarse consciousnesses and subtlest mind interact and cooperate. The coarse mind is used to learn the meditation techniques and apply them to make manifest the subtlest mind. Manifesting the subtlest mind enables meditators to control the coarser levels of mind.

To experience the manifest clear light, or *rigpa*, dzogchen practitioners must first have an initial glimpse of it by receiving the blessings and inspiration from a spiritual mentor who has these realizations. Then they must withdraw the mind from external objects by controlling the flow of the winds through meditation on the cakras, channels, and drops.

One technique used in dzogchen is for practitioners to shout the syllable *Phat!* with great force. It is said that when this syllable is uttered, the entire chain of thought processes is instantly severed, and practitioners experience sudden, spontaneous realization. This experience is described as a sense of wonderment and nonconceptuality, a state free from thoughts. At this time, they experience the clear light, which is also called emptiness. For some people, this experience is only momentary, but if the wonderment is accompanied by inspiration from the spiritual mentor and a great collection of merit, practitioners can perfect the experience so that they experience rigpa, the foundational pristine mind. When they experience this clear light, they perceive the whole world fused in the nature of emptiness.

Bliss and Emptiness

Bliss (*sukha*)[115] is mentioned in diverse contexts, beginning with ordinary, polluted happiness arising from sense pleasure and extending to the bliss of full awakening. On the path, many types of bliss may be experienced; some will be explained below. In the context of serenity (*śamatha*) and concentration (*samādhi*) meditation,[116] bliss may arise due to physical or mental pliancy. This blissful experience is characterized by a sense of freedom from physical and mental lethargy and the suppression of obstructive factors that make the body and mind unserviceable. Once these hindrances are overcome, physical and mental pliancy arise, which lead to physical and mental bliss. This was experienced by Gowo Geshe Nyima from Gaden Jangtse Monastery, who left the Tibetan refugee camp at Buxa, India. Living as a hermit in Bhutan for a long time, he attained serenity, and at one point experienced a tremendous surge of bliss while meditating. This appears to be the bliss induced by physical and mental pliancy.

A second type of bliss is the bliss of a bodhisattva attaining the first bhūmi, the Very Joyful. This bliss is a sense of great satisfaction. A third type of bliss is that experienced during the Highest Yoga Tantra practice of retaining vitality-exertion when conceptuality has been subdued. Great bliss is induced by the melting of the drops in the central channel, which has the special function of forcefully stopping the coarser minds.[117]

Another type of bliss is one that arises with the cessation of conceptuality and the fabrications that our minds tend to obsessively focus on. This bliss is a sense of respite from the clutter of wrong views and distractions that disturb the mind and cause anxiety and confusion. When practitioners gain some respite from these proliferating conceptions and fabrications, they experience a sense of bliss and calm. Tsarchen Losal Gyatso (1502–56), a master in the Sakya lineage of the lamdre teachings, spoke of this bliss in an aspirational prayer he wrote to have a vision of Vajrayoginī:[118]

> But no matter how much I searched, Noble Lady, I could find no certainty of your being truly existent. Then this youthful mind, weary of conceptual elaborations, sought respite in the forest of ineffable truth.

Here, ineffability refers to the emptiness of inherent existence. It is the freedom from all fabrications of inherent existence that Nāgārjuna mentions in his homage at the beginning of the *Treatise on the Middle Way*:

> I prostrate to the perfect Buddha,
> the best of all teachers,
> who taught that that which is dependent arising

> is without ceasing, without arising,
> without discontinuation, without permanence,
> without coming, without going,
> without difference, without identity,
> and peaceful—free from [conceptual] fabrications.

This respite from the commotion brought on by the fabrications of inherent existence is a blissful experience.

In Vajrayāna, bliss arises by deliberately dissolving the coarser winds into the central channel, causing the subtle drops to melt and flow down the central channel. The meditations on the generation stage ripen into being able to do this on the completion stage. For example, focusing on the visualization of the deity couple in union generates a blissful mind. If practitioners are already familiar with meditating that all phenomena are empty and like illusions, that blissful mind makes the mind understanding illusion-like emptiness subtler. Another example is the generation-stage visualization of deities or syllables on the sense organs. One purpose of this is to contemplate the contact of a sense faculty with its object as being blissful and then use that bliss to contemplate emptiness. This also helps to generate the winds associated with the sense faculties into the shape of the deities. The blissful mind meditating on the deities in union is then used to contemplate emptiness. This draws those winds into the central channel.

In Tsongkhapa's *Completing the Five Stages in a Single Sitting*, he discusses temporarily engaging in the meditation on bliss without meditating on emptiness and gives the analogy of someone wishing to cut grass who first needs to sharpen the sickle. His purpose is to cut the grass, but before doing that he must prepare his tool. Similarly, although meditators' ultimate purpose is to realize the union of bliss and emptiness, they must first cultivate the blissful mind. Here, the experience of bliss is the bliss that results from the melting of the drops in the central channel. In *Lamp Illuminating the Five Stages*, Tsongkhapa details a complex explanation of how this process works: When the drops melt and flow, an internal tactile sensation arises. This is the objective condition for the physical feeling of bliss. This experience of tactile bliss becomes the catalyst for the arising of mental bliss, which is then used to realize emptiness. Among the other types of union Tsongkhapa discusses—the union of two truths, the union of method and wisdom, and so on—this explanation comes in the context of the indivisibility of bliss and emptiness. This indivisibility of bliss and emptiness is not a union in the sense of the bliss being empty in nature but rather the blissful mind is the apprehending consciousness and the emptiness of this mind is its object—just as occurs in the meditative equipoise on emptiness.

This union of bliss and emptiness can also be explained through the meaning of a Sanskrit mantra found in many tantric sādhanas at the point where one meditates on emptiness before generating oneself as the deity. This mantra is *oṃ śūnyatā jñāna vajra svabhāvātmako 'haṃ*, and the explanation of its meaning is from Tsongkhapa's *Great Treatise on the Stages of the Tantric Path* (*Sngag rim chen mo*).

Śūnyatā refers to emptiness; *jñāna* indicates the wisdom realizing emptiness. *Vajra* means diamond-like or adamantine and refers to the indivisibility of emptiness and the wisdom realizing it. *Svabhāva* means nature and indicates that this indivisibility of wisdom and emptiness is a wisdom that realizes its own nature. That is, this wisdom realizing emptiness realizes the ultimate nature, emptiness, of one's own mind. Because the ultimate nature of the mind is emptiness, emptiness and the mind itself are indivisible. The moment a mental state arises its emptiness is also present. They are never separate. The wisdom itself is a conventional truth and its emptiness is an ultimate truth. They are one nature but nominally different; the indivisibility of the two truths is already there. The mind realizing its own ultimate nature is an extraordinary experience.

A similar understanding is also found in an etymological explanation of the mantra *Śrī Heruka*. Here the syllable *ka* indicates the indivisibility of wisdom and emptiness. The mind realizing its own ultimate nature—emptiness—is very different from the mind realizing the emptiness of an external object such as a table. The mind realizing its own emptiness and that emptiness are already indivisible because a conventional truth (the mind realizing emptiness) and an ultimate truth (the emptiness of that mind) are one nature. Although the emptiness of the mind and the emptiness of the table are the same in terms of being emptiness, there is a difference from the perspective of the subjects realizing these emptinesses. In one case, the wisdom is realizing its own ultimate nature, in the other it is not.

When wisdom directly experiences emptiness in meditative equipoise, the subject and object are experienced as nondual—not as two separate things that are touching, like an apple sitting on a table. *Vajra* indicates that this dissolution of subject-object duality is indestructible. This realization is not vulnerable to the destructive power of conceptual fabrications and grasping at true existence. In the Yamāntaka sadhana, the fourth immeasurable is: May all sentient beings be placed in a state of equanimity unperturbed by preconceptions of apprehender and apprehended or by the eight worldly concerns. In other words, may sentient beings possess this vajra-like indestructibility that is impervious to fabrications of true existence.

15 | A Song of the Four Mindfulnesses and the Culmination of the Path

THE SEVENTH DALAI Lama Kalsang Gyatso composed the "Rain Shower of Attainments" to lead qualified practitioners to the Madhyamaka view of emptiness in their tantric practice. In this short poem, he set out four mindfulness practices—of the spiritual mentor (guru, T. lama), compassion, our body as a divine body, and emptiness—in a five-stanza poem so that we could easily memorize and integrate it into our practice.

Initially, we contemplate the duḥkha of saṃsāra, and with the aspiration to be free from it, take refuge in the Three Jewels and engage in guru yoga, visualizing the objects of refuge and requesting them to remain in the world and teach the Dharma. This is mindfulness of the guru. Then we observe the duḥkha of other sentient beings in saṃsāra and, seeing their kindness, generate love and compassion. This induces bodhicitta—the aspiration to attain full awakening for their benefit. This is the second mindfulness. Due to this, the guru dissolves into us, transforming our body, speech, and mind into that of the deity—the third mindfulness. Meditation on the correct view of emptiness constitutes the actual session—the fourth mindfulness—and the union of serenity and insight is cultivated in conjunction with Tantra.

Mindfulness of the Guru

On the unwavering cushion of the union of method and wisdom
sits the kind lama who is the nature of all protectors.
There is a buddha in the state of culmination of realizations and
cessations.

> Beseech him (her) in the light of admiration, through casting away critical thoughts.
> Don't let your mind go astray, but place it in admiration and reverence;
> through not losing mindfulness, hold it in admiration and reverence.

Because our spiritual mentors or lamas, especially those who give us tantric empowerments and instructions, possess a union of method and wisdom—compassion and the wisdom realizing emptiness—he or she abides on the seat of the immutable union of method and wisdom. The seat is our own heart and is comprised of the red and white drops, indestructible until awakening and thus immutable. On this seat sits our kind guru. The practice of thinking the guru is present in our heart is conducive to conceiving our body, speech, and mind as undifferentiated from the guru's.[119]

Our spiritual mentors are seen as meditational deities, ḍākinīs, buddhas, and bodhisattvas—the essence of all objects of refuge. Though the great masters of the past, such as Nāgārjuna, were extremely kind to compose great texts, they are now objects of memory. Even if we wanted to meet Nāgārjuna, we could not. Without spiritual guidance we are like sick people unable to walk, even with a cane; we are like infants and the elderly, unable to sustain ourselves. In this dire situation, we turn to our spiritual mentors to teach, guide, and support us on the path. For this reason they are viewed as the essence of all sources of refuge.

Try to always think of the spiritual mentor as abiding in your heart. In this way, the Buddha who has abandoned all obstructions and attained all realizations is not sought externally but identified in the center of your heart. This is the ultimate guru, the innate wisdom of the ultimate mode of existence of all phenomena. This guru is not a flesh-and-bones person but is the wisdom of all buddhas. The persons who are our tantric gurus are seen as a manifestation of this wisdom.

Since the guru is seen as a fully qualified buddha, we should forsake the notion that they have defects. Holding such an ordinary view prevents us from paying attention and taking seriously their teachings and guidance. Therefore, with mindfulness and awareness we should train in admiration and respect.

Mindfulness of Compassion and Bodhicitta

> In unending saṃsāra, the prison of suffering,
> wander the sentient beings of the six realms, bereft of happiness.
> They are your parents, who reared you with affectionate kindness.
> Meditate on compassion and affection by relinquishing attachment and aversion.
> Don't let your mind go astray, but place it within compassion;
> through not losing mindfulness, hold it within compassion.

Sentient beings want happiness but are bereft of the happiness they seek. They do not want suffering but are continuously tormented by suffering. The six classes of beings wander in limitless saṃsāra under the control of afflictions and polluted actions. These suffering beings are not unrelated to us; they have been continuously kind to us in our beginningless lifetimes and will continue to be kind. We are responsible for them, we cannot abandon them.

The sentient beings wandering in saṃsāra can't be divided into groups, with some desired and others hated; we must develop a heart that cares for all of them. Forsaking attachment and antipathy, we must train our minds to cherish them more than ourselves and continuously generate the compassionate wish that they be freed from saṃsāra's duḥkha and its causes.

Contemplating the disadvantages of saṃsāra impels us to generate the determination to be free of saṃsāra. The thrust of the second mindfulness is to generate compassion for all others equally. This is the root of bodhicitta. If we lack a compassionate attitude, we are devoid of the very basis of the Mahāyāna.

How can we relieve these sentient beings from duḥkha and its causes? Providing vast benefit entails attaining buddhahood and working for their welfare as an awakened being. Therefore, we must put energy into creating the causes for buddhahood.

Mindfulness of the Body as a Divine Body

> In the celestial mansion of great bliss, joyous to sustain,
> there exists the divine form of the body, which is a purified state of the aggregates.

> There is a deity in the nature of union of the three divine bodies.
> Don't view it as ordinary, but train in divine identity and immaculate appearance.
> Don't let your mind go astray, but place it within profundity and clarity;
> through not losing mindfulness, hold it in an attitude of profundity and clarity.

When our bodhicitta is so strong that we cannot bear the thought of delaying working for others' welfare even for an hour, we will view our present ineffectual situation as a waste of valuable time. Training in Mantrayāna is the method for quickly attaining the wisdom of nondual bliss and emptiness, and through this we can attain buddhahood in a single lifetime. This involves making manifest the subtlest mind that realizes emptiness, generating it as a blissful entity, and developing the special concentration of bliss and emptiness. To do this, the base of the bliss—our body—must be visualized as a deity's body. This involves stopping both the appearance of ordinariness and grasping at ordinariness.

By dissolving the appearance of our ordinary body and meditating on emptiness, whatever appears is seen as empty, whatever is empty is experienced as bliss, and whatever is blissful appears as the sport or play of the deity. When we realize this, the objects of the six senses act as aids in generating bliss and thus are said to be pleasant to feel.

Everything appears as endless purity. The environment appears as the sport of bliss, and the beings in it are the play of the blissful mind. Our impure mental and physical aggregates and constituents shine as the sport of the deity. Our deity body is not to be identified as something outside ourselves. In our meditation, our flesh-and-blood body has dissolved into emptiness and the wisdom realizing emptiness now manifests as the deity. This is the divine entity that now acts as the basis of designation for imputing "I."

When we practice generating ourselves as the meditational deity and train in this vivid appearance and divine identity until they become firm, similitudes of the three buddha bodies—the truth body, enjoyment body, and emanation body—are present. For instance, when cultivating the generation stage of Highest Yoga Tantra, we gradually manifest a similitude of the three bodies, and the divine identity thinking "I am the deity" arises. Due to this divine identity, we do not conceive of ourselves as ordinary but sustain a firm sense of being the deity within clearly appearing as such. We maintain our mind in awareness of the profound—emptiness—and the manifest—the divine body of the deity.

Mindfulness of the View of Emptiness

Since this poem is mainly concerned with cultivating and stabilizing our wisdom on the correct view of emptiness, it has two stanzas on this topic, one for sustaining space-like meditative equipoise and another for sustaining the illusion-like subsequent realization.[120]

> The sphere of appearing and existing phenomena
> is pervaded by the space of the ultimate clear light of suchness.
> There is an ineffable ultimate reality.
> View this nature of emptiness through abandoning mental contrivances.
> Don't let your mind go astray, but place it in the ambiance of reality;
> through not losing mindfulness, hold it in the ambiance of reality.

> At the crossroads of the six collections (of consciousness) that have diverse perceptions,
> are seen the hazy dualistic phenomena that are baseless.
> There is a magical show, which is by nature deceptive.
> Don't believe it to be true, but view it as having the nature of emptiness.
> Don't let your mind go astray, but place it in the nature of appearance-emptiness;
> through not losing mindfulness, hold it in the nature of appearance-emptiness.

All phenomena exist within the sphere of emptiness of inherent existence, devoid of any inner essence. Thus, although the sphere of appearing and existing phenomena is limitless, they are all of one taste in having the nature of emptiness; there is no object not pervaded by this empty nature.

Emptiness pervades all knowable objects; it is their mode of being. It is not newly created by the mind. From its very inception the nature of every phenomenon is its emptiness of inherent existence. Emptiness is inexpressible, beyond terms and thoughts. The empty nature of all phenomena cannot be expressed with words or experienced conceptually by ordinary beings in the way that āryas perceive it.

There is no need to search for the mode of being of objects elsewhere; it is right with these people and things in and around us. Āryadeva's *Four Hundred* (*Catuḥśataka*) says, "All *these* are empty of inherent existence." The term "these" indicates that the phenomena that are the bases of emptiness are here right now. The ultimate truth exists as the nature of all appearances; upon analysis, we see the mode of being is right here.

Although scriptures say that all phenomena are merely imputedly existent, we must first analyze whether phenomena appear as only imputedly existent. They certainly do not; they appear to exist in the opposite way—objectively, with their own intrinsic essence that makes them what they are. If they did exist in the concrete way that they appear to, they would be findable when sought with ultimate analysis. However, when we train in the modes of analysis taught in Nāgārjuna's *Treatise on the Middle Way*, we arrive at the conclusion that although phenomena appear to be self-established, they do not exist that way at all. This deep, vivid ascertainment eliminates any possibility that phenomena exist inherently; objective existence cannot be posited in the face of this ascertainment. When the mere vacuity that is the negation of inherent existence is experienced, we should focus on it one-pointedly. This is the mode of practicing the space-like meditative equipoise.

When we later relax our concentration and loosen the mode of observation of emptiness, the objects qualified by this nature appear as if they could be posited: this is a cup, this is a cat, and so on. These various appearances—pure buddhas, impure sentient beings, habitats, inhabitants, earth, water, fire, wind—shine forth as the objects of the six senses—the visual, auditory, olfactory, gustatory, tactile, and mental consciousnesses. However, when we analyze whether these various appearances have their own self-established nature, such a nature cannot be found. All things that are seen, heard, smelled, tasted, and touched are baseless, without their own inherent nature, lacking their own independent way of existing.

Although they are baseless, they falsely appear to have their own inherent nature. We obscured sentient beings who adhere to these objects as existing the way they appear are deceived, like people who believe that a magician's illusions are real. Previously in meditative equipoise, noninherent existence was clear to the mind, but now, subsequent to meditative equipoise, phenomena appear to exist in their own right, whereas they do not. This illusion-like subsequent realization is the composite of the appearance of objects as inherently existent and the knowledge that they are empty of inherent existence.

We must repeatedly meditate on the empty nature of objects and then, within this realization, practice the union of appearance and emptiness—persons and phenomena appear to our senses and at the same time they are empty of any inherent existence. However, they exist. How do they exist? Dependently. Now we meditate on and gain deeper ascertainment of dependent arising. This increases our understanding that all phenomena exist by being merely designated by terms and concepts, and through that, the ascertainment that phenomena do not exist in their own right becomes more powerful. By its force, after meditative equipoise, the ascertainment that whatever appears is the play of emptiness becomes stronger.

With the two realizations of emptiness and dependent arising helping each other in this way, we will progress through the four levels of the path of preparation—heat, peak, fortitude, and supreme mundane qualities. As the veil of conceptual appearance fades, emptiness appears even clearer and our realization becomes more profound, whereupon the emptiness of inherent existence—the ultimate truth—is realized directly.

Why Vajrayāna Is the Culmination of the Path

I would like now to explain how and why Vajrayāna, and in particular Highest Yoga Tantra, is the essential culmination of the path to full awakening. Our coarse sense consciousnesses and coarse mental consciousness are adventitious; their continuums are not sustained and thus cannot serve as the basis to attain omniscience, a mind that is everlasting. For this reason, except for the subtlest mind—the fundamental innate mind of clear light—no other mind can serve as the basis for omniscience. Furthermore, without the mental consciousness itself becoming subtler, it would be extremely difficult to eliminate all dualistic appearances and cognitive obscurations. Only the wisdom of inseparable bliss and emptiness can do this.

Even in Pāramitāyāna the wisdom realizing emptiness must be conjoined with the strong method aspect of the path to be able to eradicate cognitive obscurations. This is why we hear the expression "emptiness conjoined with all supreme aspects of method." The wisdom directly realizing emptiness in the continuums of śrāvaka āryas and solitary-realizer āryas cannot serve as the antidote to cognitive obscurations. On the one hand, this is because they do not meditate on emptiness using limitless reasonings like bodhisattvas do. But more important, their wisdom realizing emptiness is not conjoined with all the aspects of supreme method, and for the wisdom directly realizing emptiness to become the antidote to cognitive obscurations, it must be conjoined with the extensive accumulation of merit.

In Tantrayāna the general principle is the same: the wisdom directly realizing emptiness must be conjoined with an extensive accumulation of merit for it to become the antidote to the cognitive obscurations. But the difference is that in Sūtrayāna, the collection of merit cannot be done while in meditative equipoise. Practitioners must rise from meditative equipoise and then engage in activities that accumulate extensive merit. The collections of merit and wisdom are practiced separately, whereas in Tantrayāna, due to the wisdom of great bliss, the ordinary subtlest clear-light mind can be generated into the nature of the path so that merit and wisdom are not practiced separately.

This subtlest mind—the fundamental innate mind of clear light—is possessed by all sentient beings. However, in ordinary sentient beings, it is not in the nature of the path. But when it is generated in the nature of the path, it becomes the wisdom of great bliss. At this time, yogis can harness the subtlest consciousness so that it can carry out all the activities of benefiting sentient beings. Likewise, at the time the mind arises as great bliss, the wind that is its mount is also brought under control and can be utilized according to the yogis' wish. In that way, they can attain the illusory body and are able to control the winds as they wish. Through controlling the winds, they can generate a vast variety of emanations that can serve countless sentient beings in accord with each one's disposition. The ability to harness the subtlest wind-mind and generate it into the nature of the path, thereby gaining control over it, enables the great bodhisattvas to accomplish the aims of countless sentient beings with comparatively little effort, although still not in the way a buddha can. This is why it is said that with the attainment of the illusory body yogis can create merit in one lifetime equal to that created in three countless great eons in Pāramitāyāna. In this way, by meditating with the wisdom of inseparable bliss and emptiness, the power of the collection of merit is made complete without yogis needing to arise from meditative equipoise—by meditating in equipoise itself, they can fulfill the collection of merit so that their wisdom of bliss and emptiness becomes the complete antidote to cognitive obscurations.

For this uncommon special feature to occur, the coarse mind and wind must cease. In this fortunate eon, in our world we can speak of womb-born human beings who possess a body with the six elements that is able to traverse the path of Highest Yoga Tantra. The only way for them to forcefully stop the coarse wind and mind and make manifest the subtlest mind and wind is by taking the bliss of union into the path with the aid of a wisdom or action mudrā.

16 | Epilogue: Advice for My Disciples

In recent years I have taught in many countries, and although I did not seek to have students, there may be some people who consider me their spiritual mentor and would like guidance on how to approach their Dharma practice. It is to them that I now speak.

The three principal aspects of the path—the determination to be free from saṃsāra (renunciation), bodhicitta, and the correct view of emptiness—are the bedrock of the path, so put energy into developing deep experience of them. When meditating on renunciation, focus mainly on the three types of duḥkha, especially the pervasive duḥkha of conditioning. Recognizing the destructive nature of afflictions will help you understand the disadvantages of the pervasive duḥkha of conditioning. The stronger you feel that, the greater your interest in the possibility of eliminating afflictions will grow. This will lead you to investigate emptiness, and from this you will gain conviction that the realization of emptiness will overcome the wrong views that nourish saṃsāra. Since you want to remove afflictions and know that there is a path to do so, you will automatically generate renunciation of saṃsāra and the aspiration for liberation.

Then turn your attention to other sentient beings and see the harm that afflictions cause them. Their situation and yours are similar. You both want to be happy and avoid suffering; you both have the potential to do so. Seeing this, and remembering the kindness of others, generate the altruistic intention of bodhicitta. To bring to fruition your wish to attain awakening to benefit sentient beings most effectively, exert effort to gain the correct view of emptiness and meditate on that single-pointedly.

Make it a point to cultivate these two most important practices: bodhicitta and the wisdom realizing emptiness. Directing your mind to these two shows you have great merit. The guru is fortunate to have the opportunity to teach bodhicitta. You, the disciples, are fortunate to hear about this precious altruistic mind that cherishes others more than yourself. (At this point in the teaching, His Holiness wept.)

Whoever generates this altruistic intention will find themselves setting out on the path to true happiness. Since we all want happiness and don't want suffering, if you wish for real peace and harmony, there is nothing more to ask for than bodhicitta. Bodhicitta is our best friend; it protects us from harm and hindrances, and brings all attainments of the Mahāyāna. A verse from the "Guru Pūjā" (v. 53), accentuates this.

> You are my gurus, you are my yidams, you are my ḍākinīs and Dharma protectors. From now until awakening, I seek no refuge other than you. In this life, the bardo, and all future lives, hold me with your hook of compassion, free me from saṃsāra's and nirvāṇa's fears, grant all attainments, be my constant friends, and guard me from hindrances.

The bodhicitta, this kind heart, is *our gurus, our meditational deities, our ḍākinīs, and our protectors*. It helps us *in this life and in the bardo*. If you can maintain this altruistic mind while actively dying, your next life will certainly be a fortunate one. Why? An unfortunate rebirth results from destructive karma, and generating bodhicitta purifies this karma. A fortunate rebirth comes about due to merit, and there is nothing greater than bodhicitta to create merit.

Bodhicitta delivers you from revolving in saṃsāra—*this life, the bardo, and all future lives*. When self-grasping ignorance leads to the arising of afflictions, it prevents the collection of merit and destroys the merit you have created, causing you to be tossed around in saṃsāra. Understanding this, intelligent bodhisattvas have disdain for ignorance, do not let it overpower them, and make every effort to eliminate it. By motivating you to overthrow the dictator of self-grasping, bodhicitta *frees you from saṃsāra's fears*. By overcoming self-centeredness, bodhicitta releases you from the complacency of the personal peace of nirvāṇa that prevents you from directly benefiting others. Bodhicitta spurs you to attain the nonabiding nirvāṇa of a buddha where your awakened activities can benefit all sentient beings. No other path can do that.

Bodhicitta fulfills all your temporary and ultimate Dharma goals in this life and the next, and in this way *grants all attainments*. To have even ordinary happiness, a kind heart is necessary. If you cultivate the altruistic mind, you will be happy. When you are happy you will be healthier, you will sleep peacefully, and food will taste better. Your calm, cheerful behavior will make the environment and the beings around you more peaceful. Everyone will be your friend, including birds and animals. You will live longer and will not age prematurely or die an untimely death. If you cultivate bodhicitta when you are young, this good heart will enable you to live harmoniously with others; in middle age you will be kindhearted, not troublesome; and in your senior years you will feel fulfilled knowing your life has had meaning.

Bodhicitta is *your constant friend* in all situations. A compassionate heart is an offering that pleases the Buddha and bodhisattvas. Your loving heart will be your friend forever, bringing you comfort and courage in difficult circumstances. Bodhicitta also *guards you from all hindrances*. By cherishing others, you stop creating destructive karma that brings problems in future lives, and you cease disturbing behavior that antagonizes others in this life.

I haven't met people who tried to harm me. If they did come to me, I am not sure that I could react with bodhicitta. However, when I am relaxed, I think, "Who are my enemies? Where are they?" Contemplating their suffering, I have compassion for them. Cultivate the attitude that all beings are your friends. Do not exclude enemies or beings who act with harmful intentions from your compassion.

The mind of all-encompassing yoga (see chapter 4) combines the practices of bodhicitta and the wisdom realizing emptiness. If you reflect on these two every day, you'll become one of my true disciples. Otherwise it doesn't make sense to go around saying "The Dalai Lama is my teacher" but not practice my instructions. Your guru is your role model, just as the Buddha, Nāgārjuna, Candrakīrti, and Tsongkhapa are my role models. So make the decision as my disciple to practice bodhicitta and wisdom as best you can. These two are my main practices, so by making them your main practices you will become a true disciple of the Dalai Lama. Don't be anxious or unhappy, but have a happy mind, smile, and be cheerful when you practice bodhicitta and wisdom.

Avoid being content or self-satisfied with your Dharma practice, thinking you have enough bodhicitta and wisdom. Continuously try to deepen your experience of them. Don't fall into the trap of thinking, "Oh, now I am a bodhisattva. How great I am!" If you think like this, you have succumbed to arrogance rather than deepened your spiritual understanding.

Entering Tantrayāna

When the time comes to emphasize the practice of serenity, cultivate it in relation to Tantra. Objects of meditation such as your deity body, the sound of mantra, and syllables at various parts of the divine body have special advantages when used as the object to cultivate serenity.

When you are grounded in the stages of the path, receive empowerment and enter Tantrayāna. Until you have bodhicitta and a correct understanding of emptiness, you will not be able to achieve results through tantric practice. However, beginning to practice it will prepare you to later gain tantric realizations, because familiarization with a practice is crucial to be able to actualize it one day.

I recommend beginning with the deity yoga of Action Tantra. Practice a deity that corresponds to your disposition and interests. In some cases, receiving Highest Yoga Tantra empowerment may be helpful. However, for most people, although serious tantric practice is out of the question at the beginning, laying the foundation and gaining familiarity with the practice is worthwhile. Once you reach a certain understanding of emptiness and bodhicitta, your visualization of the deity will be stable. At that time, it will be easier to enter Highest Yoga Tantra.

To prepare for death, train the mind in the five forces described in the seven-point mind training.[121] In addition, people who have received an Action Tantra empowerment can practice according to the *Three Essential Moments*, by the Second Dalai Lama.[122] This is a practice of transference of consciousness (*saṃkrānti*, T. *'pho ba*) that relates to Chenrezig and will help practitioners to take rebirth in Tushita Pure Land.

The meditation on the eight absorptions that occur at the time of death is found only in Highest Yoga Tantra. In general, without an empowerment in the practice of a particular deity, you may not do that deity's practice. Although people who have not received a Highest Yoga Tantra empowerment can do the general visualization of the elements dissolving at the time of death, the visualization of the absorption in the context of deity yoga is more elaborate and cannot be done by those who have not received the appropriate empowerment.

Even without empowerment into Highest Yoga Tantra, you may study the three foundational kāyas—death, intermediate state, and rebirth—and how tantric practice correlates these with the actual three kāyas—the truth body, enjoyment body, and emanation body. You may hear the explanation, although you may not do the self-generation visualization of transforming death, bardo, and rebirth in the path to the three kāyas without the appropriate empowerment and instructions. Nowadays Highest Yoga Tantra is an open "secret," so many misunderstandings about it exist. To avoid these, I would like my sincere students to study and intellectually understand tantric methods of practice, even though they may not do those practices before receiving the appropriate empowerment.

Some students have received empowerment into Highest Yoga Tantra practices and have done the approximation retreat in which you recite a certain number of the appropriate mantras. Unfortunately, reciting the correct number of mantras often becomes the emphasis, and the retreatant becomes like a parrot reciting a phrase over and over again. This cheapens the retreat experience and does not accomplish the purpose of retreat. Try to avoid this by practicing with sincerity.

Those of you who have Highest Yoga Tantra empowerment and meditate on the sādhana daily should do the practice of transforming death, bardo, and rebirth into the three kāyas so that at the time of death, if your memory is clear you can recollect the signs of the dissolution of the elements with one corner of your mind. Gaining familiarity with this during your life depends on having stable concentration, as does practicing the three mixings during the waking state. But at the time of death it may be possible to recognize the signs because the dissolution process naturally occurs.

Some of you are serious practitioners who have received an empowerment and completed the approximation retreat. I advise that you continue your meditation on bodhicitta and emptiness and focus on cultivating serenity. Do a month-long retreat each year, or if this is not possible, do a five-day retreat each month. In these short retreats, it is not necessary to set up the boundary and so forth, as is done for formal retreats, but a few days of more intense meditation gives you the opportunity to cultivate concentration. Serenity is like an instrument that gives you the ability to do other activities. Without it you cannot have sustained meditation experiences. With it, other practices become much easier.

In my case, intellectually I know the path to become a buddha and how to make manifest the subtlest mind and transform it into the path. I've studied and understood this. In terms of developing bodhicitta, my practice is okay, and similarly my understanding of emptiness is okay. The awareness that the self does not exist is fairly constant in my mind. Now I want to spend some time focusing on the practice of serenity to integrate the Dharma more thoroughly in my mindstream and to deepen and sustain my meditation.

Learning, Reflecting, and Meditating

I strongly encourage you to study and practice the meditations found in Śāntideva's *Engaging in the Bodhisattvas' Deeds*, especially those in chapters 6 and 8. The former speaks of fortitude and patience, and the latter describes how to generate bodhicitta through equalizing and exchanging self and others. To cultivate the correct view of emptiness, please rely on the following works by learned scholar-adepts and seek teachings on them. The wisdom contained in these texts is extraordinary: The second chapter of Dharmakīrti's *Commentary on the Compendium of Reliable Cognition* contains a wonderful analysis of why the Buddha is a reliable guide on the path to awakening. It also explains the sixteen aspects of the four truths, a topic that sharpens our meditation on saṃsāra and the path to nirvāṇa. Other texts that are important for you to study are Nāgārjuna's *Treatise on the Middle Way*, Candrakīrti's commentary on it, *Supplement to the "Treatise on the Middle Way,"* and Āryadeva's *Four Hundred Stanzas on the Middle Way*. They will give you a grounded and correct understanding of the Madhyamaka view.

If you are unable to read a whole text, it's fine to read it selectively. Go directly to chapter 2 in *Pramāṇavārttika*, and if you cannot study the complete texts on emptiness recommended above, at least study the following chapters in the *Treatise on the Middle Way*. I myself read this text and teach it to others by reading a few chapters in the following order: Chapter 26 explains how we enter and leave saṃsāra by the twelve links of dependent arising, chapter 18 discusses how we circle in saṃsāra under the influence of grasping true existence, chapter 24 explains emptiness and generating the wisdom that realizes it, and chapter 22 clarifies that the Tathāgata and all phenomena are dependently designated. These chapters clearly demonstrate that self-grasping ignorance is the source of our ruin and the wisdom realizing emptiness eradicates it. Later you can read the remaining chapters of the text slowly, beginning with chapter 1.

Regarding commentaries to use when studying the *Treatise on the Middle Way*, although Buddhapālita's *Commentary* on it (*Buddhapālitamūlamadhyamakavṛtti*) is brief and does not contain much decisive analysis, it is very good. To study it with decisive analysis, interweave two texts—Bhāvaviveka's *Lamp of Wisdom* (*Prajñāpradīpa*) and Candrakīrti's *Clear Words* (*Prasannapadā*). With the help of these texts, you will understand the distinctions between the Prāsaṅgika Madhyamaka and Svātantrika Madhyamaka systems. This is beneficial to correctly identify the object of negation when meditating on emptiness.

For the study of tenets, Bhāvaviveka's *Heart of the Middleway* (*Madhyamakahṛdayakārikā*) and autocommentary *Blaze of Reasoning* (*Tarkajvālā*) are worthwhile. These texts, composed by a great Indian scholar, follow the tradition of Nāgārjuna.

I read a portion of many of these texts every day. When I wake up, I generate bodhicitta by contemplating Śāntideva's teachings on equalizing and exchanging self and others. With the wish to dedicate my life to the welfare of all sentient beings and thus to strive to attain full awakening for their benefit, I take the bodhisattva vow. Then, to see how the I exists, I investigate, Who am I? When I can't find an inherently existent I, I know that the I exists by dependent designation. Dependent arising is the Buddha's main teaching, so I recite Tsongkhapa's *Praise to Dependent Arising*. The deepest meaning of dependent arising is dependent designation; since all phenomena exist by mere dependent designation, they are empty of inherent existence. To emphasize this, I recite Nāgārjuna's homage to the Buddha from his *Treatise on the Middle Way*, which praises the Buddha for teaching dependent arising.

I prostrate to the perfect Buddha,
the best of all teachers, who taught:
that which is dependent arising is
without ceasing, without arising,
without discontinuation, without permanence,
without coming, without going,
without difference, without identity,
and peaceful—free from [conceptual] fabrication.

Then I reflect on the four absurd consequences of not accepting the ultimate nature of all phenomena to be their emptiness of inherent existence.[123] With bodhicitta and the understanding of emptiness as my foundation, I then do my tantric sādhanas.

These are my usual practices. In general, students who consider themselves the students of a particular teacher should try to follow their teacher's practice.

As Buddhists, think seriously about these texts, familiarize yourselves with them, and make their ideas part of your lives so that when you go about your daily activities, one corner of your mind recollects them. In formal meditation, do more in-depth contemplation and analysis. If you make effort to practice this way, over time your understanding will increase and your mind will become happier and calmer. Then when problems or even illness and death occur, you will be able to accept these situations and incorporate them into the path to awakening.

At the beginning, just comprehending the general ideas of the material presented by these great masters is difficult. But giving up due to discouragement is a mistake. Despite difficulties, you must make effort. Only in this way will practice become easier until eventually these views are living perspectives in your mind. I say this according to my little experience.

Even if your realization is equal to the deities, your behavior should conform to that of ordinary people. My late tutor Takdrak Rinpoche counseled me to follow this wise advice from the Kadampa tradition, and I pass it on to you. In this day and age when some people make claims of possessing extravagant spiritual abilities, yet their daily behavior is disgraceful, remaining a humble practitioner who is kind and wise is extremely important.

Along this line, you should not wear strange or elaborate robes and costumes or practice in a flamboyant manner. As the Kadampa practitioners said, you should be externally pure, internally pure, and always reliable. The seven-point mind training in particular counsels us, "Change your attitude while remaining normal (in behavior)." We should not make our Buddhist practice or the giving of teachings into a show.

Keep your precepts as best as you can. Be fair, kind, wise, and good-natured in your dealings with people. It is disgraceful to claim to be a Buddhist practitioner if your behavior contradicts the Dharma. We should be aware of our faults and correct them. Those of you who have attended the large teachings I have given in Dharamsala and in South India know that sometimes I speak strongly about the faults in our Buddhist community. Even when I'm too old to walk and must use a wheelchair, I will continue to speak about these. When my last days come, make sure you have made me content with what you have done. Otherwise all the long-life pūjās are meaningless. All of us know I cannot live thousands of eons, so we need to be realistic and not deceive ourselves or take things for granted.

Having a nonsectarian attitude is important, but we should understand this correctly. Being nonsectarian does not mean indiscriminately saying that you accept whatever teachings you hear literally. This is foolishness, isn't it? In principle, all four major Tibetan Buddhist traditions are pure and authentic. All have the Nālandā spirit, whether they are written as philosophical treatises or as songs of spiritual experience. For example, Milarepa's writings are expressed very simply. He never studied the texts on logic or philosophy, but his teachings contain the essence of these great texts. The basic meaning of Milarepa's teachings comes from Indian Buddhism and accords with the Nālandā tradition. Therefore, it is wrong to say that since he didn't study the major philosophical texts, he didn't hold the essential Buddhist ideas. You should accept and practice the meaning of his songs.

At the same time, you must not accept all statements and texts that someone says are pure according to dzogchen, mahāmudrā, or whatever. For example, someone may say that a small text containing pith instructions is the true teaching of Nyingma, Kagyu, Sakya, or Gelug. Simply because someone claims this does not mean it is true. You must carefully study and check the meaning. Not everything everyone says or writes is reliable, and we must remain skeptical until we have sufficiently investigated these claims.

For example, I have full conviction in the teachings of the Nyingma,

Sakya, Kagyu, and Gelug traditions. While each has its own unique qualities, all are authentic and perfect teachings. Nonetheless, some texts appear to contain contradictions. When I read them, I remain mindful of Nāgārjuna's view of emptiness. I am aware that there may be differences in terminology or meditations according to the tantric tradition. In some texts I see that the meaning is authentic and correct, no matter what terminology is used. However, other books contain lofty and fancy-sounding words whose meaning is vague or insignificant. In these cases, there is danger of misunderstanding, and we must supplement the unclear portions of such texts with the clear and correct explanations from other texts. In this way, we will not be led astray.

For example, the emphasis of many mahāmudrā and dzogchen works is the clear light. Emptiness is not fully explained in them. This is because the great masters who authored these texts taught disciples who were already familiar with the correct view of emptiness. They had no need to repeat or elaborate on the teachings on emptiness because those disciples already understood them and were in no danger of misunderstanding their meaning. Thus these masters briefly reviewed the meaning of emptiness in a few words before they delved into the new subject—the clear light—with which their disciples were unfamiliar. They knew their students would understand the clear light in terms of emptiness. For people nowadays who have not studied emptiness thoroughly and have only a rough or insufficient understanding of it, the explanations found in those texts is not sufficient.

Similarly, Tsongkhapa does not describe emptiness in detail in his tantric texts. This is because the view of emptiness is common to both Sūtra and Tantra, and he already explained it in his lamrim and philosophical texts. Assuming that the students were well-versed in emptiness, he focused on the unique qualities of Tantra in his tantric explanations. Someone who skips the in-depth study of lamrim will not understand emptiness correctly by simply studying Tsongkhapa's tantric expositions.

It seems that many Westerners and Chinese students dive into tantric sādhanas without having heard many teachings about emptiness or the method to cultivate serenity and insight. They spend time visualizing deities and imagining various objects emanating from and absorbing into those deities. Not understanding Vajrayāna very well, they think it's just about visualizing exotic beings and chanting mantras and prayers in other languages. Some Tibetans as well have this superficial view of tantric practice. This is a pity.

In Tibet some monasteries had *ngakpa dratsang*, a college especially for tantric studies and practice. Unfortunately, some lay followers got the impression that the monks' main practice was tantric rituals and that they did not study philosophy. Some monks entered the tantric colleges after studying the philosophical texts in the *tsenyi dratsang* (philosophical colleges) or *shedra* (Buddhist institutes), whereas others entered the tantric colleges directly and therefore lacked sufficient preparation in Buddhist philosophy. Although the latter monks memorized many tantric sādhanas and rituals, unfortunately their teachers did not always explain their meaning. It was better when explanation and memorization occurred together.

Knowing only how to chant rituals without understanding the philosophy and purpose of Tantra has many disadvantages, in addition to being unable to meditate correctly on sādhanas. There is a story about a monk from a tantric college who memorized rituals but studied little. His teacher was a realized practitioner, and when the teacher died and his breath stopped, he sat in meditation position. The student didn't know the tantric meditations to do at death and was frightened by his dead teacher still sitting upright. Apprehensive that the body would stand up like a zombie, he pushed his teacher's body down and ran from the room!

On the other hand, the monks and geshes who enter the tantric colleges from a shedra or a philosophical college know Buddhist philosophy and teachings but do not know how to perform rituals. As a result, sometimes when laypeople ask for rituals, these monks do not know how to do them. When these monks go to the prayer assemblies, they remain silent and do not chant with the others because they have memorized only philosophical texts, not prayers and sādhanas.

Try to be a well-rounded practitioner. Although you may have your own specialties and areas of interest, having a broad education is useful. We should be twenty-first-century Buddhists. That means trying to gain full knowledge of Buddhism, including the essences of the Pāli tradition and Sanskrit tradition, including Tantrayāna, as well as some knowledge of science. This is the first step. The next step is to translate this knowledge into experience, otherwise it becomes just empty words. Practicing and applying the teachings to the state of your mind is crucial. When you have a solid foundation and are prepared, cultivate some experience of renunciation, bodhicitta, emptiness, and Tantra. In that way you will truly fulfill the purpose of this precious human life. If some members of a monastery, temple, or Dharma center study and practice well and have deeper inner experiences of the Dharma, then the real purpose of that Dharma institution has been fulfilled.

Skillful Practice

Learning to practice in a skillful, balanced way is crucial for progressing on the path. Some people want to dispense with the earlier steps of the path and focus on developing serenity and insight, as only the union of these two will cut the root of saṃsāra. However, if we ignore the earlier steps of the path, we run the risk of overlooking important points and getting confused later on. It is best to develop an overall understanding of the entire path and be convinced of its efficacy.

Our practice is on the right track if, when we meditate on the initial steps, we become more eager to cultivate the later steps, and if, when we study the later steps, our wish to practice the initial steps increases. The path becomes very interesting the more we see the interrelationships among the various topics of the stages of the path, and our mind becomes enthusiastic to practice and to actualize the various steps. At the same time, we realize doing so will take time, so we cultivate patience, enjoying each small insight as it comes without grasping on to it.

The lamrim enables you to become a doctor for your own mind. There is a Dharma remedy for whatever affliction may invade your mind, bringing suffering or confusion. As you learn the Buddha's teachings, starting from the beginning and gradually proceeding to more difficult topics, you will learn these Dharma medicines. But knowing them isn't sufficient; you must remember them and call them to mind when you need to calm and rebalance your mind.

The more we are familiar with the topics of the stages of the path, the more we will see their validity and applicability in our daily lives. We will learn how to handle our problems by contemplating on the appropriate topic. Being responsible for our own state of mind is a sign of maturity. We should not think that every time we have a problem we must ask our spiritual mentors what to do. All along they have been teaching us the antidotes to afflictions, and we must learn how and when to apply them.

Someone once asked me how to use the teachings on emptiness in difficult situations when our mind is already overwhelmed with a particular affliction. Although the wisdom realizing emptiness is the ultimate antidote for all afflictions, this takes time and effort to understand and experience. Given that we are not bodhisattvas or āryas, we need to be familiar with antidotes that are easier to understand and apply in such situations. For example, when we face strong attachment, contemplate impermanence and the defects of saṃsāra; when we are criticized, generate fortitude and compassion; when situations do not turn out the way we would like, think of the defects of the self-centered attitude and cultivate the mind that cherishes others; when jealousy strikes, rejoice at others' good fortune and pray that they use their good fortune to benefit others.

In short, we have a long history of misapprehending reality—a history that is beginningless and so deeply ingrained that it constitutes our way of seeing the world. To counteract this, we must rejoice that we have met the Buddha's teachings and good spiritual mentors so that we can learn the Dharma and familiarize ourselves with the antidotes to afflictions and defilements for a long time.

The Importance of Daily Practice

I would like to again emphasize the importance of making daily effort on the path, so that gradual, integrated change will come about. The transmitted or scriptural Dharma is taught and studied; the realized Dharma is preserved through practice.[124] When you commemorate special days associated with lineage masters, remember that the proper way to celebrate is to study the teachings and put them into practice so that they become integrated with your mind. Practice is not a matter of putting on this or that color hat, it's about studying and incorporating what you learn in your heart and mind.

Owing to the kindness of my teachers—principally Kyabje Yongzin Ling Rinpoche—over the course of many years I memorized the *Ornament of Clear Realizations* and *Supplement to the "Treatise on the Middle Way."* I received the oral transmission of both these books and even today can recite them from memory. In addition, I read from Candrakīrti's autocommentary to the *Supplement* every day.

With the clear long-term objective of buddhahood, practice day by day and gradually subdue and transform your physical, verbal, and mental actions. This is the proper way to practice. Reading the works and biographies of the great scholar-adepts, yogis and yoginīs, and siddhas shows the sincerity and effort necessary to accomplish the path. Tsongkhapa told us in *Destiny Fulfilled* (v. 4):[125]

> In the beginning, I sought much learning.
> In the middle, all teachings dawned on me as spiritual exhortation.
> In the end, I practiced day and night.
> I dedicated all this virtue for the Dharma to flourish.
>
> Thinking this over, how well my destiny is fulfilled!
> I am grateful to Noble Lord Wisdom Treasure (Mañjuśrī)!

All of us are the Buddha's followers. Whatever progress I have made has been achieved on the basis of the texts that all of us can read. We still have access to the Buddha's teachings; their lineages of transmission have survived to this day; we have encountered qualified spiritual mentors. Our job is to learn and put the teachings into practice. As we do, mental transformation will occur. When we create the causes, the results will naturally arise.

Now the Library of Wisdom and Compassion is complete and my responsibility is fulfilled. Your problems remain with you—I cannot remove them. But the Dharma I have shared with you—and especially bodhicitta and the wisdom realizing emptiness—are the most effective methods to tackle these problems. Such teachings are more valuable than all the wealth in the world.

I consider all of you to be my friends and hope that you see me in that way too. I have dedicated my entire life to the well-being of all sentient beings and continuously think of how to serve and benefit them. If you consider yourself to be my friend, then I ask you, please, think about these teachings on compassion and wisdom. Since one of your close friends, Tenzin Gyatso, is committed to working for the benefit of all sentient beings, please, my friends, try to care for others in whatever large or small way you can.

We have the tradition of ending an important teaching or project with some auspicious lines. I would like to share with you what is in my heart. Bodhicitta is my practice while I'm alive. Bodhicitta will be my practice when I am about to die. And bodhicitta will be my practice in my next life, too! This is what I say and what I feel too.

Motivated by bodhicitta, together let's do our best to fulfill Tsongkhapa's dedication verse in the *Great Treatise on the Stages of the Path to Awakening*:

> In regions where the supreme, precious teaching has not spread
> or where it has spread but then declined,
> may I illumine that treasure of happiness and benefit
> with a mind deeply moved by great compassion.

Notes

1. This is according to the Mahāyāna viewpoint.
2. The first two stages are often combined into one, the isolated speech.
3. Shangri-la is a fictional, mystical, and harmonious place described in *Lost Horizon*, the 1933 novel by James Hilton.
4. See *Saṃsāra, Nirvāṇa, and Buddha Nature*, chapter 1, for a fuller explanation of these.
5. The tantric teachings in the Sakya tradition that speak of the union of clarity and emptiness are explained in connection with the third turning of the wheel of Dharma. The Jonang teachings of "other emptiness" also derive from this turning. For a fuller discussion, see chapter 14.
6. See chapter 9 of *Approaching the Buddhist Path.*
7. This refers to the pure illusory body, a subtle body produced from its substantial cause, the subtlest wind, with the subtlest clear-light mind that directly realizes emptiness as its cooperative condition.
8. The Tibetan term for "outer lucidity" may also be translated as "outward radiance" and the term for "inner lucidity" as "inner luminosity."
9. These are the four complete purities of the resultant state.
10. Vajrayāna is also practiced in Japan as the Shingon tradition. Vajrayāna spread to China in the eighth century but was not widely practiced there.
11. Sometimes this title is abbreviated as *Supplement.*
12. In group situations, practitioners use different vajras, bells, and drums, not their personal ones.
13. In Tantra, saying a consciousness dissolves or absorbs means that it ceases to function and a subtler mind manifests.
14. *Ālaya* has different meanings in different contexts. The fundamental innate mind of clear light is not to be confused with the foundation consciousness asserted by Yogācāra, although both are called *ālaya*. Similarly, Samantabhadra has different meanings according to the context. Sometimes Samantabhadra is seen as a primordial buddha, while in other contexts he is a bodhisattva. In Highest Yoga Tantra, Samantabhadra is the wisdom of nondual bliss and emptiness, the ultimate bodhicitta in Tantra.
15. For more information, see Kachen Yeshe Gyaltsen, *Manjushri's Innermost Secret* (MIS).

16. His Holiness does not intend to confuse newcomers with many new terms that they do not understand. Rather, he is illustrating the diversity among tantras. At the same time, he is emphasizing that tantric practices from all the Tibetan traditions have much in common despite the different terminology. As your studies proceed, you will encounter these terms and will learn their meanings at that time. For people who have studied these topics in more depth, the meanings of the terms are clear, as are the associations His Holiness makes among them.
17. "The Root Manual of the Rites of Mañjuśrī," chapter 11, revision 1.21.28, 84000, last modified 2023, https://read.84000.co/translation/toh543.html#UT22084-088-038-chapter-11/.
18. These are substances that one imagines transforming into unpolluted nectar on the generation stage. At advanced levels of the completion stage, one is able to actually transform them and partake of them.
19. See chapter 5, "Saṅgha: The Monastic Community," in *Following in the Buddha's Footsteps*, 132–36, where full ordination for women in the Tibetan tradition is discussed.
20. The consort of Hevajra.
21. Also see chapters 4 and 5 in *The Foundation of Buddhist Practice*, which address spiritual mentors conducting themselves in unusual ways.
22. Candrakīrti continues by speaking about three types of great compassion. See *In Praise of Great Compassion*, chapter 6.
23. For more on the superknowledges, see *Following in the Buddha's Footsteps*, chapter 8.
24. See chapter 4 of *Realizing the Profound View* for more on these logical inconsistencies and chapters 8–10 for an explanation of dependent designation.
25. *Duḥkha* means unsatisfactory experiences and circumstances. It is often translated as "suffering," but its meaning is broader.
26. See chapter 2 of *Realizing the Profound View* for an explanation of this important verse.
27. These may be found in *In Praise of Great Compassion*.
28. If you can't completely avoid eating these foods, do your Kriyā and Caryā Tantra practices early in the day before eating any of these foods.
29. For more on counteracting afflictions, see chapter 4 of *Saṃsāra, Nirvāṇa, and Buddha Nature*.
30. This self-generation practice of Avalokiteśvara is explained more elaborately in Thubten Chodron, *Cultivating a Compassionate Heart: The Yoga Method of Chenrezig*.
31. The "next hand" is the lower hand and the third hand is the second hand.
32. This is a play on words: "self-generation" is pronounced *dag kye* and "mouth generation" is *ka kye*.
33. See *Realizing the Profound View* for more on how to meditate on emptiness and the compatibility of emptiness and dependent arising.
34. The Buddhist deity Sarvavid Vairocana, or the All-Knowing Buddha, is the personification of awakening.

35. See *Following in the Buddha's Footsteps* for an extensive explanation of how to cultivate serenity.
36. Seeing *Courageous Compassion* for an explanation of the five paths and ten grounds of the Perfection Vehicle.
37. See chapters 9–12 in *The Foundation of Buddhist Practice* for more on karma and its effects.
38. The Vaibhāṣikas differ, saying the last moment of consciousness of a dying person may be virtuous, neutral, or nonvirtuous.
39. How to cultivate serenity in the Sūtrayāna is explained in *Following in the Buddha's Footsteps*.
40. When sādhanas are done together in a group, the chant leader usually does not pause here to meditate on emptiness. However, I recommend that they stop here briefly to reflect on emptiness.
41. See *Following in the Buddha's Footsteps*, chapter 7.
42. For more on the general I and specific I, see chapter 3 of *Realizing the Profound View*.
43. These long-time meditators are concerned that placing electrodes on their heads and other scientific instruments on or in their bodies will disturb their meditation, especially at the time of death.
44. In another presentation found in *The Tibetan Book of the Dead* (TBD 37), the coarse body is our material body of the five elements of earth, water, fire, wind, and space; the subtle body consists of the channels, winds, and drops; and the subtlest body is the wind accompanying the fundamental innate clear-light mind in the indestructible drop. The coarse mind is the sense consciousnesses (visual, audio, olfactory, gustatory, and tactile) and the everyday conceptualizing mental consciousness; the subtle mind is the mind of the eighty conceptions; and the subtlest mind is the fundamental innate clear-light mind.
45. There is discussion below on whether the subtlest mind in ordinary beings has an object.
46. This interest began in His Holiness's childhood and expanded with the Mind and Life conferences that began in the 1980s to bring science and contemplative wisdom together. See the chapter "Karma, the Universe, and Evolution" in *Saṃsāra, Nirvāṇa, and Buddha Nature*. Also see His Holiness's book, *The Universe in a Single Atom*.
47. It's important to respect that Buddhism and science are different disciplines, each with its own perspectives and areas of expertise. We should not use science to prove Buddhism or use Buddhism to prove science.
48. In general, the fundamental innate clear-light mind (T. *gnyug ma lhan cig skyes pa'i 'od gsal gyi sems*) and innate clear-light mind (T. *lhan cig skyes pa'i 'od gsal gyi sems*) refer to the same mind.
49. Even a wrong consciousness is generated in the aspect of its appearing object and is considered a reliable cognizer with respect to its own appearing object. Konchog Jigme Wangpo gives the example of a conceptual mind apprehending permanent sound. Its appearing object is a conceptual appearance of permanent sound, even

though permanent sound does not exist and therefore cannot appear. Nevertheless, this mind is considered reliable with respect to permanent sound because it notices and can induce a memory of this conceptual appearance. However, even though this mind is said to be a reliable cognizer with respect to its appearing object, the conceptual appearance of permanent sound, it is not a reliable cognizer because it is not incontrovertible. It does not correctly cognize permanent sound, because permanent sound does not exist. See CTA 313.

50. "Mindfulness" is the literal translation. It is very subtle and is not the same mindfulness as used when cultivating serenity or when doing the four establishments of mindfulness. It also does not refer to mindfulness in terms of our coarse memory of past things and events.
51. As mentioned before, *luminous* does not mean the mind radiates light. Rather, it refers to the mind's ability to reflect an object.
52. This explains why, in the Tripiṭaka classification, Vajrayāna belongs to the Basket of Concentration.
53. See DIR for an in-depth explanation of these three events.
54. In the practice of Highest Yoga Tantra, the eternal indestructible drop is associated with the syllable *ah*. The *Magical Net Tantra*, which is within the *Mañjuśrī Tantra*, says "the perfect buddhas arise from *ah*" and "*ah* is the supreme among syllables." A general explanation of this, which agrees with Pāramitāyāna, is that the syllable *ah* is a negative particle and indicates emptiness, the absence of inherent existence. Thus, the defilements in your continuum are extinguished in the sphere of reality, which is the emptiness of inherent existence, as indicated by *ah*. Because *ah* indicates the ultimate nature, it is the supreme means of expression. "The perfect buddhas arise from *ah*" means that the buddhas arise from meditation on the emptiness of inherent existence.

    In Highest Yoga Tantra, the syllable *ah* also refers to the short *ah* that is the indestructible drop. Buddhahood comes about from concentrating on this indestructible drop; therefore, buddhahood is said to arise from that drop. Because the buddhas' body has the nature of the indestructible drop—the subtlest wind-mind—it is said that the perfect buddhas arise from the letter *ah*.
55. The definition of the generation stage comes from *The Essence of the "Ocean of Attainments of the Generation Stage"* (*Bskyed rim dnogs grub rgya mtsho'i snying po*) by Losang Chokyi Gyaltsen, which addresses the main points of the generation stage.
56. See *Realizing the Profound View*, 87 and 194, for the meaning of these mantras.
57. While meditating on the initial phase of the self-generation practice, some sādhanas have you visualize your wisdom realizing emptiness appearing in the form of a ray of light, a syllable, an implement, or a deity that is the causal vajra-holder. This is part of the meditation of taking the bardo into the path to the enjoyment body. The process of the self-generation continues with other visualizations until the meditator arises in the full form of the deity, known as the resultant vajra-holder. This is taking rebirth into the path to the emanation body.
58. The five clarifications are so-called because as you meditate on the five stages, the

appearance of the deity evolves and become clearer. These five are meditation on suchness, a moon, a seed syllable, an implement or symbol, and full emergence as the deity.

59. See *Following in the Buddha's Footsteps* for instructions on how to cultivate serenity.
60. There are three samādhis in the Supreme Triumphant Maṇḍala: the initial application, the samādhi of the Supreme Triumphant Maṇḍala, and the Supreme Triumphant Actions.
61. On the generation stage, practitioners meditate to develop serenity, insight, and the union of serenity and insight. Practitioners are usually on the path of accumulation and may attain the path of preparation. Dissolution of the winds is imagined.
62. The stage of slight power over pristine wisdom has periods of both the generation stage and completion stage.
63. Nāgārjuna is the parent and Āryadeva is his spiritual child.
64. There are four ways of describing deities' natural abode: their dharmakāya; the state of their enjoyment body; Ogmin (the place where the wisdom being abides); and the sphere of emptiness.
65. See Robert A. F. Thurman, trans., *The Brilliantly Illuminating Lamp of the Five Stages by Tsong Khapa Losang Drakpa* (Somerville, MA: Wisdom Publications, 2019).
66. Yael Bentor and Penpa Dorjee, trans., *The Essence of the Ocean of Attainments: The Creation Stage of the Guhyasamāja Tantra according to Panchen Lobsang Chokyi Gyaltsen* (Somerville, MA: Wisdom Publications, 2019).
67. The five aggregates that are generated as the five buddha families are form as Vairocana, feelings as Ratnasambhava, discrimination as Amitābha, miscellaneous factors as Amoghasiddhi, and consciousness as Akṣobhya.
68. The four elements are visualized in the aspect of the four consorts: earth as Locanā, water as Māmakī, fire as Pāṇḍaravāsinī, and wind as Tārā.
69. The six sources are imagined in the aspect of the six bodhisattvas: eye source as Kṣitigarbha, ear source as Vajrapāṇi, nose source as Ākāśagarbha, tongue source as Lokeśvara, body source as Sarvanivāraṇa-viṣkambhini, and mental source as Mañjuśrī.
70. The five objects become the five goddesses: forms as Rūpavajra, sounds as Śabdavajra, odors as Gandhavajra, tastes as Rasāvajra, and tangibles as Sparśavajra.
71. Here is an example of how the twenty coarse phenomena, which transform into the twenty deities, are divided into five. Vairocana is the purified aspect of the aggregate of form. There are five form aggregates, one for each of the five lineages. Thus, there is a Vairocana of the Vairocana family, a Vairocana of the Ratnasambhava family, a Vairocana of the Amitābha family, a Vairocana of the Amoghasiddhi family, and a Vairocana of the Akṣobhya family. The purified form aggregate of each of the five lineages is Vairocana. It is the same with all the other buddhas.

72. In some maṇḍalas, Vairocana and Akṣobhya exchange places, and their corresponding consorts and elements are also exchanged.
73. See *Searching for the Self*, 143, for a list of various types of elaboration.
74. It is called "vitality" because it concerns the breath, and by slowing the breathing rate, the lifespan can be increased.
75. In Sūtrayāna, all paths are consciousnesses. In Tantrayāna, an impure illusory body is a path, but it is not a consciousness. It is a form that has the nature of blissful pristine wisdom.
76. In addition to this tantric method of transference of consciousness, there is a Sūtra method as well. It is explained as one of the mind-training practices. See *The Foundation of Buddhist Practice*, 226–27.
77. For the other similes, see Cozort 1986, 101.
78. The common supernormal powers are detailed in *Following in the Buddha's Footsteps*, 246.
79. In some contexts, the minds of white appearance, red increase, and black near-attainment are said to be conceptual, but in other contexts they are referred to as nonconceptual. In this instance, saying that they are nonconceptual doesn't mean they perceive their object without a conceptual appearance. Rather, it means that compared to the eight indicative conceptions, their minds and winds have only a little dualistic appearance. Although these three minds are called nonconceptual in this context, they are obscured and still have dualistic appearances.
80. This is a conceptual understanding of emptiness. If yogis who initially had the Yogācāra view later attain the actual clear light, it indicates that they have the Prāsaṅgika understanding of emptiness. This change in view happened not because of learning and analysis, as it would in Sūtrayāna, but due to deepening experience through tantric practice, specifically through dissolving the winds in the central channel.
81. Chapters 8–11 describe how the Pāramitāyāna sets out the five paths that bodhisattvas travel to buddhahood.
82. The layout of the paths and grounds in the Kālacakra Tantra differs due to its unique features.
83. This is according to the Dagpo Kagyu, Sakya, and Gelug traditions in Tibet.
84. Georg Roerich identified this as Amarāvatī in South India.
85. Analogous to major steps in a child's development, the seven empowerments of entering like a child chart practitioners' development in the Kālacakra path. Each of the following seven empowerments is followed by its analogous event in a child's life: (1) water (a child's first bath), (2) crown (binding a child's hairlocks), (3) ribbon (piercing a child's ear and putting on ornaments), (4) vajra and bell (child laughing and talking), (5) discipline (a child's enjoyment of the five sense objects), (6) name (naming the child), and (7) mantra authorization (eliminating obstacles and attaining the four powers: pacification, increase, control, and ferocity).
86. Rahula causes eclipses.
87. According to Prāsaṅgikas, the basis for carrying karmic seeds is the mere I, the I that is merely designated in dependence on the mental and physical aggregates

and that goes from one life to the next. In Highest Yoga Tantra, the subtlest wind-mind is the final basis of designation of the mere I and this wind-mind is associated with the drops.

88. The five certainties of the enjoyment body according to Kālacakra practice are: (1) certainty of time: the fact that this comes at the conclusion of the complete ten signs of night and day; (2) certainty of place: it happens inside the upper tip of the central channel; (3) certainty of nature: it does not come from a collection of tiny particles but merely from the appearance of your mind; (4) certainty of its body: the body is that of Vajrasattva; and (5) certainty of its aspect: the aspect is that of a mother and father deity facing each other in union.
89. Bon is a Tibetan tradition but is not usually considered a Buddhist tradition. It predates the arrival of Buddhism in Tibet and was influenced by Buddhism.
90. Contemporary scholars say that Nālandā most likely began in the fifth century CE, and was destroyed in 1198 by invaders. At its peak it had two thousand teachers and over ten thousand students, including some non-Buddhists. The great seventh-century Chinese pilgrim Yijing reported that nuns also studied at Nālandā.
91. See chapter 2 of *Searching for the Self* for more about the seventeen great Nālandā masters.
92. "Khenpo Shenga," Rigpa Wiki, last modified July 4, 2017, at 21:26, http://www.rigpawiki.org/index.php?title=Khenpo_Shenga.
93. See *Searching for the Self*, chapter 2, for the prayer of supplication.
94. An excellent explanation of dzogchen is found in HM.
95. See the end of the section "The Inseparability of Wisdom and Method" in chapter 1 of this volume for a concise summary of the basis, path, and result according to dzogchen.
96. While early translators considered the *Akutobhayā* to be Nāgārjuna's autocommentary on the *Treatise on the Middle Way*, later Tibetans did not. This text was an essential Madhyamaka text in China.
97. This text may be found at https://tibetanclassics.org/wp-content/uploads/2020/09/Garland-of-Views.pdf. English translation by Geshe Thupten Jinpa, 2004.
98. Buton Rinpoche, who is known for his historical writings, was from the Shalu tradition, an offshoot of Sakya; he also held the Prāsaṅgika view.
99. This text is available from Rangjung Yeshe Publications in three volumes. The quote is from section 4. "Analysis of All: The Logical Argument of Great Interdependence," https://www.lotsawahouse.org/tibetan-masters/mipham/four-great-logical-arguments. Translated by Adam Pearcey, 2005.
100. For a discussion of diamond slivers, see chapter 6 in *Realizing the Profound View*.
101. These are different mahāmudrā practices in the Kagyu tradition.
102. See *Appearing and Empty*, chapter 3, for more on object-ultimate and concordant-ultimate.
103. For an explanation of affirming and nonaffirming negatives, see chapter 7 of *Searching for the Self* and chapter 1 of *Realizing the Profound View*.

104. For more on conceptualizations and elaborations, see chapter 7 of *Searching for the Self.*
105. For more on these two types of meditation, see *The Foundation of Buddhist Practice*, 132–33.
106. See chapter 11 of *Realizing the Profound View* for more on illusion-like appearances.
107. One of the eight-four mahāsiddhas, Ratnākaraśānti (late-tenth-to-mid-eleventh centuries), also known as Śāntipa, was an abbot of Vikramaśīla Monastery in India and was one of Atiśa's teachers.
108. Abhayākaragupta (eleventh to twelfth centuries) was a scholar and abbot of Vikramaśīla Monastery and a tantric master (*vajrācārya*).
109. Dolpopa first spoke of "other-empty," but the meaning of this term has changed over time, so that now there are several meanings. See Anne Burchardi's "A Look at the Diversity of the Gzhan stong Tradition," for the translation of "The Full Moon Dialogue" by the early twentieth-century Jonang scholar Pema Bidza for more on this point.
110. His Holiness emphasizes that if one is going to discuss similarities and differences in the views of proponents of other-emptiness (*zhentong*) and those who do not accept this view, one must compare them on an equal level, comparing apples to apples. To do this, it is essential to speak of the view presented in the Perfection of Wisdom sūtras in tandem with Tantra.
111. The most famous work Dolpopa composed to present his controversial interpretations of Buddhist doctrine is *Mountain Dharma: An Ocean of Definitive Meaning (Ri chos nges don rgya mtsho)*, written in 1330 for learned Vajrayāna meditators in mountain retreats. See Cyrus Stearns, *Mountain Dharma: An Ocean of Definitive Meaning*, by Dölpopa Sherab Gyaltsen (New York: Wisdom Publications, forthcoming 2025).
112. The other eight are *Dhāraṇī for Entering the Nonconceptual* (*Avikalpapraveśadhāraṇī*), *Sūtra of the Lion's Roar of Śrīmālādevī* (*Śrīmālādevī Siṃhanāda Sūtra*), *Great Drum Sūtra* (*Mahābherī Sūtra*), *Sūtra to Benefit Aṅgulimāla* (*Aṅgulimālīya Sūtra*), *Sūtra of Great Emptiness* (*Śūnyatānāmamahā Sūtra*), *Sūtra Presenting the Great Compassion of the Tathagata* (*Tathāgatamahākaruṇānirdeśa Sūtra*), *Sūtra Presenting the Inconceivable Qualities and Primordial Awareness of the Tathagata* (*Tathāgataguṇajñānācintyaviṣayāvatāranirdeśa*), and *Extensive Sūtra of the Great Cloud* (*Mahāmegha Sūtra*).
113. That is, it is not known or defined by means of a negation.
114. See chapter 10 of *Realizing the Profound View* for an explanation of dependent arising dawning as the meaning of emptiness and emptiness dawning as the meaning of dependent arising.
115. *Sukha* is also translated as "happiness" and "pleasure."
116. See chapter 7 of *Following in the Buddha's Footsteps.*
117. Using this on the path to cultivate the union of bliss and emptiness, some yogis may start out by generating great bliss and gradually directing it to emptiness, whereas advanced yogis automatically experience great bliss the moment they recall emptiness. The subtler the great bliss of Highest Yoga Tantra, the more

clarity that mind has, whereas in the form and formless absorptions, the subtler the mind becomes, the more obscure it is.

118. There are different types of visions of a deity: a hallucination caused by the energy-winds, a vision in a dream, the deity appearing to the mental consciousness in meditation, and actually knowing the deity with one's sense consciousnesses. It is said that Tsongkhapa's vision of Mañjuśrī is the latter.
119. See chapters 4 and 5 in *The Foundation of Buddhist Practice* for an explanation of how to properly rely on a spiritual mentor.
120. See *Searching for the Self*, *Realizing the Profound View*, and *Appearing and Empty* to learn more about the Madhyamaka view of emptiness.
121. See *The Foundation of Buddhist Practice*, 226–27, where this practice is referred to as the Seven-Point Thought Transformation.
122. See Glenn Mulin, *Meditations on the Lower Tantras* (Dharamsala: Library of Tibetan Works and Archives, 1983), 51–67.
123. See MMA 6.34–36 and GR 262. These verses are explained in chapter 4 of *Realizing the Profound View.*
124. See chapter 1 of *Following in the Buddha's Footsteps* for more about the scriptural and realized Dharma.
125. Translated by Tenzin Tsepag.
126. Sometimes the second type of dependent arising is said to be dependence on parts.

Glossary

absolutism (*eternalism* or *view of permanence*, *śāśvatānta*, P. *bhavadiṭṭhi*, T. *rtag lta*). The belief that phenomena inherently exist.

Action Tantra. *See* Kriyā Tantra.

action seal. *See* karmamudrā.

actual clear light (T. *don gyi 'od gsal*). The mind of great bliss that directly realizes emptiness.

afflictions (*kleśa*, T. *nyon mongs*). Mental factors that disturb the tranquility of the mind. These include disturbing emotions and wrong views.

afflictive obscurations (*kleśāvaraṇa*, T. *nyon sgrib*). Obscurations that mainly prevent liberation; afflictions and their seeds.

aggregates (*skandha*, T. *phung po*). The four or five components that make up a living being: form (except for beings born in the formless realm), feelings, discriminations, miscellaneous factors, and consciousnesses.

all-pervading wind (*vyāna*, T. *khyab byed kyi rlung*). A wind that abides in the heart but pervades the entire body and controls all motor functions of the body.

analysis (*vicāra*, T. *dpyod pa*). A mental factor that examines an object in detail.

analytical meditation (*vicārabhāvanā*, T. *dpyad sgom*). Meditation done to understand an object.

appearing object (*pratibhāsa-viṣaya*, T. *snang yul*). The object that actually appears to a consciousness. The appearing object of a conceptual consciousness is a conceptual appearance of something.

apprehended object (*muṣṭibandha-viṣaya*, T. *'dzin stangs kyi yul*). The main object with which the mind is concerned, the object that the mind is getting at or perceives. Syn. engaged object.

arhat (foe destroyer, T. *dgra bcom pa*). Someone who has eliminated all afflictive obscurations and attained liberation.

ārya (P. *ariya*, T. *'phags pa*). Someone who has directly and nonconceptually realized the emptiness of inherent existence.

bardo (intermediate state, T. *bar do*). The state in between one life and the next.

base of emptiness. The object whose mode of existence is being analyzed.

basis of designation (*basis of imputation*, T. *gdags gzhi*). The collection of parts or factors in dependence on which an object is designated or imputed.

basis of negation (T. *dgag gzhi*). The object on which a quality is being negated.

black near-attainment (T. *nyer thob nag lam pa*). A subtle mind experiencing complete darkness that arises in the seventh of the eight stages of dying. When it dissolves, the subtlest clear-light mind manifests.

bodhicitta (altruistic intention, T. *byang chub sems*). A main mental consciousness induced by an aspiration to bring about the welfare of others and accompanied by an aspiration to attain full awakening oneself.

bodhisattva (T. *byang chub sems dpa'*). Someone who has uncontrived bodhicitta.

bodhisattva ground (*bhūmi*, T. *byang chub sems dpa'i sa*). A consciousness in the continuum of an ārya bodhisattva characterized by wisdom and compassion. It is the basis for the development of good qualities and the basis for the eradication of ignorance and mistaken appearances.

breakthrough (*trekcho*, T. *khregs chod*). The system of attaining buddhahood through immediate liberation as a directly perceived realization that is not connected to appearances. A tantric practice in the Nyingma tradition that creates the causes to actualize the truth body and is the practice of clear light.

buddha nature (*buddhagotra*, T. *sangs rgyas kyi rigs*). A phenomenon that is suitable to transform into a buddha's exalted body; sentient beings' potential to become fully awakened.

cakra. Energy centers along the central channel. Branch channels enter the central channel at these places.

Caryā Tantra (Performance Tantra, T. *spyod rgyud*). The second of the four classes of tantra, which places equal emphasis on external and internal yogas.

central channel (*avadhūti*, *susumnā nāḍī*, T. *rtsa dbu ma*). The subtle channel that runs from the forehead to the tip of the sexual organ.

channel (*nāḍī*, T. *rtsa*). A subtle channel in the body through which the winds may run.

channel knot (T. *rtsa mdud*). Coils of smaller channels around the central channel that cause blockages to the winds entering and flowing freely in the central channel.

character (*lakṣaṇa*, T. *mtshan nyid*). Nature.

characteristics (svalakṣaṇa, T. rang gi mtshan nyid). Attributes of an object. Things have characteristics, but they do not exist by their own characteristics.

child clear light (T. *bu'i 'od gsal*). The subtlest mind that realizes emptiness and arises when the winds have dissolved in the central channel through the force of meditation.

clear appearance (T. *gsal snang*). The clear appearance of having the body of the deity that is then used as an object to cultivate serenity.

clear light (*prabhāsvara*, T. *'od gsal*) (1) the emptiness of the mind, (2) the clear and cognizant conventional nature of the mind in which the defilements are adventitious, (3) the subtlest mind that is one nature with the subtlest wind.

cognitive obscurations (*jñeyāvaraṇa*, T. *shes sgrib*). Obscurations that mainly prevent full awakening; the latencies of ignorance and the subtle dualistic appearance that they give rise to.

collection of merit (*puṇyasaṃbhāra*, T. *bsod nams kyi tshogs*). A virtuous action motivated by bodhicitta that is a main cause of attaining the form body of a buddha.

collection of wisdom (*jñānasaṃbhāra*, T. *ye shes kyi tshogs*). A virtuous mental action motivated by bodhicitta that is a main cause of attaining the truth body of a buddha.

commitment being (*samayasattva, T. dam tshig pa).* The deity meditators imagine themselves as during a sādhana.

commitments. In Tantra, practices associated with the five buddha families. There are also commitments given by the tantric master for daily mantra or sādhana recitations.

common paths. Sometimes this refers to Dharma understandings that practitioners seeking full awakening cultivate along with practitioners seeking a good rebirth or arhatship. Sometimes it refers to Dharma understandings cultivated in common between practitioners of Sūtra and Tantra.

completion stage (T. *rdzogs rim*). A yoga in the continuum of a learner that arises from having caused the entering, abiding, and dissolving of the winds in the central channel by the force of meditation.

conceived object (*adhyavasāya-viṣaya*, T. *zhen yul*). The object conceived by a conceptual consciousness. Syn. apprehended or engaged object of a conceptual consciousness.

concentration (*samādhi*, T. *ting nge 'dzin*). A mental factor that dwells single-pointedly for a sustained period of time on one object; a state of deep meditative absorption; single-pointed concentration that is free from discursive thought.

conceptual appearance (*artha-sāmānya*, T. *don spyi*). A mental image of an object that appears to a conceptual consciousness.

conceptual fabrications. False modes of existence and false ideas imputed by a conceptual consciousness.

conceptuality (*kalpanā*, T. *rtog pa*). Thought; a mind that knows its object via a conceptual appearance.

conceptualizations (*vikalpa viparyāsa*, T. *rnam rtog*). Distorted thoughts that range from exaggerating the desirability or beauty of an object to grasping impermanent things as permanent, and so forth.

consciousness (*jñāna*, T. *shes pa*). That which is clear and cognizant.

conventional existence (*saṃvṛtisat*, T. *kun rdzob tu yod pa*). Existence.

conventional truths (*saṃvṛti-satya*, T. *kun rdzob bden pa*). See veiled truths.

cooperative conditions (*sahakāri-pratyaya*, T. *lhan cig byed pa'i rkyen*). Causes that aid the main or substantial cause in producing its result.

death (*maraṇa*, T. *'chi ba*). The last moment of a lifetime when the subtlest clear-light mind manifests.

deceptive (*moṣa*, *visaṃvādaka*, T. *slu ba*). (1) erroneous, (2) not existing in the way it appears.

defilement (stain, *mala*, T. *dri ma*). Either an afflictive obscuration or a cognitive obscuration.

definitive (*nītārtha*, P. *nītattha*, T. *nges don*). Prāsaṅgika: A sūtra or statement that mainly and explicitly teaches ultimate truths; the ultimate truth itself.

deity (T. *yi dam, lha*). A manifestation of a buddha that is used as an object of meditation that practitioners seek to become.

dependent arising (*pratītyasamutpāda*, T. *rten cing 'brel bar 'byung ba, rten 'byung, rten 'brel*). This is of three types: (1) causal dependence—things arising due to causes and conditions, (2) mutual dependence—phenomena existing in relation to other phenomena,[126] and (3) dependent designation—phenomena existing by being merely designated by terms and concepts.

dependent designation (*upādāya prajñapti*, T. *brten nas gdags pa*). Being designated by term and concept.

dhyāna (P. *jhāna*, T. *bsam gtan*). A meditative stabilization of the form realm.

different (*nānātva*, T. *tha dad*). Phenomena that are diverse.

different nature (T. *ngo bo tha dad*). Two things that can exist at different times and different places.

direct perceiver (*pratyakṣa*, T. *mngon sum*). Sautrāntikas: A nonmistaken knower that is free from conceptuality. Prāsaṅgikas: An awareness free from conceptuality; a manifest phenomenon.

direct reliable cognizer (*pratyakṣa-pramāṇa*, T. *mngon sum tshad ma*). Lower schools: A nondeceptive awareness that newly knows its object directly. Prāsaṅgikas: A nondeceptive awareness that knows its object directly or conceptually without depending on a reason.

distorted conception (inappropriate attention, *ayoniśo-manaskāra*, T. *tshul bzhin ma yin pa'i yid la byed pa, tshul min yid byed kyi rnam rtog*). Incorrect thoughts that project exaggerations and erroneous qualities on objects and that lead to the arising of afflictions.

divine identity (*devamāna*, T. *lha'i nga rgyal*). In tantric practice, the meditator's holding the identity of being the deity and having the compassion, wisdom, and skillful means of an awakened deity.

dream state (*svapnadarśana*, T. *rmi lam mthong ba*). One of the six yogas of Nāropā as set out by Gampopa.

drop (*bindu*, T. *thig le*). Subtle elements composed of red and white substances derived from the sperm and ovum of our parents that exist in the channels and cakras of human bodies. White drops are more prominent at the top of the head, and red drops below the navel.

dualistic appearance (*dvayābhātā*, T. *gnyis snang*). (1) The sense that subject and object are distinct and cut off, (2) the appearance of inherent existence.

duḥkha (P. *dukkha,* T. *sdug bsngal*). The unsatisfactory experiences of cyclic existence.

dzogchen. A tantric practice emphasizing meditation on the nature of mind, practiced primarily in the Nyingma tradition.

eight worldly concerns (*aṣṭalokadharma*, T. *'jig rten chos brgyad*). Attachment to material gain, fame, praise, and pleasure, and aversion to loss, disrepute, blame, and pain.

elaborations (proliferations, *prapañca*, P. *papañca*, T. *spros pa*). Ignorance and other mental fabrications that obscure the ultimate nature of phenomena, their emptiness.

empowerment (*abhiṣeka*, T. *dbang*). A ceremony conducted by a tantric master that introduces disciples to a deity and initiates them into the practice of that deity.

emptiness (*śūnyatā*, T. *stong pa nyid*). Madhyamaka: The lack of true existence.

engaged object (*pravṛtti-viṣaya*, T. *'jug yul*). The main object with which the mind is concerned. Syn. apprehended object.

enjoyment body (*saṃbhogakāya*). The buddha body that appears in the pure lands to teach ārya bodhisattvas.

erroneous (*viparyaya*, T. *log pa*, *phyin ci log pa*). Wrong, incorrect, perverted.

ethical restraints (*samaya*, T. *dam tshig*). In Yoga Tantra and Highest Yoga Tantra, the fourteen root precepts, eight heavy infractions (T. *sbom po*), and branch precepts. Also includes precepts for Mother Tantra. In the Sūtrayāna, these are the prātimokṣa precepts. In Kriyā and Caryā Tantras, they are the bodhisattva precepts.

example clear light (*metaphoric clear light*, T. *dpe'i 'od gsal*). The completion stage from the generation of the pristine wisdom of appearance that has arisen due to the dissolution of the winds in the indestructible drop at the heart—having untied the channel knots at the heart in dependence on (1) the internal conditions of vajra recitation and the stages of withdrawal of the two concentrations and (2) an external condition—a seal—until the achievement of an impure illusory body.

existent (*bhāva*, *sat*, T. *yod pa*). That which is perceivable by mind. Syn. phenomenon.

external objects (*bāhyārtha*, T. *phyi don*). (1) Sense objects. (2) In Yogācāra and Yogācāra-Svātantrika: Objects that appear distant and cut off from the consciousness perceiving them; objects that do not arise from the same latency as the consciousness cognizing it.

focal object (*ālambana*, T. *dmigs pa*). The main object the mind refers to or focuses on.

forceful projection (*parakāya-praveśa*, T. *grong 'jug*). Transference of one's consciousness into the body of a deceased being.

form body (*rūpakāya*). The buddha body in which a buddha appears to sentient beings; it includes the emanation and enjoyment bodies.

foundation-of-all (*ālaya*, T. *kun gzhi*). Yogācāra: A storehouse consciousness on which all latencies and karmic seeds are placed. It carries karmic seeds and latencies from one life to the next and is the self according to the Yogācāra-Scripture proponents. Sakya: The subtlest mind that is the basis of saṃsāra and nirvāṇa.

four empties. Four subtle consciousnesses—the empty, great empty, very empty, and all empty—that are used to realize emptiness but are not themselves emptiness.

four truths of the āryas (*catvāry āryasatyāni*). The truth of duḥkha, its origin, its cessation, and the path to that cessation.

free from conceptuality (*kalpanā-apoḍha*, T. *rtog bral*). Without the appearance of a conceptual appearance.

fruition (*vipāka*, T. *rnam smin*). A result; a neutral phenomenon included in the continuum of a sentient being that arises from a cause that is not neutral—that is, it arises from a cause that is either virtuous or nonvirtuous.

full awakening (*samyaksaṃbodhi*, T. *yang dag par rdzogs pa'i sangs rgyas*). Buddhahood; the state in which all obscurations have been abandoned and all good qualities developed limitlessly.

fundamental innate mind of clear light (T. *gnyug sems*). The subtlest level of mind, or consciousness, which has existed from beginningless time and abides perpetually in a latent form when coarser levels of mind are manifest.

Fundamental Vehicle (T. *theg dman*). The path leading to the liberation of śrāvakas and solitary realizers.

generation stage (T. *skyed rim*). A yoga that (1) is a meditation that newly and mentally imagines an aspect similar to any of the three—death, bardo, and rebirth—and that (2) does not arise from causing the winds to enter, abide, and dissolve in the central channel through the power of meditation but ripens the continuum so that one can progress to the completion stage in which that is done.

grasping inherent existence (*svabhāvasiddhi-graha*, T. *rang bzhin gyi grub pa 'dzin pa*). Grasping persons and phenomena to exist truly or inherently. Syn. grasping true existence (Prāsaṅgikas).

grasping true existence (*true-grasping, satyagrāha*, T. *bden 'dzin*). A consciousness grasping persons and phenomena to exist with an intrinsic essence.

ground (*bhūmi*, T. *sa*). Synonymous with path and exalted wisdom; one of ten divisions of an ārya bodhisattva's path to buddhahood.

Guhyasamāja (T. *gsang ba 'dus pa*). A deity of Highest Yoga Tantra.

having-ceased (*naṣṭa*, T. *zhig pa*). An affirming negative that is the "having happened" or "having ceased" of an event or an object.

Highest Yoga Tantra (*anuttarayoga tantra*, T. *rnal 'byor bla na med pa'i rgyud*). The most advanced of the four classes of tantra.

ignorance (*avidyā*, T. *ma rig pa*). A mental factor that is obscured and grasps the opposite of what exists. There are two types: ignorance regarding ultimate truth and ignorance regarding karma and its effects.

illusion-like emptiness (T. *sgyu ma lta bu'i stong nyid*). Having realized emptiness, things appear truly existent in break times between meditation sessions on emptiness, but practitioners know they aren't.

illusory body (*māyādeha, T. sgyu lus).* The form of the deity a meditator on the completion stage arises in. It may be pure or impure.

immediately preceding condition (*samanantara-pratyaya*, T. *de ma thag pa'i rkyen*). A moment of mind that acts as a cause for a perceiving consciousness to arise in the next moment.

impermanence (*anitya*, P. *anicca*, T. *mi rtag pa*). Momentariness; not remaining in the next moment. Coarse impermanence is the ending of a continuum; subtle impermanence is something not remaining the same in the very next moment.

imputedly existent (*prajñaptisat*, T. *btags yod*). (1) Prāsaṅgika: Something that exists by being merely designated by term and concept; (2) things imputed by thought that are abstract, conceptual entities; (3) something that can be identified only by cognizing one of its parts or attributes.

indestructible drop (*akṣarabindu*, T. *mi shigs pa'i thig le*). A tiny drop, white on top and red on the bottom, located inside the central channel at the heart cakra. It is of two types: (1) the eternal indestructible drop—the very subtle wind-mind that has existed from beginningless time and will remain until awakening; and (2) a lifetime indestructible drop—a subtle material object composed of the red and white drops received from our parents, which will cease at death. The former is enclosed within the latter.

independent (*sva-tantra*, T. *rang dbang*). Prāsaṅgikas: Inherent, self-powered, not dependent on anything else. Other tenet systems: Not dependent on causes and conditions.

indicative conceptions. Conceptions associated with the white appearance, red increase, and black near-attainment.

individual withdrawal (*pratyāhāra*, T. *sor sdud*). In Guhyasamāja, an isolated body practice that involves viewing sense objects as manifestations of bliss and emptiness. In Kālacakra, the first of six branches of the completion stage that newly establishes the deity body of empty form.

inference (*anumāna*, T. *rjes su dpag pa*). A conclusion reached through a syllogism on the basis of evidence and reasoning.

inherent existence (*svabhāvasiddhi*, P. *sabhāvasiddha*, T. *rang bzhin gyis grub pa*). Existence with its own self-powered nature able to set itself up.

innate (*sahaja*, T. *lhan skyes*). Existing with the mind from beginningless time; something not acquired anew in this life.

inner heat (*caṇḍālī*, T. *gtum mo*). *See* tummo.

insight (*vipaśyanā*, P. *vipassanā*, T. *lhag mthong*). A wisdom of thorough discrimination of phenomena conjoined with special pliancy induced by the power of analysis and conjoined with serenity.

interpretable (*neyārtha*, P. *neyyattha*, *T. drang don*). Prāsaṅgika: A scripture or statement that mainly speaks about the variety of phenomena; conventional truth.

isolated body (*T. lus dben*). The completion-stage practice done to isolate twenty coarse factors—the five aggregates, four elements, and so on—from ordinary appearance and grasping.

isolated mind (*T. sems dben*). The third level of the completion stage, during which one dissolves the winds into the indestructible drop at the heart.

isolated speech (*T. ngag dben*). The second level of the completion stage that involves uniting the sounds of breathing (inhaling, pausing, and exhaling) with the mantra *om ah hum*.

karma. Intentional action of body, speech, or mind.

karmamudrā (action consort). An actual consort who has accomplished the same stage of spiritual development as the yogi.

karmic seeds (T. *las kyi sa bon*). The potencies from previously created actions that will bring their results.

knowable object (*jñeya*, T. *shes bya*). That which is suitable to serve as an object of an awareness.

Kriyā Tantra (Action Tantra). A class of tantra that contains either the yoga with signs or the yoga without signs and emphasizes external activities, such as cleanliness, more than internal ones.

lamdre (path and result, *lam 'bras*). The path to awakening as set forth in the Sakya tradition.

latencies (*vāsanā*, T. *bag chags*). Predispositions, imprints, or tendencies.

leap-over (T. *thod rgal*). A tantric practice in the Nyingma tradition that creates the causes to actualize the form body and involves seeing all appearances as arising naturally and spontaneously from rigpa.

learners' union (T. *slob pa'i zung 'jug*). The fifth level of the completion stage, during which one attains a pure illusory body and abandons all afflictive obscurations.

liberated path (*vimuktimārga*, T. *rnam grol lam*). (1) Actual: induced by the uninterrupted path preceding it, a wisdom directly realizing emptiness that has completely eradicated a portion of defilements. (2) Similitude: a path that has temporarily suppressed a portion of the manifest afflictions.

liberation (*mokṣa*, T. *thar pa*). A true cessation that is the abandonment of all afflictive obscurations; nirvāṇa, the state of freedom from cyclic existence.

liberation (*vimukti*, P. *vimutti*, T. *rnam grol*). Sanskrit tradition: complete freedom from saṃsāra. Pāli tradition: a conditioned event that brings nirvāṇa.

light drop (*ābhāsabindu*, T. *'od thig*). A subtle drop of light visualized at the upper tip of the central channel while practicing vajra recitation.

Madhyamaka (T. *dbu ma*): A Mahāyāna tenet system that refutes true existence.

Mahāmudrā (Great Seal, T. *phyag rgya chen po*). A type of meditation that focuses on the conventional and ultimate natures of the mind; in Kriyā Tantra, meditating on method and wisdom.

mahāsiddhas (T. *grub chen*). Great adepts who have profound realizations and meditative attainments. Ancient propounders of the Vajrayāna textual tradition.

maṇḍala (*T. dkyil 'khor*). A circular diagram depicting either the ordinary universe or the environment of a deity.

manifest (*pratyakṣa*, T. *mngon gyur*). An existent is a manifest object in relation to an awareness that clearly realizes it; a phenomenon that can be known for the first time without relying on a correct reason is a manifest object.

manifest afflictions (T. *nyon mongs mngon gyur*). Afflictions active in the mind at the present moment (contrasted with seeds of afflictions).

mantra (T. *sngags*). Literally, protection for the mind. Sanskrit syllables recited during certain meditation practices.

mantra drop (*mantrabindu*, T. *sngags thig*). A subtle drop visualized at the heart cakra while doing completion-stage practice to bring winds from the upper and lower parts of the body to the area of the heart.

meditative equipoise on emptiness (T. *stong nyid rtogs pa'i mnyam bzhag ye shes*). An ārya's mind focused single-pointedly on the emptiness of inherent existence.

mental consciousness (*mano-vijñāna*). A consciousness that knows mental and sense objects in contradistinction to sense consciousnesses that know only sense objects.

mental continuum. See mindstream.

mental factor (*caitta*, T. *sems byung*). An aspect of mind that accompanies a primary consciousness and fills out the cognition, apprehending particular attributes of the object or performing a specific function.

merely designated by name (T. *ming du btags pa tsam*). The mode of existence asserted by Prāsaṅgikas.

mind (*citta*, T. *sems*). That which is clear and cognizant. The part of living beings that cognizes, experiences, thinks, feels, and so on. In some contexts it is equivalent to primary consciousness.

mindfulness (*smṛti*, P. *sati*, T. *dran pa*). A mental factor that brings to mind a phenomenon of previous acquaintance without forgetting it and prevents distraction to other objects.

mindstream (*cittasaṃtāna*, T. *sems kyi rgyun*). The continuum of a mind from one moment to the next, even spanning lifetimes.

mind-vajra (T. *sems rdo rje*). Dzogchen: Fundamental innate mind of clear light that is the basis of all phenomena of saṃsāra and nirvāṇa. Its manifestations in coarse forms are conventional truths that are its sport or play. It has the nature of being the truth body at buddhahood. Kālacakra: The subtlest clear-light mind.

mistaken (*bhrānta*, T. *'khrul ba*). (1) Conceptual consciousnesses whose objects appear by means of conceptual appearances; (2) consciousnesses apprehending conventional truths that cannot recognize the appearance of inherent existence as false.

momentary (*kṣaṇika*, T. *skad cig ma*). Not enduring to the next moment without changing.

monastic (*pravrajita*, *T. rab tu byung ba*). Someone who has received monastic ordination; a monk or nun.

mother clear light (T. *ma'i 'od gsal*). The subtlest mind that is naturally empty of inherent existence. It is always present and arises naturally at the time of death.

mudrā (*seal*, T. *phyag rgya*). Hand gestures used in tantric practices; partners used in higher completion-stage practices, either real (action seals) or visualized (wisdom seals).

nature truth body (*svabhāvika dharmakāya, svabhāva-kāya*, T. *ngo bo nyid sku*). The buddha body that is the emptiness of a buddha's mind and the true cessations in that buddha's continuum.

negative (*pratiṣedha*, T. *dgag pa*). An object comprehended by an awareness upon the explicit elimination of an object of negation. Equivalent with exclusion (*apoha*, T. *sel ba*), other exclusion (*anyāpoha*, T. *gzhan sel*), and isolate (*vyatireka*, T. *ldog pa*).

ngondro (T. *sngon 'gro*). Preliminary practices in Vajrayāna, such as prostrations, maṇḍala offering, taking refuge, recitation of the Vajrasattva mantra, and so forth.

nihilism (*ucchedānta*, P. *vibhavadiṭṭhi*, T. *med mtha'*). The belief that our actions have no ethical dimension; the belief that nothing exists.

nirvāṇa (T. *mya ngan las 'das pa*). The state of liberation of an arhat; the emptiness of a mind that has been totally cleansed of afflictive obscurations.

nominally different (T. *tha snyad du tha dad*). Two phenomena are nominally different when they are not the same thing and can be distinguished by conception.

nonabiding nirvāṇa (*apratiṣṭhita-nirvāṇa*, T. *mi gnas pa'i myang 'das*). A buddha's nirvāṇa that does not abide in either the extreme of cyclic existence or the extreme of personal liberation.

nonaffirming negative (*prasajyapratiṣedha*, T. *med dgag*). A negative phenomenon in which, upon the explicit elimination of the object of negation by an awareness, an affirmative phenomenon or an affirming negative is not suggested or established in place of the object of negation.

nonconceptual consciousness (*nirvikalpaka*, T. *rtog med shes pa*). A consciousness that apprehends its object directly, not by means of a conceptual appearance.

nondeceptive (*avisaṃvādi, amoṣa*, T. *mi slu ba*). (1) Incontrovertible, correct; (2) existing the way it appears to a reliable cognizer directly realizing it.

nonduality (T. *gnyis snang nub pa*). The nonappearance of subject and object, inherent existence, conventional truths, and conceptual appearances in an ārya's meditative equipoise on emptiness.

nonerroneous (*aviparīta*, T. *phyin ci ma log pa*). Correct, right.

nonexistent (*asat*, *abhāva*, T. *med pa*). That which is not perceivable by mind.

nonlearners' union (T. *mi slob pa'i zung 'jug*). Buddhahood; the final result of Highest Yoga Tantra practice in which all obscurations have been abandoned and all excellent qualities have been perfected.

non-mentation (T. *sems med pa*). A state in which, to a third party, a person appears to be without the normal mental functions of the waking state.

object (*viṣaya*, T. *yul*). That which is known by an awareness.

objective existence (*viṣayasiddhi*, T. *yul ngos nas grub pa*, *yul steng nas grub pa*). Existence by its own nature without being posited through the power of conventional designation.

object of negation (*pratiṣedhya*, T. *dgag bya*). What is negated or refuted.

one (*ekatva*, T. *gcig*). A singular phenomenon; a phenomenon that is not diverse; identical.

one nature. Two phenomena are one nature when they arise, abide, and cease simultaneously, and do not appear separate to direct perception.

ordinary appearance (T. *tha mal snang ba*). The appearance of ourselves as ordinary, limited sentient beings with afflictions and faults. Its tantric antidote is clear appearance—dissolving yourself into emptiness and your wisdom mind arising in the form of a deity.

ordinary being (*pṛthagjana*, T. *so so skye bo*). Someone who is not an ārya.

Pāramitāyāna (Perfection Vehicle). The non-tantric vehicle to full awakening practiced by bodhisattvas.

path (*mārga*, T. *lam*). An exalted knower that is conjoined with uncontrived renunciation.

path of accumulation (*sambhāramārga*, T. *tshogs lam*). The first of the five paths. In the Fundamental Vehicle it begins when one aspires for liberation day and night. In Pāramitāyāna, it begins when one has uncontrived bodhicitta. In Tantrayāna it extends from the common paths up to but not including the ability to directly induce the empties by causing the winds to enter and dissolve in the central channel by the power of meditation.

path of meditation (*bhāvanāmārga*, T. *sgom lam*). The fourth of the five paths. In the Fundamental Vehicle and Pāramitāyāna it begins when a meditator begins to eradicate innate afflictions from the root. In Tantrayāna it extends from the learners' union up to but not including the attainment of nonlearners' union.

path of no-more-learning (*aśaikṣamārga*, T. *mi slob lam*). The last of the five paths. In the Fundamental Vehicle it is arhatship or buddhahood. In Pāramitāyāna and Tantrayāna it is buddhahood.

path of preparation (*prayogamārga*, T. *sbyor lam*). The second of the five paths. In the Fundamental Vehicle and Pāramitāyāna it begins with attaining the union of serenity and insight on emptiness. In Tantrayāna it extends from directly inducing the empties by causing the winds to enter and dissolve in the central channel by the power of meditation up to but not including the illusory body directly realizing suchness with bliss.

path of seeing (*darśanamārga*, T. *mthong lam*). The third of the five paths. In the Fundamental Vehicle and Pāramitāyāna it begins when a meditator first has direct, nonconceptual realization of the emptiness of inherent existence. In Tantrayāna it extends from the actual clear light up to but not including the attainment of union.

Performance Tantra. *See* Caryā Tantra.

permanent (*nitya*, P. *nicca*, T. *rtag pa*). Unchanging, static, not momentarily changing. It does not mean eternal.

permissory ritual (T. *rjes gnang*). A meditative ceremony in which the recipient receives the inspiration of an awakened deity's body, speech, and mind and is qualified to do the practice of that deity.

person (*pudgala*, T. *gang zag*). A living being designated in dependence on the four or five aggregates.

pervasion (*anvayavyāpti*, T. *rjes khyab*). The major premise of a correct syllogism; the relationship between the reason and the predicate: whatever is the reason is necessarily the predicate.

pollutant (*āsrava*, P. *āsava*, T. *zag pa*). A set of three or four deeply rooted defilements: sensual desire, existence (craving to exist in a saṃsāric form), and ignorance. Some lists add view.

polluted (*āsrava*, P. *āsava*, T. *zag bcas*). Under the influence of ignorance or its latencies.

positive (affirmative, *vidhi*, T. *sgrub pa*). A phenomenon that is not realized by the conceptual consciousness apprehending it by explicitly eliminating an object of negation.

potency (*śakti*, T. *nus pa*). The energy or ability to bring a result.

Prāsaṅgika Madhyamaka (T. *dbu ma thal 'gyur ba*). A Mahāyāna tenet system that asserts that all phenomena lack inherent existence both conventionally and ultimately.

pristine wisdom (*jñāna*, T. *ye shes*). A realization in the continuum of someone who has entered a path.

probing awareness (reasoning consciousness, *yuktijñāna*, T. *rigs shes*). A consciousness using reasoning to analyze the ultimate or conventional nature of an object. It can be either conceptual or nonconceptual.

pure land (*kṣetraśuddhi*, T. *dag zhing*). Places created by the unshakable resolve and merit of buddhas where all external conditions are conducive for Dharma practice.

reality (*dharmatā*, T. *chos nyid*). The emptiness of inherent existence.

realization (*adhigama*, T. *rtogs pa*). An awareness that eliminates superimpositions on an object and is able to induce ascertainment of a phenomenon. It may be either inferential or direct.

reason (sign, *liṅga*, T. *rtags*). The part of a syllogism that proves the thesis.

red increase (T. *mched pa dmar lam pa*). A subtle mind that arises in the sixth stage of the death process, a clear vacuity filled with red light like when the sun sets.

reliable cognizer (*pramāṇa*, T. *tshad ma*). Prāsaṅgika: A nondeceptive awareness that is incontrovertible with respect to its principal object and that enables us to accomplish our purpose.

retention (T. *'dzin pa).* A completion-stage practice of holding the winds inside the central channel that is done to facilitate attaining a buddha's vajra speech.

rigpa. Dzogchen: The subtlest level of awareness, untainted by stains and devoid of coarser levels of mind, although it permeates them.

sādhana. A tantric liturgical manual containing instructions to carry out the practice of a meditational deity.

samādhi. See concentration.

samaya. The commitments (close bonds) of tantric precepts that those who have received empowerment in Highest Yoga Tantra pledge to keep.

Sautrāntika (T. *mdo sde pa*). A Fundamental Vehicle tenet system that asserts that functional things are ultimate truths and phenomena that exist by being imputed by thought are conventional truths.

seed (*bīja*, T. *sa bon*). The potency to bring a result.

self (*ātman*, P. *attā*, T. *bdag*). (1) a person, (2) inherent existence, (3) a permanent soul.

self-generation (T. *bdag bskyed*). The deity that one becomes after meditating on emptiness and imagining the wisdom realizing emptiness appearing as that deity.

self-grasping (*ātmagrāha*, T. *bdag 'dzin*). Grasping a wrong mode of existence of persons or other phenomena. Prāsaṅgikas: Grasping inherent existence.

sentient being (*sattva*, T. *sems can*). Any being with a mind, except for a buddha.

serenity (*śamatha*, P. *samatha*, T. *zhi gnas*). Sanskrit tradition: Concentration arisen from meditation that is accompanied by the bliss of mental and physical pliancy in which the mind abides effortlessly without fluctuation for as long as we wish on whatever virtuous object the mind has been placed. Pāli tradition: One-pointedness of mind; the eight attainments (meditative absorptions) that are the basis for insight.

signlessness (*animitta*, T. *mtshan ma med pa*). The emptiness that is the absence of inherent existence of the cause of any phenomenon.

six perfections (*ṣaḍpāramitā*, T. *phar phyin drug*). The practices of generosity, ethical conduct, fortitude, joyous effort, meditative stability, and wisdom that are motivated by bodhicitta.

solitary realizer (*pratyekabuddha*, T. *rang rgyal*). A person following the Fundamental Vehicle who seeks liberation, emphasizes understanding the twelve links of dependent arising, and does not rely on a spiritual guide during their last rebirth before attaining liberation.

śrāvaka (hearer, P. *sāvaka*, T. *nyan thos*). Someone practicing the Fundamental Vehicle path leading to arhatship who emphasizes meditation on the four truths.

stabilizing meditation (*sthāpyabhāvanā*, T. *'jog sgom*). Meditation to focus and concentrate the mind on an object.

subsequent mindfulness (*anusmṛti*, T. *rjes su dran pa*). The fifth branch of the Kālacakra completion stage that involves practicing with either an imaginary or actual seal and engaging in the three conducts, causing the inner heat (tummo) to blaze.

substance drop (*dravyabindu*, *T. rdzas thig*). A subtle drop composed of red and white drops imagined at the lower tip of the central channel in completion-stage practice to facilitate the winds entering the indestructible drop at the heart. In some contexts, it is called the seminal drop.

substantial cause (*upādāna-kāraṇa*, T. *nyer len gyi rgyu*). The cause that becomes the result, as opposed to cooperative conditions that aid the substantial cause in becoming the result.

subtle afflictions (T. *nyon mongs phra mo*). Afflictions stemming from grasping inherent existence (contrasted with coarse afflictions).

suchness (*tattva*, T. *de kho na nyid*). Emptiness, the way things really are.

superimposition (*samāropa*, T. *sgro btags, sgro 'dogs*). The imputing or projecting of something that does not exist: for example, a self of persons.

supporting and supported maṇḍala. The supporting maṇḍala is the deity's environment, the supported maṇḍala are the deities in the maṇḍala.

supramundane (transcendental, *lokottara*, P. *lokuttara*, T. *'jig rten las 'das pa*). Pertaining to the elimination of fetters and afflictions; pertaining to āryas.

Svātantrika Madhyamaka (T. *dbu ma rang rgyud pa*). A Mahāyāna tenet system asserting that phenomena do not exist inherently on the ultimate level but do exist inherently on the conventional level.

Tantra (T. *rgyud*). An advanced form of Mahāyāna Buddhism with special techniques to attain awakening; a text on Tantra; the tantric path in contrast to Sūtra, the sūtric path; continuum. Syn. Vajrayāna; Mantrayāna.

tathāgata (T. *de bzhin gshegs pa*). A buddha.

tenet (*siddhānta*, T. *grub mtha'*). A philosophical assertion or belief.

tenet system/school (T. *grub mtha'i lugs*). A set of philosophical assertions regarding the basis, path, and result that is shared by a group of people.

thing (*bhāva*, *vastu*; T. *dngos po*). (1) something that can perform a function, syn. product; (2) phenomenon.

thought (*kalpanā*, T. *rtog pa*). Conceptual consciousness.

three conducts (T. *spyod pa gsum*) Practices that are with, without, or completely without elaboration done by yogis to enhance their practice of the path.

three natures (*trisvabhāva*, T. *mtshan nyid gsum*). A classification of all phenomena in the Yogācāra presentation into imaginary, dependent (other-powered), and consummate natures.

three realms (*tridhātuka*, P. *tedhātuka*). Desire, form, and formless realms.

transference of consciousness (*saṃkrānti*, T. *'pho ba*). (1) A meditative practice done at the time of death to transfer the mental continuum to a pure land; (2) a meditative practice, which is no longer done, to transfer the consciousness into the body of a deceased being in order to continue Dharma practice without having to take another rebirth.

true cessation (*nirodhasatya*, T. *'gog bden*). The cessation of a portion of afflictions or all afflictions; the cessation of a portion of cognitive obscurations or all cognitive obscurations.

true existence (*satyasat*, T. *bden par yod pa*). Prāsaṅgika: Existence in its own right without being merely imputed by name and concept. Svātantrika: Establishment as its own mode of abiding without being posited through the force of appearing to a nondefective awareness.

true-grasping. See "grasping true existence."

truth body (*dharmakāya*, T. *chos sku*). The buddha body that includes the nature truth body and the wisdom truth body.

tsog offering (*gaṇacakra*, T. *tshogs kyi 'khor lo*). A tantric offering ritual that is often done on the tenth and twenty-fifth days of each lunar month.

tummo (*caṇḍālī*, T. *gtum mo*). The completion-stage practice of inner heat, done to generate a blissful subtle mind that realizes emptiness.

twelve links of dependent origination (*dvādaśāṅga-pratītyasamutpāda*, T. *rten 'brel yan lag bcu gnyis*). A system of twelve factors that explains how we take rebirth in saṃsāra and how we can be liberated from it.

two truths (*satyadvaya*, P. *saccadvaya*, T. *bden pa gnyis*). Ultimate truths and veiled (conventional) truths.

ultimate analysis (T. *don dam pa'i dpyod pa*). Analysis that examines what an object really is and its deeper mode of existence.

ultimate existence (*paramārthasiddhi*, T. *don dam par grub pa*). Prāsaṅgika: Existence such that when the object is sought with ultimate analysis, it is found. Svātantrika: Existence by an object's own uncommon mode of subsistence without being posited by the force of appearing to a nondefective awareness.

ultimate truth (*paramārthasatya*, P. *paramattha-sacca*, T. *don dam bden pa*). The ultimate mode of existence of all persons and phenomena; emptiness; objects that are true and appear true to their main cognizer, a wisdom nonconceptually and directly realizing emptiness.

uninterrupted path (*ānantarya-mārga*, T. *bar chad med lam*). (1) Actual: a wisdom directly realizing emptiness that is in the process of eliminating some portion of defilements; (2) similitude: a path that is in the process of temporarily suppressing some portion of manifest afflictions.

union of bliss and emptiness. An indivisible union of the mind of great bliss and the wisdom realizing emptiness, where the two minds are integrated and become one entity.

union of serenity and insight (*śamatha-vipaśyanā-yuganaddha*, T. *zhi lhag zung 'brel*). Absorption on emptiness in which the bliss of mental and physical pliancy has been induced by analysis. This marks the first moment of the path of preparation.

union with abandonment (T. *spangs pa zung 'jug*). Union of the pure illusory body and the abandonment of all afflictive obscurations attained on the fifth level of the completion stage.

union with realization (T. *rtogs pa zung 'jug*). Union of the pure illusory body and the actual clear light attained on the fifth level of the completion stage.

unpolluted (*anāsrava*, T. *zag med*). Not under the influence of ignorance; not under the influence of ignorance and the latencies of ignorance.

vajra body (T. *rdo rje sku*). A pure illusory body with the signs and marks of a buddha that is not associated with afflictive obscurations and can continue to buddhahood.

vajra recitation (T. *rdo rje'i bzlas pa*). The practice of linking mantra recitation with the breath.

vase breathing (*kumbhaka*, T. *rlung bum pa can*). A practice that involves holding or containing the breath in a way that is analogous to a vase. It is used in the practice of tummo and in cultivating serenity.

vast and profound. Meditation on the method aspect of the path (vast) combined with the wisdom aspect of the path (profound).

veiled truths (*saṃvṛtisatya*, P. *sammuti-sacca*, T. *kun rdzob bden pa*). Objects that are true only from the perspective of ignorance; objects that appear to exist inherently to their main cognizer. This includes all phenomena except ultimate truths. Syn. conventional truths.

Vinaya (T. *'dul ba*). Monastic discipline.

vitality-exertion (*prāṇāyāma*, T. *srog rtsol*). A practice found in all tantric classes for gaining control over the wind. In Highest Yoga Tantra, it is done to move the winds from the side channels into the central channel. Also known as wind yoga, breath control.

white appearance (T. *snang ba dkar lam pa*). A subtle mind that arises in the fifth stage of the death process, a vacuity filled with white light like moonlight.

wind (*prāṇa*, T. *rlung*). Subtle energy on which levels of consciousness ride. One of the four elements; energy in the body that influences bodily functions.

wind yoga. *See* vitality-exertion.

wisdom being (*jñānasattva, T. ye shes sems dpa'*). Deities throughout the universe that are invoked and dissolve into the meditator, who is visualized as the commitment being.

wisdom mudrā/seal (*jñānamudrā*, T. *ye shes kyi phyag rgya*). A visualized partner who helps to dissolve winds into the indestructible drop at the heart.

wisdom truth body (*jñāna dharmakāya*, T. *ye shes chos ku*). The buddha body that is a buddha's omniscient mind.

withdrawal (*pratyāhāra*, T. *sor sdud*). The practice of withdrawing or dissolving the winds into the central channel. It is of two types: (1) gradual (final dissolution, T. *rjes gbig*), and (2) instantaneous (holding the body entirely, T. *ril 'dzin*).

yoga (T. *rnal 'byor*). A practice to connect with what is authentic. Highest Yoga Tantra: A union, in one consciousness, of bliss and emptiness.

Yoga Tantra (T. *rnal 'byor rgyud*). The third class of Tantra that emphasizes internal activities and includes some external activities.

yoga with signs (T. *mtshan bcas kyi rnal 'byor*). The meditative techniques of deity yoga that are separate from meditation on emptiness.

yoga without signs (T. *mtshan med kyi rnal 'byor*). The meditative techniques of deity yoga that are done together with meditation on emptiness.

Yogācāra (*Cittamātra*, T. *rnal 'byor spyod pa, sems tsam pa*). A Mahāyāna tenet system that asserts the true existence of other-powered natures but does not assert external objects.

yogi/yoginī (T. *rnal 'byor pa/ma*). A meditator on suchness.

yogic direct reliable cognizers (T. *rnal 'byor mngon sum tshad ma*). Nondeceptive mental consciousnesses that know their objects by depending on a union of serenity and insight.

Recommended Reading

Tantras

Vajra Rosary Tantra. Śrī Vajramālā Tantra. Translated by David R. Kittay and Lozang Jamspal as *The Vajra Rosary Tantra: An Explanatory Tantra of the Glorious King of Tantras, the Esoteric Community Tantra.* Somerville, MA: Wisdom Publications, 2020.

Sources for Study by Indian Authors

Āryadeva. *Four Hundred Stanzas on the Middle Way. Catuḥśataka.*

———. *Lamp for Integrating the Practices. Caryāmelāpakapradīpa.* Translated by Christian K. Wedemeyer as *Āryadeva's Lamp That Integrates the Practices: The Gradual Path of Vajrayana Buddhism according to the Esoteric Community Noble Tradition.* New York: American Institute of Buddhist Studies, 2007.

Asaṅga. *Śrāvaka Grounds. Śrāvakabhūmi.*

Bhāvaviveka. *Blaze of Reasoning. Tarkajvālā.*

———. *Heart of the Middleway. Madhyamakahṛdayakārikā.*

———. *Lamp of Wisdom. Prajñāpradīpa.*

Buddhapālita. *Commentary on "Treatise on the Middle Way." Buddhapālitamūlamadhyamakavṛtti.*

Candrakīrti. *Clear Words. Prasannapadā.*

———. *Supplement to the "Treatise on the Middle Way." Madhyamakāvatāra.*

Dharmakīrti. *Commentary on the Compendium of Reliable Cognition. Pramāṇavārttika.*

Kamalaśīla. *Stages of Meditation. Bhāvanākrama.*

Maitreya. *Discrimination of the Middle and Extremes. Madhyānta-vibhāgakārikā.*

———. *Ornament of Mahāyāna Sūtras. Mahāyānasūtrālaṃkāra.*

———. *Sublime Continuum. Uttaratantra.*

Nāgabodhi. *The Twenty Procedural Points of the Generation-Stage Maṇḍala.*

Nāgārjuna. *Precious Garland. Ratnāvalī.* Translated by John Dunne and Sara McClintock as *Nāgārjuna's Precious Garland*. Boston: Wisdom Publications, 2024.

———. *Treatise on the Middle Way. Mūlamadhyamakakārikā.*

Śāntideva. *Engaging in the Bodhisattvas' Deeds. Bodhicaryāvatāra.*

Sources for Study by Tibetan Authors

Clarifying the Meanings of Kriyā Tantra. Bya rgyud dongsal.

Dalai Lama. *Deity Yoga: In Action and Performance Tantra*. Ithaca, NY: Snow Lion Publications, 1981.

———. *Dzogchen: The Heart Essence of the Great Perfection*. Boulder, CO: Shambhala Publications, 2020.

———. *The Heart of Meditation: Discovering Innermost Awareness*. Translated and edited by Jeffrey Hopkins. Boulder, CO: Shambhala Publications, 2016.

———. *The Union of Bliss and Emptiness: Teachings on the Practice of Guru Yoga*. Translated by Thubten Jinpa. Ithaca, NY: Snow Lion Publications, 1988.

———. *The Universe in a Single Atom*. New York: Harmony, 2006.

Dalai Lama, Tsong-ka-pa, and Jeffrey Hopkins. *Tantra in Tibet*. Ithaca, NY: Snow Lion Publications, 1977.

Deschung Rinpoche. *The Three Levels of Spiritual Perception: A Commentary on The Three Visions*. Translated by Jared Rhoton. Somerville, MA: Wisdom Publications, 2003.

Dodrup Jigme Tenpai Nyima. *General Exposition of the "Secret Essence Tantra." Gsang snying spyi don.*

Gampopa. *Jeweled Ornament of Liberation. Dam chos yid bzhin gyi nor bu thar pa rin po che'i rgyan.*

Gyaltsen, Kachen Yeshe. *Manjushri's Innermost Secret: A Profound Commentary of Oral Instructions on the Practice of Lama Chopa*. Translated by David Gonsalez. Somerville, MA: Wisdom Publications, 2019.

Kensur Jampa Tegchok. *Practical Ethics and Profound Emptiness*. Translated by Steve Carlier, edited by Thubten Chodron. Boston, MA: Wisdom Publications, 2017.

Khedrup Gelek Palzang. *General Exposition of Tantras. Rgyud sde spyi'i rnam gzhag.*

———. *Ocean of Attainments of the Generation Stage. Bskyed rim ngo bsgrub rgya mtsho.*

Khedrup Norsang Gyatso. *Lamp for Clarifying the Samaya. Dam tshig gsal ba'i sgron me.*

Kirti Tsenshap Rinpoche. *Principles of Buddhist Tantra*. Translated and edited by Ian Coghlan and Voula Zarpani. Boston, MA: Wisdom Publications, 2011.

Kongtrul, Jamgon. *Creation and Completion: Essential Points of Tantric Meditation*. Translated by Sarah Harding. Boston, MA: Wisdom Publications, 1996.

Lingpa, Jigme, Patrul Rinpoche, and Getse Mahapandita. *Deity Mantra and Wisdom: Development Stage Meditation in Tibetan Buddhist Tantra*. Translated by the Dharmachakra Translation Committee. Ithaca, NY: Snow Lion Publications: 2006.

Lodoe, Yangchen Gawai. *Paths and Grounds of Guhyasamaja according to Arya Nagarjuna*. Dharamsala, India: LTWA, 1995.

Longchenpa. *Mind at Ease. Sems nyid ngal gso.*

———. *Treasury of Philosophical Tenets. Grub mtha' mdzod.*

———. *Treasury of the Supreme Vehicle. Theg mchog mdzod.*

———. *Treasury of the Ultimate Expanse. Chos dbyings mdzod.*

———. *Treasury of the Wish-Fulfilling Jewel. Yid bzhin mdzod.*

Losang Chokyi Gyaltsen. *Essence of the Five Stages. Rim lnga snying po.*

———. *The Essence of the "Ocean of Attainments of the Generation Stage." Bskyed rim dngos grub rgya mtsho'i snying po*. Translated by Yael Bentor and Penpa Dorjee as *The Essence of the Ocean of Attainments: The Creation Stage of the Guhyasamāja Tantra according to Panchen Lobsang Chokyi Gyaltsen*. Somerville, MA: Wisdom Publications, 2019.

Patrul Rinpoche and Dilgo Khyentse Rinpoche. *The Heart Treasure of the Enlightened Ones: The Practice of View, Meditation, and Action*. Boston: Shambhala Publications, 1992.

Rabjam, Longchen. *The Practice of Dzogchen*. Translated by Tulku Thondup. Ithaca, NY: Snow Lion Publications, 1989.

Sakya Paṇḍita. *Clear Differentiation of the Three Ethical Codes* (*Sdom gsum rab dbye*). Translated by Jared Douglas Rhoton. Albany: State University of New York, 2002.

Samten, Geshe Ngawang, and Jay L. Garfield, trans. *Ocean of Reasoning by rJe Tsong Khapa*. New York: Oxford University Press, 2006.

Tharchin, Sermey Khensur Lobsang. *Six-Session Guru Yoga: An Oral Commentary with a Detailed Explanation of the Bodhisattva and Tantric Vows*. Howell, NJ: Mahayana Sutra and Tantra Press, 1999.

Trijang Rinpoche, and Aku Sherab Gyatso. *Healing Nectar of Immortality: White Tara Healing & Longevity Practices and Commentary*. Translated by David Gonsalez. Seattle, WA: Dechen Ling Press, 2012.

Tsering, Geshe Tashi. *Tantra: The Foundation of Buddhist Thought, Volume 6*. Somerville, MA: Wisdom Publications, 2012.

Tsongkhapa. *Commentary to the Fifty Verses on the Guru. Bla ma lnga bcu pa'i rnam bshad.*

———. *Explanation of the Root Downfalls in Tantra. Snags kyi rtsa ltung gi rnam bshad.*

———. *Explanation of the Systematic Stages [of Guhyasamāja]. Rnam bzhag rim pa'i rnam bshad.*

———. *Great Exposition of Secret Mantra. Sngags rim chen mo.* Translated by Thomas Freeman Yarnall as *Great Treatise on the Stages of Mantra: Chapters XI–XII, The Creation Stage.* New York: American Institute of Buddhist Studies, 2013.

———. *Great Treatise on the Stages of the Path to Awakening. Lam rim chen mo.*

———. *Lamp Illuminating the Five Stages of the Completion Stage. Rdzogs rim rim lnga gsal sgron.* Translated by Gavin Kilty as *A Lamp to Illuminate the Five Stages: Teachings on Guhyasamāja Tantra.* Somerville, MA: Wisdom Publications, 2013. Also translated by Robert A. F. Thurman as *The Brilliantly Illuminating Lamp of the Five Stages by Tsong Khapa Losang Drakpa.* Somerville, MA: Wisdom Publications, 2019.

———. *Ocean of Reasoning. Rigs pa'i rgya mtsho.*

———. *Praise to Dependent Arising. Rten 'brel bstod pa.*

———. *Tantric Ethics: An Explanation of the Precepts for Buddhist Vajrayāna Practice.* Translated by Gareth Sparham. Somerville, MA: Wisdom Publications, 2005.

Yeshe, Lama. *Becoming the Compassion Buddha: Tantric Mahāmudrā for Everyday Life.* Edited by Robina Courtin. Somerville, MA: Wisdom Publications, 2003.

———. *Becoming Vajrasattva: The Tantric Path of Purification.* Somerville, MA: Wisdom Publications, 2004.

———. *Introduction to Tantra: The Transformation of Desire.* Somerville, MA: Wisdom Publications, 2001.

Zopa Rinpoche. *Abiding in Retreat: A Nyung Nä Commentary.* Boston: Lama Yeshe Wisdom Archive, 2017.

———. *A Chat about Heruka*. PDF only: https://www.lamayeshe.com/article/teaching-heruka. Access restricted to those with full Heruka or Vajrayogini empowerment.

———. *A Chat about Yamantaka*. PDF only: https://www.lamayeshe.com/shop/teaching-yamantaka-download-only-0. Access restricted to those with Yamantaka empowerment.

Sources by Western Authors

Burchardi, Anne. "A Look at the Diversity of the Gzhan stong Tradition." *Journal of the International Association of Tibetan Studies* 3 (2007): 1–24. http://www.thlib.org?tid=T3128.

Chodron, Thubten. *Cultivating a Compassionate Heart: The Yoga Method of Chenrezig*. Ithaca, NY: Snow Lion Publications, 2005.

———. *How to Free Your Mind: The Practice of Tara the Liberator*. Boston: Snow Lion Publications, 2013.

Cozort, Daniel. *Highest Yoga Tantra*. Ithaca, NY: Snow Lion Publications, 1986.

Guarisco, Elio, and Ingrid McLeod, trans. *Systems of Buddhist Tantra: The Indestructible Way of Secret Mantra*. Ithaca, NY: Snow Lion Publications, 2005.

Hopkins, Jeffrey. *Ngag-wang-pal-dan's "Grounds and Paths of the Four Great Secret Tantra Sets."* Palmyra, VA: UMA Institute for Tibetan Studies, 2018.

———. *Tantric Techniques*. Ithaca, NY: Snow Lion Publications, 2008.

Jackson, Roger R. *Mind Seeing Mind: Mahāmudrā and the Geluk Tradition of Tibetan Buddhism*. Somerville, MA: Wisdom Publications, 2019.

Mullin, Glenn. *Selected Works of the Dalai Lama I: Bridging the Sutras and Tantras*. Ithaca, NY: Snow Lion Publications, 1985.

Preece, Rob. *Preparing for Tantra: Creating the Psychological Ground for Practice*. Ithaca, NY: Snow Lion Publications, 2011.

———. *The Psychology of Buddhist Tantra*. Ithaca, NY: Snow Lion Publications, 2006.

Roberts, Peter Alan, trans. *Mahāmudrā and Related Instructions: Core Teachings of the Kagyu Schools.* Somerville, MA: Wisdom Publications, 2011.

Stearns, Cyrus, trans. *Taking the Results as the Path: Core Teachings of the Sakya Lamdre Tradition.* The Library of Tibetan Classics 4. Somerville, MA: Wisdom Publications, 2006.

Wilson, Martin. *In Praise of Tara: Songs to the Savioress.* Somerville, MA: Wisdom Publications, 1996.

Index

A

Abhayākaragupta, 93, 310, 364n108
Abhidharma, 163
absolutism, 77, 320
action seal. *See* karmamudrā
Action Tantra. *See* Kriyā Tantra
actual clear light, 8, 192, 245, 247
  and example, differences in, 195, 230
  in Highest Yoga Tantra, 15, 41
  and illusory body, uniting, 14, 25–26, 30, 161, 195, 197, 229, 357n7 (*see also* union with realization)
  manifesting, xvii, 130–31, 197, 201–2, 242
  meaning of, 240
  as substantial cause of truth body, 21
  as ultimate meaning, 241
affirmative phenomenon, 304, 318–19, 364n113
affirming negation, 17, 304
afflictions, 5, 18, 174–75
  as adventitious, 3, 7, 14
  clear-light nature of, 291, 325
  five primary, correlates, 217
  mind-vajra and, 303
  in Pāramitāyāna and Guhyasamāja, distinctions, 308
  recognizing, 341
  in subtle mind, 159
  two ways of understanding, 131–32
  ultimate and temporary antidotes, distinctions, 11–12
  utilizing in path, 134–36
afflictive obscurations, 197
  cessation, 195, 201
  in completion stage, 20
  direct antidote, 240, 242
  eradicating, 243, 245
  in example clear light, 230
  Pāramitāyāna and Highest Yoga Tantra in eradicating, distinctions, 29–30
aggregates, 89, 333
  correlates, 93, 216, 217, 361n67
  in deity yoga, 17–18
  as deity's sport, 334
  dissolution, imagined, 218
  emptiness of, 112
  impermanence of, 135
  rebirth and, 323
  self and, 321–22
  at time of death, 166–68
Akaniṣṭha Pure Abode, 78, 123–24
Ākāśagarbha, 361n69
Akṣobhya, 93, 96, 119, 216, 361n67, 362n72
Aku Sherab Gyatso; *Sacred Words of Akṣobhya*, 154
alcohol and intoxicants, 78–79, 83
all-encompassing yoga, xvi, 85
  advice on, 343–44
  instructions, 87–90
Amitābha, 93, 98, 119, 216, 361n67
Amitāyus, 96

Amoghasiddhi, 93, 119, 216, 361n67
analogies and examples
  binoculars, 159
  child holding fragile cup, 75
  crystals, 325
  insect born in wood, 134
  magician's illusions, 337
  mother stricken with grief, 23
  pond water, 325
  reflections, 37, 113, 232
  sandalwood, lighting fire to, 42
  sesame seed and oil, 325
  sprout and seed, 293
  tortoise contracting limbs, 101
  two wings of bird, 9
  water mixed with water, 228
  wind and flame, 134
Analapramohani, 96
analytical meditation, 21, 28
  in Action Tantra, 100
  in generation stage, 187
  in Highest Yoga Tantra, 188
  in mahāmudrā, 297
  in Sakya, 298
  in self-generation, 137
  and stabilizing, alternating, 19, 104–5, 109–10, 116, 121
  in Sūtra and Tantra, distinctions, 163
  tantric practice and, 68, 296, 297
Ānandagarbha, 117, 123, 124
anger, 5, 49, 259
  antidote, temporary, 11–12
  correlates, 217
  taking into path, 38, 134, 135
  winds and, 153, 164
Anuttarayoga Tantra. *See* Highest Yoga Tantra
Anuyoga tantra, 82, 279
appearing objects, 141, 162–63, 359n49
apprehended objects, 11, 162, 229
arhats, 15, 197, 243, 245
arrogance, 4, 5, 42, 51, 70, 177, 217, 344
ārya bodhisattvas, 8, 16, 18, 22–23, 122, 172, 205, 210
Ārya Parent and Child tradition, 195, 196, 212, 251, 361n63
Āryadeva, 35, 171
  Four Hundred Stanzas on the Middle Way, 36, 275, 287, 336, 346
  Lamp for Integrating the Practices, 302–3
Asaṅga, 7, 273, 310, 318
  Compendium of Knowledge, 275
  Śrāvaka Grounds, 105
Aśvaghoṣa; *Fifty Verses on the Guru*, 47, 49
Atiśa, 55, 82, 272. See also *Lamp for the Path to Enlightenment*
Atiyoga tantra, 82, 279. *See also* dzogchen
attachment, 5, 18, 38, 47, 49, 333, 353
  correlates, 217
  preliminary practices and, 61
  to sense objects, 259
  to tantric practice, 80
  utilizing on path, 134–35
  winds and, 101, 151
attainments. *See* siddhis (feats, attainments)
Avalokiteśvara (Chenrezig), 94–95, 96, 97–99, 257, 344. *See also* One-Thousand-Armed Avalokiteśvara
awakening, 39, 42–43, 55, 200. *See also* full awakening

B

bardo (intermediate state), 175–76, 201, 232
  awakening in, 148, 242, 254
  correlates, 234, 235
  generation stage and, 143, 181
  mixed with enjoyment body, 204
  ordinary and realized beings in, distinctions, 130
  purifying, 174–75, 189, 192
  taking into path to enjoyment body, 144, 172–73, 345, 360n57
bardo body/bardo being, 156, 171, 172, 174, 201, 231, 232

Bhāvaviveka, 274, 314, 315, 347
black near-attainment
  bardo and, 174, 231
  as conceptual, 362n79
  in dying process, 8, 165, 175–76, 218, 230
  impure illusory body and, 233
  latencies of, 243
  two phases, 162, 165, 170–71
  as yogic experience, 203, 209, 219, 242, 303
bliss, 197, 237, 364n115
  as antidote, 296
  without emptiness, 328
  in four tantra classes, 127
  method of, 12–13
  of pliancy, 105
  types of, 326–28
  See also great bliss; union of bliss and emptiness
Bodhgaya, 9
bodhicitta, 10, 334
  benefits of, 343
  in Buddhist practices, 40
  contrived and actual, 11
  in devotional practices, 39
  importance of practicing, 73, 85, 268, 341, 342, 354, 355
  mindfulness of, 333
  in Pāramitāyāna and Vajrayāna, compared, 15–16
  as preliminary practice, 62
  reinforcing, 125
  samādhi of not forgetting, 117
  in self-generation, 76
  in Sūtra, 22–23
  symbols of, 90
  in utilizing afflictions, 135
  in Vajrayāna, 1, 42, 50–53, 68
  and wisdom, relationship of, 3
  See also conventional bodhicitta; ultimate bodhicitta
bodhicitta drops
  bliss from, 135, 228
  melting, 142, 157, 219, 249–50, 253
  red and white, 154, 157, 165
  in refined generation stage, 138
  See also subtle drops
Bodhisattva Vehicle, xiii, 10, 278. *See also* Pāramitāyāna
bodhisattva vow, 347
bodhisattvas, 9, 15, 18, 22–24, 78. *See also* ārya bodhisattvas
body
  course, 75, 133, 153, 154, 359n44
  course winds and, 160
  defilements, coarse and subtle, 128–29
  formation of, 158
  and mind, relationship of, 40, 153–55
  and mind, separation of, 230–31
  self and, 321–22
  subtlest, 30, 40–41, 133, 153, 155, 159, 175, 198, 206, 359n44
  at time of death, 164, 166–68
  See also subtle body
body maṇḍala, 66, 93, 180, 260
Bon tradition, 363n89
brain, 152, 153, 158, 159, 324
breakthrough (T. *khregs chod*), 27, 279–80, 282–83, 297, 304, 309
breath, cessation of, 202–3
buddha families
  five, 58, 63, 65, 93, 111, 117, 118
  numbers of, 216–18, 361n71
  three, 96
buddha nature, 133, 276. *See also* tathāgatagarbha
Buddha Śākyamuni, 172, 315
  asceticism of, 277
  faith in, 266
  first teaching of, 6
  parinirvāṇa of, 9
  as principal of family, 96
  as role model, 343
  tantric teachings from, 34–35, 257
  on teaching Dharma, 5
  three secrets of, 26
  visualizing, 84, 132
  Yoga Tantra awakening of, 123–24
Buddhaguhya, 108, 117, 123

buddhahood, 128–30, 198, 202, 247, 333
appearances at, 142
compassion and, 85–86
four perfect results at, 21, 29, 357n9
in four tantra classes, 27–28, 121, 123
in four Tibetan traditions, 309
Highest Yoga Tantra method for, 26, 193
indestructible drop and, 360n54
method and wisdom at, 22, 114, 115
potential for, presence of, 292
in single lifetime, 43, 82–83, 123, 180, 193, 253–54, 334
tantric aspiration for, 20–21
See also full awakening
Buddhajñāna; *Means of Attainment Called "All Good"*, 140
Buddhapālita, 274, 289, 314, 315, 318, 347
Buddhism
body and mind in, 152–53
broad education in, 351
and science, commonality between, 158, 359nn46–47
traditions of, xiii, 271
See also Tibetan Buddhism
Buton Rinpoche, 119, 281, 363n98

C

cakras, 154, 156–57, 169, 260–61, 262. *See also individual cakras*
Cakrasaṃvara system, 26, 126, 180, 252, 286, 287, 309
Candrakīrti, 113, 274, 284, 285, 314
Autocommentary on the "Supplement to the 'Treatise on the Middle Way'", 274, 354
Clear Lamp, 311
Clear Words, 347
Jonang critiques of, 318
misunderstanding, 315
as role model, 343
Tsongkhapa and, 289
See also *Supplement to the "Treatise on the Middle Way"*
Caryā Tantra, 81, 127, 278
attainments of, 106, 108, 117
close approximation practice, 112–16
diet in, 71
empowerments in, 58, 63, 93
ethical restraints in, 94, 112
function of, 80
lamas' outer qualities in, 47–48
main texts, 111
precepts of, 70
samayas of, unique, 95, 358n28
stabilizing and analytical meditations in, 19
suitability for, 53, 111–12
celibacy, 52, 67, 71, 132
central channel, 71, 199
dissolution of winds in (chart), 247–48
isolated mind and, 176
location, 156
in refined generation stage, 138, 146
in subtle hand implement visualization, 120
winds dissolved in, 30, 131, 151, 203
channels, 26, 156, 260. *See also* central channel
Chanting the Names of Mañjuśrī, 260
Chekawa, 272
Chenrezig. *See* Avalokiteśvara
cherishing others, 15, 87, 333, 342, 343
China, xiv, 15–16, 33, 126, 357n10
Christianity, 40–41
circle of three, 22–23, 29, 39
clear appearance, 129, 183
analytical meditation in developing, 188–89
as antidote, 192, 219–20
confidence in, 236
emptiness and, 137
importance of, 144–45, 184
in Kriyā Tantra, 101–2
serenity and, 127
in sixfold self-generation, 109
Clear Differentiation of the Three Ethical Codes (Sakya Paṇḍita), 64, 181, 258, 276

clear light of death, 172, 204, 207, 240–41
bardo and, 232
correlations, 234, 235
illusory body and, 200, 230–31, 254
at moment of death, 166, 230
in nine mixings, 211
of ordinary beings and yogis, distinctions, 130, 170–71, 173
returning from, 176
subtle I at, 323
clear light/clear-light mind, 12–14, 129, 245
brain function and, 153
coarse, arising of, 207
continuum of, 316–17
in dying process, 8, 44, 166, 170, 175–76 (*see also* clear light of death)
in Jonang, 319–20
meanings of, 240–41
mother and child, 170, 241, 242, 304
object, 6, 7, 13, 240, 282, 301, 313
potential of, 198
in Sakya, 288
subject, 7, 13, 240, 282, 316
in Sūtra and Tantra, differences, 45, 158
varying perspectives on, 324–26
See also actual clear light; example clear light; fundamental innate mind of clear light
close approximation
in Action Tantra, 96–104
in Performance Tantra, 112–16
in Yoga Tantra, 118–21
Cloud of Jewels Sūtra, 141
coarse generation stage, 185–86, 187–88, 248
difficulty of, 235
meditations in, 137–38
purpose of, 192
realizing, 146, 184, 219
cognitive obscurations, 122, 202, 244
in Action Tantra, 29
in completion stage, 20
direct antidote, 240, 339
eradicating, 197–98, 210, 245, 338
Highest Yoga Tantra and, 15, 26
in Pāramitāyāna and Highest Yoga Tantra, 30
in Sūtra and Tantra, 20–21
Vajrayāna and, 128
Commentary on "Compendium of Reliable Cognition" (Dharmakīrti), 153, 276, 346
commitment beings, 209
compassion
anger and, 135
cultivating, 85–86, 87, 353
for enemies, 343
great bliss as, 228–29
impartial, 102
mindfulness of, 333
in Pāramitāyāna, 228
in Vajrayāna, 15
and wisdom, relationship of, 3, 85–86, 226
Compendium of Principles of All the Tathāgatas, 117, 118, 119
Complete Fulfillment of All Deeds, 91, 95
completion stage, 16, 31, 41, 129, 148
analytical and stabilizing meditations in, 20, 139, 163
appearances in, 142
attaining, 193–94
bliss in, 228, 328
clear light in, levels of meaning, 241
common features, 252–53
complete power over pristine wisdom stage, 186, 187, 189, 190
definition, 147–48, 195, 245
dissolutions in, 170, 205, 218
empowerments for, 180
emptiness meditation in, 298
foundation, 191–93
and generation stage, relationship of, 151, 181, 193
in Guhyasamāja, 45, 56, 63, 132, 176, 199, 215
in Guhyasamāja and Kālacakra, differences, 263, 265–66

of Highest Yoga Tantra, 78
learners' union stage in, 26
main practices (chart), 247–48
method and wisdom in, 17
purification in, 175
between sessions, 147
speed of, 30
stages of, xvi, 196–98, 357n2
starting points within (chart), 245–46
suitability, 148
training for dying in, 170
two realizations of, 161
concentration (*samādhi*), 127–28, 129, 131, 187–88, 265, 326–27
conceptuality, types of, 44–45
conduct, tantric, 348–49
attained capacity, 79
enhancing, four occasions for, 235–36
misunderstanding about, 238–39
purposes of, 237–38
three types, 23–237, 244, 264
consciousness, 41
adventitious, 337
coarse, 322–23, 324–26
coarse and subtle, distinctions, 155
deity's body and, 108–9
dissolution of, 45, 357n13
eight types, 309–11
without objects, variant views, 161–63
for omniscience, 14
as path, 308, 362n75
scientific and Buddhist views of, 152–53
six types, 155
in Vajrayāna and Pāramitāyāna, distinctions, 12–14, 127
See also foundation-of-all; mental consciousness
consort practices, 52, 138, 196–97, 200
difficulty of, 236–37
"great seal of empty form," 263
misunderstandings about, 226
purpose of, 224–25
suitability for, 226–27
three recognitions, 225
in vitality-exertion, 221–22
See also karmamudrā (action seal); wisdom mudrā (*jñānamudrā*)
contact, internal state of, 153
continuum of inspiration (blessings), 46
conventional bodhicitta, 66, 85, 90
conventional truth, 10, 24, 115, 126, 194, 275, 286, 298. *See also* two truths
creators, 39, 311–12
crown empowerment, 58, 63, 93, 124

D

Dagpo Kagyu tradition, 284
daily practice, 11, 62, 66, 353–54
ḍākinīs, 75, 78, 82, 227, 332, 342
death, 161, 201
bodhicitta at, 342
correlates, 234, 235
drops at, 158
final isolated mind at, 223
generation stage and, 143, 181
indestructible drops at, 157
mixed with truth body, 203, 204
mixing with three buddha bodies, 210, 211
moment of, 166, 230
of ordinary and realized beings, comparison, 130–31
overcoming, 233
preparing for, 344–45
purifying, 174–75, 189, 192, 259–60
stages of, 164, 166–70, 194, 218
state of mind at, 168
subtlest mind at, 7–8, 166, 204, 211, 240–41
sudden, 164
taking into path of truth body, 171, 172–73, 230, 345
without fear, 268
of yogis, 130, 170–71, 173, 200, 231
See also clear light of death
debate tradition, 274–75, 300
dedication, 268, 355
deep sleep, 158, 160
awareness maintained during, 209–10
correlates, 234–35

emptiness meditation in, 205
latencies activated (Kālacakra), 262
in nine mixings, 203, 204
definitive meaning, 56, 126, 274, 318
deities, tantric
actual and imagined, 201
closeness to, 39
cultural adaptation, 67
generation by mouth, 108, 358n32
as meditational deities, 38–39
number of, 37–38
principal, emphasizing, 55
in sexual union, 37, 38, 132–33
visions of, 327, 365n118
as wisdom realizing emptiness, 322
See also self-generation
deity yoga, 40, 68, 141, 249, 310
analytical and stabilizing meditation in, 19
daily sessions, number of, 31
focus of, 69
in Highest Yoga Tantra, 41
in Kālacakra, 259–60
method and wisdom in, 17–18, 24
mind understanding emptiness in, variant views, 113–15, 116
in Nyingma, 279
profundity and clarity in, 102–3
and sādhanas, relationship of, 74
speed of, 29
and Sūtra deity meditation, differences, 24–25
two truths in, 143, 182
See also generation stage
dependent arising, 89, 327–28, 347, 365n126
in deity yoga, 69
and emptiness, unity of, 113, 281–82, 283, 286
free from eight extremes, 6–7
meditating on, 337
in sādhana practice, awareness of, 76–77
See also twelve links of dependent origination
dependent designation, 347
Descent to Laṅka Sūtra, 274
desire, 249
sexual, 225–26
taking into path, 38, 131–32, 134–35, 136
Dezhung Azom, 289
Dhānyakaṭaka, 35, 257, 362n84
Dharamsala, 75, 349
Dharma, scriptural and realized, 353
Dharma practice, 4, 266–68, 344, 351–52
Dharma Wheel, 5–7
first turning, 267
second turning, 35, 318, 321
third turning, 318
Dharmadodhe, 323–24
dharmakāya. *See* truth body (*dharmakāya*)
Dharmakīrti, 192, 273–74, 276. See also *Commentary on "Compendium of Reliable Cognition"*
Dharmashri, 320
dhyāna. *See* meditative stability (*dhyāna*)
diet
for dream yoga, 206–7
in Kālacakra, 258
in lower tantras, 71, 95, 358n28
Dignāga, 273–74, 276
direct reliable cognizers, 135, 162
discriminating awareness, 104, 114, 239
discriminating wisdom, 189, 217
divine identity, 17–18, 92, 246, 334, 335
as antidote, 188, 220
in Caryā Tantra, 113
confidence in, 236
defilements overcome by, 129
as factually concordant awareness, 145
in Highest Yoga Tantra, 137–38
importance of, 144–45, 183
instructions on, 102
in isolated body, 196
in Kriya Tantra, 101–2
in nine mixings, 209
purposes of, 184, 192–93
serenity and, 127
in sixfold self-generation, 109

ultimate and conventional aspects, 141
Dodrup Jigme Tenpai Nyima (Dodrupchen), 282, 292, 301, 307, 316. See also *General Exposition of the "Secret Essence Tantra"*
Dolpopa Sherab Gyaltsen, 317, 318, 321, 364n109, 364n111
Dombipa, 252
Dorji Damdul, xviii
doubt, three levels of, 135–36
dream bodies, 176, 206–7, 209
dream state
  correlates, 234–35
  drops in, 158
  latencies activated (Kālacakra), 261, 262
  level of mind in, 160
  in nine mixings, 204–5
dream yoga, 205–6, 207, 209–10
dreams, value of content, 208
Drom Tonpa, 272, 285
Drop of the Great Seal Tantra, 62–63
drops. *See* subtle drops
duḥkha, 3, 6, 50, 88–89, 333, 341, 358n25
dzogchen, 53, 138, 350
  on awakening, 148, 291–92
  clear-light mind in, 161–62, 307–8, 309, 314, 325–26
  empowerment in, 64
  Highest Yoga Tantra perspectives in, 313
  and lamdre, parallels, 291
  and Madhyamaka, comparing, 300, 301, 303–4
  method and wisdom in, 26–27
  methods of, 13, 133–34, 279–80
  mind as creator in, 302–3, 312
  misunderstanding, 299–300
  New Translation traditions and, 305–6
  second Dharma Wheel and, 321
  subject clear light in, 282
  terminology of, 8
  three categories of practices, 282–83
  See also breakthrough (T. *khregs chod*); leap-over (T. *thod rgal*); rigpa

E

eight antidotes, 105, 137
eight signs of dissolution (internal visions), 176
  correlates, 217, 218–19
  in stages of death, 164, 166–71, 218, 230
  in two stages, visualizing, 170, 205, 209, 210
eighty conceptions. *See* indicative conceptions
Ekajaṭī (blue), 98
elements, 112
  of coarse body, 359n44
  correlates, 216, 217, 218–19, 361n68
  internal, 153–54
  signs of dissolution, 203, 218
  at time of death, 166–68
emanation bodies, 8
  mixing birth with, 204, 205
  rebirth as path to, 144, 172–73, 345, 360n57
empowerments, 31, 57, 58–59, 249
  abhiṣeka, meaning of, 65
  actually receiving, 51
  all-encompassing yoga in, 90
  cultural adaptation, 67
  Dalai Lama's emphasis in, 65
  deity affiliation in, 118
  of five buddha families, 58, 63, 65, 93, 111, 117, 118
  in four tantra classes, 93–94
  gathering indiscriminately, 55
  importance of, 62–63, 92–93, 344
  in Kālacakra Tantra, 258, 362n85
  lamas' importance in, 46–47
  and permissory rituals, differences, 58
  premature, 72–73
  remote transmission of, 59–60
  suitability for, 52–53, 54
  terms and connotations, 64
  See also four empowerments; vajra-master empowerment
emptiness, 8, 90, 116, 147, 350
  with all supreme aspects, 338
  analytic approach to, 13

awareness of, reaffirming, 184
and clarity, inseparability of, 288–89, 298, 313
common view, 12, 275
conceptual and direct realization, progression of, 104
correct inferential understanding of, 121
correct view of, xv, 8, 13, 51, 60, 73, 139, 154, 212, 290, 297, 346–47
and dependent arising, unity of, 113, 281–82, 283, 286
in dying process, variant views, 130, 170–71
in isolated mind, 197
in Jonang, 319
in Pāramitāyāna and Tantrayāna, 127
and pure appearance, relationship of, 295
in sādhana practice, awareness, 76–77
subtlest mind's realization of, 13, 30, 45, 129, 132, 154, 195, 197, 297, 301, 312
in tenet systems, distinctions, 45
emptiness meditation, 87, 304
appearances in, 17–18
in clear appearance and divine identity, 102
erroneous, 320
in four Tibetan traditions, 296–98, 305
in generation stage, 68–69, 140, 143–44, 145, 182–83
in Performance Tantra, 113–14
in sādhana practice, 68
and self-generation, relationship of, 92
in Sūtra, variant views, 24–25
in Sūtra and Tantra, distinctions, 13–14, 296–97
at time of death, 205
in Vajrayāna, two features, 139–41
engaged objects, 162. *See also* apprehended objects
Engaging in the Bodhisattvas' Deeds (Śāntideva), 4–5, 86, 125, 275, 346, 347
enjoyment body, 8, 16, 124
bardo as path to, 144, 172–73, 345, 360n57
dream state and, 205
five certainties (Kālacakra), 263, 363n88
special dream body and, 206
Ensapa, 231
equalizing and exchanging self with others, 15, 346, 347
ethical conduct, 2, 22–23, 69–70, 129, 268. *See also* precepts
ethical restraints and commitments, 31
ability to commit to, 72–74
in consort practices, 226
in empowerments, 46–47, 58
of five buddha families, 118
importance of, 75
in Kālacakra, 258–59
keeping, 65, 71–72, 80, 94–95
purpose of, 70–71
restoring, 72
example clear light, xvi, 192, 200–201
attaining, 200
as hidden meaning, 241
in isolated mind, xvi, 176, 197, 224
manifesting, 130–31, 195
meaning of term, 230, 240
Extensive Play Sūtra, 5
external objects, terminology regarding, 309–11

F

faith, 266
based on reason, 40
others loss of, 73, 79, 80
of tantric disciples, 53
familiarity, power of, 213
fire pūjās, 58, 121, 185
five clarifications, 144, 183, 190, 360n58
five degenerations, 49, 123, 180, 253, 254–55, 266–67
five faults, 105, 137
five manifest awakenings, 124
five meats and five nectars, 71, 358n18
five paths, 11
in Action Tantra, 105, 123
in Highest Yoga Tantra, 201, 250–51

in Pāramitāyāna and Tantra, differences, 30–31, 250
in Yoga Tantra, 121
five wisdoms, 63, 166–68, 217
form body (*rūpakāya*), 8, 37, 40, 195
actualizing, 161, 243
compassion and, 85
creating causes for, 21, 27
in Highest Yoga Tantra, 128
method and, 10
substantial cause, 21, 253
in Sūtra and Tantra, 16–17
formless meditative absorptions, 127, 364–65n117
fortitude, 5, 22–23, 183, 194, 346, 353
foundation-of-all
in Sakya, 288, 290, 291, 292, 294, 307, 312
in Yogācāra and other traditions, 322
four activities, 42, 52, 222, 238, 253, 259
four attentions, 105, 137
four empowerments, 14, 63, 64, 93, 180. *See also* secret empowerment; vase empowerment; wisdom empowerment; word (fourth) empowerment
four empties, 45, 203, 204, 219, 248, 253, 290
four immeasurables, 88, 330
four joys, 26, 133, 148, 219, 248, 253, 309
four purities, 16, 21, 357n9
four tantric classes, xvi, 14–15
empowerments in, 93–94
four types of bliss in, 80
practices of, 112
study of, 82
ways of differentiating, 127
See also Caryā Tantra; Highest Yoga Tantra; Kriyā Tantra; Yoga Tantra
four thoughts that turn the mind, 60, 284
four truths of the āryas, 1, 5, 6, 10, 267
fourfold recitation, 106
in Action Tantra, 99–101, 109
in Performance Tantra, 112
as yoga with signs, 110
full awakening, 251, 131
actualizing, 195
body and mind at, 26
in four tantra classes, 27–30
gender in, 78
in Highest Yoga Tantra, 27–28, 29–30, 82–83, 121, 133, 180, 242–43, 262–63
three ways of attaining, 253–54
fundamental innate mind of clear light, xvi, 21, 154, 155, 160, 293, 324, 359n44, 359n48
arising, two ways, 162–63
as basis for omniscience, 337
and causal continuum, relationship of, 291, 292
in consort practices, 225
in four Tibetan traditions, 307–8, 309, 313–14
generated in nature of path, 338–39
in Highest Yoga Tantra, 133
in New Translation traditions, 302, 305
in Nyingma practices, 131
in Prāsaṅgika, 322
rigpa and, 301
subtlest wind and, 153–54, 155–56
transforming, 20, 41–42
and Yogācāra foundation consciousness, distinctions, 357n14
yogic experience of, 205
See also subtlest mind/subtlest clear light
Fundamental Vehicle, xiii, xiv, 1–2, 33, 82

G

Gaden Jangtse Monastery, 327
Gaden Monastery (Tibet), 263
Gampopa, 131, 252, 272, 284, 285. See also *Jeweled Ornament of Liberation*
Gandhavajra, 361n70
Gateway to Knowledge (Mipham), 281–82
Gelug tradition, 80, 284, 289–90, 314
coarse and subtle mind in, 291
empowerments in, 58
emptiness meditation in, 298

Marpa's transmission in, 286–87
Sūtra preliminaries in, 60
union of bliss and emptiness in, 138
Gen Lobsang Gyatso, 161
gender discrimination, 78
General Exposition of the "Secret Essence Tantra" (Dodrupchen), 294, 306
generation stage, 16, 29, 31, 41
abandonments of, 182–83, 188
analytical meditation in, 20
bliss in, 228, 328
and completion stage, relationship of, 151, 181, 193
definition, 181, 189–90
dissolution analogy in, 170, 205, 218, 230
empowerment for, 63, 64–65, 180
emptiness meditation in, 68–69, 140
enhancing, 235–36
foundation, 129
great yoga of self-completion and, 120
in Highest Yoga Tantra, overview, 143–46
in Kālacakra, 259–60
nine mixings in, 210
Nyingma three concentrations and, 173–74
purpose of, 182, 361n61
serenity in, 137, 187, 189
between sessions, 147
starting point, 246
three buddha bodies in, 334–35
See also coarse generation stage; refined generation stage
generosity, 22–23, 24, 87, 122, 183, 194
Ghaṇṭāpa; *Five Stages of Cakrasaṃvara*, 131
Glorious Supreme Primal Tantra Paramādhyā, 118
Go Lotsawa, 212
Gorampa Sonam Senge, 289
Gowo Geshe Nyima, 327
great bliss, 139, 338
as antidote, 15
in consort practices, 224–26
desire as support for, 134
in Highest Yoga Tantra, 20, 21, 27–28, 30, 127, 128, 327, 364n117
in refined generation stage, 138
subtlety of, 14
in subtle drop meditation, 157
in vase empowerment, 65
wisdom realizing emptiness and, 51, 80
Great Madhyamaka, 318
Great Nirvāṇa Sūtra, 318
Great Tantra of the Primordial Buddha, 51
Great Treatise on the Stages of the Path to Awakening (Tsongkhapa), 12, 23, 46, 61, 72, 355
great yoga of self-completion, 118, 119, 120
Guhyagarbha system, 126
Guhyasamāja (deity), 286
Guhyasamāja Root Tantra, 212, 268, 309
Guhyasamāja system, 26, 30, 56, 126, 158
body maṇḍala in, 180
buddhahood in, 148
clear light in, 309, 314
completion stage, 45, 56, 63, 132, 176, 199, 215
conduct in, 236
four empties in, 45, 160–61
Madhyamaka in, 300–301
major traditions, 251
preliminaries for, 61
principal approach of, 133
See also Ārya Parent and Child tradition
Guhyasamāja Tantra, 38, 286, 306
on three meanings of *tantra*, 287–88, 292
on ultimate reality, 161
on women, awakening of, 78
Guṇaprabha; *Vinayasūtra*, 275
Gungthang Rinpoche, 42
"Guru Pūjā," 342
Guru Rinpoche. *See* Padmasambhava
guru yoga, 62, 64, 331. *See also* Six-Session Guru Yoga
guru-disciple relationships, 49–50, 55, 227

Gyaltsab Darma Rinchen; *Way to Practice the Two Stages of Kālacakra*, 145
Gyuto Tantric College, 170, 231

H

heart cakra, 157, 168, 169, 231, 323
  in all-encompassing yoga, 88
  in completion stage, 20, 199–200
  in dream yoga, 205
  in Highest Yoga Tantra, 28, 78, 129, 151
  in Kriyā Tantra, 103
  in three isolates, 176, 195, 196–97, 219, 225
  in vitality-exertion, 221
Hevajra system, 126, 252, 287, 309
Hevajra Tantra, 287, 293
Highest Yoga Tantra, 15, 36, 41, 127, 225
  afflictions utilized in, 134–36
  ah in, 360n54
  aspiration and result, 203
  awakening in, 27–28, 29–30, 82–83, 121, 133, 180, 242–43, 262–63
  behavior in, 78–80
  bliss in, 327, 364n117
  bodhicitta in, 68
  clear-light mind in, 12–13, 241, 307–8
  as culmination of path, 337–39
  deity practices of, 38, 251–52
  empowerments in, 14, 58, 63 (*see also* four empowerments)
  emptiness meditation in, 296–97
  entering, 344
  ethical restraints and commitments in, 70, 180–81
  final basis of designation in, 362–63n87
  five meats and five nectars in, 71, 358n18
  five paths in, 30
  focus of, 295
  in Gelug, 289–90
  gender in, 78
  generation stage, 181–89
  great bliss in, 228, 229
  karma in, 303
  lamas' inner qualities in, 48–49
  levels of meaning, 126
  and lower tantras, relationship of, 80–81
  maṇḍalas in, 66
  method and wisdom in, 25–26
  misunderstanding, 83, 345
  nature of mind meditation in, 312–13
  ngondro for, 62
  permissory rites, 57–58
  in Sakya, 287, 288–89
  Samantabhadra in, 357n14
  secrecy in, 54
  serenity and insight in, 19–20, 128, 137–39
  special qualities of, 123, 128, 133, 151, 188
  subtle defilements and, 129
  subtlest mind in, 34, 40–41
  suitability, 51–52, 53, 179–80, 198
  and Sūtra, differences, 20–21
  texts to study, 189
  three levels of practitioners, 148–49
  three main methods, 133–34
  two truths in, 302
  vast and profound in, 194–95
  See also union of bliss and emptiness
Hindu Tantra, xiii, xiv, 36, 39–40, 133
Hopkins, Jeffrey, xviii

I

  general and specific, 145
  as merely designated, 89, 154
  See also self
ignorance (afflictive), 3, 217
ignorance grasping inherent existence, 2, 88–89, 129. *See also* self-grasping ignorance
illusory body, 41, 148, 204, 311, 338
  with action mudrā, 232–33
  advancing to, 230–32
  arising apart from former aggregates, 173, 231–32, 233
  attaining, two views, 231
  and course body, separating, 175
  defilements overcome by, 129
  description, 232, 362n75

empowerment for, 63
form body and, 21
and mental body, distinctions, 18
merit of, 339
as path, 308
perception in, 293
pure and impure, differences in, 195, 230
similes about, 233
substantial cause for, 16
See also impure illusory body; pure illusory body
impermanence, 2, 60, 284, 353
as antidote, 353
awareness of, 207
of mind, 323
perceiving, 287, 304
of phenomena, 65, 315, 319
yogic direct perceivers of, 135–36
impure illusory body, xvi, 195, 246, 247
appearance of, 197
attaining, 224, 233
bardo appearance of, 231
cessation, 241, 242, 245
manifesting, 200–201
as path, 362n75
of yogis, 176–77, 241–42
indestructible drops, 78, 129, 157, 359n44
actual clear light and, 195, 245
ah and, 360n54
in isolated mind, 223–24
organ transplants and, 323
at time of death, 165–66, 169–70
in vitality-exertion, 221–22
India, 35–36, 54, 66, 132–33, 271
indicative conceptions, 8, 151, 159, 160, 165, 169, 194, 218, 230, 359n44
individual withdrawal, 263–64
Indrabhūti, 236
inferential cognizers, 142
inseparability of bliss and emptiness. *See* union of bliss and emptiness
inseparability of clarity and emptiness, 288–89, 298, 313
inseparability of saṃsāra and nirvāṇa, 64, 138, 288, 290, 295, 298, 312, 313
insight (*vipaśyanā*), xiv, 19, 21, 103, 128, 137–39. *See also* union of serenity and insight
Instruction on the Jeweled Garland of Views (Padmasambhava), 280
interpretable meaning, 126, 274
introspective awareness, 128, 210, 213, 285
isolated body, 196, 220, 246, 248
basis of purification, 216–18
beginning of, 199, 215–16
dissolutions in, 176
four empties and four blisses in, 219
in lower tantras, 101
meaning of name, 219–20
ripening of, 202
isolated mind, 196–97, 223, 231, 246, 247
beginning, 222
behavior during, 78–79
dissolutions in, 222–23
example clear light and, 176, 200
final, equipoise of, 233
in lower tantras, 101
ripening of, 202
two types, 223
isolated speech, 196, 246, 248
beginning, 220, 221
in lower tantras, 101
ripening of, 202
vajra recitation in, 199, 220–22

J

Jain tradition, 36
Jambel Rolway Dorje, 316
Jampel Drakpa, 257
Jamyang Dewai Dorje, 239
Jamyang Khyentse Chokyi Lodro, 314
Jamyang Khyentse Wangchug, 289
Jamyang Khyentse Wangpo, 306
Jamyang Shepa, 14, 15–16
Japan, xiv, 1, 33, 126, 357n10
jealousy, 4, 5, 153, 217, 353
Jeweled Ornament of Liberation (Gampopa), 309, 310

Jigme Lingpa, 283, 292
jñānamudrā. *See* wisdom mudrā (*jñānamudrā*)
Jñānapada tradition, 251
Jokhang temple (Lhasa), 239
Jonang tradition, 357n5
  influence of, 289
  origins, 317
  refutations of, 319
  view of, 318–20

K

Kadam tradition, 284, 285, 289, 348, 349
Kagyu traditions, 14, 80
  coarse and subtle mind in, 291
  empowerments in, 58
  emptiness in, 285–86
  Gelug and, 289
  mahāmudrā in, 284–85, 309
  origins of, 284
  Sūtra preliminaries in, 60
Kālacakra (deity), 263
Kālacakra Root Tantra, 257
Kālacakra system, 51, 126, 252, 257
  buddhahood in, 148
  clear light in, manifesting, 309
  empowerment in, 54, 57, 93–94
  generation stage, 259–60
  rules of conduct in, 70–71
  six-branch completion stage, 263–65
  suitability, 258
  three wheels of, 259
  twenty-five rules of ethical conduct, 258–59
  unique methods of, 253, 265
  vajra body (completion stage), 260–62
Kālacakra Tantra, 38, 306
  on empty form, 305
  on four types of drops, 157–58
  on gurus, 49
  on householders, precepts of, 268
  on karmic winds, 164
  on tantric teachings, origins of, 35
Kalsang Gyatso, Seventh Dalai Lama
  "Rain Shower of Attainments," xvii–xviii, 330
  "Song of the Direct View," 76–77
Kamalaśīla, 141, 274. See also *Stages of Meditation*
Kapilavastu, 124
karma, 139, 174–75, 303
  course body and, 154
  mind and, 312
  ripening of, 198
  seeds of, 10, 154, 261, 322, 362n87
  in spiritual practices, creating, 131
  tantric gurus and, 55
  at time of death, 164, 168
  two illusory bodies and, 230
  winds of, 15, 151, 164, 264–65
karmamudrā (action seal), 138, 339
  in illusory body, 229, 242, 243
  in Kālacakra, 264
  permission for, 225
  suitability, 227
  in three isolates, 200, 221–22, 223, 247
  when not to practice with, 237
Khasarpaṇi (Avalokiteśvara), 98
Khedrup Gelek Palzang, 263
  General Exposition of Tantras, 108
  Miscellaneous Works, 289, 299
  Ocean of Attainments of the Generation Stage, 189
Khedrup Norsang Gyatso, 170, 304
  on illusory body, 231
  Lamp for Clarifying the Samaya, 181, 258
  Ornament for "The Stainless Light", 225
King of Concentrations Sūtra, 320
knowledge-holders, 106–7, 108, 117, 121
Konchog Jigme Wangpo, 359n49
Kriyā Tantra, 127, 278
  ascetic practices in, 94–95
  attainments, 106–8
  awakening in, 28–29
  beginning with, 81, 83, 344
  buddha's body, speech, mind in, 108–9
  and Caryā, comparisons, 111, 112, 117
  diet in, 71

empowerments, 58, 63, 93
function, 80
lamas' outer qualities in, 47–48
main texts of, 91
meditative concentration with mantra recitation, 96–103
meditative concentration without mantra recitation, 103–4
method and wisdom in, 24
permissory rites, 57, 58
precepts, 70
samayas of, unique, 95, 358n28
stabilizing and analytical meditations in, 19
suitability, 53, 92–94
Kṛṣṇācārya tradition, 252
Kṣitigarbha, 186, 218, 361n69
Kūkai, xiv
Kunga Drolchok, 321

L

lamdre, 64, 282, 287–88, 291, 292, 294, 298, 312
Lamp for the Path to Enlightenment (Atiśa), 36, 51–52, 88, 285
Lamp Illuminating the Five Stages of the Completion Stage (Tsongkhapa), 30, 56, 61, 203–4, 212, 250, 295, 328
Langdarma, 272, 299
language and terminology, 161, 194, 274–75
confusion about, 309–11
as contextual, 44–45, 302
in cultural adaptation, 67
in tantric systems, 126–27, 350
teachers' role in explaining, 308–9
laxity, 144, 183, 187, 203, 285, 296
leap-over (T. *thod rgal*), 27, 280, 283, 309
learners' union, 26, 197, 202, 241, 243–44, 245, 247, 251
Lhodrak Drubchen Namkha Gyaltsen, 299
liberated path, 201, 202, 240, 243, 245
Library of Wisdom and Compassion, 354
Appearing and Empty, 105
Following in the Buddha's Footsteps, 105
Foundation of Buddhist Practice, 46, 47
Praise of Great Compassion, 87
Realizing the Profound View, 104, 321
Searching for the Self, 104, 321
lifespan, 27, 29, 42, 82, 87, 254
Ling Rinpoche, 55, 170, 173, 353
Lobsang Chokyi Gyaltsen
Discussion between Self-Grasping and the Wisdom Realizing Selflessness, 116–17
Essence of the Five Stages, 212
Root Verses for the Precious Gaden Oral Transmission of Mahāmudrā, 300, 307
Locanā, 218, 361n68
Lokeśvara, 361n69. *See also* Avalokiteśvara (Chenrezig)
Longchenpa Rabjampa, 280–81, 283
Lower Tantric College, 231
lucid dreams, 206, 207
lucidity, outer and inner, 27, 357n8
Luipa tradition, 252

M

Madhyamaka, 198, 295
and dzogchen, comparing, 300, 301, 303–4
in mahāmudrā, 284
on mind as creator, 311
studying, importance of, 283
texts to study, 306, 346–47
Yogācāra refutations in, 310
See also Great Madhyamaka; Prāsaṅgika Madhyamaka; Svātantrika Madhyamaka
Magical Net Tantra, 148, 360n54
Mahācakra Vajrapāṇi completion stage, 252
mahāmudrā, 53, 138, 287, 290, 350
in Action Tantra, 92
approach of, 13, 133–34
clear-light mind in, 161
four yogas of, 297–98

Highest Yoga Tantra perspectives in, 313
in Kagyu, 284–85, 309
method and wisdom in, 26
mind as creator in, 312
Mahāvairocana, 124
Mahāyāna, xiii
common paths of, 31
entering, 128
time in accomplishing, 82
and Vajrayāna, relationship of, xiv, 1, 33
See also Pāramitāyāna
Mahāyoga tantra, 82, 279
Maitreya, 275
Discrimination of the Middle and Extremes, 104–5, 120, 302
Ornament of Clear Realizations, 33, 61, 275, 302, 313, 353–54
Ornament of the Mahāyāna Sutras, 104–5, 120, 275
Sublime Continuum, 7, 133, 158, 275, 293
Maitrīpa, 284, 285
Māmakī, 361n68
maṇḍala offering, 66
maṇḍalas
elaborate, 223
general meaning and usage of term, 66
in Highest Yoga Tantra, 93
in Kriyā Tantra, 92–93
of meditative concentration, 180
sexual union in, 224–25
supporting and supported, 185–86, 190, 231, 248
supreme conqueror, 187, 361n60
types, 65–66, 180
See also body maṇḍala
Mangtho Lhudrup, 289
Mañjuśrī, 37, 75, 83, 96, 107, 117, 361n69, 365n118
Mañjuśrī Root Tantra, 69–70, 111
mantras
all sound as, 294
in all-encompassing yoga, 90
emptiness, 76, 113, 182, 313, 328
language of, 74
lotus family, 99
mental recitation, 100, 109, 112
om mani padme hum, 100
one-hundred-syllable Vajrasattva, 73
purpose of reciting, 42, 185
Śrī Heruka, 329
types of recitation, 146
whispered recitation, 100, 109, 112
See also fourfold recitation; vajra recitation
Mantrayāna, 34, 151. *See also* Vajrayāna
Marīci, 96
Marpa Lotsawa, 193–94, 203, 212, 234, 238, 272, 284, 285, 286–87
Medicine Buddha, 83
meditation
in dark, 263
formal, 348
life force of, 213
and post-meditation, relationship of, 147
research on, 152, 359n43
on skeletons, 18
and study, relationship of, 267, 353
meditation objects
in mahāmudrā, 285
night and day signs, 263
subtle, 139
in Sūtrayāna and Vajrayāna, distinctions, 137
in Tantra, advantages of, 344
meditative absorption
on emptiness, 202
formless, 124
illusion like, 311
meditative concentration (*samādhi*), 28
with mantra recitation, 96–103
without mantra recitation, 103–4, 106, 109
in yoga with and without signs, types, 110
meditative equipoise
on actual clear light, 197

and bodhisattva activities, alternating, 22–24
on emptiness, 159–61, 205, 237, 286, 329–30
space-like, 335, 336
meditative stability (*dhyāna*)
in form realm, four, 127, 364–65n177
in fourfold mantra recitation, 100
in generation stage, increasing, 184–85
loss of, 104
memory, 101, 162, 170–71, 323–24, 332, 345, 359–60n49
mental body, 16, 18, 123–24
mental consciousness, 109, 154, 155, 359n44
becoming subtler, 337–38
in generation stage, 184, 186–87, 188
levels of, 160–61
objects of, 153
subtlest mind as, 322
at time of death, 156
mental factors, 10, 131, 153, 207
merit, 70, 266
of benefactors, 268
collection of, 9, 10
during five degenerations, 267
illusory body and, 198–99, 231, 232, 243–44
preventing and destroying, 342
Meru, Mount, 124
method and wisdom, xv, 10–11, 84, 332
necessity of both, 12
relationship of, 2–4
in Sūtra and Tantra, distinctions, 17–18, 22–27, 50–51, 114
symbols of, 38, 132, 226
in Vajrayāna, 12, 21, 22, 24–27, 41, 50–51, 114, 229
as vast and profound, 92, 194
Mikyo Dorje, Eighth Karmapa, 315
Milarepa, 349
awakening of, 254
on benefactors, 268
with Gampopa, 131
hailstorms of, 238
illusory body of, 232
lineages, 272, 284
with Marpa, 193–94
with Rechungpa, 238–39
self-blessing of, 234
"Song to the Five Long-Life Sisters," 285–86
mind, 161–62
as basis of purification, 174–75
as creator, 311–12
defilements of, coarse and subtle, 128–29
emptiness of, 76–77, 297, 312, 329
in nature of bliss, 143
ordinary (*sem*), 279
reflexive quality of, 162
science on, 86–87
tantric levels of, 7–8, 155, 158–60, 359n44
See also subtlest mind/subtlest clear light
mindfulness, 101, 128, 210, 285
of body as divine body, 333–35
of compassion and bodhicitta, 333
of guru, 331–32
importance of, 212–13
innate (dzogchen), 162, 360n50
of view of emptiness, 335–37
mind-vajra, 301–2, 303, 305
Mipham, 315. See also *Gateway to Knowledge*
mirror-like wisdom, 166, 217, 265
miserliness, 112, 217
Mithupdawa, 252
monastics, 52, 227, 267
Mongolia, 1, 15, 126
mother tantras, 133
motivation, 36, 42, 60, 83, 85, 147
My Land and My People (Tenzin Gyatso), 9

N

Nāgabodhi, 189
Nāgārjuna, 171, 189, 273, 285, 315, 350
Akutobhayā, 280, 363n96

awakening of, 254
Compendium of Sūtras, 310
Five Stages, 293, 306, 311
as object of memory, 332
Praise to the Ultimate Expanse, 318
reasoning of, 113
as role model, 343
tantric practice of, 36
on two truths, 320
See also *Treatise on the Middle Way*
Nairanjana River, 123
Nairātmya, 78, 358n20
Nālandā Monastery, 272, 273, 284, 287, 317, 363n90
Nālandā tradition, 4, 273–74, 275, 277, 349
Nāropa, 79, 208, 272, 284, 285, 286. *See also* six yogas of Nāropā
natural abodes of deities, 209, 361n64
natural purity, 280, 295
nature of mind, 7, 130–31, 136, 279–80, 311, 325
nature truth body, 8, 171
navel cakra, 157, 165, 169, 202, 207, 219
near-death experiences, 176–77
New Translation traditions, 272, 284, 300
empowerments in, 58
emptiness and clear light in, 304
four tantra classes in, 80
mind-vajra in, 302
subtle body in, 158
subtlest mind meditation in, 26
Ngawang Palden; *Presentation of the Grounds and Paths of Mantra*, 122
nihilism, 3, 77, 140, 320
nine mental abidings, 105, 137
nine mixings
Guhyasamāja system, 203–7
Marpa's instructions, 208–10, 211
nirvāṇa, 7, 159
natural, 279
nonabiding, 279, 343
three types of, 133
See also inseparability of saṃsāra and nirvāṇa
nonaffirming negative, 141, 158, 304, 319
nonconceptuality, 44, 133–34, 194–95, 197, 228, 261, 292, 325
nonlearners' union, 14, 30, 198, 241, 244, 245, 247, 251
nonsectarianism, 349
Nyengon Sungrab Tulku, 316
Nyingma tradition, 14
empowerment in, 64
emptiness in, 280–84
equality of basis and result in, 293
heart's drop practice, 282
monastic universities of, 276
nine vehicles, 81–82, 278–79
origins, 272
Sakya and, 288, 295
Sūtra preliminaries in, 60
sūtras held authoritative by, 274
taking death, bardo, rebirth into paths in, 173–74
See also dzogchen; primordial purity; rigpa

O

objects of negation, 198, 297, 303, 304, 320–21, 347
Oḍḍiyāna, 35
Old Translation tradition, 158, 272. *See also* Nyingma tradition
omniscience, 13–14, 37, 42, 56, 85, 106, 135–36, 243, 337
One-Thousand-Armed Avalokiteśvara, 83, 84, 98–99
oral transmission, 59, 69
ordinary appearances
abandoning, 182, 294
antidote to, 183–84, 188, 192
body, speech, mind isolated from, 196
dissolving, 140–41, 144
in Highest Yoga Tantra, 83, 137
in lower tantras, 25, 101–2, 109
protection from, 151
in three isolates, 219–20

ordinary grasping
  abandoning, 182, 294
  antidote to, 183–84, 192
  body, speech, mind isolated from, 196
  in Highest Yoga Tantra, 83, 137
  in lower tantras, 25, 101–2, 109
  protection from, 151
  in three isolates, 219–20
orgasm, 207–8, 225–26
other-empty (*gzhan stong*), 8, 316, 364n109, 364n110
  four empties and, 290
  Jonang view, 289, 318–19
  Jonang view, refutations, 320–21
  Nyingma use of term, 321

P

Padma Karpo, 79, 257
Padmasambhava, 82, 272, 280
Pāṇḍaravāsinī, 361n68
Pāramitāyāna, xiii, 2, 15–16, 81, 278, 284
  afflictions in, 134
  body and mind in, 308
  clear light in, 240, 241
  compassion in, 228
  emptiness meditation in, 142, 338
  as foundation, 104–5, 113
  limitations of, 243
  method and wisdom in, 10, 11
  sleep transformation in, 207
  stabilizing and analytical meditation in, 296
  supersensory perception in, 163
  time in accomplishing, 13, 15, 29–30, 82
  and Vajrayāna, comparisons, 12–15, 80, 122–23, 188, 198
path of accumulation, 11, 29, 246, 250, 361n61
path of meditation, 136, 202, 243, 245, 251, 265
path of no-more-learning, 195, 245, 251
path of preparation, 28, 29, 201, 246, 250–51, 337, 361n61
path of seeing, 28, 29–30, 202, 242, 245, 251, 265
paths and grounds texts, 212
Patrul Rinpoche, 40, 290–91
Perfection of Wisdom Sūtra in One Hundred Thousand Verses, 257
Perfection of Wisdom sūtras, 6, 283
  as definitive, 318
  emptiness in, 320
  levels of meaning in, 126
  mahāmudrā and, 286
  Mantra Vehicle and, 12
  natural nirvāṇa in, 279
  Tantra and, 364n110
Performance Tantra. *See* Caryā Tantra
permanence, 77, 158, 281
  of clear light continuum, 316–17
  in Jonang, 319–20
  meanings of, 302
  of mind-vajra, 301
  sound example, 135–36, 359n49
permissory ritual, 57–58, 59
Phagmo Drupa, 215, 252
phenomena
  dependent arising of, 337
  and emptiness, inseparability of, 3
  as illusion-like, 205
  impermanent, 65, 315, 319
  as lacking inherent existence, 77, 87, 139, 336–37
  permanent, 158
  qualified by emptiness, appearance of, 142
  ultimate nature of, 6, 89–90
pliancy, 19, 20, 105, 109, 127, 228, 327
post-meditation, 16–17, 146–47
Potowa, 272
prāṇāyāma (binding wind)
  in Caryā Tantra, 112
  in Kriyā Tantra, 28, 99, 100
Prāsaṅgika Madhyamaka, 139
  emptiness in, 12, 275, 289, 313, 362n80
  foundation-of-all in, 322
  in four Tibetan traditions, 298–99
  Jonang and, 319
  in Kagyu, 285–86
  on karmic seeds, basis for, 362n87

on mind, 161, 162
mind as creator in, 311, 312
in Nyingma, 280–82
in Sakya, 287, 289
studying, importance of, 198, 347
view, necessity of realizing, 321
Prātimokṣa Sūtra, 275
precepts
bodhisattva, 70, 72, 94, 95, 112, 118
duration of, 72
five lay, 67, 70, 94
keeping, 349
monastic, 70
prātimokṣa, 69, 72, 94, 118, 200
women in tantric, 78
precious human life, 198, 352
preliminary practices, 60–61, 62, 292, 297
primordial purity, 26–27, 131, 132, 279–80, 282, 316, 321
profound path, 92
psychology, Buddhist, 87
pūjās, purpose of, 66–67
Puṇḍarīka; *Cluster of the Ultimate Meaning*, 49
pure appearance, 16, 261–62, 287, 288, 294, 295
pure illusory body, xvii, 25–26, 195, 245
actual clear light manifesting as, 201
arising of, 197, 241, 243
and clear light, union of, 14, 25–26, 30, 161, 195, 197, 229, 357n7 (*see also* union with realization)
pure lands, 210, 232, 344

R

Ra Lotsawa, 235
rainbow body, 148
Rasāvajra, 361n70
Ratnākaraśānti, 310, 364n107
Ratnasambhava, 93, 119, 216, 361n67
reason and logic, 4, 113, 116
rebirth
bodhicitta and, 342
consciousnesses and winds in, 156
correlates, 234, 235
generation stage and, 143, 181
preserving good qualities in, 177
purifying, 174–75, 189, 192, 259–60
taking into path to emanation body, 144, 172–73, 345, 360n57
wind-mind in, 231
Rechungpa, 238–39
red increase
as conceptual, 362n79
in dying process, 8, 165, 169, 175–76, 218, 230
latencies of, 243
as yogic experience, 203, 209, 219, 242, 303
refined generation stage, 186, 188, 248
bliss in, 193
completing, 146, 148, 184, 219
meditations in, 138
purpose of, 192
reflections
on all-encompassing yoga, 90
on completion-stage realizations, 199
on conduct, 239
on consort practices, 227–28
on deity yoga, 105–6
on Dharma practice, 269
on divine identity, 185, 194
on dying process, 175
on four activities, 255
on generation stage, 190
on Highest Yoga Tantra, 136–37, 146
on illusory body, 239
on lower tantras, 124
on method and wisdom, 22
on ordinary appearance and ordinary grasping, 185
on pure appearance, 296
on self-generation, 194
on tantric gurus and students, 56
on three isolates, 224
on Tibetan traditions, 296
on union, types of, 255
on Vajrayāna, entering, 77
on yoga with and without signs, 124

refuge, 40, 68, 70, 94, 118
rejoicing, 125, 353
reliable cognizers, 135, 359n49
Rendawa, 289, 319
restlessness, 144, 183, 187, 285, 296
result taken into path, 16, 18
Resultant Vehicle, 34. *See also* Vajrayāna
retreats, 43, 181
  advice for, 346
  approximation, 185, 345
  close-approximation, 106, 107–8
  on deity yoga, 185
  empowerments for, 58
  ngondro for, 62
  three-year, 67
rigpa, 279–80, 288, 325
  attaining, 290, 291–92
  fundamental innate mind of clear light and, 301
  meditation on, 304, 305–6
  sport of, 294, 295, 303, 306
  two principal qualities, 26–27
Rinchen, Khenpo, 314
Rinchen Zangpo, 272
Ripa Damtsig Dorje, 301
rituals, 66, 67
Rongsom Paṇḍita, 280
Rūpavajra, 218, 361n70

S

Śabdavajra, 361n70
sādhanas, 39
  commitment to, 73, 75
  emptiness meditation in, 139–41, 359n40
  long and short versions, 74–75
  purpose of, 66–67
Sakya Chokden, 289
Sakya Paṇḍita, 14, 276, 287. See also *Clear Differentiation of the Three Ethical Codes*
Sakya tradition, 80, 357n5
  clear light in, 324
  coarse and subtle mind in, 291
  empowerments in, 14, 58, 64
  emptiness in, 287–89, 298
  Gelug and, 289
  mind as creator in, 312
  Nyingma and, 288, 295
  origins, 272, 287
  scholars of, 289
  Sūtra preliminaries in, 60
  See also inseparability of saṃsāra and nirvāṇa; lamdre
Śākyamitra, 117, 123
Samantabhadra, 45, 288, 357n14
Samantabhadra couple, 279
Śambhala, 35, 257
Sāṃkhya tradition, 293
saṃsāra, 2, 3, 115, 151, 154, 159, 333, 353. *See also* inseparability of saṃsāra and nirvāṇa
Samye Monastery, 272, 273
Śāntarakṣita, 35, 82, 272–73, 274, 280
Śāntideva. See *Engaging in the Bodhisattvas' Deeds*
Sarasvatī, 78
Śāriputra, 267
Sarvanivāraṇa-viṣkambhini, 361n69
Sarvavid Vairocana, 117, 119–20, 358n34
Sautrāntika system, 161
science, 86–87, 152, 351
secrecy, 1, 43, 54, 83, 181, 222
secret cakra, 157, 169, 207
secret empowerment, 48, 51–52, 58, 63, 64, 180, 233
Secret Essence Tantra, 299
Secret Vehicle (Guhyayāna). *See* Vajrayāna
seeds and latencies, 244
  from bodhicitta, 125
  cleansing, 243
  of compassion, 85
  and consciousnesses, variant views, 154, 322, 324, 362n87
  from empowerments, 65
  eradicating, 3, 11–12
  four drops and, 261–62
  in mental body, 16
  from practice, 51, 69, 177, 182, 193

in similitudes of collections, 11
self
aggregates and, 321–22
coarse and subtle, 322–23
as dependent designation, 323–24, 347
emptiness of, 112, 312, 322
self-blessing stage, 233–34
self-centeredness, 5, 38, 43, 60, 86, 342–43, 353
self-empowerment, 49, 58, 72, 185
self-empty (*rang stong*), 316, 317, 319, 320–21
self-generation, 92, 137, 334–35, 360n57
empowerment for, 58, 59
emptiness meditation in, 113–14, 144
gender and, 75–76
in generation stage, 183, 226
in Nyingma, 279
restrictions, 345
of Śākyamuni Buddha, 84
sixfold, 96, 97–99, 108, 109
self-grasping ignorance, 38, 137, 143–44, 154, 198, 342, 347
selflessness, xiv, xv, 6, 45, 135
sense consciousness, 155, 359n44
coarse winds and, 159
in generation stage, 184, 186–87
at time of death, 156, 164
sense faculties, 328
coarse minds and, 159
correlates, 216, 217, 361n69
at time of death, 166–68
sense objects
bliss and, 334
correlates, 216, 217, 361n70
in subsequent realization, 336–37
sentient beings, 2, 86, 341
as awakened, 292–94, 303, 318
contemplating, 87
as empty of inherent existence, 3
final basis of designation, 311
variations in, 37–38
serenity, 3–4, 346
in Action Tantra, 28, 103, 109
attaining prior to tantric practice, 92, 192, 344
bliss in, 228, 326–27
in four tantra classes, distinctions, 127–28
in generation stage, 137, 187, 189
and insight, simultaneous cultivation, 19, 21, 128, 137–39
See also union of serenity and insight
seven destructive actions, 129
seven-point mind training, 344, 349
sexual union, 83
of deities, 37, 38, 132–33
latencies activated (Kālacakra), 261, 262
and ordinary sexuality, distinctions, 208, 224–25
See also consort practices
Shangri-la, 2, 357n3
Sharawa, 272
Shenga, Khenpo, 276
siddhas, behavior of, 79
siddhis (feats, attainments), 253
according to signs, 107
in Action Tantra, 28–29
common and transcendent, 36
in Highest Yoga Tantra, 180
special actual, three types, 106–7
signlessness, 115, 141
Siṃhamukhā, 78
single mindfulness of deity, 185–86, 193
single-minded concentration, 115, 196, 263–66. *See also* concentration (*samādhi*)
Śiva with consort, 132–33
six boundaries, 126
six perfections, 12, 16, 31, 54–55, 122, 129, 147, 278
six powers, 105, 137
Six-Session Guru Yoga, 74, 75, 181
six yogas of Nāropā, 224, 232, 252, 282, 284, 287
skepticism, 349–50
sleep, 207, 209, 211. *See also* deep sleep; dream state

Solitary Realizer Vehicle, xiii, 9, 10, 81, 128, 278, 300, 338
Sonam Drakpa, 25
Sparśavajra, 361n70
sphere of reality, 217
spiritual mentors, 352–53, 354
abuse by, 227
advice on, 267
dreaming of, 208
mindfulness of, 331–32
as role model, 343–44
See also guru-disciple relationships; tantric lamas
spiritual songs, 310–11
spontaneous presence, 26–27
Śrāvaka Vehicle, xiii, 9, 10, 81, 128, 278, 295, 300, 338
stabilizing meditation, 13
and analytical meditation, alternating, 19, 104–5, 109–10, 116, 121
in generation stage, 137
in Highest Yoga Tantra, 163
in mahāmudrā, 297–98
at time of death, 171
Stages of Meditation (Kamalaśīla), 35–36, 109–10, 120
stages of the path (*lamrim*), 60, 61, 70, 76, 92, 350, 352–53
study
advice on, xv, 4, 191–92
and practice, relationship of, 267, 353
six alternatives and four modes of meaning, 212
subsequent attainment, 22, 205
subsequent dissolution, 201, 222–23
subsequent mindfulness, 264–65
subsequent realization, illusion-like, 335, 337
Subsequent Tantra of Guhyasamāja, 215
subtle body, 148, 154, 359n44
advice on, 212–13
extremely, 154
overview, 156–58
See also cakras; channels; subtle drops; winds
subtle drops, 26, 29, 157–58
bliss from, 328
in completion stage, 196
in isolated body, 215–16
in Kālacakra, four, 261–62
meditation on, 187, 188–89, 248
melting, 142, 157
in refined generation stage, 138
See also bodhicitta drops
subtle nervous system, 40
subtle thought, 290–91
subtlest mind/subtlest clear light
abiding in, 303
ascertaining emptiness, 13, 30, 45, 129, 132, 154, 195, 197, 297, 301, 312
and coarse consciousness, relationship of, 322–23, 324–26
continuity of, 177
as empty form (Kālacakra), 305
external objects and, 311
four empties and, 160
illusory body and, xvi, 17, 28, 201, 231, 233
manifesting, 81, 129, 142, 156, 291, 334
meanings of, 44, 158–59
meditating with, different modes, 300–306
on path of seeing, 251
and study, necessity of, 198
subtlest wind and, 16, 17, 40–41, 133, 151, 243
at time of death, 7–8, 166, 204, 211, 240–41
yogic experience of, 219
See also fundamental innate mind of clear light
Sucandra, 257
Sufi tradition, 40–41
Sukhāvatī, 198
supernormal powers, 80, 238
supersensory perception, 163–64
Supplement to the "Treatise on the Middle Way" (Candrakīrti), 33, 275
on compassion, 85
on enthusiastic perseverance, 266

on erroneous emptiness meditation, 320
on mind as creator, 311, 312
studying, 87, 346, 353–54
translation, 280
viewpoint of, 313
Sūtra Unraveling the Thought, 274
Sūtrayāna
afflictions in, 136
analytical meditation in, 13, 163, 296
appearances and emptiness in, 114
approaches of, 33
body and mind in, 153, 156, 308
deity meditation in, 24–25
on dying process, 130, 359n38
as foundation, 43, 111
gender in, 78
method and wisdom in, 9–10, 12, 16, 22–24
on mind as creator, 311
nirvāṇa in, types of, 133
paths as consciousness in, 362n75
permanence in, 302
preliminaries for, 60–61
serenity and insight in, 19, 137
serenity in, 127–28
and Tantra, combining, 68
and Tantra, differences, 20–21, 300–301
three vehicles of, 81
two emptinesses in, 312
vast and profound in, 194
Svātantrika Madhyamaka, 280, 347

T

Takdrak Rinpoche, 55, 348
taken-all-together dissolution, 201, 222, 223
Taklungdrak Hermitage, 55
Taktsang Lotsawa, 38, 315–16
Tantra Requested by Subāhu, 69, 91
Tantra/Tantrayāna
Buddhist and non-Buddhist, distinctions, 39–40, 41–42
non-Buddhist, xiii, xiv, 36, 133
See also Vajrayāna
tantric lamas, 31, 49
in empowerments, 64
importance of, 42, 46, 80
interpretive and definitive, differentiating, 62
qualities of, 47–48, 75
tantric practitioners
behavior of, 79
motivation of, 53–54
qualities of, 50–53
three levels of, 148–49
Tārā, 75, 78, 83, 96, 361n68
Cittamaṇi Tārā, 58
green, 98
Tathāgata Essence Sūtra, 7, 318
tathāgatagarbha, 7. *See also* buddha nature
tathāgatagarbha sūtras, 318, 364n112
Teaching of Akṣayamati Sūtra, 274
ten grounds, 11, 123
eighth, 29–30
first, 242, 245, 265, 327
five paths and, 202, 251
in Pāramitāyāna and Tantra, differences, 30–31
second, 245
tenth, 13, 15, 128
ten nonvirtuous actions, 94, 112
tenet systems, 274, 283, 347
Tenzin Gyatso, Fourteenth Dalai Lama, 9
daily readings, 347–48
interest in science, 158, 359nn46–47
personal practices, 85, 90, 288, 343–44, 346
Theravāda Buddhism, xiv
Three Baskets (*Tripiṭaka*), 33, 276, 360n52
three buddha bodies
aspiration for, 88
correlates, 234–35, 345
death, bardo, rebirth and, 171–73
four drops and (Kālacakra), 262
nine mixings and, 208–10, 211

similitudes of, 334–35
three concentrations, 173–74
three empties, 154, 155
three higher trainings, 31, 33, 129
three principal aspects of path
after empowerments, 68
as foundation, 46, 51, 60, 117, 215, 222
importance of, 39, 341
three samādhis (Yoga Tantra), 118, 120
three samādhis of three isolated states, 196
three vehicles, xiii, 10, 14–15, 81
throat cakra, 157–58, 199, 207, 219, 221
Tibet, 1
Atiśa in, 82
romanticizing, 2, 357n3
Tantra in, 54–55, 61, 69, 117, 351
translation efforts in, 273
Tibetan Book of the Dead, 359n44
Tibetan Buddhism
approaching, 277–78
diversity of, 274
four principal traditions, xiv
Highest Yoga Tantra in, 126
inappropriate behavior in, 227
misunderstandings, 4, 271–72, 273, 299
misunderstandings among traditions, 314–16
nonsectarianism in, 349
similarities among traditions, 290–91, 307
texts in common, 275–77
Vajrayāna in, 33
Tibetan medical texts, 158
Tilbupa, 180
Tilbupa (Gandhapada) tradition, 252
Tilopa, 79, 284
Togden Jampel Gyatso, 37
transference of consciousness, 149, 232, 323, 344, 362n76
Treasury of Knowledge (Vasubandhu), 198, 275
Treatise on the Middle Way (Nāgārjuna), 7, 275, 320
on aggregates, 89
analysis in, 336
homage, 327–28, 347–48
on saṃsāra and nirvāṇa, equality of, 313
studying, importance of, 346, 347
in Tibet, 280
trekcho. *See* breakthrough (T. *khregs chod*)
truth body (*dharmakāya*), 27, 40, 195
actualizing, 161, 243
causes for, 104
compassion and, 85
and form body, unity of, 17, 133
in Highest Yoga Tantra, methods for attaining, 128
one's own purpose and, 37
substantial cause of, 21, 253
in Sūtra and Tantra, 16–17
wisdom and, 10
See also nature truth body; wisdom truth body
Tsarchen Losel Gyatso, 289, 327
Tsen Kawoche, 317
tsog offering, 234, 236
Tsongkhapa, 36, 212, 272
awakening of, 200, 231
Commentary to Fifty Verses on the Guru, 180–81
Completing the Five Stages in a Single Sitting, 158, 328
Destiny Fulfilled, 354
dzogchen transmissions of, 299
Essence of Eloquence, 319
Explanation of the Root Downfalls in Tantra, 181, 258
Explanation of the Systematic Stages, 189
on four empowerments, 63–64
Great Exposition of Secret Mantra, 108, 114, 119, 120
Great Treatise on the Stages of the Tantric Path, 329
misunderstanding, 315
Ocean of Reasoning, 116

Opening the Eyes to View the Hidden Meaning, 131–32
Praise to Dependent Arising, 347
as role model, 343
on six yogas, 252, 362n83
Small Stages of the Path, 22, 23
sūtras held authoritative by, 274
tantric works of, 350
view of, 289
visions of, 37, 365n118
See also *Great Treatise on the Stages of the Path to Awakening*; *Lamp Illuminating the Five Stages of the Completion Stage*
Tulku Tsullo (Tsultrim Zangpo), 282, 316
tummo (inner heat), 148, 264
bliss in, 249
in Hevajra, 309
in Hindu Tantra, 36
in Kagyu, 285
in six yogas, 252
subtle drops and, 157, 253
in three isolates, 196, 224, 248
Tushita Pure Land, 344
twelve deeds of a buddha, 124
twelve links of dependent origination, 113, 154
two collections, 114, 122–23, 244, 338–39
two dissolutions, 242, 244, 247. *See also* subsequent dissolution; taken-all-together dissolution
two obscurations, 129, 133, 224–25, 226, 265. *See also* afflictive obscurations; cognitive obscurations
two stages
advice on, 212–13
demarcation between, 191
four stages in generating path, 186–89, 190, 361n62
sustaining view in, 142
taking death, bardo, rebirth into paths in, 172–73
See also completion stage; generation stage
two stages of withdrawal, 231, 247
two truths, 3, 102, 320
completion-stage practices of, 229
in deity yoga, 143, 182
in Jonang, 319
method and wisdom in, 10
simultaneous perception, 21, 30
union of, Highest Yoga Tantra, 63, 249–50, 329
union of, lower tantras, 104, 110, 113, 116–17
variant views on, 301–2

U

ultimate analysis, 77, 89, 310, 336
ultimate bodhicitta, 85, 89–90, 93, 180, 357n14
ultimate truth, 115, 286, 302, 336, 337
uninterrupted path, 201, 240, 242, 245
union of bliss and emptiness, 13, 21, 138, 142–43, 226, 249–50, 289–90, 328–30, 338–39, 364n117
union of serenity and insight, 11, 19–20, 52, 84, 331
in Highest Yoga Tantra, 21, 29, 138, 189
in Kriyā, 104–5, 109–10
lower tantras, 28, 121
union of vast and profound, 195
union with abandonment, 197, 202, 243–44, 245, 247, 251
union with no-more-learning, 198, 202. *See also* nonlearners' union
union with realization, 197, 244, 245, 247, 251
Upadhaya, Jaganath, 36

V

Vaibhāṣika system, 359n38
Vairocana, 93, 119, 216, 218, 317n67, 361n71, 362n72. *See also* Sarvavid Vairocana
Vairocana Abhisaṃbodhi, 112
vajra body, 201, 231, 245, 254, 260–62
Vajra Garland, 52–53
Vajra Īśvarī, 117

vajra recitation, 148, 231, 246, 247
in completion stage, 199–200
in Kālacakra, 264
methods for, 222
three wind yogas in, 220–22
while dying, 229
Vajrabhairva, 252, 259–60
Vajrabodhi, 108
Vajradhara, 75, 210, 233, 268
arising as, 209
buddha family of, 218
in nine mixings, 210, 211
peaceful and wrathful forms of, 37
principle, 144
state of, 198, 253, 254
teachings from, 9, 34, 35, 268
visualizing, 199, 209
Vajradhātu practice, 117
vajra-holders, causal and resultant, 144, 183, 360n57
Vajrakīlaya, 126
vajra-master empowerment
conduct of, 52
in Nyingma tradition, 64
in Yoga Tantra, 58, 93, 117, 118
Vajrapāṇi, 35, 83, 96, 98, 186, 361n69
Vajrapañjara Tantra, 80
Vajrayāna, 1–2, 351
afflictions utilized in, 134–36
avoiding pitfalls, 42–43
bliss in, 228–29, 328
body and mind in, 153–55, 164–66, 308
Buddha in, 9
as culmination of path, 337–39
degeneration of, 66
emptiness, importance of understanding in, 139–40
entering, considerations for, 51, 215, 344
expectations of, 53
external objects in, 310
foundation for, 54–55, 56, 104
humility in, 177
and Mahāyāna, relationship of, xiv, 1, 33
meaning of term, 24, 34
method and wisdom in, 12, 15–18, 22, 24–27, 41, 50–51, 114
mind as creator in, 311
misconceptions about, xiii, xiv, 4, 36, 350–51
newcomers, advice for, 68, 73–74, 81, 83
origin and evolution of, 34–36
and Pāramitāyāna, differences, 12–15, 80
prescribed for individuals, 35
purpose, 40–41
serenity and insight in, 19
skillful methods of, 234
suitability, xviii, 50, 63, 80
superiority of, 14, 31
and Sūtra, combining, 68
and Sūtra, differences in, 20–21, 300–301
third Dharma Wheel and, 7
three results of, 253–54
time in accomplishing, 27–30
Tripiṭaka classification of, 360n52
two presentational styles, 126
Vajrayāna and the Culmination of the Path
aims of, xiv–xv, 2
overview, xv–xvii
Vajrayoginī, 58, 78, 126, 232, 259–60, 327, 365n118
Varanasi Sanskrit University, 36
vase breathing, 148, 264
vase empowerment, 58, 63, 64, 65, 93
vase-like meditation, 205
vast path, 92
Vasubandhu, 7. See also *Treasury of Knowledge*
view
in four Tibetan traditions, comparing, 298
in Sūtra and Tantra, comparing, 14
varying perspectives on, 313–14
Vikramaśīla Monastery, 364nn107–8
Vinaya, 50, 227, 273, 276, 277

gender in, 77–78
importance of, 49
remote ordination, 59
on sexual conduct, 132
vipaśyanā. *See* insight
Virūpa, 272, 287
Viśvamāta, 263
vitality-exertion (wind yoga), 28, 99–100, 215, 221, 248, 252, 264, 327, 362n74
Vulture's Peak, 35, 257

W

waking state
clear-light mind and, 155–56
correlates, 234–35
latencies activated (Kālacakra), 261, 262
level of mind in, 160
mixed with three buddha bodies, 209, 211, 345
in nine mixings, 204, 205
winds in, 155
yogas of, 147
water empowerment, 63, 93
white appearance
as conceptual, 362n79
in dying process, 8, 165, 169, 175–76, 218, 230
latencies of, 243
as yogic experience, 203, 209, 219, 221, 223, 242, 246, 303
wind yoga, 112, 133–34, 148, 163–64, 205, 206, 249, 309. *See also* vajra recitation
wind-mind, subtlest, 201, 232, 338–39
as deity, 173
in dying process, 171, 172, 176, 231, 323
as indestructible drop, 157, 165–66, 174
manifesting, 161
purifying, 164
in rebirth, 231
in transference, 232
two ways to access, 243
as ultimate basis of designation, 159, 362–63n87
winds, 26
all-pervasive, 200, 222, 223, 261
as basis of purification, 174–75
binding (*see* prāṇāyāma)
coarse and subtle, 155, 159
controlling, 338
dissolution, 12–13, 28, 30, 203
dissolution, results of, 176–77
emotions and, 153, 154, 165
functions and names, 157
in Kālacakra, 261, 264
karmic, 15, 151, 164, 264–65
and mind, relationship of, 20, 99, 159, 193
purposes of utilizing, 151
in stages of death, 169–70
subtlest, as voice, 41
tantric understanding of, 152–56
in three isolated practices, 202
uses of term, 101
wisdom
collection of, 9, 10
and compassion, relationship of, 3, 85–86, 226
higher training of, 129
See also wisdom realizing emptiness
wisdom beings, 99, 103–4, 209
wisdom empowerment, 51–52, 58, 63, 64, 180, 241
wisdom mudrā (*jñānamudrā*), 138, 221–22, 223, 225, 237, 247, 264, 339
wisdom of accomplishment, 168, 217
wisdom of discrimination, 167
wisdom of equality, 167, 217
wisdom realizing emptiness, 2, 20, 80, 194
as antidote, 3, 151, 353
in Buddhist practices, 40
great bliss generated into, 229
in Highest Yoga Tantra, 41
importance of cultivating, 268, 342, 354
in isolated body, 215–16, 246
manifesting as deity, 102
nonconceptual, 44

in Sūtrayāna, 10
in Tantra, 69, 322
wisdom truth body, 8, 171
word (fourth) empowerment, 58, 64, 180
wrathful deities, 38, 39
wrong consciousness, 18, 134, 144, 145, 183, 359n49
wrong views, 36, 125, 145, 327–28, 341

Y
Yamāntaka, 38, 75, 135
Yamāntaka system, 26, 126, 181, 252, 286, 330
Yoga Tantra, 81, 127, 278
attainments in, 121
close approximation in, 118–21
diet in, 71
empowerments, 58, 93
ethical restraints and commitments, 70, 118
four seals in, 119–20
function of, 80
lamas' inner qualities in, 48–49
main texts of, 117
origin of, 35, 124
stabilizing and analytical meditations in, 19
suitability, 53, 117
yoga with signs, 84, 110
with coarse visualization, 118–20
practices of, 112
as separate from emptiness meditation, 113
with subtle hand implement visualization, 120
yoga without signs, 28, 84, 109, 110, 112
and deity yoga, distinctions, 115, 116
emptiness meditation and, 113, 141
in Yoga Tantra, 121
Yogācāra school, 117, 287, 294, 309–11
emptiness in, 139, 249, 362n80
foundation consciousness in, 322, 357n14
tantra and, 50
three natures in, 7
view of, 321
Yogācāra-Svātantrika, 280, 309
Yumo Mikyo Dorje, 317

Z
Zen, xiv
zhentong. *See* other-empty (*gzhan stong*)

About the Authors

THE DALAI LAMA is the spiritual leader of the Tibetan people, a Nobel Peace Prize recipient, and an advocate for compassion and peace throughout the world. He promotes harmony among the world's religions and engages in dialogue with leading scientists. Ordained as a Buddhist monk when he was a child, he completed the traditional monastic studies and earned his geshe degree (equivalent to a PhD). Renowned for his erudite and open-minded scholarship, his meditative attainments, and his humility, Bhikṣu Tenzin Gyatso says, "I am a simple Buddhist monk."

Peter Aronson

BHIKṢUṆĪ THUBTEN CHODRON has been a Buddhist nun since 1977. Growing up in Los Angeles, she graduated with honors in history from the University of California at Los Angeles and did graduate work in education at the University of Southern California. After years studying and teaching Buddhism in Asia, Europe, and the United States, she became the founder and abbess of Sravasti Abbey in Washington State. A popular speaker for her practical explanations of how to apply Buddhist teachings in daily life, she is the author of several books on Buddhism, including *Buddhism for Beginners*. She is the editor of Khensur Jampa Tegchok's *Insight into Emptiness*. For more information, visit sravastiabbey.org and thubtenchodron.org.

Also Available from the Dalai Lama and Wisdom Publications

Buddhism
One Teacher, Many Traditions

The Compassionate Life

Ecology, Ethics, and Interdependence
The Dalai Lama in Conversation with Leading Thinkers on Climate Change

Essence of the Heart Sūtra
The Dalai Lama's Heart of Wisdom Teachings

The Essence of Tsongkhapa's Teachings
The Dalai Lama on the Three Principal Aspects of the Path

The Fourteenth Dalai Lama's Stages of the Path, vol. 1
Guidance for the Modern Practitioner

The Fourteenth Dalai Lama's Stages of the Path, vol. 2
An Annotated Commentary on "Oral Transmission of Mañjuśrī"

The Good Heart
A Buddhist Perspective on the Teachings of Jesus

Imagine All the People
A Conversation with the Dalai Lama on Money, Politics, and Life as It Could Be

Kalachakra Tantra
Rite of Initiation

The Life of My Teacher
A Biography of Kyabjé Ling Rinpoché

Meditation on the Nature of Mind

The Middle Way
Faith Grounded in Reason

Mind in Comfort and Ease
The Vision of Enlightenment in the Great Perfection

MindScience
An East-West Dialogue

Opening the Eye of New Awareness

Practicing Wisdom
The Perfection of Shantideva's Bodhisattva Way

Science and Philosophy in the Indian Buddhist Classics, vol. 1
The Physical World

Science and Philosophy in the Indian Buddhist Classics, vol. 2
The Mind

Science and Philosophy in the Indian Buddhist Classics, vol. 3
Philosophical Schools

Science and Philosophy in the Indian Buddhist Classics, vol. 4
Philosophical Topics

Sleeping, Dreaming, and Dying
An Exploration of Consciousness

The Wheel of Life
Buddhist Perspectives on Cause and Effect

The World of Tibetan Buddhism
An Overview of Its Philosophy and Practice

Also Available from Thubten Chodron

Insight into Emptiness
Khensur Jampa Tegchok
Edited and introduced by Thubten Chodron

"One of the best introductions to the philosophy of emptiness I have ever read."—José Ignacio Cabezón

Practical Ethics and Profound Emptiness
A Commentary on Nagarjuna's Precious Garland
Khensur Jampa Tegchok
Edited by Thubten Chodron

"A beautifully clear translation and systematic explanation of Nagarjuna's most accessible and wide-ranging work. Dharma students everywhere will benefit from careful attention to its pages."—Guy Newland, author of *Introduction to Emptiness*

Awakening Every Day
365 Buddhist Reflections to Invite Mindfulness and Joy

Buddhism for Beginners

The Compassionate Kitchen

Cultivating a Compassionate Heart
The Yoga Method of Chenrezig

Don't Believe Everything You Think
Living with Wisdom and Compassion

Guided Meditations on the Stages of the Path

How to Free Your Mind
Tara the Liberator

Living with an Open Heart
How to Cultivate Compassion in Daily Life

Open Heart, Clear Mind

Taming the Mind

Working with Anger

About Wisdom Publications

Wisdom Publications is the leading publisher of classic and contemporary Buddhist books and practical works on mindfulness. To learn more about us or to explore our other books, please visit our website at wisdom.org or contact us at the address below.

Wisdom Publications
132 Perry Street
New York, NY 10014 USA

We are a 501(c)(3) organization, and donations in support of our mission are tax deductible.

Wisdom Publications is affiliated with the Foundation for the Preservation of the Mahayana Tradition (FPMT).